New Directions in German Studies

Vol. 37

Series Editor:

IMKE MEYER

Professor of Germanic Studies, University of Illinois at Chicago

Editorial Board:

KATHERINE ARENS
Professor of Germanic Studies, University of Texas at Austin

ROSWITHA BURWICK
Distinguished Chair of Modern Foreign Languages Emerita, Scripps College

RICHARD ELDRIDGE
Charles and Harriett Cox McDowell Professor of Philosophy, Swarthmore College

ERIKA FISCHER-LICHTE
Professor Emerita of Theater Studies, Freie Universität Berlin

CATRIONA MACLEOD
Frank Curtis Springer and Gertrude Melcher Springer Professor in the College and the Department of Germanic Studies, University of Chicago

STEPHAN SCHINDLER
Professor of German and Chair, University of South Florida

HEIDI SCHLIPPHACKE
Associate Professor of Germanic Studies, University of Illinois at Chicago

ANDREW J. WEBBER
Professor of Modern German and Comparative Culture, Cambridge University

SILKE-MARIA WEINECK
Grace Lee Boggs Collegiate Professor of Comparative Literature and German Studies, University of Michigan

DAVID WELLBERY
LeRoy T. and Margaret Deffenbaugh Carlson University Professor, University of Chicago

SABINE WILKE
Joff Hanauer Distinguished Professor for Western Civilization and Professor of German, University of Washington

JOHN ZILCOSKY
Professor of German and Comparative Literature, University of Toronto

A list of volumes in the series appears at the end of this book.

Germany from the Outside
Rethinking German Cultural History in an Age of Displacement

Edited by Laurie Ruth Johnson

BLOOMSBURY ACADEMIC
NEW YORK • LONDON • OXFORD • NEW DELHI • SYDNEY

BLOOMSBURY ACADEMIC

Bloomsbury Publishing Inc
1385 Broadway, New York, NY 10018, USA
50 Bedford Square, London, WC1B 3DP, UK
29 Earlsfort Terrace, Dublin 2, Ireland

BLOOMSBURY, BLOOMSBURY ACADEMIC and the Diana logo are trademarks of
Bloomsbury Publishing Plc

First published in the United States of America 2022
This paperback edition published 2024

Copyright © Laurie Ruth Johnson, 2022

Each chapter copyright © by the contributor, 2022

Cover design by Andrea Federle-Bucsi
Cover image courtesy of the Earth Science and Remote Sensing Unit, NASA Johnson Space
Center / NASA World Wind / https://eol.jsc.nasa.gov/

All rights reserved. No part of this publication may be reproduced or transmitted in any
form or by any means, electronic or mechanical, including photocopying, recording,
or any information storage or retrieval system, without prior permission in writing from
the publishers.

Bloomsbury Publishing Inc does not have any control over, or responsibility for, any
third-party websites referred to or in this book. All internet addresses given in this book
were correct at the time of going to press. The author and publisher regret any inconvenience
caused if addresses have changed or sites have ceased to exist, but can accept no responsibility
for any such changes.

Library of Congress Cataloging-in-Publication Data

Names: Germany from the outside (Conference) (2019 : Champaign, Ill.) | Johnson, Laurie
Ruth, editor.
Title: Germany from the outside : rethinking German cultural history
in an age of displacement / edited by Laurie Ruth Johnson.
Description: New York : Bloomsbury Academic, 2022. | Series: New directions in German
studies | Conference proceedings of Germany from the Outside held in September 2019 at the
University of Illinois Urbana-Champaign. | Includes bibliographical references and index. |
Summary: "Illuminates our understanding of the nation and the role of culture in the nation, in
an era of extreme displacement and increased migration, in "German" geopolitical and
linguistic-cultural spaces"— Provided by publisher.
Identifiers: LCCN 2022009679 (print) | LCCN 2022009680 (ebook) | ISBN 9781501375903
(hardback) | ISBN 9781501375897 (paperback) | ISBN 9781501375934 | ISBN 9781501375910
(epub) | ISBN 9781501375927 (pdf)
Subjects: LCSH: German literature—20th century—History and criticism—Congresses. | German
literature—21st century—History and criticism—Congresses. | German literature—Minority
authors—History and criticism—Congresses. | National characteristics, German, in literature—
Congresses. | Emigration and immigration in literature—Congresses. | LCGFT: Literary
criticism. | Conference papers and proceedings.
Classification: LCC PT405 .G459 2022 (print) | LCC PT405 (ebook) | DDC 830.9/3552—dc23/
eng/20220525
LC record available at https://lccn.loc.gov/2022009679
LC ebook record available at https://lccn.loc.gov/2022009680

ISBN:	HB:	978-1-5013-7590-3
	PB:	978-1-5013-7589-7
	ePDF:	978-1-5013-7592-7
	eBook:	978-1-5013-7591-0

Series: New Directions in German Studies

Typeset by RefineCatch Limited, Bungay, Suffolk

To find out more about our authors and books visit www.bloomsbury.com
and sign up for our newsletters.

Contents

List of Illustrations   vii
Notes on Contributors   viii

Introduction   1
Laurie Ruth Johnson

I Reading German Cultural History Differently

1. Finding Odysseus's Scars Again: Hyperlinked Literary Histories in the Age of Refugees   13
   B. Venkat Mani
2. Between the Court and the Port, but Never Part of a Nation: Friederike Brun's Domesticated Cosmopolitanism   37
   Birgit Tautz
3. On the Inside Looking Out: Fichte, the University, and the Psychopolitics of German Idealism   61
   Laurie Ruth Johnson
4. Rewriting German Literary History from the Outside In: J. M. Coetzee's *Elizabeth Costello*   85
   David D. Kim

II Stories of Expulsion, Exile, and Displacement

5. Looking for Heinrich Heine with Nâzım Hikmet and E. S. Özdamar   109
   Azade Seyhan
6. Between Times and Places: Mobility and National Identity in Albert Vigoleis Thelen's Refugee Memoirs from Spain and Portugal (August 31 – September 1, 1939)   129
   Carl Niekerk
7. Writing Germany with Brazil: Julia Mann's Memoir   151
   Veronika Fuechtner
8. From Vienna to the Midwest: Austrian Refugees and Quaker Rescue Efforts after 1938   169
   Bettina Brandt

9 Keeping Time: Trauma as Intimate Alienation in
   Hans Keilson's Writing 191
   Anna M. Parkinson

III Rewriting German Culture

10 Tracing the Continual Present: Yoko Tawada and Vilém Flusser 215
   Gizem Arslan
11 Mobilizing the Archive: Marica Bodrožić and Deniz Utlu's
   Unterhaltungen deutscher Eingewanderten 237
   Claudia Breger
12 Constructing an "Inside": Transcultural Laughter Communities
   in Fatma Aydemir's *Ellbogen* (2017) and Olga Grjasnowa's
   Der Russe ist einer, der Birken liebt (2012) 261
   Lucas Riddle
13 Screening Urban Space and Belonging in Berlin: Contemporary
   Berliners in Sheri Hagen's *Auf den zweiten Blick/At Second
   Glance* (2013), Ines Johnson-Spain's *Becoming Black* (2019),
   and Amelia Umuhire's *Polyglot* (2015) 281
   Berna Gueneli
14 Bertolt Brecht's *Me-ti* or the Aesthetics of Translation:
   Universal Love, Mutual Benefits, and Transience 303
   Chunjie Zhang
15 Clowns in Exile: *Hamletmaschine* and the (In)human 323
   Olivia Landry

Index 343

Illustrations

11.1   Screenshot from *Unterhaltungen deutscher Eingewanderten.*   240
11.2   Screenshot from *Unterhaltungen deutscher Eingewanderten.*   253

Contributors

Gizem Arslan is Assistant Teaching Professor of German at Worcester Polytechnic Institute, USA. Her research and teaching interests include postwar literatures in German, French, and Turkish, translation studies, migration studies, theories of language, and writing systems of the world. She has published articles on Paul Celan, Ernst Jandl, José F. A. Oliver, Emine Sevgi Özdamar, and Yoko Tawada. Her current work investigates the Paris-based OuLiPo group's influence on German-American poet Uljana Wolf's interlingual play with German and English, and a book project tentatively titled "(Il)Legibility in Translation" on literary experimentation with writing systems as a form of resistance to ethno-nationalist ideas about language.

Bettina Brandt is Teaching Professor of German and Jewish Studies, Director of Undergraduate Studies and Honor's Advisor at Penn State University, USA. Her most recent article in the area of Holocaust Studies is entitled "Nelly and Trudie: Deciphering a Transatlantic Holocaust Correspondence from Vienna" (in *On Being Adjacent to Historical Violence*, ed. Irene Kacances, 2021) Brandt is co-editor of *Tales that Touch: Migration, Translation and Temporality in Twentieth- and Twenty-First-Century German Literature and Culture* (with Y. Yildiz, forthcoming 2022); *China in the German Enlightenment* (with D. Purdy, 2016); and *Herta Müller: Politics and Aesthetics* (with V. Glajar, 2013).

Claudia Breger is the Villard Professor of German and Comparative Literature at Columbia University, New York, USA. Having received her PhD and Habilitation from Humboldt University, Berlin, she taught at the University of Paderborn, Germany, and Indiana University, Bloomington, USA, before joining Columbia in 2017. Her research and teaching focus is on modern and contemporary culture, with emphases on film, performance, literature, and literary and cultural theory, as well as the intersections of gender, sexuality, and race in a transnational framework. Her most recent book is *Making Worlds: Affect and Collectivity in Contemporary European Cinema* (2020).

Veronika Fuechtner is Associate Professor of German at Dartmouth College, USA, where she also teaches in Comparative Literature, Jewish Studies, Women's, Gender and Sexuality Studies and the Geisel School of Medicine. She is the author of *Berlin Psychoanalytic* (2011) and the co-editor of *Imagining Germany, Imagining Asia* (2013) and *A Global History of Sexual Science 1880–1960* (2017). Her research interests include the history of psychoanalysis and sexology, discourses on race and ethnicity, German-language modernism, contemporary culture, German-language film, and global cultural and scientific histories.

Berna Gueneli is Associate Professor of German in the Department of Germanic and Slavic Studies at the University of Georgia, Athens, USA. In addition to her book *Fatih Akın's Cinema and the New Sound of Europe* (2019), she has published articles and co-edited two special issues on Turkish German studies. Her second book-length study explores Orientalism's impact on film and visual culture in the Weimar Republic.

Laurie Ruth Johnson is Professor of German with affiliations in Criticism and Interpretive Theory and Comparative and World Literature at the University of Illinois at Urbana-Champaign, USA, where she also directs the Campus Honors Program. She works on eighteenth- through twenty-first-century intellectual history, literature, philosophy, and film, with emphasis on Romanticism and its afterlives. She is the author of *Forgotten Dreams: Revisiting Romanticism in the Cinema of Werner Herzog* (2016; 2019), *Aesthetic Anxiety: Uncanny Symptoms in German Literature and Culture* (2010), and *The Art of Recollection in Jena Romanticism* (2002). Her articles cover topics ranging from *Harry Potter* to psychological aspects of Kant's philosophy.

David D. Kim is Professor in the Department of European Languages and Transcultural Studies at the University of California, Los Angeles, USA. He is the author of *Cosmopolitan Parables: Memory and Responsibility in Contemporary Germany* (2017). His edited and co-edited publications include, among others, *Imagining Human Rights* (2015), *The Postcolonial World* (2017), *Reframing Postcolonial Studies: Concepts, Methodologies, Scholarly Activisms* (2021), and *Globalgeschichten der deutschen Literatur* (2021). His latest articles have appeared in the *German Quarterly, Gegenwartsliteratur, Monatshefte*, and *Jahrbuch der Deutschen Schillergesellschaft*. Kim is the recipient of the Alexander von Humboldt Research Fellowship and the American Council of Learned Societies Fellowship.

x   Contributors

Olivia Landry is Assistant Professor of German at Lehigh University, USA, where she also directs the Film and Documentary Studies Program. She is author of *Movement and Performance in Berlin School Cinema* (2019), *Theatre of Anger: Radical Transnational Performance in Contemporary Berlin* (2020), and *A Decolonizing Ear: Documentary Film Disrupts the Archive* (forthcoming 2022/2023). Her most recent articles have appeared in the *Contemporary Theatre Review*, the *Journal of Middle East Women's Studies*, the *German Quarterly*, *Discourse*, and *Feminist Media Studies*.

B. Venkat Mani is Professor of German and World Literature and Race, Ethnicity and Indigeneity Senior Fellow at the Institute for Research in the Humanities at the University of Wisconsin–Madison, USA. He is the author of *Cosmopolitical Claims: Turkish German Literatures from Nadolny to Pamuk* (2007) and *Recoding World Literature: Libraries, Print Culture, and Germany's Pact with Books* (2017; winner of GSA's DAAD Prize and MLA's Aldo and Jeanne Scaglione Prize for Best Book in German Studies 2018). Mani has edited five volumes, including *A Companion to World Literature* (2020), and for *German Quarterly*, "Against Isolationist Readings: A Forum on World Literature" (Fall 2021). His public humanities essays can be read in *Inside Higher Ed*, *TeloScope*, *The Wire* (Hindi), the *Hindustan Times*, and the *Indian Express*.

Carl Niekerk is Professor of German, Comparative and World Literature, and Jewish Studies at the University of Illinois at Urbana-Champaign, USA. His research covers German culture from the Enlightenment through today, focusing in particular on the construction of Otherness. He has edited the *German Quarterly* and is currently the editor of the *Lessing Yearbook*. Niekerk's most recent publications include *Die Ökonomie des Skandals. Gesellschaft, Sexualität, Gender und Judentum bei Arthur Schnitzler*, edited with Margrit Vogt (2020), and *The Radical Enlightenment in Germany: A Cultural Perspective* (2018).

Anna M. Parkinson is Associate Professor of German at Northwestern University, USA, where she is a core member of the Critical Theory Cluster and Jewish Studies Program, and affiliated with the Gender and Sexuality Studies Program. She is author of *An Emotional State: The Politics of Emotion in Postwar West German Culture* (2015) and has contributed to journals including *New German Critique*, *German Politics and Society*, *Exilforschung*, and *Psychoanalysis and History*, as well as peer-reviewed volumes on topics such as affect in literature, exile and cosmopolitanism, postwar Jewish-German literature, German film, feminism, memory studies, and psychoanalysis.

Contributors   xi

Lucas Riddle is the Andrew W. Mellon Postdoctoral Fellow in German at Bowdoin College, USA. He holds a PhD in Germanic Studies from the University of Illinois, Chicago. His dissertation is entitled "Laughter from the Margins: Minority Humor in Contemporary German-Language Literature," while his research interests include contemporary German literature, especially contemporary transcultural fiction and writing by often minoritized authors; humor; pop culture; communities, forms of belonging, and subcultures; and cinema.

Azade Seyhan is Research Professor in German Studies and Comparative Literature at Bryn Mawr College, USA. She is the author of *Representation and Its Discontents: The Critical Legacy of German Romanticism* (1992), *Writing Outside the Nation* (2001), *Tales of Crossed Destinies: The Turkish Novel in a Comparative Context* (2008), and *Heinrich Heine and the World Literary Map: Redressing the Canon* (2019). She has published on Romantic Idealism, transnational literatures, translation theory, modern Turkish literature, and exiled writers and academics, such as Heinrich Heine, Alexander Rüstow, Walter Benjamin, and Nâzım Hikmet, among others.

Birgit Tautz is the George Taylor Files Professor of Modern Languages and Professor of German at Bowdoin College, USA. She is the author of the award-winning *Translating the World: Toward a New History of German Literature around 1800* (2018) as well as of *Reading and Seeing Ethnic Differences in the Enlightenment: from China to Africa* (2007), and she edited *Colors 1800/1900/2000: Signs of Ethnic Difference* (2004). The author of numerous articles and chapters, Tautz recently co-edited *Social Capital, Material Cultures, Reading: German and European Networks around 1800*, and is working on a new book on "Small Things, Narrative Episodes."

Chunjie Zhang is Associate Professor of German at the University of California, Davis, USA, and the author of *Transculturality and German Discourse in the Age of European Colonialism* (2017). In addition to her research in eighteenth-century studies, postcolonial studies, global modernisms, and refugees and migration, she currently is writing an intellectual history of the reformulation and repurposing of Confucian ethics in the early twentieth century in the West and China.

Introduction

Laurie Ruth Johnson

Practitioners of German Studies grapple frequently with relations between geopolitical, linguistic, and cultural spaces. *Germany from the Outside: Rethinking German Cultural History in an Age of Displacement* brings current discussions about these intersections together with reflections on the relation between nation, language, and culture. Just as "Germany" never has been one discrete entity, "German culture" and "German language" never have been the property of one ethnic or national group. Emphasizing current issues of migration, displacement, systemic injustice, and belonging, the chapters in this volume explore new opportunities for understanding and shaping community in new ways at a time when many are questioning the ability of cultural practices to effect structural change. And, located at the nexus of cultural, political, historiographical, and philosophical discourses, these essays also can help inform our institutional discussions about next directions for our discipline.

Scholars in language, literature, and culture studies departments in the United States and around the globe are now, as perhaps always, discussing the very definitions of our fields even as we perform work within these fields' shifting borders. It is generally accepted that the humanities are in a state of fluctuating yet remarkably constant "crisis,"[1] but since the fall of the Berlin Wall at the very latest, teachers and researchers in German Studies have turned even more explicit attention to the extent to which national identity and national borders should determine the shape of our departments and work, especially given that language rarely is confined within national boundaries. Since the early 1990s, the debate about the relationship between language,

---

1 For one of the latest comprehensive engagements with this issue, see Paul Reitter and Chad Wellmon, *Permanent Crisis: The Humanities in a Disenchanted Age* (Chicago: University of Chicago Press, 2021).

culture, and the nation has intensified in general, but arguably especially in German Studies.[2] The field's history is an interesting subject in its own right: shaped inside and outside of Germany by those who, after 1871, committed intensely to the German national project, and then developed further in part by those who viewed the study of literature, culture, and language as a refuge *from* the national project (during and after World Wars I and II), work in German Studies always has been work at the boundaries, in the margins, or at the troubled center of a shifting physical and psychological geography.

The notion that the German cultural canon is limited to the borders of a German nation-state has long been challenged; nevertheless, our language, literature, and culture departments also have been based on the nation-state model for a long time.[3] The nation-state is largely a European invention of the eighteenth and nineteenth centuries. In the case of the German nation in particular, this invention was tied closely to the idea of a homogeneous German culture with a strong normative function. Consequently, histories of German culture and literature often are told from the "inside"—as the unfolding of a canon of works representing certain core values, with which every person who considers him- or herself "German" necessarily must identify. To be sure, critiques of nationalism and of identifying a particular culture with a particular nation have been plentiful: Lessing, Heine, Nietzsche, and numerous other figures strongly associated with "German culture" all have questioned the notion that culture must be tied to political geography; scholars long have pointed out that "nations" are, if not sheerly imagined, then also certainly not ageless or fixed. As Helmut Walser Smith puts it in his study of nationalism and the concept of the nation in Germany, "nations, like many other historical phenomena, are real or true in different ways in different periods [. . .] there was no transhistorical concept of the German nation. There was only a nation in its time."[4] The essays here, then, explore and perform direct and indirect engagements with a sense of the "German" and "Germany" in various times, from the eighteenth century to the present.

---

[2] For instance, Yasemin Yildiz discusses the role of the nation-state in shaping the construction of language as belonging within national borders, and the role of language education in shaping the modern nation-state, in *Beyond the Mother Tongue: The Postmonolingual Condition* (New York: Fordham University Press, 2013).

[3] On the role not only of the nation-state, but of nationalism in the development of German Studies—and vice-versa—see, for instance, Jakob Norberg, "German Literary Studies and the Nation," *German Quarterly*, vol. 91, no. 1 (Winter 2018): 1–17.

[4] Helmut Walser Smith, *Germany: A Nation in its Time: Before, during, and after Nationalism, 1500–2000* (New York: W.W. Norton, 2020), xi.

While recognizing that the "nation," with all its shifting and even chimerical meanings and associations, still does have immense significatory power—perhaps especially in our current era of accelerated globalization, transnationalism, neo-nationalisms, fiercely asserted regionalisms, and identity politics—the essays here approach German culture and its history from the "outside," as something heterogeneous and shaped by multiple and diverse sources, many of which are not connected overtly to things traditionally considered "German." They represent work on perspectives on Germany that emanate, in one way or another, from outside the borders of Germany itself, or that reflect how those within Germany's borders were influenced by "outsiders." Included here is work on authors who write in German but do not identify as German themselves; on how literature or cinema produces reflections on the changing nature of the nation-state; or on authors who live in Germany but are perceived in some way as "outsiders."

My use of quotation marks around "outside/r" refers to the intentional choice of *Germany from the Outside* as the volume's title, a choice that nevertheless needs to be problematized. We still construct identity (whether psychological, social, or political) in terms of what things are and what they are not; this is a starting point for our thinking about where and who we are. But, while acknowledging this, the volume's essays also deconstruct the implicit binary relationship between "inside" and "outside," and the ways in which those terms shape identities. As Edward Said understands it in *Freud and the Non-European* (2003), "identity cannot be thought or worked through itself alone; it cannot constitute or even imagine itself without that radical originary break or flaw which will not be repressed."[5] For Said, Freud's portrayal of Moses as a non-European who helped to define seminal aspects of what we consider a "European" identity is an exemplary understanding of the ways identity is constituted, not only from the outside, but, ever after, via a collective attempt to repress something we always knew: that the outsider is central to whomever "insiders" believe they are, purchase, or possess.

In addition to locating this mechanism of identity constitution in the psyche, Said locates it in history. He reads nineteenth-century nationalism in particular as relying on a very material construction of insides

---

[5] Edward Said, *Freud and the Non-European* (2003), cited here in *The Selected Works of Edward Said, 1966–2006*, ed. Moustafa Bayoumi and Andrew Rubin, 2nd ed. (New York: Vintage, 2019), 494–517, here 517. Tacitus's *Germania* (98 CE) is an analogous example to the example of Moses helping construct a European sense of identity, as *Germania*, the work of an "outsider," influenced the idea of the German nation and its culture.

and outsides. In his seminal reading of Jane Austen's *Mansfield Park*, "Jane Austen and Empire" (in *Culture and Imperialism*, 1993), Said notes that nationalism is inextricably connected with "'nation-making,'" which often involved imperialist expansion.[6] The estate of Mansfield Park and the intense inwardness of Fanny Price's focus on the social class to which she aspires are unthinkable without the support of Sir Thomas Bertram's slaves and plantation in the Caribbean. Said identifies a "curious alternation of outside and inside" in the novel that ultimately culminates in "the outside *becoming* the inside [. . .]. What was wanting *within* [within the estate, within the nationally landed but also internationally slave-owning gentry] was in fact supplied by the wealth derived from a West Indian plantation and a poor provincial relative [Fanny], both brought in to Mansfield Park and set to work."[7] The psychoanalytic mechanism of bringing the outside in, in order to supplement or sustain something missing, or wanting, within the self, is manifest in the political and social geography of Austen's novel and her age.

An essential hypothesis of the present volume is that the above-mentioned understandings of how identity is constituted mean that complex "outside" perspectives also always must have existed; at times, these perspectives have assumed the characteristics of productive cultural criticism. That criticism in turn can reflect a more complex and nuanced view of the nation, as well as of the role culture plays in the formation and functioning of nations. The contributions here develop an analytical vocabulary for the many ways in which Germany and its culture have been and can be understood "from the outside." The essays build on critical approaches developed over the past few decades that create a more diverse view of the impact of mobility on the nation-state, including exile studies, postcolonial studies, ethnic studies, and migration studies. At the same time, there are independent approaches represented here, as well as a concomitant critical vocabulary that demonstrates that the "outside" of the German nation was always part of its "inside"—that the history of German culture can be written as highly heterogeneous, as the product of many different "outside" influences and perspectives. The approaches and arguments in several essays herein correspond well with recent studies that trace aspects of the global or transnational history of "German" literature and culture, including Sandra Richter's *Eine Weltgeschichte der deutschsprachigen Literatur (A*

---

[6] Edward Said, "Jane Austen and Empire" (1990; appeared in *Culture and Imperialism* in 1993), cited here in *The Selected Works of Edward Said*, 351. Said quotes Walter Bagehot's use of the term "nation-making" from *Physics and Politics* (1887).

[7] Said, "Jane Austen and Empire," in *The Selected Works of Edward Said*, 361.

World History of German-Language Literature, 2017). Richter traces various historical culture migrations, and in so doing describes, for instance, how parts of what became the German literary canon originated in France and elsewhere. A move analogous to the one Said identifies in the early to mid-nineteenth century, of the "outside" world becoming the "inside" via imperialism and an economically driven process of nation-making, was happening in the late seventeenth and eighteenth centuries as well; and, according to Richter, as the outside came in, it also became identified as "German."[8]

By continuing to question and probe the constructed boundaries between inside and outside, this book offers, arguably, a cosmopolitan approach to German culture and literature. However, by grounding this cosmopolitanism in specific historical and material conditions, such as the histories of exile, expulsion, and displacement, the essays implicitly acknowledge that a cosmopolitan perspective can come at a cost. In this sense, they align well with Emily Apter's critique of "world literature" as espousing "identifying over differing" and with her advocacy of a world-oriented pursuit of cultural meanings that breaks open the notions of "inside" and "outside," ownership and dispossession, rootedness and displacement, belonging and exclusion, and that thus participates in actively remaking our collective and disrupted spaces.[9]

In addition to presenting specific case studies in German cultural history, then, the essays here co-create a fundamental methodological reflection on the vocabulary used to analyze community, culture, and language in the early twenty-first century. *Germany from the Outside* looks through the lenses of German culture, broadly understood, to help rethink German Studies by offering:

- models for reshaping our understanding of the nation-state and its relationship with culture, problematizing the latter's deployment to in- and exclude groups and individuals;
- an updated exploration of what German Studies means today, within the context of a global history of mobility (both voluntary and involuntary); and

---

[8] See Sandra Richter, *Eine Weltgeschichte der deutschsprachigen Literatur* (Munich: C. Bertelsmann, 2017), especially 77–122.
[9] Emily Apter, *Against World Literature: On the Politics of Untranslatability* (London and New York: Verso, 2013), 335. In a different argument that parallels Apter's in some respects, B. Venkat Mani calls for "an open, porous, border-crossing, discipline-trespassing methodology" in literature and culture studies that simultaneously pays painstaking attention to local and historical specificities. See the Introduction to the special forum "World Literature: Against Isolationist Readings," in the *German Quarterly*, vol. 94, no. 3 (Summer 2021): 367–70, here 370.

- a reconsideration of and renewed purpose for the humanities in the early twenty-first century, with the goal of creating non-coercive forms of community.

In a forum on German cultural studies and the nation-state model in the *German Quarterly* in 2019, Benjamin Robinson excavates the common assumption that the truth or value of what we do can be assessed relative to how well it matches things in the world. According to this view, the organization of German and other national language departments reflects aspects of organization of the world. But, Robinson asks, what if the ideas advanced in literature and culture studies are "quite independent of the actual world of the moment, being instead creative constructions suited to the inexistent ends of the imagination?"[10] Such work might, paradoxically, be a better fit for a world in which, as Marx put it in *The Communist Manifesto*, all that is solid melts (continuously) into air. And it certainly could relieve us of the burden of needing to be "relevant" in a world of electronic financial markets, global trade, and agglomerated service economies. However, Robinson acknowledges that without pursuing some relation to the structures of the world, no matter how quickly they shift, we will fossilize—and not necessarily in a museum-worthy way. One productive avenue of "matching" things in the world while also advancing our understanding of diversity, injustice, and the need for equity and inclusion might be to use our knowledge of the histories of the nation (or, of the nation in its times, to rephrase Helmut Walser Smith) to illuminate the contemporary world.

However: already in 1998, Slavoj Žižek identified the timeliness of Marx's warning (or, hope) that

> In place of the old local and national seclusion and self-sufficiency, we have intercourse in every direction, universal interdependence of nations. And as in material, so also in intellectual production. The intellectual creations of individual nations become common property. National one-sidedness and narrow-mindedness become more and more impossible, and from the numerous national and local literatures, there arises a world literature.[11]

For Marx, the end of narrow-minded nationalism was not a bad thing, but Žižek, projecting Marx's thinking into contemporary capitalism,

---

[10] Benjamin Robinson, "Which Model makes us more Adequate to the World?" *German Quarterly*, vol. 92, no. 4 (Fall 2019): 475–78, here 476.

[11] Slavoj Žižek, *The Spectre is Still Roaming Around!* (Zagreb: Arkzin, 1998), monumenttotransformation.org/atlas-of-transformation/html/c/communist-manifesto/the-specter-is-still-roaming-around-slavoj-zizek.html.

wields that idea to say that it is late capitalism's unstoppable trend toward homogeneous global markets that will end local traditions and meanings. Žižek reaffirms Marx's claim that the means of production have replaced religion as the primary means of exploiting and instrumentalizing individuals and groups, but posits that both are spectral, and a specter governs us: an "'objective,' systemic, anonymous" one, even ghostlier, if this is possible, than the ghost of the mythology of religion. Marx's prophesying of the end of the nation-state thus ends in Žižek's lament about potentially even more exploitative kinds of spectrality. Instead of chasing material advantages, we are chasing ghosts.

A project involving (specters of) national history is always also a memory project. Despite the very current nature of much of this volume's work, the essays contribute to ongoing negotiations in cultural memory about what can and should be remembered, "inside" and "outside" of the nation and its myriad subparts, and how. The essays embody the relationality that is inevitable in any memory work: that is, memory is always constituted in the present and out of a set of connections between diverse past and present events. Memoirs written during and after the Holocaust reflect the singularity of that genocide, even as, when we remember them, we relate them to other memoirs and/or to other trauma. This type of non-relativistic relation can help form solidarity and community among, say, various displaced peoples without reducing all displacement to a monolithic experience.[12]

This book's three main sections structurally reflect this consciously relational memory work, by grouping essays with similar thematic but diverse chronological foci. Part I, "Reading German Cultural History Differently," explicitly emphasizes and questions the status and (self-) definition of insiders and outsiders relative to rapidly shifting concepts of German identities. Part II, "Stories of Expulsion, Exile, and Displacement," tugs at the notion of "exile studies" to yield fresh transnational perspectives on how self-consciousness morphs in periods of displacement, whether forced or voluntary. Part III, "Rewriting German Culture," provides models for doing the disciplinary work of German Studies in ways both related to and shifted from the past. Whether examining the persistence of the traditional canon within new work or the influence of the "marginal" on how we understand the canonical, these essays analyze the multimedial as well as the multinational and

---

[12] For more on the relational and multidirectional nature of cultural memory, see Michael Rothberg, *Multidirectional Memory: Remembering the Holocaust in the Age of Decolonization* (Stanford, CA: Stanford University Press, 2009), and "Wir brauchen neue Wege, um über Erinnerung nachzudenken," interview with Elizabeth von Thadden, *Die Zeit*, March 27, 2021, zeit.de/kultur/2021-03/michael-rothberg-multidirektionale-erinnerung-buch-holocaust-rassismus-kolonialismus.

multicultural. All essays not only reflect relational memory but represent current approaches to what Édouard Glissant called the "poetics of relation": a practice of reading that understands identity as positive, as multiple (or: multiply constituted), as both specific and general, and often as something to be celebrated. And, for this volume's contributors, as for Glissant, the practice of reading itself, accompanied by an understanding of the conditions of literary and cultural production, can aid actively in the work of decolonization.[13]

The enthusiastic and energetic nature of the work in this book and in German Studies today unfortunately will mean less if our discipline continues to lose students. The essays in *Germany from the Outside* are scholarly but speak to the classroom as well: this is the kind of transnational exploration that could inspire recalibrated curricula and redefined departments—departments that may remain "German" but which could be loosened from the nation-state model, depending on the student needs, faculty expertise, and other institutional considerations in the places where we write and teach.[14]

In the above-mentioned piece on "Which Model makes us more Adequate to the World?", Benjamin Robinson asks: what world-adequate, but also imagination-adequate, structures are we, in German Studies, creating now? He argues that contemporary humanists are "not disruptors and purveyors of shock, but mediators and kindlers of epiphany."[15] I understand Robinson to mean that we are in part stewards as well as re-creators of the world, working in spaces where the "nation" undeniably still exists and helps define what we do, but in ways that we can assess critically and constructively. In this age of displacement, we also are makers of places—whether in the Zoom classroom or in pandemic-wary in-person lecture halls—places of refuge, and of shelter.

---

[13] Édouard Glissant, *Poetics of Relation*, trans. Betsy Wing (Ann Arbor: University of Michigan Press, 1990).

[14] Per Urlaub argues compellingly for a "transnational orientation of the field [of German Studies, that] has more potential to result in attractive curricula and resonates more strongly with teaching philosophies and research activities of the majority of the current and future professoriate," while noting that "decisions that relate to departmental structures must be calibrated to local particularities, including size of program and institution, enrollment trends, shifts in local student demographics, faculty interests and strengths, availability of robust partners, and the level of overall enthusiasm (or lack thereof) for language education among the campus's senior leadership." See "The Nation-State Model and German Studies: An Applied Linguistics Perspective," *German Quarterly*, vol. 92, no. 4 (Fall 2019): 490–4, here 493–4.

[15] Robinson, "Which Model makes us more Adequate to the World?" 476.

Acknowledgments

I am privileged to serve on the Board of Directors of the American Friends of Marbach (AFM), a support organization for the Deutsches Literaturarchiv (DLA). The DLA is hugely important to so many of us, and to the work of German Studies on this side of the Atlantic. The AFM regularly hosts conferences either at a US institution where one of the board members is employed, or at the DLA. The AFM-affiliated conference on *Germany from the Outside* took place in September 2019 here at the University of Illinois Urbana-Champaign; we are indebted to the support of then-AFM President Paul Michael Lützeler, current President Meike Werner, and to all my fellow Board and AFM members, as well as to staff at the DLA itself.

My thanks also go to Imke Meyer, the editor of the series *New Directions in German Studies*, as well as to Rachel Moore, Haaris Naqvi, Ronnie Hanna and Merv Honeywood at Bloomsbury. Jeff Castle assisted with the early stages of editing. I deeply appreciate the thoughtful work of the various anonymous reviewers who read the volume's pieces with care and provided excellent suggestions, all of which the authors used to improve their essays. And I am grateful for the supporters of the above-mentioned conference on *Germany from the Outside*, including the Max Kade Foundation, the German Academic Exchange Service, and the College of Liberal Arts and Sciences as well as various schools, centers, and programs at the University of Illinois. The conference jump-started the book process, and it has been very rewarding to have been able to engage additional scholars with the project since then. Carl Niekerk, as ever, made it all work.

Works Cited

Apter, Emily. *Against World Literature: On the Politics of Untranslatability* (London and New York: Verso, 2013).

Bayoumi, Moustafa, and Andrew Rubin, eds. *The Selected Works of Edward Said, 1966–2006*, 2nd ed. (New York: Vintage, 2019).

Glissant, Édouard. *Poetics of Relation*, trans. Betsy Wing (Ann Arbor: University of Michigan Press, 1990).

Mani, B. Venkat, ed. "World Literature: Against Isolationist Readings," a special forum, in *German Quarterly*, vol. 94, no. 3 (Summer 2021): 367–96.

Norberg, Jakob. "German Literary Studies and the Nation," *German Quarterly*, vol. 91, no. 1 (Winter 2018): 1–17.

Reitter, Paul, and Chad Wellmon. *Permanent Crisis: The Humanities in a Disenchanted Age* (Chicago: University of Chicago Press, 2021).

Richter, Sandra. *Eine Weltgeschichte der deutschsprachigen Literatur* (Munich: C. Bertelsmann, 2017).

Robinson, Benjamin. "Which Model makes us more Adequate to the World?" *German Quarterly*, vol. 92, no. 4 (Fall 2019): 475–8.

Rothberg, Michael. *Multidirectional Memory: Remembering the Holocaust in the Age of Decolonization* (Stanford, CA: Stanford University Press, 2009).

Rothberg, Michael. "Wir brauchen neue Wege, um über Erinnerung nachzudenken," interview with Elizabeth von Thadden, *Die Zeit*, March 27, 2021, zeit.de/kultur/2021-03/michael-rothberg-multidirektionale-erinnerung-buch-holocaust-rassismus-kolonialismus.

Smith, Helmut Walser. *Germany: A Nation in its Time: Before, during, and after Nationalism, 1500–2000* (New York: W.W. Norton, 2020).

Urlaub, Per. "The Nation-State Model and German Studies: An Applied Linguistics Perspective," *German Quarterly*, vol. 92, no. 4 (Fall 2019): 490–4.

Yildiz, Yasemin. *Beyond the Mother Tongue: The Postmonolingual Condition* (New York: Fordham University Press, 2013).

Žižek, Slavoj. *The Spectre is still Roaming Around!* (Zagreb: Arkzin, 1998).

I Reading German Cultural History Differently

One Finding Odysseus's Scars Again: Hyperlinked Literary Histories in the Age of Refugees

B. Venkat Mani

We are living, once again, in times of forced migrations and refuge. For the year 2020, the United Nations High Commission for Refugees estimated that there were 82.4 million forcibly displaced people around the world—the highest number on record since the two world wars.[1] The proliferation of refugees and stateless people in the world has coincided with the resurgence of ethno-religious nationalism and divisive rhetoric centered on securing and insulating borders. The year 2019 also marked thirty years since the iconic fall of the Berlin Wall, and from India to Hungary to the United States, we witnessed a worldwide fixation on construction of new walls and barbed-wire fences along national borders.[2]

In addition, new migration plans and migration bans are using refugees as instruments to shape and transform national self-representation, as well as the very definition of citizenship. In the US, this includes the so-called Muslim Ban, also known as the Travel Ban, which had been introduced in various forms since 2016, until finally receiving approval from the Supreme Court, in 2018, and then being rescinded by the US House Committee.[3] In Germany, the CSU politician Horst

---

[1] "Figures at a Glance," UNHCR, updated June 18, 2021, www.unhcr.org/figures-at-a-glance.html.
[2] Elisabeth Zerofsky, "Viktor Orbán's Far-Right Vision for Europe," *New Yorker*, January 14, 2019, www.newyorker.com/magazine/2019/01/14/viktor-orbans-far-right-vision-for-europe; Lucy Rodgers Zurcher and Anthony Dominic Bailey, "Trump's Border Wall—in seven Charts," BBC News, September 27, 2019, www.bbc.com/news/world-us-canada-46824649.
[3] Rebecca Rainey, "House Committee votes to rescind Trump Travel Ban," *POLITICO*, February 2, 2020, www.politico.com/news/2020/02/12/house-committee-votes-to-rescind-trump-travel-ban-114649.

Seehofer's Masterplan Migration (2018)[4] has led to a large-scale deportation of Afghan asylum seekers by placing limitations on migration in the name of national cultural cohesion.[5] India's discriminatory Citizenship Amendment Act (2019) has likewise weaponized the very idea of citizenship, creating an internal wall between the majority Hindu and the minority Muslim communities in a two-tier citizenry, through a two-tier refugee profile.[6]

In other words, we live in a time when the figure of the forced migrant, the refugee, rendered homeless due to political upheaval or natural disaster and on a treacherous journey to find safety, becomes the figure from whom we need to guard our relatively safer homes by shutting doors or closing borders. In addition, minority citizens, be they recent immigrants, as millions are in the United States, or members of populations with longer histories of residency, as in the case of India's Muslim communities, are being rendered stateless and homeless. Migration has become the anathema of nationalism, as the Indian historian Romila Thapar has recently reminded us, because it works against purist notions of national composition.[7] Citizenship is being weaponized so that populist political discourse can operate without any challenges to the state's attempts to manipulate history in order to willfully erase heterogeneity of national formations from public memory.[8] Processes of willful and forced migration, and slow sedimentation, through which national communities and nation-states were created, are being proactively suppressed by denouncing histories of migration, and consequentially migratory futures. In the US, the closing of international borders and the massive restrictions on visa processes in the

---

[4] Florian Gathmann, "Innenminister Seehofer stellt Migrationskatalog vor. Der Desaster-Plan," *Spiegel Online*, July 10, 2018, www.spiegel.de/politik/deutschland/innenminister-und-csu-chef-seehofer-stellt-migrationskatalog-vor-masterplan-des-desasters-a-1217421.html.

[5] Waslat Hasrat-Nazimi, "Afghanische Flüchtlinge verzweifeln an Europas Außengrenze," *DW.COM*, March 3, 2020, www.dw.com/de/afghanische-fl%C3%BCchtlinge-verzweifeln-an-europas-au%C3%9Fengrenze/a-52623524.

[6] Nayanima Basu, "CAA, NRC could render Huge Numbers of Indian Muslims stateless, says Ashutosh Varshney," *ThePrint* (blog), March 5, 2020, theprint.in/india/caa-nrc-could-render-huge-numbers-of-indian-muslims-stateless-says-ashutosh-varshney/376008.

[7] Romila Thapar, "They peddle Myths and call it History," *New York Times*, May 17, 2019, www.nytimes.com/2019/05/17/opinion/india-elections-modi-history.html.

[8] Sahana Ghosh and Sara Shneiderman, "New Laws weaponize Citizenship in India," *The Conversation*, December 22, 2019, theconversation.com/new-laws-weaponize-citizenship-in-india-129027.

midst of the global coronavirus pandemic, all under the guise of protecting national public health and safety, is just the latest indication of the uncertain journey ahead for migrants and refugees aspiring to make the United States their home.

At this conflict-ridden and volatile moment at the beginning of the third decade of the twenty-first century, it is urgent for scholars of literature to reclaim and reinsert histories of human migration, and to grant these their rightful place in studies of "national literatures." Reading literature in the institutional context of a university today necessitates the charting out of new pathways to resist natalist-nativist, racist, and ethnonationalist imaginations of literary studies. Today more than ever before, there is an urgent need to hypothesize linkages among various national and regional histories to challenge further a monolingual, homogeneous cooptation of literatures and their histories into the nationalist discourse.

These ideas form the core of this chapter, in which I underscore the need for a global history of German literature by proposing a transnational arrangement of literary history around borderlines, walls, and the figure of the refugee. There are three central ideas that guide my proposal. First, any attempt at tracing a "globally connected" literary history of a national or linguistic-cultural sphere must aspire to engage a global, discerning readership rather than a specialized set of professional readers (i.e., students and scholars of a single national literature). Second, such a broadly oriented literary history should offer its readers an account of global historical forces—which may include a set of globally influential ideas, significant political events, and/or state- and non-state actors—locating authors, readers, and critics within these forces. Finally, a global history of German or any other "national" literature should try to emancipate itself from a territorially bound imagination of transnationalism that still privileges the native over the migrant in the national imaginary. To this end, merely treating authors of "migrant backgrounds" or authors in exile as additions or supplements—that is, optional, or exceptional enrichments—to a national literature otherwise written by authors of majority (ethnic German) communities will not suffice. New modes of global history must proactively seek, and uncover, "hyperlinks"—a term that I will explain later—between national and global political histories, and in doing so work to bring literature written by authors with histories of comparatively recent migrations onto an equal footing with literature written by so-called native or majoritarian authors. What I am essentially arguing for in this chapter is a way of thinking about literary history that presents literatures of and by the native, the migrant, the refugee, and the foreign author as an essential condition for, and not an exception to, the formation of national or world literatures.

By locating the need for a paradigm shift in the study of literature and literary history in our current political realities, my thoughts extend a project whose foundations were laid by Edward Said. In his celebrated essay "Secular Criticism," Said pointed out that "academic literary history is a descendant of such nineteenth-century specialties as scholarship, philology, and cultural history."[9] Said's new formulations for criticism in the last two decades of the twentieth century—the essay was first published in 1983—were framed by his poignant observation that the "cultural realm and its expertise are divorced from their real connections with power."[10] Said traces the roots of power inequities in tandem with the realm of culture by locating them in the nineteenth-century Eurocentric project of creating national cultures, based very much on the notion of inside and outside: "The readiest account of place might define it as a nation, and certainly in the exaggerated boundary drawn between Europe and the Orient [. . .] [through which] the idea of a national-cultural community as a sovereign entity and place set against other places, has its full realization."[11] Said identifies modes in which literary criticism and literary history are embedded in multiple formations of borders and hierarchies: "The entire history of nineteenth-century European thought [. . .] is made between what is fitting for us and what is fitting for them, the former designated as inside, in place, common, belonging, in a word, *above*, the latter, who are designated as outside, excluded, aberrant, inferior, in a word, *below*."[12]

There are multiple ways in which we can imagine upsetting the vertical hierarchies of above and below and the horizontal discriminations of inside and outside, thus breaking up nineteenth-century national-cultural formations. Focusing on different ways in which political borders are punctured and cultural expertise engages with real connections of power can lead us to think about ways in which national spaces are connected through wars, trade, state-sponsored or state-independent cultural exchanges, and more. For the purpose of this chapter, I will focus on the figure of the refugee. For reasons stated at the beginning of the chapter, the figure of the refugee has become the litmus test for our global humanity, for our politics of recognition, inclusion, and exclusion. Contained in, and disseminated through, the figure of the refugee are *longue durée* histories of empire and nation-state formations, wars, insurgencies, terrorism, religious and sectarian violence, poverty, pandemics,

---

[9] Edward W. Said, "Secular Criticism," in *The Selected Works of Edward Said, 1966–2006*, ed. Moustafa Bayoumi and Andrew Rubin (New York: Vintage Books, 2019), 220–44, here 221.
[10] Said, "Secular Criticism," 222.
[11] Said, "Secular Criticism," 228.
[12] Said, "Secular Criticism," 230 (emphasis in original).

and, more recently, climate, environmental, and health-related crises through which nations, as political and social units, are inextricably connected with one another. An engagement with the figure of the refugee, especially in a literary historical context, would mean, extending my previous thought, recognizing the refugee, conditions that lead to the formation of refugees, management of refugee populations, and narratives about and by refugees as central to—rather than an episodic or momentary enrichment of—national literature and its literary history. Consistent with Said, I want to consider the refugee as a figure that is constantly out of place, and that therefore paves the way for us to upset vertical hierarchies and horizontal discriminations between Europe and the Orient, the nation and its others. This is the second set of assertions that I want to present in this chapter, albeit through a few questions.

What ensues when the figure of the refugee is imagined not at the periphery but at the center of our historical and literary historical investigations? What does it mean to cross borders, establish relations, and enable exchanges through "borderless" readings of historical events and literary texts? How would a literary history based on borderless reading help us to rethink our understanding of literary history in a globally comparative context?

I want to approach my proposals, assertions, and these questions in three steps. First, I want to briefly discuss two models of literary history published in the first decade of the twenty-first century—one in the national and the other in the world literary context. Second, I turn to a brief discussion of the term *global history* from the discipline of history, which opens up space for a discussion of archives as a concept and practice in the context of a global literary history. This will lay the ground for me to present a "hyperlinked" history of German literature, with a focus on connections to the history of Afghanistan and Afghan refugees. My chapter ends with a discussion of Erich Auerbach's *Mimesis* and Edward Said's "Reflections on Exile," examining how refuge, exile, and displacement can be "hyperlinked" to frame historical and literary events.

World Literary Histories

In his introduction to the volume *A New Literary History of German Literature* (2004), David Wellbery cites Paul Celan's famous dictum, "Every poem is datable" ["Jedes Gedicht ist datierbar"].[13] In the same context, Wellbery argues that

---

[13] David E. Wellbery, ed., *A New History of German Literature* (Cambridge, MA: Harvard University Press, 2004), xvii.

> [...] traditional literary histories treat individual texts and performances not as singular occurrences, but as illustrative instances of some force, tendency, or norm such as the spirit of an age or a nation, a class bias, or an aesthetic ideal. To grasp the historical character of a literary text is, according to this way of thinking, to see the individual case as something typical of something else, and therefore replaceable. This operation effaces literature's 'datable' singularity and contingency. A major aim of *A New Literary History of German Literature* is to find a mode of presentation that restores access to this dimension of literature.[14]

Moving away from a literary history that presents a work as an example for or typical of something, Wellbery proposes a reorganization based on specific dates—of an important court case, a publication date, a performance date, or a political or cultural event—which coincide with and therefore help to reflect on the historical, temporal situation of a literary work. Multiple modes of production and circulation of literary works in the electronic age, both physical and digital, and the creation of a new, more inclusive readership drive Wellbery's model of datability. The task of such a literary history is formidable, spotlighting the singularity of the date while providing "multiple points of entry and allowing for various reading agendas."[15] The datable event, the encounter of a reading experience, and the constellation of media in storage and transmission become central to this literary historical enterprise, which aspires to construct German literary history in relation with various other literary histories. Wellbery calls this form of literary historical writing "random access history."

Wellbery's model of the narrative writing of "national" literary histories, framed through significant time periods or specific years, shifts the focus from spatiality to temporality, thus opening the possibility of a transnational evaluation of literatures that is not territorially bound. However, the decided focus on German language and the German-speaking world in general curbs that ambition significantly. Consequently, "random access history" remains sparse and selective in its aspiration to access political or literary histories beyond Europe that might be connected in some way to the German-speaking world.

While Wellbery's literary history focuses on literature in the German-speaking world, a different model of arranging literary history is offered in a special issue of *New Literary History* (2008), which focused on "world literary history." This model also draws attention to the

---

[14] Wellbery, *A New History of German Literature*, xxi.
[15] Wellbery, *A New History of German Literature*, xxii.

particularity of literary texts, but the project gains its richness through its much larger temporal and spatial scale, and contextualizes the production, circulation, and translation of literature in the larger context of world literary space. Key to this collection are two opposing positions.

Hans Ulrich Gumbrecht, in an essay tellingly entitled "Shall we continue to write Histories of Literature," traces a history of literary history from early nineteenth-century Germany to late twentieth-century Anglo-American theory, only to reveal an Auerbachian anxiety over the very loss of historicity and the purpose of literary history today. "How [. . .] such new ways of experiencing the historicity of literature may relate to each other—I don't know," writes Gumbrecht, but he points out that we will have to "think, experiment, and [. . .] wait" if we want to write histories of literature.[16] Admittedly, Gumbrecht does not reject outright the possibility of writing literary histories in the future. However, in questioning the relevance of traditional modes of writing literary history, Gumbrecht opens up ways of thinking and experimenting. Juxtaposed with Said's ideas, such experimentation should involve undoing the national-cultural paradigm.

A counter-position to Gumbrecht's comes from David Damrosch, whose "Definition," "Design," and "Purpose" of a world literary history somewhat intersect with ideas proposed by Wellbery. A "full history of world literature," Damrosch proposes, "should unfold the varied processes and strategies through which writers have individually and collectively furthered the long negotiation between local cultures and the world beyond them."[17] This very formulation brings Damrosch into conversation with Said about the significance of moving beyond a simple national-cultural, isolationist model. Multiple points of entry, multiple modes of writing—in other words, the plurality of languages, critical approaches, and literary traditions, as well as modes of production and circulation, encompassing scripts, media, and forms—remain foundational to Damrosch's model. Instead of conceptualizing a "random access history," Damrosch mentions Wikipedia as providing "hyperlinks" that connect literary works on a larger scale.

At the risk of generalizing, let me point out three commonalities among the approaches to literary history proposed above. The first is the centrality of the literary terrain. Wellbery's "random access history" still privileges German—as a marker of linguistic-cultural specificity— for its conceptualization of national literature, which, in turn, cannot be

---

[16] Hans Ulrich Gumbrecht, "Shall we continue to write Histories of Literature?" *New Literary History*, vol. 39, no. 3 (2008): 519–32, here 531.

[17] David Damrosch, "Toward a History of World Literature," *New Literary History*, vol. 39, nos. 3–4 (2009): 481–95, here 485.

dissociated from geographical borders, even if they change over time. The *New Literary History* model emphasizes multilingualism, but here as well, language, at least in the scope of the essay, is largely linked to territory. The second commonality is the positioning of a literary work: born in the local but read in relation to the extra-local—whether it is regional, international, or really on a global scale. One can sense an evolutionary perspective, which goes from natal-residential to migrant. There is more room in this model to think about migration along with, and despite, worldwide projects of nation-building. The third, and most important, commonality is history itself: a) the changing nature of our relationship, especially the younger generation's relationship, to history, and b) the changing nature of the very discipline of history—its design, definition, and purpose. What I find noteworthy here is that a newer generation's relation to history seems to be in flux, as, perhaps, do the design, definition, and purpose. But historical specificity seems to be traceable largely to place—that is, to a singular territory. A national space, defined by territorial boundaries, becomes open to pluralistic imagination and examination through its connection to other national spaces, also defined by territorial boundaries. A sense of permanency in natality and residency, and of insecurity in itinerancy, migrancy, and especially exile informs such modalities of thinking about literary history. Underlying these observations is more than a hunch. A tradition of intellectual investment in settlement, residency, and citizenship can be noted in European, especially German, literary history and historiography. This sense of privileging space can be seen in the periodization model of multiple edited volumes, such as *Deutsche Literaturgeschichte von den Anfängen bis zur Gegenwart* (2019, first published in 1979), edited by Wolfgang Beutin et al.

It should be noted that in his review of the first edition, the prominent US-based Germanist Jost Hermand hailed the volume as the first "useable project" ("brauchbares Projekt") with a "'readable' representation" ("'lesbare' Darstellung") and a clear pedagogical purpose of cultural education.[18] For Hermand, the volume was geared toward students in the (former) Federal Republic of Germany, who did not read books, go to the theater, or even know what "lyric" might mean, a generation Hermand claimed had grown up in an era of cultural regression ("Kulturzurückstufung").[19] Hermand had less of an issue with the singularly

---

[18] Jost Hermand, "Book Review: Deutsche Literaturgeschichte. Von den Anfängen bis zur Gegenwart," *Monatshefte für deutschsprachige Literatur und Kultur*, vol. 73, no. 3 (1981): 338–40, here 338.
[19] Hermand, "Book Review," 338–39.

German-oriented nature of this cultural product; understandably so, as at the very outset of his review, he thought of this literary history as the perfect source for German literature and culture for his students in the United States. Nonetheless, Hermand found it problematic that a 500-page volume had reduced the discussion of post-1945 literatures to a mere 100 pages.

Hermand's description, as well as his critique, of the volume, could be useable for the 2019 edition, albeit for different reasons. The jacket carries the following formidable description:

> From medieval singers and epic writers to Martin Opitz, Gotthold Ephraim Lessing, Friedrich Schiller and Johann Wolfgang von Goethe, to Heinrich Heine, Georg Büchner and Bertolt Brecht to Günter Grass, Martin Walser, Uwe Tellkamp, Herta Müller and Ursula Krechel. All well-known writers are recorded. This literary history captures poetry, novels, prose and other literary genres and currents in the mirror of the epochs, shows the authors, their work and the literary business in close interweaving with the social, cultural and political zeitgeist. A lively reference work, which thanks to the successful combination of text and illustrations, ensures great reading pleasure for the curious and the connoisseurs alike.
>
> [Von den mittelalterlichen Sängern und Epikern über Martin Opitz, Gotthold Ephraim Lessing, Friedrich Schiller und Johann Wolfgang von Goethe, über Heinrich Heine, Georg Büchner und Bertolt Brecht bis Günter Grass, Martin Walser, Uwe Tellkamp, Herta Müller und Ursula Krechel. Alle namhaften Schriftsteller sind erfasst: Die Literaturgeschichte fängt Lyrik, Roman, Prosa und andere literarische Gattungen und Strömungen im Spiegel der Epochen ein, zeigt die Autoren, ihr Schaffen und den Literaturbetrieb in enger Verflechtung mit dem gesellschaftlichen, kulturellen und politischen Zeitgeist. Ein lebendiges Nachschlagewerk, das durch die gelungene Verknüpfung von Text und Illustrationen bei Neugierigen und Kennern gleichermaßen für großes Lesevergnügen sorgt.]

The volume promises a national-cultural pedagogy steeped in the traditions of the nineteenth century. Trends of each decade in this volume are defined by continuous waves of "original" national artistic tendencies that provide a national literature its character—from *Aufklärung* and *Sturm und Drang* to *Expressionismus*, or even the *Bitterfelder Weg*, all the way up to *Wendeliteratur*. *Migrationsliteratur* finds an extremely brief mention and is not connected to *Exilliteratur*. This literary historical form of "trending now," to use a contemporary phrase, is highly place-based and obligated to the nation. *Exilliteratur* is extolled because it was written in exile, in a place where somebody settled, but still remained connected to the place that was left behind, to which one hoped or longed to return. "Literatur der Migration" (usually referring to literature that comes out of voluntary or forced migrations) is appreciated because it enriches ("bereichert") the language and literature of a place. There is little room for the figure of the refugee within these spaces. There is no attention paid to the possibility that instead of enriching an already existing national tradition, the figure of the refugee within a narrative, or the refugee author may actually be modifying the existing tradition, or contributing to the creation of a new tradition, one that in turn may be connected to many other literary traditions previously ignored or willfully neglected.

Following Gumbrecht's cue of thinking and experimenting, what if we disarrange the particular imagination of a "rooted" connectivity that I have mentioned in the previous modalities and give equal significance to "uprootedness" and "unsettlement"—by force, not just by volition—as essential to our conceptualization of networks of histories? What if we accord primacy to a series of "hyperlinked" bases that are formed and informed by the itinerancy of the human subject, instead of disentangling historical connections by tracing and restoring genealogies to singularly space-bound, sociocultural headquarters? To approach these questions, it might be productive to consider the development of the framework of global history within the discipline of history.

Global Histories, Refugees, and the Question of Archives

The notion of territoriality and global history is taken up most compellingly by historian Sebastian Conrad in his monograph *What is Global History?* (2016), in which he underlines the complexity of history in our time, when "the relevance of territorial boundaries has been called into question."[20] As an alternative to the "compartmentalization of historical reality—into national and world history, into history and area studies"[21]—Conrad presents global history as one of the ways to "come to terms with the connectivities of the past."[22] Instead of presenting global history as "what happens worldwide," or casting it in terms of an "omnivorous perspective [through which] everything that ever

---

[20] Sebastian Conrad, introduction to *What Is Global History?* (Princeton, NJ: Princeton University Press, 2016), 15.
[21] Conrad, *Global History*, 5.
[22] Conrad, *Global History*, 6.

happened on the earth is a legitimate ingredient of global history,"[23] Conrad proposes global history as a perspective and as a process.[24] Cross-border exchanges, connections, conditions, concepts, or phenomena that shape human societies in different parts of the world become central for thinking through the perspectival and processual approach and scope of global history. However, instead of just reducing the project of global history to a perspective or a process, Conrad privileges contextualization as a mode of global historical inquiry: "Any attempt to contextualize globally needs to consider the degree and quality of the entanglements in its purview."[25] A preliminary test of the degree and quality of such entanglements can be found in Conrad's underlining of the significance of links:

> As the world has evolved more and more into a single political, economic, and cultural entity, casual links on the global level have become stronger. And as a result of the proliferation and perpetuation of such links, local events are increasingly shaped by a global context that can be understood structurally or even systematically.[26]

The complexity of the model of global history and its promise, scope, limitations, and impact within the field of history are too vast to summarize here. Nonetheless, the perspectival and processual opening that Conrad presents could serve well to develop a conceptual framework for a global literary history for our times.

A global history of literature need not rely on a worldwide coverage model, but it would be helpful to identify the degree and quality of entanglements in the purview of a literary historian in order to escape a compartmentalized, partially focused examination of ideas, concepts, and phenomena in the larger literary field. While the field of comparative world literature has succeeded in constructing frameworks within which the development of genres such as the novel, poetry, and drama is traced in specific locations around the world, the focus on the territorially-bound local specificities has curtailed the globality of the project. A prime example of such an exercise would be Franco Moretti's much discussed two-volume project *The Novel* (2007), which relies on the synthesis of scholarship on the novel from various local interlocutors from the Chinese (linguistic and national), Indian (national, subsuming all

---

[23] Conrad, *Global History*, 7.
[24] Conrad, *Global History*, 11.
[25] Conrad, *Global History*, 13.
[26] Conrad, *Global History*, 11.

Indian languages into one), and African (continental, subsuming all literatures of Africa into one) contexts (as well as others), establishing the primacy of the distinctions between various European novels, such as French, German, and English. A global literary history would afford the possibility of moving beyond such territorially-based, territorially-bound models of arranging literature, which, on the one hand, operate according to cross-border, worldwide exchanges and influences and, on the other hand, erase the migratory, hybrid origins of aesthetic forms and flatten the nuances that occur when aesthetic forms acquire different shapes and forms, after the border-crossings have taken place. Moretti's model also reduces the agency of the scholar: by limiting the scholar to local expertise, this form of tracing the globality of a genre allows little space for the identification and articulation of connectivities of the past.

While I do not discount the significance of a narrative of global history with a genre at its center, I am more interested in seeing how the inherent mobility of a figure that by nature is not bound to a place or a space—a figure that exists though deterritorialization, whose very identity is defined by forced displacement and the lack of acceptance into the text of a nation, or national literature—could become productive for a model of global literary history that privileges contextualization and linkages in a much more flexible, borderless way. That is why the figure of the refugee, the unwanted, an always already erased outsider, whose primary teleological trace is often limited to the co-optation into the national text, becomes so fascinating for thinking through global literary history. However, instead of reducing the refugee to an "ingredient" of a global literary history, I want to speculate on the position of the refugee and refugee narratives through the notion of the archive. For a history requires its archives, and in the context of a global historical project, or the globalization of German literary archives, the question remains: whose history, whose archive? Which past is remembered, and which conveniently subjected to amnesia?

A focus on refugees and refugee narratives immediately draws attention to the dual meaning of a literary archive: first, as a house of "authentic" documents, a repository of records, a collection of artifacts pertaining to an author, place, movement, political organization, or collective such as the nation-state, in a physical or digital space; and second, as a collection of forms of aesthetic expression—verbal, visual, and aural, physical and digital—that may serve as a surrogate to narratives absent from regular archives.

In their comprehensive *Handbuch Archiv. Geschichte, Aufgaben, Perspektive* (2016), Marcel Lepper and Ulrich Raulff list several definitions of *archive*. An archive, they state, is "a building, a repository" ["ein Gebäude, ein Aufbewahrungsort"], "an institution or a form of organization" ["eine Institution oder Organizationsform"], or "the material that is stored or processed in an archive building" ["das Material, das im Archivgebäude belagert, oder verarbeitet wird"].[27] Lepper and Raulff's definitions correspond to those of the Society of American Archivists, but with one major difference. The SAA's disciplinary definition emphatically states that archival materials are those "maintained using the principles of provenance, original order, and collective control" and must have "enduring value."[28]

The design and purpose of an archive—as a safe or right place for documents—its contents, as well as the notion of its enduring value underwent contestation in the late twentieth century. In *Archive Fever* (1996), Jacques Derrida invokes the Greek word *arkheion*, which is a place, an address, a domicile that houses "authentic documents."[29] Derrida uses this definition as a point of departure to challenge the notion of archive, as well as the authenticity of documents. Roughly two decades before Derrida's publication of *Archive Fever*, Hayden White, in his *Metahistory* (1973), called an archive a place that contains bits of "unprocessed historical record," making the radical declaration that an archive cannot be considered the "arbiter of truth."[30] Extending some of White's concerns, in *History and Criticism* (1985), Dominick LaCapra warned of the fetishization of the archive as "a literal substitute for the 'reality' of the past which is always already lost on the historian," and "a stand in for the past."[31] While White's phrasing serves as an important reminder to question the very authority of the house of documents, as historical truths emerge from rigorous examination and careful interpretation and narrativization of documents present in the archive, LaCapra subjects the archive to an even more stringent scrutiny, admonishing against the givenness of the archive and the conflation of the archive with the past, rather than seeing it as a space meant for a critical analysis of documents that represent parts of that past.

But which truth? And whose past? The sufficiency of the archive was subject to sharp scrutiny by postcolonial theorists. Here, the main question was, how does one create postcolonial narratives from colonial

---

[27] Marcel Lepper and Ulrich Raulff, eds., *Handbuch Archiv* (Stuttgart: J.B. Metzler, 2016), 1.
[28] "What are Archives?" Society of American Archivists, www2.archivists.org/about-archives.
[29] Jacques Derrida, *Archive Fever: A Freudian Impression*, trans. Eric Prenowitz (Chicago: University of Chicago Press, 2005), 2.
[30] Hayden V. White, *Metahistory* (Baltimore, MD: Johns Hopkins University Press, 1973), 5.
[31] Dominick LaCapra, *History & Criticism* (Ithaca, NY: Cornell University Press, 1985), 92, n. 17.

archives? Valentin Y. Mudimbe's groundbreaking study *The Invention of Africa* (1988) begins by tracing the etymological roots of colonialism and colonization to the Latin word *colĕre*, meaning to cultivate and design, to argue that the cultivation and design came from the tendency to "organize and transform non-European areas into fundamentally European constructs."[32] Focusing on three figures—the explorer, the soldier, and the missionary—Mudimbe disarranges the European epistemic archive, literal and figurative, in medicine, geography, and anthropology, which produce otherness relentlessly. In the *Critique of Postcolonial Reason* (1999), Gayatri Chakravorty Spivak insists on a continuous vigilance toward the historicity of the archive and its ordering of knowledge, in literature and in history. There are two moments in Spivak's discussion of archives that are worth noting here. First, in taking issue with LaCapra, Spivak proposes that "in establishing the relationship between the 'literary' and the 'colonial,' the reading of literature can supplement the writing of history with suspicious ease."[33] Second, she states, "To me, literature and the archives seem complicit in that they are both a crosshatching of condensations [. . .]. The authority of the author is there matched by the control of the archon, the official custodian of truth."[34]

If Mudimbe and Spivak focus on the archive as a collection of documents, broadly defined, Ann Laura Stoler shifts the focus from objects to a process. In the opening chapter of *Along the Archival Grain* (2007), which tellingly begins with a discussion of Pramoedya Ananta Toer's novel *House of Glass* (1988), Stoler makes a case for "archiving-as-process rather than archives-as-things."[35] To distinguish the two forms of engagement with archives, Stoler offers the term "archival form": "prose style, repetitive refrain, the arts of persuasion, affective strains that shape 'rational' response, categories of confidentiality and classification, and not least, genres of documentation."[36] She proposes that archives are "condensed sites of epistemological and political anxiety rather than skewed and biased sources," and that "colonial archives were both transparencies on which power-relations were inscribed and intricate technologies of rule themselves."[37]

By outlining differences between processes of archiving and the archive itself, by questioning the very authority of the archon, and by revealing the power relations contained in and disseminated throughout the archives, Mudimbe, Spivak, and Stoler provide valuable insights

---

[32] Valentin Yves Mudimbe, *The Invention of Africa: Gnosis, Philosophy, and the Order of Knowledge* (Bloomington: Indiana University Press, 2010), 1.
[33] Gayatri Chakravorty Spivak, *A Critique of Postcolonial Reason: Toward a History of the Vanishing Present* (Cambridge, MA: Harvard University Press, 1999), 205.
[34] Spivak, *Postcolonial Reason*, 205.

into the governance of the archives, the legitimization of documents, and the truth narratives that are created through careful critical analysis. In the context of our discussion, these scholars point out the limitations of a representative, national-cultural consideration of literature and literary histories, and, consequently, the possibilities of using the very archives that are inscribed with power to unravel power relations, by shedding light on boundaries, hierarchies, and discriminations.

The postcolonial critique of archives, however, is not limited to colonial archives that are present. The authority of the colonial archon that determines the admittance or presence of documents within an archive is concomitant with the willfully created absence thereof, which makes the creative assemblage of new archives for writing hitherto unwritten histories and representing hitherto underrepresented historical connections essential. In his essay on recollection and narration of histories that are neither officially blessed nor ordained, Dipesh Chakrabarty draws our attention to instances of absence of archives. In "Minority Histories, Subaltern Pasts," an essay in *Provincializing Europe* (2001), Chakrabarty confronts the "problems of telling the stories of groups hitherto overlooked—particularly under circumstances where usual archives do not exist," to ask, quiet directly, "How do you construct the narrative of a group or class that has not left its own sources?"[38]

Chakrabarty's essay, as I have considered elsewhere, presents a rich discussion of the responsibility and ambition of democratizing the discipline of history.[39] In the context of refugees and forced migrants, his question can be reformulated as, "How do you construct the narrative of a group or a class that has left all of its sources behind?" And herein lies the tension between forced migration, its archive, and the narrative histories, literary and political, that we create from it. An archive, by definition, is a space or an act of collection—a *Sammlung*. Migration, by definition, involves dispersal: *Zerstreuung*. Narratives of refuge that we choose to read in relation to otherness should work out the tension between *sammeln* and *zerstreuen*: first, in their creation, as we account for legacies of war, partitions, and the creation of borderlines; second, in

---

[35] Ann Laura Stoler, *Along the Archival Grain: Thinking through Colonial Ontologies* (Princeton, NJ: Princeton University Press, 2009), 20.
[36] Stoler, *Archival Grain*, 20.
[37] Stoler, *Archival Grain*, 20.
[38] Dipesh Chakrabarty, "Minority Histories, Subaltern Pasts," in *Provincializing Europe: Postcolonial Thought and Historical Difference* (Princeton, NJ: Princeton University Press, 2000), 97–113, here 98.
[39] B. Venkat Mani, *Cosmopolitical Claims: Turkish-German Literatures from Nadolny to Pamuk* (Iowa City: University of Iowa Press, 2007), 89.

their reception, as we read narratives that recount lives of individuals and groups who are forced to leave their collections behind and are dispersed across the world; and third, through their bibliomigrancy, as literary works are catapulted into the world literary space, in their original languages or in translation.[40] But what would the narrative construction of such a random-access, hyperlinked, multilingual, bibliomigrant literary history look like?

Afghanistan and Germany: An Attempt at a Globally Connected Literary History

In 1857, the same year the first revolt against the British East India Company took place in India, German author Theodor Fontane published a poem with the title "Afghanistan. Ein Trauerspiel." The poem depicts the catastrophic defeat of the British army at the end of the First Anglo-Afghan War (1839–42). Led by the so-called "Fighting Bob," Sir Robert Sale, whom Fontane mentions in celebratory tones, the poem recounts from the perspective of the aggressors, in a somber, almost sympathetic tone, their disastrous defeat at the hands of the resistance army of Pashtuns, led by Sirdar Akbar Khan. The reason for the First Anglo-Afghan War was territorial control over Pashtun and Baloch territories, a way of controlling the local territory to impact the extra-local project of expanding imperial power. Fontane, who was working as a journalist in England at the time, took the title of the poem from a history book, Karl Friedrich Neumann's *Das Trauerspiel in Afghanistan*, published in Leipzig in 1848. Neumann and Fontane's term "Trauerspiel" anticipates by almost sixty years Rudyard Kipling's novel *Kim* (1900–01), in which Kipling uses the term "the Great Game" to describe the power struggle in western South Asia, as the British Empire tried to curb the influence of two other empires: Russia, to the north, and Persia, to the west of what is Pakistan and Afghanistan today. The first war led to the second one. The Second Anglo-Afghan War was fought between 1878 and 1880, at the end of which the Peace Treaty of Gandamak was signed, and eventually the Durand Line was drawn, in 1896, cutting through the hearts of the Pashtun communities in northern and northwestern Pakistan, and southern Afghanistan. The "Frontier Policy" of the Russians and the British was captured in one fleeting line by the Nobel laureate Rabindranath Tagore in his short story "Kabuliwala" (1894), which recounts events in the life of Rahmat Khan, an Afghan migrant trader of dry fruit and spices in Calcutta.

---

[40] B. Venkat Mani, *Recoding World Literature: Libraries, Print Culture, and Germany's Pact with Books* (New York: Fordham University Press, 2017), 33–37.

While the Great Game might have found its closure in 1896, it reappears in the form of the Cold War in the late twentieth century, when Afghanistan became a much less discussed but very crucial pawn. The US–Soviet struggle and the repercussions of the fights between the Russian soldiers and the Mujahideen, funded by the US, regularly appear as frame stories in the French-Afghan author Atiq Rahimi's works. The novella *Earth and Ashes* (2000), originally composed and published in Dari as *Khâkestar-o-Khâk* (1999), is set in the years following the Soviet invasion of Afghanistan, in 1979. The unnamed protagonist is an old man whose son works for a coal mine run by the Afghan state. The Soviet army bombards the village and everyone in the family dies, except for the old man and the five-year-old grandson Yassin, who goes deaf. Incapable of understanding why he cannot hear anyone anymore, Yassin asks, "Grandfather, have the Russians come and taken away everyone's voice? What do they do with all the voices? Why did you let them take away your voice? If you hadn't would they've killed you?"[41]

The history of Afghanistan, entangled and inseparable from the history of many Western nations—Great Britain, the Soviet Union, as well as imperial, divided, and reunited Germany—acquires an epic treatment in the German-Afghan author Masssum Faryar's novel *Buskaschi, oder der Teppich meiner Mutter*. Published in 2015, the year that saw record numbers of refugees arriving in Germany from Syria, but also from Afghanistan—a fact that is hardly recognized in literary and refugee studies—the novel begins in 1919, with the end of World War I, when the Western-oriented Afghan king Amanullah resumes power. It ends in the late twentieth century, when the aftermath of the rivalries between superpowers empowers the Mujahideen, and, later, the Taliban. The narrator, who finds refuge in Germany in the 1980s, recounts the lives of his mother, Khurschid, and father, Scharif, the protagonists of the novel, over the course of the twentieth century and into the twenty-first. A pattern on the carpet of the narrator's mother, which depicts the game of Buzkashi, an equestrian precursor to polo in which riders fight for the body of a headless sheep, emerges early in the novel as a motif that drives the narrative forward. Afghanistan, and the refugees created over the course of a century, become the metaphorical headless sheep, thrown around by superpowers from the outside, and by powerful factions from the inside. Faryar's novel is the first in the German language that is bookended by the history of British colonialism in South Asia and the East German support for the Soviet invasion

---

[41] Atiq Rahimi, *Earth and Ashes*, trans. Erdag M. Göknar (New York: Other Press, 2010; Kindle ed.), 32.

of Afghanistan, which culminated in the German army's presence alongside NATO forces after the US invasion of Afghanistan, in 2001.

Refugees from Afghanistan created by the Great Games appear in Navid Kermani's journalistic photo essay *Einbruch der Wirklichkeit* (2016). They traverse the trail from Greece to Germany, and their stories document the mass arrival of Syrian refugees in Germany in the summer of 2015. Kermani himself in this book is neither aware of nor interested in historical connections between Germany and Afghanistan. Suffice it to say—as he comments on "a strangely softer Germany" ["seltsam weichgewordenes Deutschland"] with its "welcome culture" ["Willkommenskultur"][42]—he quickly realizes that the arrival of the "bogeyman" ["Schreckgespenst"] figure of the young Muslim, whom he knows, will push Europe into the onset of a new reality.[43]

At a distance from Kermani's specter of the figure of the young Muslim is a collective of refugee poets in contemporary Germany, writing under the auspices of the Poetry Project, who are drawing attention to the contemporary histories of the *Trauerspiel* of Afghanistan in the twenty-first century. The project was founded by the journalist Susana Koelbl, who served as foreign correspondent for the German political magazine *Der Spiegel* in Afghanistan, in collaboration with Afghanistan-born German lawyer Aarash Spanta. It serves as a creative writing platform as well as a forum for cultural and social integration into German society for refugees from Afghanistan, Syria, and Iran. Much like Tagore's Rahmat Khan, Rahimi's Yassin, and Faryar's narrator, these poets shed light on the unfinished business of borders and borderlines.

This sketch of a global literary historical process through multiple points of historical and literary entry, and some hyperlinks, stresses the need for a new kind of *Vergangenheitsbewältigung* of Germany/Europe in tandem with the non-European world. In resonance with Conrad's thoughts, this is a way to come to terms with the connectivities with the past formed through forced migration and displacement.

Finding Odysseus's Scars, Again: Hyperlinking Literary Histories

The tension between settlement as a norm, on the one hand, and exile and forced migration as aberration, on the other, is expressed most beautifully in Erich Auerbach's *Mimesis* (1946). While a detailed discussion of

---

[42] Navid Kermani, *Einbruch der Wirklichkeit. Auf dem Flüchtlingstreck durch Europa* (Munich: C. H. Beck, 2015), 5. Navid Kermani, *Upheaval: The Refugee Track through Europe*, trans. Tony Crawford (Cambridge, UK and Malden, MA: Polity Press, 2017), 1.

[43] Kermani, *Einbruch*, 11; Kermani, *Upheaval*, 7.

Auerbach's work is not possible here, it is important to note that the opening chapter of the book is titled "Odysseus' Scar"—Auerbach's poignant reading of Odysseus's return home and his recognition by his nurse Euryclea. The entire project is a literary history of Europe that is inaugurated in the shadow of imminent war and violence, as faced by Odysseus and his interpreter, Auerbach, who is writing in exile. In tracing this scar on the body of a war-torn Europe, Auerbach reveals toward the end of his book a temporally moving genealogy:

> Basically, the way in which we view human life and society is the same whether we are concerned with things of the past or things of the present. A change in our manner of viewing history will of necessity soon be transferred to our manner of viewing current conditions. When people [. . .] come to develop a sense of historical dynamics, of the incomparability of historical phenomenon and their constant inner mobility [. . .] when finally, they accept the conviction that meanings of events cannot be grasped in abstract and general forms of cognition [. . .] but also in the depths of the workday world and its men and women [. . .] then it is to be seen that those insights will be transferred to the present, and that, in consequence, the present too will be seen as incomparable and unique.[44]

Representation and representability, as connected to time and space, put history and the present on an equal footing. But tracing Odysseus's scar from Homer to Thomas Mann or Virginia Woolf cannot happen in a linear, orderly path. Rather, such a journey is best described as a constant, moving, back and forth, a series of proactive "hyperlinkings."

I am using this term intentionally, for its genealogy can be traced to the same year in which Auerbach finished *Mimesis*. "The term hyperlink, or simply a link, is a reference to data that the reader can follow by clicking or tapping. A hyperlink points to a whole document or to a specific element within a document. The text that is linked from is called anchor text."[45] A hyperlink, in other words, opens up the possibility of thinking about history and literature through multiple entry points, created communally by readers and experts—but also by individuals—and it gives rise to a collective of authors and works, a trail of related information. The hyperlink is multi-sourced rather than

---

[44] Erich Auerbach, *Mimesis: The Representation of Reality in Western Literature* (Princeton, NJ: Princeton University Press, 2003), 443–4.
[45] Wikipedia, s.v. "Hyperlink," last modified July 11, 2021, en.wikipedia.org/w/index.php?title=Hyperlink&oldid=948004191.

single-sourced, much like the coding of a nation or national history is built over time. To borrow from Auerbach, it is a trail of specific events, constituting an epoch, that brings history and the present on an equal footing through the recognition of violence. After all, by the end of *Mimesis* it is clear that the project is as much about the dramatic transformation of European realism starting in the early nineteenth century as it is about the destruction of humanity and human values and the creation of exilic subjectivities en masse when Auerbach wrote his text, in the first half of the 1940s.

Coda

In his essay "Reflections on Exile," Edward Said draws attention to the "unhealable rift between a human being and a native place, between the self and its true home."[46] In tracing this rift, Said does not want us to focus merely on exile literature:

> You must think of refugee-peasants with no prospect of ever returning home, armed only with a ration-card and an agency number [...], the hopelessly large numbers, the compounded misery of the "undocumented," [...] without a tellable history.[47]

This "tellable history," I want to argue, cannot be constructed just by reading the refugee—that is, by their representation—but by reading with the refugee figure as the primary frame story. What this involves is a willful disarranging of refugee narratives and world historical events and a subsequent rearranging in an imperfect constellation aimed at rethinking the idea of a literary home, puncturing chronologies of national, political, and literary histories. Reading with refugees to surmise a postcolonial archive of globally connected histories reveals that nation-states and empires are ephemeral, and refugees are perennial. Concepts of temporary or permanent stay, of integration or isolation, of hopes and angst, of old homes and new ones, of old friends and strangers, of old objects and newly founded objects, start acquiring relief as we see the whole world as a fractured entity, with fissures and wounds weeping from the follies of imperfect historical triages. Locating refugees at the center of world literature, history, and literary history calls upon us to see the world not as a place of permanent dwellers, homeowners, or renters but as a place where human beings are one political, military, or environmental disaster away from becoming refugees. In

---

[46] Edward W. Said, "Reflections on Exile," in *Reflections on Exile and Other Essays* (Cambridge, MA: Harvard University Press, 2000), 137–49, here 137.
[47] Said, "Reflections" 139.

the third decade of the twenty-first century, when the cacophony of populist voices reverberates against borders and walls—already existing, or new ones—thus demarcating new insides and outsides, refugees, who are always already out of place, ask us to dismantle the long-standing validation and legitimization of national-cultural hierarchies of the nineteenth century. A focus on the figure of the refugee reveals the limitations of place-based literary and cultural studies, opening up possibilities for a new Humanities that considers willful and forced migration as critical frameworks for crossing boundaries and bringing down disciplinary insides and outsides.

Refugees are at the front and center of every society, revealing the internal fissures of the place of settlement and carrying wounds and scars from their places of departure. In being undocumented, in having left everything else but their stories, refugees become the *arkheion*—the place that holds authentic documents. They are the documents themselves. Refugees remind us what our last home looks like: an alias, a place of eternal sorrow, or a home whose address we ask every stranger. Instead of asking what we can say about refugees from the safety of our homes, it is time to ask what refugees tell us about our literatures, our literary histories, our homes, our worlds.

Works Cited

Auerbach, Erich. *Mimesis: The Representation of Reality in Western Literature* (Princeton, NJ: Princeton University Press, 2003).

Basu, Nayanima. "CAA, NRC could render Huge Numbers of Indian Muslims Sstateless, says Ashutosh Varshney," *ThePrint* (blog), March 5, 2020, theprint.in/india/caa-nrc-could-render-huge-numbers-of-indian-muslims-stateless-says-ashutosh-varshney/376008.

Beutin, Wolfgang, ed. *Deutsche Literaturgeschichte von den Anfängen bis zur Gegenwart* (Stutgart: J. B. Metzlersche Verlagsbuchhandlung und Carl Ernst Poeschel Verlag, 2019).

Chakrabarty, Dipesh. "Minority Histories, Subaltern Pasts," in *Provincializing Europe: Poscolonial Thought and Historical Difference* (Princeton, NJ: Princeton University Press, 2000), 97–113.

Conrad, Sebastian. Introduction to *What Is Global History?* (Princeton, NJ: Princeton University Press, 2016), 1–16.

Damrosch, David. "Toward a History of World Literature," *New Literary History*, vol. 39, nos. 3–4 (2009): 481–95.

Derrida, Jacques. *Archive Fever: A Freudian Impression*, trans. Eric Prenowitz (Chicago: University of Chicago Press, 2005).

Faryar, Massum. *Buskaschi, oder, Der Teppich meiner Mutter. Roman* (Cologne: Kiepenheue & Witsch, 2015).

Fontane, Theodor. *Gedichte*, ed. Joachim Krueger (Berlin: Aufbau, 1995).

Gathmann, Florian. "Innenminister Seehofer Stellt Migrationskatalog Vor: Der Desaster-Plan," *Spiegel Online*, July 10, 2018, www.spiegel.de/politik/deutschland/innenminister-und-csu-chef-seehofer-stellt-migrationskatalog-vor-masterplan-des-desasters-a-1217421.html.

Ghosh, Sahana, and Sara Shneiderman. "New Laws weaponize Citizenship in India," *The Conversation*, December 22, 2019, theconversation.com/new-laws-weaponize-citizenship-in-india-129027.

Gumbrecht, Hans Ulrich. "Shall we continue to write Histories of Literature?" *New Literary History*, vol. 39, no. 3 (2008): 519–32.

Hasrat-Nazimi, Waslat. "Afghanische Flüchtlinge verzweifeln an Europas Außengrenze," *DW.COM*, March 3, 2020, www.dw.com/de/afghanische-fl%C3%BCchtlinge-verzweifeln-an-europas-au%C3%9Fengrenze/a-52623524.

Hermand, Jost. "Book Review: Deutsche Literaturgeschichte. Von den Anfängen bis zur Gegenwart," *Monatshefte für deutschsprachige Literatur und Kultur*, vol. 73, no. 3 (1981): 338–40.

Kermani, Navid, and Moises Saman. *Einbruch der Wirklichkeit. Auf dem Fluchtlingstreck durch Europa* (Munich: C. H.Beck, 2016).

Kermani, Navid, and Moises Saman. *Upheaval: The Refugee Trek through Europe*, trans. Tony Crawford (Cambridge, UK and Malden, MA: Polity Press, 2017).

LaCapra, Dominick. *History & Criticism* (Ithaca, NY: Cornell University Press, 1985).

Lepper, Marcel, and Ulrich Raulff, eds. *Handbuch Archiv* (Stuttgart: J. B. Metzler, 2016).

Mani, B. Venkat. *Cosmopolitical Claims: Turkish-German Literatures from Nadolny to Pamuk* (Iowa City: University of Iowa Press, 2007).

Mani, B. Venkat. "Introduction: Recoding World Literature," in *Recoding World Literature: Libraries, Print Culture, and Germany's Pact with Books* (New York: Fordham University Press, 2017), 9–47.

Moretti, Franco, ed. *The Novel* (Princeton, NJ: Princeton University Press, 2007).

Mudimbe, Valentin Yves. *The Invention of Africa: Gnosis, Philosophy, and the Order of Knowledge* (Bloomington: Indiana University Press, 2010).

Neumann, Karl Friedrich. "Das Trauerspiel in Afghanistan," in *Historisches Taschenbuch*, vol. 9, ed. Friedrich von Naumer (Leipzig: F. A. Brockhaus, 1848), 449–570.

Rahimi, Atiq. *Earth and Ashes*, trans. Erdağ M. Göknar (New York: Harcourt, 2002).

Rainey, Rebecca. "House Committee votes to rescind Trump Travel Ban," *POLITICO*, February 12, 2020, www.politico.com/news/2020/02/12/house-committee-votes-to-rescind-trump-travel-ban-114649.

Said, Edward W. "Reflections on Exile," in *Reflections on Exile and Other Essays* (Cambridge, MA: Harvard University Press, 2000), 137–49.

Said, Edward W. "Secular Criticism," in *The Selected Works of Edward Said, 1966–2006*, ed. Moustafa Bayoumi and Andrew Rubin (New York: Vintage Books, 2019), 220–44.

Society of American Archivists. "What Are Archives?" www2.archivists.org/about-archives.

Spivak, Gayatri Chakravorty. *A Critique of Postcolonial Reason: Toward a History of the Vanishing Present* (Cambridge, MA: Harvard University Press, 1999).

Stoler, Ann Laura. *Along the Archival Grain: Thinking through Colonial Ontologies* (Princeton, NJ: Princeton University Press, 2009).

Tagore, Rabindranath. *Selected Short Stories*, ed. Śaṅkha Ghosha and Tapobrata Ghosha, trans. Sukanta Chaudhuri (New Delhi and New York: Oxford University Press, 2002).

Thapar, Romila. "They peddle Myths and call it History," *New York Times*, May 17, 2019, www.nytimes.com/2019/05/17/opinion/india-elections-modi-history.html.

The Poetry Project. "The Poetry Project," thepoetryproject.de/.
UNHCR. "Figures at a Glance," UNHCR, www.unhcr.org/figures-at-a-glance.html.
Wellbery, David E. *A New History of German Literature* (Cambridge, MA: Harvard University Press, 2004).
White, Hayden V. *Metahistory* (Baltimore, MD: Johns Hopkins University Press, 1973).
Zerofsky, Elisabeth. "Viktor Orbán's Far-Right Vision for Europe," *The New Yorker*, January 14, 2019, www.newyorker.com/magazine/2019/01/14/viktor-orbans-far-right-vision-for-europe.
Zurcher, Lucy Rodgers, and Anthony Dominic Bailey. "Trump's Border Wall—in seven Charts," BBC News, September 27, 2019, www.bbc.com/news/world-us-canada-46824649.

Two Between the Court and the Port, but Never Part of a Nation: Friederike Brun's Domesticated Cosmopolitanism

Birgit Tautz

I really do not know to which nation I belong;
And this may well be the reason
that I lack any allegiance to one Fatherland *over any other,*
and this lack helped me to keep open my heart,
mind and eyes to appreciate the goodness and ailments
of people and nations, as I saw them.
And indeed my father would often say [. . .]
and nothing more eager to promote than a resolute sense of
cosmopolitanism

Zu welchem Volk ich nun eigentlich gehöre, weiß ich wirklich nicht; und daher mag wohl mein gänzlicher Mangel an ausschließender Vaterlandsliebe *herrühren, welcher mir Sinn, Herz und Augen offen gehalten hat, für die Vorzüge und Gebrechen der Völker und Länder, so ich gesehn. Auch sagte mein Vater oft [. . .] nichts eifriger zu befördern gesucht, als offenen Weltbürgersinn*
—*Friederike Brun,* Wahrheit aus Morgenträumen

Situating Friederike Brun

Friederike Brun (1765–1835) fits the theme of this volume perfectly. Forging a legacy in the German language, she was born but never lived in German lands. In Danish Copenhagen she had become a local fixture, someone who socially craved and ultimately stood for the wider world. Brun hosted salons in her city home as well as at her country estate of Sophienholm, observing, reciting, and writing among the

German-speaking community that served the Danish monarchy in what was then called the "Unitary State" ("Helstaten," 1773–1864). She was *the* Northern salonnière. Married to a wealthy merchant, she projected a cosmopolitanism that initially had been nourished by her German pastor father's preaching. But she traveled in German lands and beyond, with seemingly obsessive frequency and gusto; Brun was always *en route*. After many years of journeying between Copenhagen and Rome—with many stops and repeat visits in between—as well as to the spas from Pyrmont to Carlsbad, she permanently returned to Sophienholm in 1810. Ailing, she remained there for the rest of her life. Nevertheless, she wrote about and thereby continued to criss-cross a figurative Germany. Insisting on its unifying language, Brun asserted herself as a writer of occasional poetry, autobiographical prose, and exquisite letters that, while seeking to achieve a certain documenting authority over communal creative experiences, trace a Germany quite different from the one that has structured literary history and shaped our collective imagination. Brun's writings unveil an alternate literary and cultural history that speaks to the legacy of orality and varying registers of writing style, and that uses foreign models while achieving transnational impact.

On a conceptual level, the local situatedness of Brun's signature event (the salon) and her penchant for escape and flux (her journeys) correlate with the elements of domestication and cosmopolitanism that this chapter's title conjures and that describe, in a nutshell, Friederike Brun's German cultural legacy. The performances in her salons localized (foreign) cultural traditions—and, very much like the salons, her cultural impact was profound yet temporary and has been relegated to the graveyard of literary history. Yet in and beyond the events, Brun's gaze honed in on the court, to which she was beholden as a Danish subject, as well as the port, which stood for the often forgotten global aspirations of the Danish Crown. Those aspirations were shared by many of Brun's friends and other residents whose ethnic, cultural, and linguistic ties to German lands were strong and who remained lifelong outsiders, both in Denmark and the nascent German Culture Nation (*Kulturnation*). Friederike Brun thus evolves as an emblematic figure in a literary history that embraces alternate cognitive figures in its self-articulation—namely, the local and the global, or a "domesticized cosmopolitanism," rather than a then-absent nation. This history turns to since-eclipsed forms of literary production, as well as to marginal themes and genres, while emphasizing robust exchange and networked relations rather than an idealist narrative promoting the inward-directed homogeneity of a united Germany. Accordingly, as this chapter's goal is to introduce a critical vocabulary suitable for exploring conceptual alternatives to a unified, telos-driven national literary history, a series of examples, or episodes involving Brun, depict Germany from the outside.¹ They culminate in a discussion of Brun's oeuvre vis-à-vis philology, a discipline that like no other could ground the nation in tradition and culture, as well as her position vis-à-vis early nineteenth-century Philhellenism, a literary movement that marked the displacement of German national politics onto the Greek liberation movement; yet that too leaves Brun outside the nation.

A Ship in a Port, or Reading a Narrative Episode

Well known in the early nineteenth century,² Brun's oeuvre has been rediscovered in the past decades, mainly as part of projects that seek to restore forgotten female voices.³ Back in her day, her writing, first published in periodicals around 1800 and later in editions of her works,

---

[1] This chapter complements, in part revises, and expands upon Birgit Tautz, *Translating the World: Toward A New History of German Literature around 1800* (University Park: Pennsylvania State University Press, 2018), 104–44.

[2] For a comprehensive, recent account of Brun's nineteenth-century fame and legacy, see Kerstin Gräfin von Schwerin, *Friederike Brun. Weltbürgerin in der Zeitwende. Eine Biographie* (Göttingen: Wallstein, 2020), here 10; as well as Cora Sutton Castle, *A Statistical Study of Eminent Women* (New York: Science Press, 1913), 11. All translations are my own, except where noted.

[3] See, most recently, Gudrun Loster-Schneider, "Poetics, Politics, Gender and Pedagogics in Friederike Brun's (1765–1835) Autobiography *Wahrheit aus Morgenträumen* (1824)," in *Women from the Parsonage: Pastors' Daughters as Writers, Translators, Salonnières, and Educators*, ed. Cindy Renker and Susanne Bach (Berlin: De Gruyter, 2019), 131–51. For pioneering editorial work, see the Sophie Digital Library, a repository of women's literature housed at BYU (scholarsarchive.byu.edu/sophie/), and the work of Brian Keith-Smith: he particularly deserves credit for making Brun accessible to English speakers. Other examples include Karin Hoff, *Die Entdeckung der Zwischenräume. Literarische Projekte der Spätaufklärung zwischen Skandinavien und Deutschland* (Göttingen: Wallstein, 2003); and Angela Esterhammer, *Romanticism and Improvisation, 1750–1850* (Cambridge: Cambridge University Press, 2008); both books discuss Brun in a conventional comparative-literature context while accounting for her living in Copenhagen and for the performance aspect of her work, respectively. Many studies emphasize Brun's relationship to canonical male authors—for example, Janet Besserer Holmgren, *The Women Writers in Schiller's Horen: Patrons, Petticoats, and the Promotion of Weimar Classicism* (Newark: University of Delaware Press, 2007). Still others place Brun as travel writer, often in relation to cosmopolitanism, politics, or the places she performed or traversed (e.g., Switzerland, Rome). Examples include Karin Baumgartner, "Packaging the Grand Tour: German Women Authors Write Italy 1791–1874," in *Women in German Yearbook* 31 (2015): 1–27; Tone Brekke, "A Cosmopolitan Salon-Heiress: Friederike Brun's Revision of Schiller in *Idas ästhetische Entwicklung* (1824)," *Literature Compass*, vol. 1 (2004): 1–11; Kari Lokke, "Brun's *Briefe aus Rom* (1816): Cosmopolitanism, Nationalism, and the Politics of *Geistlichkeit*," in *Women against Napoleon: Historical and Fictional Responses to his Rise and Legacy*, ed. Waltraud Meierhofer, Gertrud Roesch,

emerged along with an increasing and personal notoriety. Brun certainly made her voice heard. Goethe and Schiller engaged with and apparently gossiped about Brun more frequently than the well-known, one-time mockery in the *Xenien* suggests.[4] But slander and biographical details are not my main interest here. Brun's work holds a key for telling the story of an alternate literary history. It begins in the port of Marseille:

> In the afternoon we visited a Danish captain on his ship belonging to the Royal West Indian Trading Company, the Caroline Tugendreich. My heart grew tender when I saw the homeland's flag, and I longed to sail to Copenhagen at this moment!
>
> [Nachmittags machten wir einem *dänischen* Schiffer einen Besuch auf seinem der Königl. Westindischen Companie gehörigen Schiffe, *Caroline Tugendreich*. Mir ward das Herz ganz weich beim Anblick der heimischen Flagge, und ich hätte in dem Augenblick nach *Kopenhagen* segeln mögen!][5]

---

and Caroline Bland (Frankfurt: Campus, 2007); Karin Klitgaard Povlsen, "Persistent Patterns: The Genre of Travel Writing in the Eighteenth Century," in *Northbound: Travels, Encounters, and Constructions 1700–1830* (Aarhus: Aarhus Universitetsforlag, 2007), 325–40; and Cindy Renker, "The Political Voice in the Writings of Friederike Brun (1765–1835)," *Women in German Yearbook*, vol. 29 (2013): 81–96.

[4] See Holmgren, *The Women in Schiller's Horen*, 95–6, on the discussion and promotion of Brun's work among the well-known men of Classical Weimar. Among the *Xenien*, no. 273 allegedly mocks Brun. However, commentary on Goethe and Schiller disputes the veracity of this claim. See *Goethes Werke*, 1.5:295–324, here 312. Overall, when perusing all references to Brun by Goethe and Schiller, in their letters, diaries, and conversations, a far more complex picture arises, calling into doubt any narratives of Brun being simply scorned in Classical Weimar. While including a full analysis exceeds the scope of this essay, a clear pattern emerges: both Goethe and Schiller appreciated the social and cultural relevancy of Friederike Brun, while Schiller's mentioning of and reference to Brun provide a glimpse into patterns of communication at the time (e.g., the delivery of letters through intermediaries) and publication practice and the agenda surrounding the *Horen*, among other works. On the former, see, for example, Goethe's letter to Kirms, April 2, 1799, in *Goethes Werke*, 14:65–7, as well as 258. See also *Tagebücher* 76. Brun's impression of Goethe, upon first meeting him, also proves instructive; see "Gespräch mit Brun, Juli 1795," in *Goethes Werke, Anhang*, 265–6. On Schiller engaging with Brun and her writing, see, among others, letters by Baggesen, June 9, 1795 (#219), in *Schillers Werke*, 35:217; by Brun herself (#105), in *Schillers Werke*, 40:101–2; in addition to a poem that Schiller dedicated to Brun, in *Schillers Werke, Gedichte*, 221. In general, use of a digital edition and database (e.g., ProQuest) is recommended to reconstruct the elaborate networks and to have easy access to the detailed commentary sections.

[5] Friederike Brun, *Prosaische Schriften*, vol. 1 (Zurich: Orell, Füssli und Compagnie), 85–6.

The episode casts homesickness as a sentimental gesture and, thus, overtly contradicts both the non-belonging of a bystander and the cosmopolitan openness Brun professed elsewhere. But through the ship, a giant material object referenced here passim, a multilayered story unfolds and enwraps the narrative detail. First, it affirms the role of the gaze in Brun's texts, which glimpses objects, for sure, but also records affective impact and a momentary, fleeting experience of the eyewitness. The detail arrests the impact of the visual and exemplifies a mode and effect of representation that we find elsewhere in Brun's works and to which we will return shortly.

Second, though far away from her Danish home, Brun's visit to the French port recalls her roots in Copenhagen's aristocratic environs, while impressing upon us—her twenty-first-century readers—that her life testifies to more than a national literary canon revolving around a native language. For Brun, Copenhagen remained a point of departure and return, underscoring the role that cities (rather than nations) played in crafting legacies. Though not writing in Danish, she has retained a place in Danish literary historiography. As a proponent of sentimental style, and an embodiment of European travel, Brun is still present in European literature, whereas her native language has done nothing to place her, in any lasting manner, in German literary history. Yet language has rendered Brun a de facto German writer. Indeed, her particular use of the German, as well as her gradual embrace of editorial praxis, define Brun as she simultaneously shuns and adheres to one of the most German of all academic disciplines—philology.

More urgently, though, the material referent of this narrative episode—a giant object rendered small in the text—gestures to a global existence and contextualizes Brun's observation further. The Royal West Indian Trade Company's ship hints at the scope and personnel of the Danish colonial enterprise: it is named for Caroline Tugendreich, who was the wife of merchant and politician Heinrich von Schimmelmann, the patriarch of a prominent German family in the service of the Danish Crown. After they made a fortune as porcelain traders in the Seven Years' War, the Schimmelmanns arrived in Copenhagen via Hamburg. They owned huge plantations in the Danish West Indies, were the leading sugar manufacturers in Hamburg and its Danish vicinity, and traded and owned slaves.

As the episode entwines others' global reach with the author's personal experience, it replicates tensions that I also see in the domesticating atmosphere of the aristocratic salons hosted by Brun and her contemporaries. Participants created the local event only to have global networks encroach upon it, over and over again—whether through conscientious or veiled efforts to account for global guilt in the slave economy, such as art sponsorship and religious redemption,[6] visible markers of these involvements,[7] or through associative encounters, like Brun's reaction in the port of Marseille. But looking at Brun's works through the metaphor of the ship and the port also unveils a more complex story of vanishing and preserving—namely, of the salon as a temporal event—while encouraging us to look at the entire corpus of German-language literature through a non-national lens.

Networks, Genres, Vanishing Acts

Just like Brun lived among transnationally, even globally, acting people, her literary works and cultural legacy (or non-legacy) preserve a position transcending the national.[8] In *Prosaische Schriften* (*Prosaic Writings*)—written at a time when Brun actually moved away from Copenhagen and toward Rome[9]—she marshals a somewhat disruptive, domesticating gesture of belonging when eyeing the ship, juxtaposing home with the ship's journey along the Atlantic triangle shipping routes that exchanged manufactured goods for people and sugar. Hinting at networked infrastructures of trade, the detail encapsulates the equivalent structures of *Prosaic Writings*. The writings give rise to, and ultimately proliferate, networked thoughts, as they point to an elaborate epistolary and multidirectional exchange even when concealing obvious rhetorical markers of the letter (e.g., opening and closing, dates and

---

[6] Tautz, *Translating the World*, 110–22; also, Birgit Tautz, "Revolution, Abolition, Aesthetic Sublimation: German Responses to News from France in the 1790s," in *Rewriting the Radical: Enlightenment, Revolution and Cultural Transfer in 1790s Germany, Britain and France*, ed. Maike Oergel (Berlin: De Gruyter, 2012), 80–3.

[7] See Jeanine Blackwell, "Sophie von La Roche and the Black Slave Poet Feuerbach: A Study in Sentimentality, Enlightenment, and Outsiderdom," in *The Enlightenment and its Legacy: Studies in German Literature in Honor of Helga Slessarev*, ed. Sara Friedrichsmeyer and Barbara Becker-Cantarino (Bonn: Bouvier, 1991), 105–15, where she references Schimmelmann's domestic slaves passim.

[8] Von Schwerin emphasizes a bridge between Scandinavia and Italy, and befitting her comprehensive biography, details Brun's journey to St. Petersburg in some length; see her *Friederike Brun*, 9, 45–56.

[9] Journeys south, including to Switzerland and Italy, have become markers in understanding Brun's biography, work, and legacy, often delineating comparative studies. See, among others, the requisite chapters in von Schwerin, *Friederike Brun*: "Erste Reise in den Süden. Frankreich und die Schweiz 1790," 71–86, and "Letzte Reise in den Süden 1805–1807," 211–22, where geography acts as a framing device; Baumgartner, "Grand Tour," establishes journeys to Italy as a point of comparison and anchor for women's literary production.

signatures) and being dedicated and addressed to only one person, who gradually fades into anonymity.[10]

Prosaic Writings marks circulation and narrative fragility—including the potential to become serial—rather than the development of a cohesive work (let alone its completion). Consisting of episodes and impressions from travel, the form suggests porousness rather than adherence to generic models and traditions. The text's style appears to be additive and observational, not deliberate in defining the author's or the work's intention. Chronicling the process of perception as much as recording its results, the writings inventory and archive moments while organizing them only partially (e.g., through chapter titles). In emphasizing their rawness, these texts resonate with the forms and genres used by other authors at the time, which, in toto, mark a shift, even a rupture, in the media landscape, as they place seemingly inferior or unfinished material next to chiseled, by now well-known, works.[11] Such texts often pay tribute to a much greater awareness of the world than their authors' status suggests today. A case in point is Johannes von Müller, Brun's long-time Swiss friend whose collected works provide unique access to *her* oeuvre through reciprocal letters, commentary, and her editorship of his correspondence.[12] Müller shows deep knowledge of the Americas in letters to Karl Viktor von Bonstetten, another mutual friend, writing, among other topics, about slavery in Jamaica, famines all over the Caribbean, and European hypocrisy in the face of transatlantic hardships and crises.[13] But the same correspondence points to other localities and local luminaries as well: Müller and Bonstetten had first become acquainted with Hamburg, northern German, and Danish-German salons through Caspar Voght, an influential Hamburg merchant, who was equally engaged in transatlantic trade and local philanthropy. His own diaries and autobiography document a proverbial grand tour straddling the lines between ruthless global enterprising, religious atonement, and quiet artistic aspiration, supplementing his recollection

---

[10] Brun ostensibly addresses *Prosaische Schriften* to her brother Friedrich Münter. Marie Isabel Matthews-Schlinzig has advanced research on eighteenth-century letters considerably, emphasizing the genre's "networked" nature over rhetorical features, per se.
[11] The most well-known example is Goethe's *Italienische Reise* (*Italian Journey*), which was published many years after Goethe actually undertook the journey.
[12] Von Schwerin, *Friederike Brun*, 148; Johannes von Müller, *Sämmtliche Werke*, vols. 13 and 14, ed. Friederike Brun (Tübingen: J. G. Cotta, 1812).
[13] Von Müller, *Sämmtliche Werke* 14: 21, 54.

of an actual grand tour that he undertook as a young man.[14] In Brun's "networked" circles, written texts act as indices for personal interaction, documenting incipience of long-lasting exchanges as well as one-time encounters, the enduring as well as the momentary.

The salons, which brought protagonists together, formed node-like entities in establishing these networks. Yet they also proved to be vanishing acts within the larger cultural landscape. Though stable locales, salons promoted a fleeting and improvised culture, constituting at best a momentary network. Moreover, they were testament to the increasingly fragile power of the aristocratic courts. Relegated to rural estates in the Danish unitary state (which included, for example, Altona), the salons stood opposite ports and urbanity (e.g., Hamburg) as centers of global economic activity. Though enacting meaningful communicative and performance spaces—something we can see as a correlate to the epistolary form—the salons' literary traces marked instability and fragility in yet another way. In this respect, Brun's *Wahrheit aus Morgenträumen* (*Truth in Morning Dreams*) actually represents a series of short prose portraits that recall the performative role and dynamics in the salons while turning the participants into static figures defined by visuality—despite being commonly labeled an autobiography.[15] But as Brun attempted to tell participants' story by casting their lives in small vignettes, she created a tableau that failed to come alive.[16] *Wahrheit aus Morgenträumen* points to but cannot fully capture the essence of the temporary salon. Consequently, for part of the nineteenth century salons can only cling to a place in literary history by being subsumed and integrated under autobiography. Here Brun performed yet another archiving task when it came to preserving their literary legacy. She committed them to the page, just as she preserved the networked

---

[14] Von Schwerin, *Friederike Brun*, 64, 148, the latter on the acquaintance between Müller, Bonstetten, and Voght. See also Caspar Voght, *Lebensgeschichte*, ed. Charlotte Schoell-Glass (Hamburg: Christians, 2001), and Doris and Peter Walser-Wilhelm, *Zeitgebirge. Karl Viktor von Bonstetten, Madame de Staël, Friederike Brun, geb. Münter. Zwei Briefgespräche 1811–1813* (Göttingen: Wallstein, 2005), 42–59.

[15] The attribution "autobiography" prevails, most recently, in Loster-Schneider, "Poetics, Politics, Gender."

[16] To the well-versed in the many crevices of German literary history, Gleim's *Bildersaal* comes to mind. Though Gleim retains his status and importance among specialists of *Empfindsamkeit* and patriotic poetry within Germanistik, in Anglo-German studies, and—less so—in German-centered comparative literature, he hardly ever enters the considerations of scholars outside Germany and maybe the United Kingdom. Gleim's fate is to be a good indicator of alternate literary canons, depending on whether they are constructed from the inside or out.

exchanges of global knowledge among locally acting protagonists through her editorial work.

Wahrheit aus Morgenträumen thus resembles *Prosaische Schriften* in that it marks a transformative moment in the media architecture of literature that does not fit with the author-, work-, or genre-centered paradigms of telling literature's story which have become anchors of national literary historiography and national canons. As Brun tried to chronicle (in prose) an instance of live performance, she fought an already lost battle for orality; oral performance culture could not be fully preserved in print format. Instead, her text traces a cultural moment through an eclipse, for it could not be absorbed into a narrative that became tasked with sustaining the nation—at first as its pure imagination and later as its retroactive origination in narrative. Conversely, though, being caught in multiplying events of recitation and occasion allowed Brun's poetry to become substrate and fuel for both *improvisation*, as a mode of cultural production, which fuses the local and transnational in a style, as Angela Esterhammer has argued,[17] and *appropriation*, as a mode of erasure.

The latter signals Brun's fate in literary history. Her poem "Ich denke dein" ("Thinking of You," 1795) was immediately set to music by Carl Friedrich Zelter and quickly anthologized, as a song, by Johann Friedrich Reichardt in *Blumenlese* (literally, *Flower Harvest*; metaphorically, *Best Poems*), before Goethe borrowed "form and motif" in "Nähe des Geliebten" ("Nearby Lover") while eclipsing variations and denigrating the original author. Goethe's rather than Brun's poem is now an established part of literary history; his insistence on invention and original authorship eradicated textual sources that had been sustained but were ultimately eclipsed by the one-time performance.[18] Though deemed selective, exemplary, and collectable by virtue of its inclusion in the anthology, Brun's poem never broke free from its "anthologized confines"; that is, it only "survived" in an anthology. Absorbed and preserved for its musical qualities, it cleared neither the threshold of the popular nor the purposefully authorial—characteristics of anthologized works that would help them succeed beyond the nineteenth century.[19]

Still, it is through inclusion in anthologies that Friederike Brun's work points beyond Germany in yet another way. Esterhammer makes a case for Brun having imported conventions of improvisation

---

[17] Esterhammer, *Romanticism and Improvisation*, 109–10.
[18] Von Schwerin, *Friederike Brun*, 92
[19] See Nora Ramtke and Seàn Williams, "Approaching the German Anthology, 1700–1850: An Introduction," *German Life and Letters*, vol. 70, no. 1 (2017): 3–5.

as stylistic features of her own poetry, especially in its awareness of audience and playing to an audience. These conventions comprise poetic diction as an element of style as well as "media management" through publication in journals and, later on, anthologies. Accordingly, she reads "Ich denke Dein" as a poem reflecting the culture of improvisation, because of its adaptability to different contexts and situations, to different forms of publication and performance.[20] She deems most interesting the *Horen*-version of the poem (1796), simultaneously directing our attention to an aspect of Brun's work that is central to foreshadowing, and ultimately anchoring, her later Philhellenic turn: "As the speaker locates herself in this evocative ancient setting (i.e., Rome 1795), its art and mythology work on her and dramatically modulate the direction of her thoughts."[21] Esterhammer observes a "du" receding into the background as the classical surroundings take center stage. The moment of improvisation vanishes in the archives of classical convention, just like the model of eighteenth-century journeys—the grand tour—changed its characters. As much as it was instrumental for the development of classical archeology, it gave way to Rome-inspired collections and antique designs.[22] Brun's voice, too, fossilizes in the face of Rome.

Clearly, Brun's transnational and performance-driven existence—not just her gender—got between her and the German literary canon. Editions more and more revolved around the sole author, as authors intentionally wrote holistically—that is, for legacy and afterlife.[23] Editions depended on editors—who managed, created, cut, and arranged in the name of an acclaimed *Gesamtwerk*—rather than on an author producing on commission for an occasion, be it for an event or for a periodical publication. In the course of the nineteenth century, the releases of collected works were further enhanced by rigorous philological standards that sought to integrate editorial genesis and multiple versions, unifying language and typesets as well as publication history and commentary. The absorption of editorial style in authorial identities finally came full circle. Yet Brun left it to others—indeed, begged others—to collect and edit her work, holding on to a staple that had defined the culture of anthologizing. Thus, Brun's literary enterprise once more defied the national literary narrative. The latter was to be

---

[20] See Esterhammer, *Romanticism and Improvisation*, 51.
[21] Esterhammer, *Romanticism and Improvisation*, 55–6.
[22] Grafton, *Classical Tradition*, 404–5.
[23] Ramtke and Williams approach research from the perspective of edition versus anthology.

contained in the ensuing collected works of famous authors, before being repackaged in editions that allowed Germany's bourgeois citizens to possess all of this history through impressive-looking shares.

In contrast to her (male) contemporaries, Brun mostly struggled to have writings transition from publication in periodicals to publisher-sponsored books. Having her first poems edited and published by Friedrich von Matthison,[24] she continued to peddle her texts to publishers (e.g., Füssli, Cotta, and Perthes), hoping to see her poems appear in a stand-alone volume, while paying attention both to the larger political contexts impairing publication (such as censorship) and to tradition. Her works survived, at least in part, in what I would call self-commissioned anthologies of her selections (rather than editions), a then-common form of self-publishing.[25] But she was also aware of emerging philological habits. Brun's ancillary correspondence promoting her texts thus becomes as much part of her work as the marginalia, notes, and letters accompanying and documenting her role as the editor of other people's writings, most prominently Müller's *Fragmente aus Briefen eines jungen Gelehrten an seinen Freund* (*Fragments from a Young Scholar's Letters to his Friend*). The previously mentioned correspondence between Müller and Bonstetten therefore testifies not only to Müller's knowledge of the world, or both authors' network of acquaintances, but also to an archive of editorial practice, eclipsed by the proliferation of collected works.

First published in 1797–1800 in *Deutsches Magazin* (*German Magazine*), the volume of letters was prepared to appear with Cotta, complete with an editor's preface and having undergone elaborate manuscript evaluation and an amicable censoring process at the hands of regulars in Brun's salons.[26] Intended to guard against any compromising details about von Müller and Bonstetten, such evaluation produced a mediated text that expunged imperfections, inconsistencies, or any traces of

---

[24] A landscape poet and anthologist, known today mainly as the subject of Schiller's essay "Über Matthisons Gedichte."

[25] Von Schwerin emphasizes that Brun's works contain traces of self-censorship, laying bare discrepancies between letters and later accounts (46), and that the second and third Roman stays were documented with considerable distance, thus replicating a practice that I mentioned before as a formative yet underappreciate feature of Goethe's Italian journey—namely, the significant delay between travel experience and recording the experience for public consumption in literary representation.

[26] The group included the aforementioned Schimmelmann as well as Carsten Niebuhr. Von Schwerin provides nuance to this story, detailing Matthison's involvement and the employment of copyists so that Brun could destroy all originals; see von Schwerin, *Friederike Brun*, 281.

incompleteness that scholars detect and attribute to her own texts.[27] Brun doubles down on her intention by prefacing a "Vorerinnnerung" to the volume, reflecting on the positive resonance of prior publication in the journal and assuring the readers of both her care and devotion as an editor and the authenticity of the letters.[28] As editor, Friederike Brun thoroughly domesticated an epistolary exchange that spoke to the world and of the world, while becoming invisible amid the book's pages, which survive today as part of Johannes von Müller's *Sämmtliche Werke* (1814).

German Language, Philology, Marginalia

The displacement of the editorial signature is but one of the hallmarks of nineteenth-century philology. But recovery of editorial work can sharpen our view of German literature from the outside, especially for a writer-editor like Friederike Brun, whose legacy has been both irrevocably German and marginalized by the German literary canon that manifested in the second half of the nineteenth century. This legacy is tied not so much to an elusive German national identity or "feeling," as Kerstin Gräfin von Schwerin asserts, and that flies in the face of Brun's own words at the opening of this chapter, but to the German language and the philological enterprise that aimed at unifying linguistic dominance and played a foundational role in the building of an author and, by extension, a nation. Homing in on such national and philological claims sheds further light on Brun's forgottenness as an author, albeit with a detour. Here we turn to classical convention one more time, although we leave Rome behind. For the national enterprise of philology co-emerged and then existed, as Tuska Benes has shown, alongside the persistence of "Hellas," a revaluation of ancient Greek philology toward classical studies (*Alterthumswissenschaft*). Though Brun did not name Germany but merely insisted on linguistic perfection, reading her through the lens of competing philological efforts and transitions adds yet another dimension to the complexity and fragility of her oeuvre.

First, Brun's editorial project is not just about codifying and controlling the legacy of the edited author but also about expunging an ominous alterity. She orders, publishes, connects, and communes toward a shared linguistic unity in editorial history. And while this philological effort primarily affirms her status as an editor of other people's work (and, thus, one "brand" of a philologist), it also and primarily situates Brun as a *German* writer. Aside from sharing philology's

---

[27] Hoff, *Entdeckung der Zwischenräume*, 225.
[28] Von Müller, *Sämmtliche Werke*, 13: v.

telos of a unifying standard, Brun's activities allowed the integration of a scholarly or erudite endeavor into the large corpus of German literary writings. Her creative writings were less fortunate, but scholars have consistently turned to language—and, thus, the ultimate philological gesture of the nineteenth century—when discussing Friederike Brun's texts, emphasizing that she wrote in German. This trend began with Rosa Olbrich, who in 1913, despite calling Brun "a German-Danish female poet," underscored that even Brun's earliest contributions to Danish journals had to be translated.[29] Brun's singular use of German was of course consistent with the language's preponderance in Danish lands, especially (but not only) among aristocratic administrators. It structured the literary market not least by serving as a vehicle to aid English-language literary imports.[30] Even authors who published in both Danish and German (e.g., Jens Baggesen and Adam Oehlenschläger) became known for their German-language texts, and one of them—Baggesen—even went on to lecture about the elevating status of German among its speakers in Denmark, as well as about translations of Danish works into German, when he was a professor of Nordic languages at the University of Kiel.[31] Though Brun clearly participated in this German takeover of Danish literary, cultural, and political life, not least by never making Denmark into a subject of her artistic representation, she is today remembered for her role as a mediator of and a traveler between national cultures. But such remembrance lingers at best outside of Germany. Like errant spellings in a scholarly edition, Brun was expelled from German literary history by a grand gesture that was as much grounded in place as it was in philology.[32]

For Brun's oeuvre effectively illustrates the work of philology. It differs from, say, Heinrich Heine's oeuvre or those of numerous German-Jewish and Yiddish writers of the nineteenth century, as well as the practice in *Editionsphilologie* of publishing medieval texts, in that it actually exposes the reservoir—in all its rawness—that philology works

---

[29] Rosa Olbrich, *Die deutsch-dänische Dichterin Friederike Brun, ein Beitrag zur empfindsam-klassizistischen Stilperiode* (Wanne-Eickel: Wolf, 1932), 55–61.
[30] Vibeke Winge, *Dänische Deutsche, Deutsche Dänen* (Heidelberg: Winter, 1992), 297.
[31] Hoff, *Entdeckung der Zwischenräume*, 22.
[32] Hoff, *Entdeckung der Zwischenräume*, 22. Strangely, though language (and, in essence, language science or philology) came to transport and sustain ideals of nation, the locations of Brun's life and writing—Copenhagen, Rome, and Switzerland—proved pivotal for declaring her a European woman writer. And it is the older model of philology, the fixation on the classical languages, that supports Brun's self-alienation from an emergent canon of German literature.

with and against and in which it seeks to intervene by shaping a norm. Brun's work thus draws attention to instances of otherness or defiance of the norms, before squaring off with philology's achievement of creating and sustaining a national, even nationalist, idea.[33] Her editorial work embraces attention to both the grammatical models and disciplinary accuracy inherited from classical philology and a uniquely German philology, fusing literature, history, law, and myth in the belief that language was "the cultural form with the most intimate connection to a preexisting national spirit."[34] Philology's tripartite task—the restoration of "the perfected text," the discerning of its "fullest meaning," and, somewhat secondary, "the evolution of its genre"—had been in service of the German nation ever since the brothers Grimm began collecting folk tales and working on their dictionary and since the grand monumental gesture, according to James Turner, that was Wilhelm von Humboldt's "Romantic conflation of language and nation."[35] Though Brun does not deal with philological remnants perused to reconstruct origins, she does seek to codify, arrest norms, and project authority. She works with fragments of oral languages, misspellings, distorted words, aberrations of rhythm and rhyme, and other non-codified uses of German. She too silences: often her own linguistic imperfections, and nearly always the upheavals and infractions of political discourse.[36] And she continues to be shaped by yet another philological tradition, no matter how unrelated it seems to her editorial work—namely, classical philology.

Classicism's moment of transformation in the early nineteenth century initially reframes Brun's frequent moaning about not knowing ancient Greek and Latin, especially when it came to poetic genres. Though considered an indicator of women's exclusion from erudition and *Bildung*, clinging to ancient Greek poetic models also stood for the "neohumanist

---

[33] More recent take-ups of philology include the special issue of *Germanic Review*, edited by Willi Goetschel and David Suchow, entitled *Displaced Philologies*. Here, editors and authors have teased out philology's translation work in the service of expunging a (religious) other ("second order secularization"), emphasizing its unifying task. Furthermore, see James Turner, *Philology: The Forgotten Origins of the Modern Humanities* (Princeton, NJ: Princeton University Press, 2014). Though preoccupied with American philology, the book references German philology passim.

[34] Tuska Benes, *In Babel's Shadow: Language, Philology, and the Nation in Nineteenth-Century Germany* (Detroit: Wayne State University Press, 2008), 121.

[35] Turner, *Philology*, 134.

[36] Philology could of course take on a decidedly political task, as Goetschel's essay on Heinrich Heine demonstrates; see *Displaced Philologies* 30–8. Brun's philological enterprise undercuts Renker's claim that all projects Brun undertook reflect political intention.

German veneration of ancient Greece [. . . that had] classical Hellas [as] the Urbild or the primordial, ideal model of cultural development and nationhood that modern Germans should emulate." Philhellenism conjured up a continuity in linguistic structure and poetic form that contributed to the representation of material circumstance, truth, and a self-image that had Germans as "interpreters and custodians of the Hellenic legacy, having been, they claimed, the only Europeans to have escaped the imprint of Latin."[37] As classical philology was transformed into a more holistic study of classics that had language as one among many historical phenomena and objects (*Sachphilologie*), it inspired and even redirected Germans to focus on their own, at times genuinely German or folk poetic models, on the one hand, while tasking them to assert the autonomy of ancient Greece, on the other. Carving out this unique status had far-reaching implications, not just for the place of ancient Greek within comparative philology or Orientalists at German universities, but also for the discourse surrounding the Greek War of Independence against the Ottoman Empire. German poetic engagement with the war appears, then, in an alternate light: not just as simultaneous displacement and enforcement of anti-Napoleonic political sentiment, as most scholars have it,[38] but also as an inward-directed, and latently apolitical, gesture that turned to poetry and literary writing—indeed, philology—to shore up the national.

It is here that the linguistic work of philology, along with its various intended or effected displacements, once more redirects our attention to Brun's incongruousness with the nineteenth-century literary field. Her *Lieder für Hellas* (*Songs for Hellas*)—also and more commonly circulating as *Scherflein für Hellas* (*A Widow's Mite for Hellas*)—underscore her marginal position in that they emphasize the formal ideals of classical philology more so than appealing to the Greek War of Independence, to anti-Napoleonic sentiment, or to the political future of the German nation. (A political turn in support of the German nation would have integrated Brun in the poetic and political movement of Philhellenism.) The circle of poems adheres to principles commensurate with an ideal

---

[37] Benes, *Babel's Shadow*, 161.
[38] This is a common scholarly opinion, especially in the context of restauration and *Vormärzforschung*. See, for example, the preface to Gilbert Heß, Elena Agazzi, and Elisabeth Décultot, *Graecomania. Der europäische Philhellenismus* (Berlin: de Gruyter, 2001), ix, where Philhellenism is contextualized within "broader European phantasms around 1800"; also Alfred Noe, "Philhellenismus im deutschsprachigen Österreich," in *Der Philhellenismus in der westeuropäischen Literatur, 1780–1830*, ed. Alfred Noe (Amsterdam: Rodopi, 1994), 189–224, where the author argues that especially in early phases of the liberation wars (1821–2), Philhellenism projected its own ideals about the birthplace of Western civilization rather than any worthwhile political understanding of the Greek situation (190).

of national unity in and through language, which relies on an unprecedented resurrection and appreciation of tradition. It praises the ancient form and poetic etiquette and ultimately celebrates classical philology. Unlike the poetry of Heinrich Heine, or of Junges Deutschland, which openly reflected the political zeitgeist, Brun's poems conjure another space amid gory images: the antiquarian nature of a fossilized ideal of a "high" culture that was, and had to remain, outside Germany.

Brun Interrogates Ancient Greece and Ends Up Writing German

The poems translate ancient Greek forms—another element under the purview of philology—into German, paying lip service to the Philhellenic gestures bubbling up everywhere across Europe.[39] Her contemporary Heinrich Döring insinuates that Brun supported the Greek liberation movement and offered donations—explaining, perhaps, the more commonly used, main title of the poems (*Scherflein für Hellas*), though Brun herself preferred using the subtitle or an abbreviated version (*Lieder für Hellas*; *Griechenlieder*).[40] But her participation in the Greek cause remains rhetorical. She herself states that only if the poems can be published as part of a larger volume will she donate the proceeds to the movement. Initially, we do not even know for sure whether she has in mind the *Lieder für Hellas* when "singing for the Greeks":

> Now to something that is extremely close and dear to my heart. I did not want to sing for the Greeks alone, but also to help them in some way. [. . .] You should help me with this. You once were kind enough to let me make a promise to you, namely to entrust you with the publication of my "Truth and Poetry from Morning Dreams, or Childhood and first Youth Memoirs." I also add "Ida's Aesthetic Development." Both would make a pretty volume. I therefore ask that you sell the manuscript for as much as possible, to the highest bidder, wherever, and to whom you want. The yield belongs to the Greeks.

---

[39] The extensive scholarship on European Philhellenism documents this movement. See, among others, Constanz Güthenke, *Placing Modern Greece: The Dynamics of Modern Hellenism 1770–1840* (Oxford: Oxford University Press, 2008); Heß, Agazzi, and Décultot, *Graecomania*; Marco Hillemann and Tobias Roth, *Wilhelm Müller und der deutsche Philhellenismus* (Berlin: Frank & Timme, 2015); Alfred Noe, *Der Philhellenismus in der westeuropäischen Literatur 1730–1830* (Amsterdam: Rodopi, 1994).

[40] Heinrich Döring, *Das Merkwürdigste aus dem Leben von Johannes von Müller, Schröckh, Jünger, Reinhold, Bertuch, ferner von Louise Brachmann und Friederike Brun* (Quedlinburg and Leipzig: Ermst'sche Buchhandlung, 1841), 171–2.

[Jetzt zu einer Sache, die mir gewaltig nahe und innig am Herzen liegt. Ich wollte gern nicht allein für die Griechen singen, sondern ihnen auch auf irgend eine Weise thätig helfen. [. . .] Hierzu sollst du mir behülflich sein. Du warst einst gütig genug, Dir von mir versprechen zu lassen, um Dir einst die Herausgabe meiner "Wahrheit und Dichtung aus Morgenträumen, oder Kindheit und erste Jugendmeinungen" anzuvertrauen. Ich füge noch "Ida's ästhetische Entwicklung" hinzu. Beides würde ein hübsches Bändchen geben. Ich bitte Dich also, das Manuscript so theuer, als möglich, zu verschachern, wo und an wen Du willst. Der Ertrag gehört den Griechen. Findest Du, des besseren Absatzes wegen, für gut, dies bekannt zu machen, so habe ich nichts dawieder. Ich wünschte dies Büchlein zur Ostermesse erscheinen zu sehen.][41]

Scherflein für Hellas is not mentioned explicitly, and a few months later, Brun apparently backed out on the offer to donate all proceeds and denied ever wanting to make the *Griechenlieder* part of the much-desired edition ("habe nie daran gedacht"). Though she cited fear of censorship because of the poem's political force, her larger concern was for her legacy and autobiography. She feared that the entire publication plan might unravel; the *Griechenlieder should* therefore be kept separate and published (or not) in support of the cause of Greek independence.[42] Despite the back-and-forth, they appeared in an appendix to *Wahrheit aus Morgenträumen und Idas ästhetische Erziehung*.

Yet Friederike Brun's contradictory directives to Matthison reflect her peculiar Graecomania. It stands removed from that of her contemporaries, who styled themselves as activists (e.g., by abdicating philology and the ideal of ancient Greece and favoring instead the modern, contemporaneous Hellas), post-nationalists who embraced a European solidarity movement (and made donations to equip volunteer fighters sent to Greece), or promoters of a cultural transfer popularized through the fantasy of a fighting poet, embodied in the most legendary way by Lord Byron.[43] Brun's attitude toward Greece is more complex; first and foremost, it thrives on Greek poetry and ancient Greek culture. Elsewhere I have read Brun's referencing of ancient poetry as a comparative gesture, setting apart the sentimental and performance-driven culture of the salons. Indeed, *ästhetische Entwicklung* reflects a conception of education and art that is critical of the impact of ancient culture and the associated formation of classical ideals in Germany, favoring instead

---

[41] Döring, *Das Merkwürdigste aus dem Leben*, 172, quoted from a letter to Matthison, November 16, 1822.
[42] Döring, *Das Merkwürdigste aus dem Leben*, 172.
[43] Heß, Gazzi, and Décultot, *Graecomania*, xi–xx.

the live performances of *tableaux vivants*. The self-depreciating verdict on her poetry in *Wahrheit*, which she deems "forever unfinished" because she lacks the pure models of Greek poetry and which I have interpreted as an indicator of networked relationships in the salons, appears in a different light when read against philological principles. Then it suddenly matters whether one can recognize, apply, and perfect such models and imitate them accordingly in writing, rather than embracing a natural talent for the meter composed by hearing and reciting. Here, too, Friederike Brun domesticates—by deliberately leaving Greek form and verse outside her written repertoire[44]—while acknowledging the dominance of philological principles inherited from the classical languages. She clearly places the written word above performance. Put differently, by delineating the limits of both salon and journey, Brun ends up putting forth a new marker of a nation and its tradition—the published book.

Yet she tries one more time, as the *Lieder für Hellas* seemingly evade the fate of performance felled by writing. They represent an aberration within Brun's oeuvre, as they are defined by an ancient classical form. Comprising four triads (poems in three stanzas) and very much in the tradition of Pindar's odes—and structured as strophe, anti-strophe, and epode—the cycle strives for erudition and expressive poetic education while simultaneously undercutting their tradition in the title. "Scherflein" suggests as much commonality and communal claim, as it remains vague and perhaps void of an actual contribution. The exaggerated form conceals a moderate intervention. While allusions to ancient myths give the poems motivic and historical gravitas, the efforts to locate them in current events appear both obvious and contrived, especially as elegant and sophisticated form intersects with vicious, even bloody (e.g., "Barbarians") and xenophobic rhetoric, beginning in the second triad, where Algerian pirate ships are let loose on the Greeks, countering the choirs of their loyal friends. Stefan Lindinger sees herein the typical pattern of German Philhellenism—namely, an interlacing of ancient Greek ideal poetry and Christian modernity; however, he also ascribes to Brun a pick-and-choose attitude when it comes to poetic motifs (e.g., the allusion to Greek tragedy via the two choirs).[45] I suggest that it is standard Philhellenic

---

[44] Brun, *Wahrheit*, 176. This is not incompatible with the turn to Greece and the larger movement of Philhellenism, especially if there is a doubling down via motif, e.g., nature. On distressed genre, where rigors of genre convention are naturalized, albeit with a flaw; see Güthenke, *Placing Modern Greece*, 109–10.

[45] Lindinger, "'O Hellas, Hellas im Blut'gen Kampf / Wie bist du schön!' Die philhellinische Lyrik Friederike Bruns und Amalie von Helvigs," in *Wilhelm Müller und der deutsche Philhellinismus*, ed. Marco Hillermann and Tobias Roth (Berlin: Frank & Timme, 2015), 48.

rhetoric, including the feminization and pronounced Christianization of Hellas, that pervades the form, only to bring it to collapse amid the invocation of context: Brun initially attempts a rather mundane transposition of the European resistance to Napoleon onto the Greek liberation movement, conjuring a unity among "Germany and Hellas" ["Germanien und Hellas"] with a somewhat empty pathos. She lets go of strict parallels in stanza length in the classical triad. She annotates with parenthetical commentary, placing her poetry in a particular contemporary moment by showing off her knowledge of events and legitimizing herself. In the final two triads, she combines prayer and elegy, only to culminate in a promise of salvation, as the last triad narrates the successful defeat of the Turks at sea. Lindinger has put forth a compelling analysis and interpretation of motif and form in each stanza and triad of the cycle and frames both tone and intention vis-à-vis Brun's Pietist worldview.[46] What strikes me as necessary for understanding the odd place that the poems take among Brun's works is her unusual attempt to appropriate and comply with inherited classical form, and also her full-fledged embrace of Christian rhetoric, including a proselytizing tone directed at non-Westerners. The poems thus circumscribe not only the limitations of her ability to translate and effectively domesticate foreign form but also the limits of her alleged cosmopolitanism. While Philhellenism lent itself to accommodating European national ideals, it also offered a space for transcendence of the raging struggles for liberation. The struggle of the Turks and Greeks appeared in the crosshairs of different discourses—namely, "as a religious war of Christianity against Islam, and as a rebellion of an oppressed people against the authorities."[47] In the German-speaking regions, the actual and imagined reverberations of these constellations were felt with more intensity in light of the complex southeast European power structure and Austria-Hungary.[48] In light of this supranational, or transnational, dimension of Philhellenism, three additional observations complicate Brun's attitude toward Greece and further help in understanding what I have called domesticated cosmopolitanism. First, her understanding and praxis of Philhellenism is shaped by her relationship to the Greek language, especially by her desire to master what she clearly lacks. Second, she transfers in toto her admiration and experience of Italy to Greece. Third, and much more covertly, Brun's life and writing intensify what marks Philhellenism as a movement. Just as recent scholarly

---

[46] Lindinger, "O Hellas," 47–57, esp. 51–57.
[47] Heß, Agazzi, and Décultot, *Graecomania*, xi.
[48] Noe, "Philhellenismus," 189–90.

discussions of the movement remind us of the regional and urban conditions of literary life, local conditions and networks refracted Brun's epistolary, poetic, and prose production—no matter how far-flung her journeys seemed to be. In many ways, Brun's work was marginal and small. Local, not to say personal, needs and conditions directed her adaption of transnational, though not global, traditions and structured her observation of global entanglements. These include her friendship with von Bonstetten and Matthison, which modeled the local, workshop-like shaping of material, as well as the forced local existence that she endured when health problems prevented her from traveling.

Cosmopolitanism Abridged and Domesticated: From the Salon to the Book

Just as her Sophienholm salon was very much a domesticating event—albeit with cosmopolitan, globally acting participants—Brun's sometimes desperate efforts to publish a book represent a domesticating act. Editing and grafting onto the naturalness of spoken and performed language strengthened the artificiality (*Kunstcharakter*) of the poetic practice. Her turn to philological models appears pronounced, even if it was merely expressed in marginalia, conversations, and ancillary genres (e.g., letters). Indeed, Brun and her network used techniques that today, in light of recent scholarship by Petra McGillen, among others, strike us as modern. And while I do not believe that Brun was motivated by complying with conventions and habits of Classical Weimar, her works hover between consolidation and displacement. The former happens via philological practice in all its facets and includes a uniform, perfected language and latently national task. It leaves the salon behind and culminates in books and collected works, though not always and not easily her own. The court and country estate are symbols of such consolidation and domestication. The latter is also expressed by Brun's perpetual avoidance of Germany except for its language. This move involves extensive travel and is hyped by Brun's commentary and reflection upon places, sites, and observations outside German territories. And her acknowledging of global overtures and existence—by herself, her friends, and the Danish Unitary State— underscores this habit and trend. Avoidance of the national flirts with the promise of cosmopolitanism, though it exposes its limitations at the horizon of Europe. The port, exemplified by the observational detail of a ship, emerges as a symbolic harbor of such cosmopolitan reach. But Brun's prosaic musings on the world are reigned in as she turns toward a quest for form. Eventually, institutional framing—Brun's nod to Classical philology—and a book—*Lieder für Hellas*—define the limits of both her cosmopolitanism and agency outside the nation.

Works Cited

Baumgartner, Karin. "Packaging the Grand Tour: German Women Authors Write Italy 1791–1874," *Women in German Yearbook*, vol. 31 (2015): 1–27.

Benes, Tuska. *In Babel's Shadow: Language, Philology, and the Nation in Nineteenth-Century Germany* (Detroit: Wayne State University Press, 2008).

Blackwell, Jeanine. "Sophie von La Roche and the Black Slave Poet Feuerbach: A Study in Sentimentality, Enlightenment, and Outsiderdom," in *The Enlightenment and its Legacy: Studies in German Literature in Honor of Helga Slessarev*, ed. Sara Friedrichsmeyer and Barbara Becker-Cantarino (Bonn: Bouvier, 1991), 105–15.

Brekke, Tone. "A Cosmopolitan Salon-Hostess: Friederike Brun's Revision of Schiller in Idas ästhetische Entwicklung (1824)," *Literature Compass*, vol. 1 (2004): 1–11.

Brun, Friederike. *Prosaische Schriften*, 4 vols. (Zurich: Orell, Füssli und Compagnie, 1799–1801).

Brun, Friederike. *Wahrheit aus Morgenträumen und Idas ästhetische Erziehung* (Aarau: Sauerländer, 1824).

Castle, Cora Sutton. *A Statistical Study of Eminent Women* (New York: Science Press, 1913).

Döring, Heinrich. *Das Merkwürdigste aus dem Leben von Johannes von Müller, Schröckh, Jünger, Reinhold, Bertuch, ferner von Louise Brachmann und Friederike Brun* (Quedlinburg and Leipzig: Ernst'sche Buchhandlung, 1841).

Esterhammer, Angela, *Romanticism and Improvisation, 1750–1850* (Cambridge: Cambridge University Press, 2008).

Goethe, J. W. von. *Werke. Herausgegeben im Auftrage der Großherzogin Sophie von Sachsen. III. Abtheilung. Goethes Tagebücher. 3. Band: 1801–1808* (Weimar: Böhlau, 1889).

Goethe, J. W. von. *Werke. Anhang. Abtheilung für Gespräche. 8. Band 1831–1832 und Nachträge* (Weimar: Böhlau, 1890).

Goethe, J. W. von. *Werke, IV. Abtheilung. Goethes Briefe, 14. Band, 1799* (Weimar: Böhlau, 1893).

Goetschel, Willi. "Heine's Displaced Philology," *Germanic Review*, vol. 93, no. 1 (2018): 30–8.

Goetschel, Willi, and David Suchow, eds. *Displaced Philologies*, *Germanic Review*, special issue, vol. 93, no. 1 (2018): 1–92.

Grafton, Anthony, ed. *The Classical Tradition* (Cambridge, MA: Belknap at Harvard University Press, 2010).

Güthenke, Constanze. *Placing Modern Greece: The Dynamics of Romantic Hellenism, 1770–1840* (Oxford: Oxford University Press, 2008).

Hering, Gunnar. "Der griechische Unabhängigkeitskrieg und der Philhellenismus," in *Der Philhellenismus in der westeuropäischen Literatur 1780–1830*, ed. Alfred Noe (Amsterdam: Rodopi, 1994), 17–72.

Heß, Gilbert, Elena Agazzi, and Elisabeth Décultot, eds. *Graecomania. Der europäische Philhellenismus* (Berlin: de Gruyter, 2009).

Heß, Gilbert, Elena Agazzi, and Elisabeth Décultot, eds. "Vorwort," in *Graecomania. Der europäische Philhellenismus* (Berlin: de Gruyter, 2009), ix–xxiv.

Hillemann, Marco, and Tobias Roth. *Wilhelm Müller und der deutsche Philhellenismus* (Berlin: Frank & Timme, 2015).

Hoff, Karin. *Die Entdeckung der Zwischenräume. Literarische Projekte der Spätaufklärung zwischen Skandinavien und Deutschland* (Göttingen: Wallstein, 2003).

Holmgren, Janet Besserer. *The Women Writers in Schiller's Horen: Patrons, Petticoats, and the Promotion of Weimar Classicism* (Newark: University of Delaware Press, 2007).

Keith-Smith, Brian. *Friederike Brun Reader: Supplement to an Encyclopedia of German Women Writers* (Lewiston: Edwin Mellen Press, 2006).

Lindinger, Stefan. "'O Hellas, Hellas im Blut'gen Kampf / Wie bist du schön!' Die philhellenische Lyrik Friederike Bruns und Amalie von Helvigs," in *Wilhelm Müller und der deutsche Philhellenismus*, ed. Marco Hillermann and Tobias Roth (Berlin: Frank & Timme, 2015), 45–68.

Lokke, Kari. "Parting Songs: Hemans, Landon, and Barrett Browning Rewrite Friederike Brun," in *Romanticism: Comparative Discourses*, ed. Larry Peer and Diane Long Hoeveler (Aldershot: Routledge, 2006), 131–41.

Lokke, Kari. "Friederike Brun's *Briefe aus Rom* (1816): Cosmopolitanism, Nationalism, and the Politics of *Geistlichkeit*," in *Women against Napoleon: Historical and Fictional Responses to his Rise and Legacy*, ed. Waltraud Maierhofer, Gertrud Roesch, and Caroline Bland (Frankfurt: Campus, 2007), 137–57.

Loster-Schneider, Gudrun. "Poetics, Politics, Gender and Pedagogics in Friederike Brun's (1765–1835) Autobiography *Wahrheit aus Morgenträumen* (1824)," in *Women from the Parsonage: Pastors' Daughters as Writers, Translators, Salonnières, and Educators*, ed. Cindy Renker and Susanne Bach (Berlin: de Gruyter, 2019), 131–51.

Matthews-Schlinzig, Marie Isabel, and Caroline Socha, eds. *Was ist ein Brief? Aufsätze zu epistolarer Theorie und Kultur—What is a letter? Essays on Epistolary Theory and Culture* (Würzburg: Königshausen & Neumann. 2018).

McGillen, Petra. *The Fontane Workshop: Manufacturing Realism in the Industrial Age of Print* (New York: Bloomsbury, 2019).

Müller, Johannes von. *Sämmtliche Werke*, vols. 13 and 14, ed. Friederike Brun (Tübingen: J. G. Cotta, 1812).

Noe, Alfred, "Philhellenismus im deutschsprachigen Österreich," in *Der Philhellenismus in der westeuropäischen Literatur, 1780–1830*, ed. Alfred Noe (Amsterdam: Rodopi, 1994), 189–224.

Noe, Alfred, ed. *Der Philhellenismus in der westeuropäischen Literatur, 1780–1830* (Amsterdam: Rodopi, 1994).

Olbrich, Rosa. *Die deutsch-dänische Dichterin Friederike Brun, ein Beitrag zur empfindsam-klassizistischen Stilperiode* (Wanne-Eickel: Wolf, 1932).

Povlsen, Karen Klitgaard. "Persistent Patterns: The Genre of Travel Writing in the Eighteenth Century," in *Northbound: Travels, Encounters, and Constructions 1700–1830*, ed. Karen Klitgaard Povlsen (Aarhus: Aarhus Universitetsforlag, 2007), 325–40.

Ramtke, Nora, and Seàn Williams. "Approaching the German Anthology, 1700–1850: An Introduction," *German Life and Letters*, vol. 70, no. 1 (2017): 1–21.

Renker, Cindy. "The Political Voice in the Writings of Friederike Brun (1765–1835)," *Women in German Yearbook*, no. 29 (2013): 81–96.

Schiller, Friedrich. *Werke. Nationalausgabe. Erster Band. Gedichte in der Reihenfolge ihres Erscheinens 1776–1799* (Weimar: Böhlau, 1992).

Schiller, Friedrich. *Werke. Nationalausgabe. Fünfunddreißigster Band. Briefwechsel. Briefe an Schiller 25.5.1794–31.10.1795* (Weimar: Böhlau, 1993).

Schiller, Friedrich. *Werke. Vierzigster Band. Briefwechsel. Briefe an Schiller 1.1.1803–17.5.1805* (Weimar: Böhlau, 1995).

Schwerin, Kerstin Gräfin von. *Friederike Brun. Weltbürgerin in der Zeitenwende. Eine Biographie* (Göttingen: Wallstein, 2020).
Tautz, Birgit. "Revolution, Abolition, Aesthetic Sublimation: German Responses to News from France in the 1790s," in *Rewriting the Radical: Enlightenment, Revolution, and Cultural Transfer in 1790s Germany, Britain and France*, ed. Maike Oergel (Berlin: de Gruyter, 2012), 72–87.
Tautz, Birgit. *Translating the World: Toward A New History of German Literature around 1800* (University Park: Pennsylvania State University Press, 2018).
Turner, James. *Philology: The Forgotten Origins of the Modern Humanities* (Princeton, NJ: Princeton University Press, 2014).
Voght, Caspar. *Lebensgeschichte*, ed. Charlotte Schoell-Glass (Hamburg: Christians, 2001).
Walser-Wilhelm, Doris and Peter, eds. *Zeitgebirge: Karl Viktor von Bonstetten, Madame de Staël, Friederike Brun, geb. Münter. Zwei Briefgespräche 1811–1813* (Göttingen: Wallstein, 2005).
Winge, Vibeke. *Dänische Deutsche, Deutsche Dänen* (Heidelberg: Winter, 1992).

Three On the Inside Looking Out: Fichte, the University, and the Psychopolitics of German Idealism

Laurie Ruth Johnson

German Idealists and Romantics were not the first intellectuals to aestheticize reality, but some of the self-conscious stylization of violence and upheaval in their work is nevertheless startling. Johann Gottlieb Fichte described the French Revolution as "a rich painting about the great text: human right and human value" ("ein reiches Gemälde über den großen Text: Menschenrecht und Menschenwert").[1] And, after the Terror had begun, Fichte attributed inspiration for the *Wissenschaftslehre* (*The Science of Knowledge*, beginning in 1794) to the revolution, comparing his "inner fight with myself" ("inner(n) Kampf mit mir selbst") to how the French nation "fought with outer force for its political freedom" ("mit äußerer Kraft die politische Freiheit erkämpfte").[2] The parallels between Fichte's psychological struggle and the revolutionaries' physical and political

---

[1] Johann Gottlieb Fichte, *Beitrag zur Berichtigung der Urteile des Publikums über die französische Revolution*, 1793, cited here in Fichte, *Schriften zur Revolution*, ed. Bernard Willms (Cologne and Opladen: Westdeutscher Verlag, 1967), 34. This essay was written before the outbreak of the Terror in September 1793, and Fichte wrote the last parts (the essay remained unfinished) around the time that the Committee of Public Safety (Comité de salut public, led by Robespierre) was installed, in the summer of 1793. Translations from Fichte's work are my own.

[2] Letter from Fichte written in 1795, probably to the Danish poet Jens Baggesen. Cited here in Fichte's *Briefwechsel 1793–1795*, in the *Gesamtausgabe der Bayerischen Akademie der Wissenschaften*, ed. Reinhard Lauth and Hans Gliwitzky (Stuttgart-Bad Cannstatt: Frommann, 1962–2012), vol. 3, no. 2, 298, letter no. 282a. References to this edition are abbreviated henceforth as GA.

battle culminated in "the first 'hints' and premonitions" ("die ersten 'Winke' und Ahndungen") of his philosophical system.[3] Reshaping reality into theory was of course part of the German Romantic and Idealist projects, but the tendency to depict external events as internal processes, and to create narratives of psychological and aesthetic geographies based in part on knowledge of political and economic events, also came to influence a particular kind of German nationalism, and a German notion of the nation, as the nineteenth century unfolded.[4]

Although we now may see connections between philosophy and politics as not only commonplace, but unavoidable, and despite Fichte's own attribution of his philosophical system to politics, in the past scholars often have resisted exploring connections between Fichte's philosophy, Idealist thought more generally, and politics. In addition, psychology has been left out of considerations of Fichte's philosophy and politics almost entirely. The lack of emphasis on the interrelation of politics and philosophy arguably corresponds to the cleft in German cultural history between politics as a phenomenon of the outside, and philosophy as belonging to the inner world. But by now there is consensus that German Idealism was a politically inflected philosophy, and that its manifestations in the "real world" had political resonances—that, in other words, in- and outside are connected.[5]

However, the relation of politics to philosophy was never straightforward. Addressing the general German public and seemingly promising national expansion based on psychic self-management, Fichte suggests an almost telepathic connection between interior psychic processes and exterior political ones: "I search in the presence of God, conscientiously, and discover—the sovereignty of your will on the inside—the expansion of your borders outward" ("Ich forsche vor Gott, gewissenhaft, und finde – Alleinherrschaft eures Willens im Innern – Verbreitung eurer Grenzen von außen").[6] The text in which this passage

---

[3] GA, vol. 3, no. 2, 298, letter no. 282a.
[4] Helmut Walser Smith discusses intersections between Romantic and Idealist aesthetics and developing German nationalism around 1800 in *Germany: A Nation in Its Time: Before, During, and After Nationalism, 1500–2000* (New York: W.W. Norton, 2020), esp. 145–9, 177–81.
[5] For just a few examples of some recent analyses of Idealist work that explicitly connects that work to politics, see Frederick Beiser, "Fichte and the French Revolution," 38–64; Jean-Christophe Merle, "Fichte's Political Economy and His Theory of Property," 199–221; and David James, "Fichte and Hegel on Recognition and Slavery," 350–73, all in *The Cambridge Companion to Fichte*, ed. David James and Günter Zöller (Cambridge: Cambridge University Press, 2016).
[6] Fichte, *Beitrag*, in *Schriften zur Revolution*, 73.

and the above-mentioned comparison of the revolution to a painting both appear is an anonymously published essay intended to counter increased anti-revolutionary sentiment in Germany. But beyond advocating for the importance and even beauty of the French Revolution specifically, the *Beitrag zur Berichtigung der Urtheile des Publicums über die französische Revolution* (*Contribution to the Rectification of the Public's Judgement of the French Revolution*, 1793) envisions psychology as central to political philosophy and practice.

Fichte's Revolutionary "I"
Psychology (and the new empirical psychology in particular) is for Fichte a pathway to politics, informing his understanding of what humans are both individually and in community.

> [. . .] as with spirits in the original state of reason, so are all people equal in terms of certain other sensuous spiritual forms. The differences among them that are due to historical period, climate, or occupation are really minimal compared to the number of similarities, and, in the hands of wise state constitutions, *must continue to fall away, if culture progresses.* [. . .] This is where experience really comes into play: not how many monarchies there were, or what day the Battle of Philippi took place, but an experience much closer to us—*empirical psychology.*—Choose yourself as your most trusted partner, follow yourself into the most secret corners of your heart, and coax all of your secrets out of yourself: *get to know yourself*—that is the first principle of this psychology. The rules that you deduce from this self-observation, about the direction of *your* drives and inclinations, and about the form of *your* sensual self, apply—you can surely believe it—to everything that has a human face.

> [[. . .] so wie der ursprünglichen Vernunftform nach alle Geister, so sind gewissen andern sinnlichen Geistesformen nach alle Menschen sich gleich. Die Unterschiede, welche Zeitalter, Klima, Beschäftigung in ihnen hervorbringen, sind gegen die Summe der Gleichheiten wirklich gering, *müssen bei fortrückender Kultur* unter den Händen weiser Staatsverfassungen *immer mehr wegfallen* [. . .]. Hier nun ist es, wo wirklich die Erfahrung eintritt: aber nicht jene, wieviel Hauptmonarchien es gegeben habe, oder an welchem Tage die Schlacht bei Philippi vorgefallen sei, sondern die uns viel nähere—die *Erfahrungsseelenkunde.* — —Wähle dich selbst zu deinem vertrautesten Gesellschafter, folge dir in die geheimsten Winkel deines Herzens, und locke dir alle deine Geheimnisse ab: *lerne dich selbst kennen*—das ist der erste

Grundsatz dieser Seelenkunde. Die Regeln, die du dir aus dieser Selbstbeobachtung über den Gang *deiner* Triebe und Neigungen, über die Form *deines* sinnlichen Selbst abziehen wirst, gelten—du darfst es sicher glauben—für alles, was menschliches Antlitz trägt.][7]

In this passage from the *Beitrag*, Fichte does not deploy the philosophical "I" so much as the psychological "I." However, this relatively early text, written when Fichte was just over thirty years old, demonstrates that the philosophical "I" was always psychological.

Fichte's reference in the above passage to "empirical psychology" ("*Erfahrungsseelenkunde*") suggests familiarity with Karl Philipp Moritz's *Magazin zur Erfahrungsseelenkunde* (*Journal of Empirical Psychology*, 1783–93).[8] Although Fichte often is considered a metaphysical theorist, his reliance on empirical psychology is less surprising than it initially may appear. The injunction to "get to know yourself" is completely compatible with the early *Wissenschaftslehre*'s emphasis on developing a code for how to act in the world. In that world, indeed, "freedom" is essential, but it is utterly grounded in lived experience. Only later does Fichte "abstract" the philosophical self from physical and historical experience.[9]

The *Beitrag* is a surprisingly empirically grounded and arguably even progressive essay in this respect, and not only due to its insistence that all people are essentially equal and that their differences are minor. The practice of looking inward, of using empirical psychology on oneself, is itself a democratic practice: it is available to everyone all the time. The command to "choose yourself as your most trusted partner," along with the assurance that the only way to self-trust and self-knowledge is to "coax all of your secrets out of yourself," certainly echoes the content and tone of any number of passages in Rousseau's *Confessions* (1782, 1789), but the *Beitrag*'s combined emphasis on internal processes and external material conditions and events also

---

[7] Fichte, *Beitrag*, in *Schriften zur Revolution*, 52.
[8] Anthony Krupp traces a compelling path from Rousseau's to Fichte's concepts of the "I" that travels through Moritz's work, while also noting the significant differences among the three, in "Other Relations: The Pre-History of *le moi* and *(das) Ich* in Jean-Jacques Rousseau, Karl-Philipp Moritz, and Johann Gottlieb Fichte," *Goethe Yearbook*, vol. 11 (2002): 111–31.
[9] See Frederick Beiser's explication of the development of the *Wissenschaftslehre* in "Fichte and the French Revolution," 38–64, and in *German Idealism: The Struggle Against Subjectivism, 1781–1801* (Cambridge, MA: Harvard University Press, 2008), esp. 217–21, 222–39.

resonates with a similar blend, in Moritz's work, of materialism, morality, and the imagination.[10]

Rousseau's influence on Fichte's thinking about the role of the state in social life, especially as manifested in *Der geschlossene Handelsstaat* (*The Closed Commercial State*, 1800), is well documented.[11] However, Fichte's reworking of Rousseau's contributions to psychology, as well as, as I am suggesting here, of Moritz's empirical psychology, largely has been ignored. This is perhaps understandable, due to the challenges of working with Fichte's philosophy and untangling his politics, not to mention the challenges of bringing his philosophy and politics together in a coherent way. But it is in the *Beitrag*, and in the early to mid-1790s in general, amid his excitement about the French Revolution, that Fichte's fascination with psychology is most evident.

Fichte's implication in the *Beitrag* is that self-knowledge will bring us closer to a radically improved individual life and to a relatively moderate political situation. A state in which the government essentially stays out of the way of its citizens' moral and psychological progress, which is in effect what Fichte advocates in the *Beitrag*, is the kind of state that enables that "rich painting" about "human right and human value" to emerge. In a sense, the only way in which Fichte could defend the increasingly violent situation in France (and, he indeed never completed the *Beitrag*)[12] was to psychologize political experience, to reframe external revolution as an internal uprising, and to reassure readers that the cost of learning one's secrets would be massively repaid with a greater understanding not only of oneself, but of others (whatever "rules that you deduce from this self-observation [. . .] apply—you can surely believe it—to everything that has a human face").

The self who is like others, and whom we can reliably know (as, by extension, we can reliably know others) via the practice of empirical

---

[10] I have discussed Moritz's empirical psychology and its intellectual contexts in *Aesthetic Anxiety: Uncanny Symptoms in German Literature and Culture* (Amsterdam: Rodopi, 2010), esp. 104–23.

[11] Isaac Nakhimovsky notes, for instance, that the characterization of *Der geschlossene Handelsstaat* as indebted to Rousseau's *Du contrat social* (*The Social Contract*, 1762) dates at least to the mid-nineteenth century. See *The Closed Commercial State: Perpetual Peace and Commercial Society from Rousseau to Fichte* (Princeton, NJ: Princeton University Press, 2011), here esp. 5–6. Reinhard Lauth and Hans Gliwitsky also address Fichte's political indebtedness to Rousseau in their introduction to Fichte's *Nachgelassene Schriften* in GA, vol. 2, no. 9, viii.

[12] Anthony LaVopa argues that the *Beitrag* "was left unfinished because it broke down, both as a philosophical exercise and as a rhetorical experiment," in "The Revelatory Moment: Fichte and the French Revolution," *Central European History*, vol. 22, no. 2 (1989): 130–59, here 134.

psychology, emerges in the *Beitrag* right around the time that Fichte enacted what Daniel Breazeale has called the "transformation of German Idealism."[13] In 1794, Fichte published a review of the book *Aenesidemus oder über die Fundamente der von dem Herrn Professor Reinhold in Jena gelieferten Elementar-Philosophie* (*Aenesidemus, or Concerning the Foundations of the Elementary Philosophy Propounded in Jena by Professor Reinhold, including a Defense of Skepticism against the Pretensions of the Critique of Reason*).[14] In this review, Fichte attempts to lay a foundation for his efforts to create a transcendental philosophy that is a true science. That foundation informed his later work on the *Wissenschaftslehre*— from then on, to put it in a reductive way, Fichte in part will be preoccupied with proving that a reliable knowledge of external things *as they are*, with no connection to our power of representation, is not only inconceivable (as he contends that we need representation to know, as well as to think of, external things), but that knowledge of such an external world is not relevant for a reliable "I" to come to reliable conclusions about itself and about other minds (or, about "everything that has a human face").

In the *Aenesidemus* review, Fichte says that any "passage from the external to the internal or vice versa is precisely what is in question. It is precisely the task of Critical Philosophy to show that no such passage is required, that everything that occurs in our mind can be completely explained and comprehended on the basis of the mind itself" ("Aber die Frage ist ja eben von einem *Uebergange* von dem Auessern zum Innern, oder umgekehrt. Est ist ja eben das Geschäft der kritischen Philosophie, zu zeigen, dass wir eines Ueberganges nicht bedürfen; dass alles, was in unserm Gemüthe vorkommt, aus ihm selbst vollständig zu erklären und zu begreifen ist").[15] The self certainly can and does posit an external reality all the time; it is confronted with external reality via encounters with limits of all sorts, mortality being not the least of these. But in order to agitate in the world—to conduct a revolution, to work at a university, to formulate a systematic philosophy—we need only "get to know" ourselves. The road inward is the way to know any kind of "outward."

---

[13] Daniel Breazeale, "Fichte's *Aenesidemus* Review and the Transformation of German Idealism," *Review of Metaphysics*, vol. 34, no. 3 (March 1981): 545–68. Breazeale concludes that the review of 1794 already contains much of Fichte's later system of philosophy, 564.
[14] *Aenesidemus*, by Gottlob Ernst Schulze, appeared anonymously in 1792.
[15] Johann Gottlieb Fichte, *Recension des Aenesidemus*, in *Sämmtliche Werke und Nachlaß*, ed. Immanuel Hermann Fichte, vol. 1 (Berlin: Veit & Co., 1845-6), 3–25, here 15. References to this edition are abbreviated henceforth as SW.

Fichte's unquestionably reliable, self-positing "I," unlike the "I" of Rousseau's and Moritz's psychology, is not historical. Anthony Krupp has argued that Rousseau and Moritz subscribe to a "gradual, continualist narrative meant to trace the development of identity from its origin," only to reveal that such a narrative fails: identity actually emerges in a discontinuous, choppy way. As Krupp puts it, "Rousseau and Moritz were among the first to articulate the modern belief that every individual lives for several years before identity, in the form of *le moi* or *das Ich*, is established." Fichte inherits the same critique of Enlightenment continualist narratives of the development of identity as Rousseau and Moritz, but he avoids dealing with the fallout of those narratives' failure by, in effect, disregarding gradualist, continuous developmental narratives as well as discontinuity and contingency. In Krupp's terms, Fichte "ignores time."[16]

But the very ahistoricity of Fichte's "I," the stability of his self-consciousness in a sort of vacuum of timelessness, is perhaps all the more reason to trust it. By stating directly, in 1795, that his *Wissenschaftslehre* was inspired by France,[17] Fichte does attribute the existence of even the most interior, inner-directed system of thinking to something "outside" not only of his own psyche, but outside of Germany as well, and, implicitly, to the radically discontinuous events of the revolution. However, Fichte's attribution of inspiration for his philosophy of the self to the revolution is matched by his projection of that stable, knowable "I" out into the world—an "I" unchallenged by demands to develop logically or by the pitfalls of contingency. Since the "I" posits the "not-I" (or, everything in the world that is not the self),[18] Fichte's politics is necessarily a psychopolitics, a projective exercise.

Fichte was certain that the revolution happened and that other minds and bodies existed. Precisely in the 1790s, he was working on a version of German Idealism that acknowledged the existence of equal others and, by extension, the ability to delineate the self as possessing not only a mind independent of those others, but its own autonomous physical body. In *Die Bestimmung des Gelehrten* (*The Vocation of the Scholar*, 1794), which in some respects can be read as part of Fichte's early thinking about the shape of the ideal university, Fichte argues

---

[16] Krupp, "Other Relations," 113.
[17] In the above-mentioned letter of 1795, Fichte says that his "system belongs in a way to the [French] nation" ("das System gehört gewißer maßen schon der [französischen] Nation"), GA, vol. 3, no. 2, 298, letter no. 282a.
[18] David James helpfully defines the "not-I" ("Nicht-Ich") as "the object which the I posits in opposition to itself and which must be introduced to explain the possibility of consciousness of the world." In "Fichte and Hegel on Recognition and Slavery," in *The Cambridge Companion to Fichte*, 350–72, here 350.

against solipsism (saying that practical, experiential principles tell us that we must act as if other minds like ours exist), and for the extension of natural rights to all others.[19] Given his own acknowledgment that the French Revolution was inspiring his philosophical work at this point, it is not a stretch to assume that the world "outside" was at least partly driving Fichte's development of a critique of radical subjectivism that manifests as a projective psychopolitics: I cannot explain how I know the world without resorting to my own reason, and I must assume that the world is governed by the same laws that govern my reason—but, my own reason would exist were it not for the encounter with the world. That encounter with the "outside" (in one example here, Fichte's encounter with knowledge of the initial ideals of the French Revolution) has in turn taught me to go further inward, to discover my own secrets, for this logically will help me (*das Ich*) to know all that is not me (*das Nicht-Ich*).

One of the many challenges to the ahistorical "I" that Fichte proposes, arguably as a counter to the time-trapped self that emerges in the work of Rousseau and Moritz, is the undeniable fact that events in the world of the "not-I" *are* time-bound and changing fast. By the late 1790s, the French Revolution had gone through the Terror, and Fichte was embroiled in the "Atheismusstreit" ("Atheism Dispute"), ultimately losing his position at the University of Jena in 1799. Scholars agree that Fichte's early enthusiasm for the revolution transformed into a passionate German nationalism no later than 1806, when the French occupied Berlin. Disagreements have ensued about just how much Fichte's *Reden an die deutsche Nation* (*Addresses to the German Nation*), delivered at the Berlin Academy in 1807 and 1808, represent a proto-racist, ethnic nationalism that pre-shadows the twentieth century.[20] The *Reden* certainly call for Germany to constitute its moral character internally, in the absence of an external political unity; moral unity will lay the

---

[19] SW, vol. 6, 289–346, here 301–11. See also Fichte's roughly contemporaneous *Grundlage des Naturrechts nach Principien der Wissenschaftslehre* (*Foundations of Natural Law According to Principles of The Science of Knowledge*, 1796), SW, vol. 3, 1–385.

[20] This scholarly debate breaks down largely along national lines: German and English/Anglophone scholars tend to dismiss or harshly criticize the *Reden an die deutsche Nation*, while French political philosophers in particular argue that Fichte's lectures are not ethno-nationalist and in fact contribute to the foundation of modern, Enlightened thinking about the role of citizens in shaping the state. See Arash Abizadeh, "Was Fichte an Ethnic Nationalist? On Cultural Nationalism and its Double," *History of Political Thought*, vol. 26, no. 2 (Summer 2005): 334–59.

groundwork for political unification. The university is central to this effort, as Fichte conceives of the university as symbolic of the entire nation, and as a site for thinking about the future.

Fichte was of course not alone in making a "nationalist turn" in the early years of the nineteenth century. Helmut Walser Smith identifies 1806 as "an important marker because for the first time in German history a handful of intellectuals began to write in an unmistakably nationalist mode," accompanied by an increasingly subjective direction in philosophy and literature. In several respects, what Frederick C. Beiser has called Idealism's (so, also, Fichte's) "struggle against subjectivism" had ended already by 1801.[21] While resistance to French occupation was a major driver of this assertive subjectivism as well as of a new nationalism and anti-cosmopolitanism,[22] Smith points out that the vestiges of past regionalism still characterized the public mood, also during French occupation: "Patriotism attached to a territorial state, like Saxony or Austria, still came more naturally [than nationalism], and was by all accounts a sentiment more widely shared."[23] Fichte's thinking in the 1790s, however, transcended regionalism, not initially in favor of nationalism, but rather in favor of advocating for a larger and more just world co-created by an eventual "league of nations" ("Völkerbund").[24]

Fichte's essay fragments on *Die Republik der Deutschen* (*The Republic of the Germans*), written in 1807–8, the same years in which he gave the *Reden an die deutsche Nation*, actually reflect a degree of pessimism about short-term national progress.[25] That pessimism could be understood in

---

[21] Beiser's analyses follow the internal workings of pre-Idealist and Idealist philosophy from 1781 to 1801, largely avoiding connections to political or social events. But the "subjective turn" in Fichte's work, and arguably also in that of other German Idealists and Romantics such as Hegel, Schelling, and Friedrich Schlegel, maps at least roughly with the "objective" focal turn among German intellectuals to, for instance, the Terror, the Haitian Revolution, and the French occupation of Germany.

[22] Smith, *Germany: A Nation in its Time*, 171.

[23] Smith, *Germany: A Nation in its Time*, 171.

[24] In 1796, Fichte argued that war was a legitimate way to ensure a state's lawful existence; in this context, he proposed the creation of a league of nations that would make the victory of the lawful more likely. See *Zweiter Anhang des Naturrechts. Grundriß des Völker- und Weltbürgerrechts* (*Second Appendix to Natural Law: Sketch of International and World Law*, 1796), SW, vol. 3, 369–85.

[25] The intended full title was *Die Republik der Deutschen zu Anfang des zwei und zwanzigsten Jahrhunderts unter ihrem fünften Reichstvogte* (*The Republic of the Germans at the Beginning of the Twenty-Second Century, under its Fifth Governor*). In the fragments, Fichte counters his immediate pessimism about the German nation with a long-term utopian optimism for a territorially and spiritually expanded Germany in the long run. See GA, vol. 2, no. 10: 377–426.

the context of the French occupation; however, already in 1799, during dismissal proceedings from the University of Jena, Fichte had referred to himself as a "young man who has abandoned his fatherland and was not bound to any state" ("ein junger Mensch, der sein Vaterland aufgegeben hatte, und an keinem Staate hing").[26] But by 1800, several years prior to the French occupation, Fichte was advocating a self-sufficient, socially and economically "closed" German state in the *Geschlossener Handelsstaat*, stating:

> It is clear that in such a secluded nation, whose members live only with one another and very rarely with foreigners, which derives its particular way of life, institutions and habits from these measures of isolation, which loves its fatherland and all that is fatherlandish with devotion, a high degree of national honor and a sharply defined national character will very soon develop. It will become another, entirely new nation. The introduction of a national currency is its true creation.
>
> [Es ist klar, daß unter einer so geschlossenen Nation, deren Mitglieder nur unter einander selbst, und äußerst wenig mit Fremden leben, die ihre besondere Lebensart, Einrichtungen und Sitten durch jene Maassregeln erhält, die ihr Vaterland und alles Vaterländische mit Anhänglichkeit liebt, sehr bald ein höher Grad der Nationalehre, und ein scharf bestimmter Nationalcharakter entstehen werde. Sie wird eine andere, durchaus neue Nation. Jene Einführung des Landesgeldes ist ihre wahre Schöpfung.][27]

Significantly, however, even in his most nationalist and isolationist work Fichte emphasizes that scholarship is not a matter for the state. Peoples of different nations should only come together in the pursuit of knowledge, and otherwise remain separate.[28] It does seem important to Fichte to use the sphere of education to carve out some autonomy for the educated individual, even as that individual is part of an immediate national community that is isolated, secluded, and rarely interacts with anything "foreign."

Fichte's work as rector of the University of Berlin (albeit only for two years, 1810–12) put him right at the core of the tensions he had helped to create between the self and the world, and between the closed state

---

[26] Fichte, *Gerichtliche Verantwortungsschriften gegen die Anklage des Atheismus*, in SW, vol. 5, 239–333, here 288.
[27] SW, vol. 3, 387–513, here 509.
[28] SW, vol. 3, 512.

and its neighbors. In some ways Fichte's university work (including his previous work as a professor) demonstrates not an ethnically or culturally restrictive nationalism, but rather a continuation of the enthusiasm he showed in the 1790s for the kind of individual psychological exploration that would lead to communal and national progress. Viewed in the context of the university and of nation-building via education, Fichte's ahistorical "I" is compatible with Wilhelm von Humboldt's portrayal in 1793 of the individual who must counteract the often chaotic changes in the world by going inward: "The more the individual is accustomed to living in ideas and feelings, the stronger and subtler his intellectual and moral power is; the more he seeks to choose only those external situations that give his internal self more material" ("Je mehr der Mensch in Ideen und Empfindungen zu leben gewöhnt ist, je stärker und feiner seine intellektuelle und moralische Kraft ist; desto mehr sucht er allein solche äußere Lagen zu wählen, welche zugleich dem inneren Menschen mehr Stoff geben").[29] Humboldt's ideal man must "bring the mass of things closer to himself, and impress the shape of his spirit upon this substance, making both more similar to one another" ("die Masse der Gegenstände sich selbst näher bringen, diesem Stoff die Gestalt seines Geistes aufdrücken").[30] The university was, for both men, the ideal venue for accomplishing this ultimately psychological ideal. And even after Fichte's "nationalist turn" some of his work continued to evince a promise of a more expansive Idealism that did not try to obliterate what was "outside" (of the self, or of the nation), but rather to acknowledge that, just as with consciousness, there is no "inside" without the "outside."

Before returning to a renewed consideration of the tensions in Fichte's philosophical and political work, in the following section I examine some of Fichte's and Wilhelm von Humboldt's thinking about the University of Berlin (founded in 1810 and renamed the Humboldt University in 1949), along with how that thinking either has or has not been remembered, to address some of the perhaps unexpected ways in which Fichte's publicly facing work prompts us to re-evaluate received ideas about German Idealism. At the beginning of the nineteenth century, as German intellectuals entered the post-Kantian, post-metaphysical world, the future was being contested, in part, at the site of the new research university. Some of Fichte's vast and not infrequently self-contradictory work evinces a potential for a trajectory within German Idealism that

---

[29] Wilhelm von Humboldt, *Wie weit darf sich die Sorgfalt des Staats um das Wohl seiner Bürger erstrecken?* in *Schriften zur Bildung*, ed. Gerhard Lauer (Stuttgart: Philipp Reclam, 2017), 126–61, here 150–1. Translation mine.
[30] Humboldt, *Theorie der Bildung des Menschen*, in *Schriften zur Bildung*, 12.

remained largely unrealized. This more enlightened, tolerant, world-oriented, outward-reaching politically and psychologically inflected Idealism was also intensely pragmatic and realistic. Among other places, its traces can be found in the viewpoints Fichte shared with Humboldt, whose work, like Fichte's, was crucial for founding the University of Berlin, an institution within Germany that was outward-oriented from its inception.

Fichte, Humboldt, and the German University

In 1807, just before Fichte began delivering the *Reden an die deutsche Nation*, he proposed the founding of a university located in Berlin, one which would teach philosophy to students in all disciplines, as a foundation for and pathway to understanding the sciences. But Fichte opens the treatise *Deduzierter Plan einer zu Berlin zu errichtenden höhern Lehranstalt* (*A Plan, Deduced from First Principles, for an Institution of Higher Learning to be established in Berlin*) by discussing the history of the transition from orality to print, and the need for in-person teaching and the persistence of the lecture even after the widespread availability of books. The treatise continues with concrete recommendations for ways in which an institution of higher education in Berlin can contribute to scientific progress, and is more of a collection of specific recommendations for institutional structures, as well as a set of arguments for the importance of presence, of the spoken word, and of in-person interactions at the future University than it is a reflection on the role of "education" ("Bildung") in the life of the nation.[31]

In this respect, the *Deduzierter Plan* is similar to the *Ideen für die innere Organisation der Universität Erlangen* (*Ideas for the Internal Organization of the University of Erlangen*, 1805–6) that Fichte penned a year earlier. In both texts, Fichte is concerned with the rationale for universities in an age when books are increasingly widely available. What can the institution give students that books cannot? Fichte's answer, consistently, is: the presence of knowledgeable, but also highly communicatively skilled, instructors whose lectures are interactive. Classes must involve "*two-way conversation*" ("*wechselseitige Unterredung*"), and the instructor should give his students active tasks to complete during class, so that each student does not merely memorize information, but rather

---

[31] Johann Gottlieb Fichte, *Deduzierter Plan einer zu Berlin zu errichtenden höhern Lehranstalt, die in gehöriger Verbindung mit einer Akademie der Wissenschaft stehe* (*A Plan, Deduced from First Principles, for an Institution of Higher Learning to be established in Berlin, connected to and subordinate to an Academy of Sciences*), in SW, vol. 8, 95–204.

demonstrates that he "has made the imparted information his own" ("das Mitgetheilte zu seinem freien Eigenthume bekommen hat").[32]

Fichte's practical plan for ideal teaching contributed to the legitimation for the university's founding, but the institution's public memory-shaping since then (not to mention its eventual renaming in honor of Wilhelm and Alexander von Humboldt) has been more overtly compatible with Wilhelm von Humboldt's portrayal of "Bildung" in his fragmentary treatise on the *Theorie der Bildung des Menschen* (*Theory of Human Education*, 1793), as well as in his other writings on educational philosophy and the state. Like Fichte, Humboldt considers the centrality of language in the development of a system of education.[33] However, Humboldt's essay is more of a manifesto that explicitly links nation-building, as well as the building of a national character, to the general idea of "education" as a form of organized mass self-development.[34] He is less concerned with classroom practice and more with a general proclamation of the importance of "development" in Germany and in Europe.

It arguably has been Humboldt's nation-oriented approach rather than Fichte's pedagogical philosophy that has informed public messaging around and memory of the institution, remarkably consistently, whether under the GDR regime or since the fall of the Wall. After 1949, the university maintained strong international contacts within the Eastern bloc, but also with Western Europe. But the early twenty-first century witnessed a move towards explicitly "branding" the university as Humboldtian in a specific sense. For instance, during the 200th anniversary celebration of Humboldt University in 2010, the marketing firm Nordsonne was hired by the institution to, as Sean Franzel puts it, link "the international brands of Berlin and Humboldt (because) the Humboldt [brothers, Wilhelm and Alexander,] serve as supposedly benign symbols of German science recognizable around the world, and the city itself remains a highly desirable draw for tourists and scholars."[35] Alexander von Humboldt in particular represented, and arguably still

---

[32] Johann Gottlieb Fichte, *Ideen für die innere Organisation der Universität Erlangen*, in SW, vol. 11, 275–94, here 278.

[33] See, for instance, Humboldt's discussion of the ways in which various modern and older languages express terms for "soul" and "spirit," and the ways in which the differences (also over time) alter our understanding of these and other concepts. Wilhelm von Humboldt, "Über den Geist der Menschheit," in *Schriften zur Bildung*, 120–5.

[34] Wilhelm von Humboldt, "Theorie der Bildung des Menschen," in *Schriften zur Bildung*, 6–19.

[35] Sean Franzel, "Branding Berlin: The Humboldt University celebrates its Founding," *Germanic Review*, vol. 85, no. 3 (2010): 250–6, here 251.

represents, the cosmopolitan and progressive face of Germany, as an outspoken critic of slavery and colonial practices—although he lived for a time with slaveowners in Cuba, and traveled to Spanish colonies in North America with the support of the Spanish king.[36] And, to bring the outside world back to Germany, Alexander also engaged in actions such as robbing South American gravesites.[37]

The positive image of the Humboldt brothers as men of progressive science and politics recurred in various media and events throughout the city during the anniversary events of 2010, but also in other contexts. Their largely congenial, transnational image may have helped simultaneously to calm anxieties about the direction of the German university in the age of the Bologna Process and to invest Berlin with the aura of a Humboldtian, Kantian disinterest: in other words, the branding of the Humboldts as disinterested, multiculturally aware scientists also brands Berlin and Humboldt University, transcending both potential over-fractionalization (feared, for instance, as a possible result of the relatively recent emphasis on competitive excellence initiatives linked to high degrees of specialization) and the kind of over-unification exemplified by neo-nationalism. Although Wilhelm von Humboldt knew Fichte's philosophy well and borrowed from Fichte's thinking when working on his own educational and institutional theory,[38] it is likely that neither Fichte's name nor image appeared, for instance, in events associated with the 200th anniversary in 2010, and that no one has ever been hired to "brand" him.[39]

---

[36] See, for instance, Dorothee Nolte, "Im Hause des Sklavenhändlers. Alexander von Humboldt und der Kolonialismus," *Der Tagesspiegel*, August 27, 2019, tagesspiegel.de/wissen/alexander-von-humboldt-und-der-kolonialismus-im-hause-des-sklavenhaendlers/24947632.html.

[37] Alexander did comment critically on his own grave-looting in a letter to Johann Friedrich Blumenbach, but nevertheless brought a number of artifacts back to Europe, including a skull from a tomb in Venezuela. The exhibition "Wilhelm und Alexander von Humboldt" at the Deutsches Historisches Museum in Berlin in 2019–20 documented the shadier side of Alexander's archaeology. See Bettina Baumann, "Two Brothers, One Exhibition: 'Wilhelm and Alexander von Humboldt' at the German Historical Museum," *Deutsche Welle*, November 21, 2019, dw.com/en/two-brothers-one-exhibition-wilhelm-and-alexander-von-humboldt-at-the-german-historical-museum/a-51349167.

[38] See Peter Uwe Hohendahl, "Humboldt Revisited: Liberal Education, University Reform, and Opposition to the Neoliberal University," *New German Critique*, vol. 38, no. 2 (2011): 159–96, here 161.

[39] The German Democratic Republic did memorialize Fichte much more proudly and explicitly, not least on the occasion of the 200 anniversary of his birth in 1962, when he was publicly honored for his contribution to the foundations of Marxist thought. An essay by Dieter Bergner on this occasion explicitly notes

Humboldt's educational vision usually is assumed to be indebted far more to Enlightenment thinking about social order than to Romantic concepts of the nation. That assumption, however, does not originate in the early nineteenth century, but in the early twentieth, when it formed part of the creation of the so-called "Humboldt myth," which, in Peter Uwe Hohendahl's phrasing, is "the use of Humboldt's aura as a [. . .] reformer in discussing [educational issues of] the twentieth century without firm grounding in the historical evidence."[40] Hohendahl notes that "recent scholarship has found a significant difference between the work and achievements of the historical figure and the reconstructed Humboldt that circulated in German debates about university reform since the 1920s. It was actually the model of the German university ascribed to Humboldt around 1900 that became the center of the twentieth-century debates."[41] But recent work has focused not only on the differences between Humboldt's reconstruction and the historical record, but also on what Alexander Schmidt calls "the plurality of competing visions for the future university around 1800."[42] Although it is the reshaping of *Humboldt's* legacy that today is considered most significant in German debates about what the research university should look like, there is a perhaps less pervasive or acknowledged, but nonetheless significant, "Fichte myth" that has affected scholarship about the role of education in nation formation as well as scholarship about the history of German Romanticism.

Like the reimagining of Humboldt, narratives of Fichte's legacy have been used to shape both conservative and progressive arguments about the ideational content and institutional structure of the university.[43] By and large, however, those narratives have been shaped by the perception of the *Reden an die deutsche Nation* of 1807–8 and Fichte's later work rather than by a consideration either of Fichte's emphasis on an interactive, arguably democratic style of teaching that would characterize the work of an entire university (and, implicitly, shape the citizens of the nation), or of his earlier outward-looking enthusiasm for the kind of

---

that Fichte has been remembered in very different ways for very different uses, and essentially boldly reclaims Fichte in this context for the GDR. "Die Deutsche Demokratische Republik würdigt Johann Gottlieb Fichte (zu seinem 200. Geburtstag am 19. Mai 1962)," *Deutsche Zeitschrift für Philosophie*, vol. 10, no. 4 (1962): 417–28.

[40] Hohendahl, "Humboldt Revisited," 160.
[41] Hohendahl, "Humboldt Revisited," 160.
[42] Alexander Schmidt, presentation at the Work-in-Progress seminar series at the Centre for Research in the Arts, Social Sciences and Humanities (CRASSH), Cambridge, UK, June 6, 2011.
[43] David James, "Fichte on the Vocation of the Scholar and the (Mis)use of History," *Review of Metaphysics*, vol. 63, no. 3 (2010): 539–66, here 540.

psychological development that took its inspiration from a passionate engagement with revolutionary ideals. In a sense, a cosmopolitan, difference-erasing Humboldtian "brand" has taken over in the public memory of state institutions, while the anti-solipsistic concept of the individual that Fichte was developing in the 1790s has been largely forgotten outside of specialized scholarship on Idealist philosophy. One consequence of this forgetting is, possibly, increased division between a radically subjective modern "internal" self that can essentially hallucinate its own reality and an increasingly specialized, fragmented, and collapsing "external" world.

Fichte's Politics as a Projection of the Psyche

The kind of citizen Fichte imagines living in the Germany he sketches in the *Reden an die deutsche Nation*, and in the secluded, homogeneous Germany of the *Geschlossener Handelsstaat*, is charged with completely remaking mankind by developing his own moral character and expanding it ever outward. In the post-Enlightened, post-metaphysical world of 1808, the psyche of this ideal German virtually replaces a deity, as nationalism supplants faith and Christianity primarily characterizes the nation on earth rather than pointing the way to heavenly salvation:

> The faith of the noble man in the eternal survival of his activity, also here on this earth, is therefore founded on the hope of the eternal survival of the nation out of which he has himself developed, and of its distinctive characteristics [. . .]. His conception of his own life as an eternal life is the bond which unites first his nation and through it and all of its needs the whole of humanity most intimately with himself, to the end of days, into his expanding heart.

> [Der Glaube des edeln Menschen an die ewige Fortdauer seiner Wirksamkeit auch auf dieser Erde gründet sich demnach auf die Hoffnung der ewigen Fortdauer des Volkes, aus dem er selber sich entwickelt hat, und der Eigenthümlichkeit desselben [. . .]. Sein Glaube und sein Streben, Unvergängliches zu pflanzen, sein Begriff, in welchem er sein eigenes Leben al sein ewiges Leben erfasst, ist das Band, welches zunächst seine Nation, und vermittelst ihrer das ganze Menschengeschlecht innigst mit ihm selber verknüpft, und ihrer aller Bedürfnisse, bis ans Ende der Tage, einführt in sein erweitertes Herz.][44]

---

[44] Fichte, *Achte Rede. Was ein Volk sey, in der höhern Bedeutung des Wortes, und was Vaterlandsliebe?*, in *Reden an die deutsche Nation*, SW, vol. 6, 377a–96, here 382–3.

Life on earth is the only life upon which Fichte comments, and in the *Reden* he also cautions against replacing moral action on earth with the promise of an afterlife. Instead, religion should make us oppose immorality *while* on earth: "although it is true, that religion is the comfort of the unlawfully crushed slave, nevertheless above all it is the purpose of religion that one resists slavery and that keeps religion from sinking to a mere consolation for the imprisoned" ("obwohl es wahr ist, dass die Religion auch der Trost ist des widerrechtlich zerdrückten Sklaven, so ist dennoch vor allen Dingen dies religiöser Sinn, dass man sich gegen die Sklaverei stemme, und, so man es verhindern kann, die Religion nicht bis zum blossen Troste der Gefangenen herabsinken lasse").[45]

But hints of the post-metaphysical were already present in Fichte's work in the early 1790s. In the section of the *Beitrag zur Berichtigung der Urteile des Publikums über die französische Revolution* entitled "Von der Kirche" ("On the Church"), Fichte emphasizes repeatedly that the world with which we must engage is the visible world. He also notes that we cannot take actions based on our judgment of the status of others' faith, present or past, or on any notion of an afterlife. In the context of a discussion about inheritance, debt, and responsibility, Fichte uses his deceased father as an example:

> He appeared to believe; whether he really believed, I do not know; whether he believes now, if he still exists, I know even less. Be this as it may; I am not referring to my father as if he were a member of the invisible world, but rather of the visible world, and especially of the state. He has died, and in the state I take his place.
>
> [Er hat zu glauben geschienen; ob er wirklich geglaubt habe, weiß ich nicht; ob er jetzt glaube, wenn er noch existiert, weiß ich noch weinger. Verhalte sich dies, wie es wolle; selbst mit meinem Vater habe ich es nicht zu tun, als mit einem Mitgliede der unsichtbaren Welt, sondern der sichtbaren, und insbesondre des Staats. Er ist gestorben, und im Staate besetze ich seine Stelle.][46]

Dead citizens of the living state live on, not necessarily in an afterlife, but rather in the form of the living citizens who are their physical descendants.

Later in the same section, Fichte again stresses the importance of understanding duty and activity in the present and visible world:

---

[45] SW, vol. 6, 379.
[46] Fichte, *Beitrag*, in *Schriften zur Revolution*, 206.

> I don't know of any church, I recognize no church; let your church prove its existence to me in the visible world; I know nothing of an invisible world; the power of your church in the invisible world has no sway over me, because I don't believe in it. [. . .] I don't know your church, and I don't know the unseen world in which your church is supposedly powerful.
>
> [Ich weiß von keiner Kirche, ich anerkenne keine Kirche; mag deine Kirche mir in der Welt der Erscheinungen ihr Dasein beweisen; von einer unsichtbaren Welt weiß ich nichts; und die Macht deiner Kirche in derselben hat über mich keine Gewalt, denn ich glaube nicht an sie. [. . .] deine Kirche kenne ich nicht, und die unsichtbare Welt, in der sie gar mächtig sein soll, kenne ich auch nicht.][47]

If I do not believe in something, it is not real (to me). Since I cannot know of a life after death, beyond the proxy life that the dead live here on earth, in their descendants, I must by default live in the present, visible world. By the time he wrote the *Beitrag*, Fichte had claimed that the world is a product of our active consciousness.[48] The political theory he develops in response to the French Revolution is an extended application of his philosophical and psychological convictions to events in the world.

Fichte's work on the university, on the state, and on the self from the early 1790s to about 1810 certainly contains tensions and inconsistencies, as well as eventually a more pronounced allegiance to an ideal of Germany proper, especially after 1806. But while he took different positions toward the French and France over time, wrote various versions of the *Wissenschaftslehre*, and eventually converted his pessimism about German reality into hope for a German ideality, there is more that binds his oeuvre together than divides it. The schism scholars have identified in Fichte's career is perhaps less of his own making than it is the result of a desire to separate political from philosophical work. The fact that Fichte is remembered differently in French scholarship than in

---

[47] Fichte, *Beitrag*, in *Schriften zur Revolution*, 207.
[48] Manfred Frank characterizes this claim as belonging to "Produktionsidealismus" ("production Idealism"): instead of thinking of the world as existing *relative* to our consciousness of it, as in Berkeley's famous pronouncement "esse est percipi (aut percipere)" (to be is to be perceived; there are no objects independent of mind), the world is a "product" of the operations of our active consciousness. See *"Unendliche Annäherung." Die Anfänge der philosophischen Frühromantik* (Frankfurt am Main: Suhrkamp, 1997), 133.

English/Anglophone and German scholarship is telling in this respect as well.[49] To be sure, in the 1790s Fichte argued for the kind of rational, creative educational system that could ultimately make nations irrelevant, while in 1808 he asserts that only the nation can make any individual's short time on earth meaningful:

> Life, simply as life, as the continuation of a changing existence, has never had value without [the divine . . .]; but only the survival of the nation assures [man] eternity; to save it, he must be willing even to die, that his nation may live, and that he may live in it the only life he has ever desired.
>
> [Das Leben, bloss als Leben, als Fortsetzen des wechselnden Daseyns, hat [. . .] ja ohnedies [das Göttliche] nie Werth gehabt, [. . .]; aber diese Dauer verspricht ihm allein die selbstständige Fortdauer seiner Nation; um diese zu retten, muss er sogar sterben wollen, damit diese lebe, und er in ihr lebe das einzige Leben, das er von je gemocht hat.][50]

But what stands out in Fichte's connection here between a willingness to die for the collective identified as a "nation," and an unshakeable belief that this sacrifice will enable eternal life, is not so much the greatness of what could become Germany, but the unthinkability of "nation" without what he calls "national character" ("Nationalcharakter"). And the German "national character" is everything that Fichte calls "foreignness" ("Ausländerei," a very pejorative term) is not. Anyone who does not believe in "an origin, and in a further development of that origin" ("ein Ursprüngliches, und an eine Fortentwicklung desselben"), but instead only believes in "an eternal cycle of the life we perceive" ("einen ewigen Kreislauf des scheinbaren Lebens"), is not an in-lander, but an out-lander, foreign, not German.[51] Despite their supposedly clear differences, Germans and those who practice "foreignness" both have an ahistorical character: foreigners (clearly non-Christians) think everything repeats itself in a circle, while Germans plot their lives on earth according to a belief in an implicitly unchanging eternity.[52]

---

[49] See note 20.
[50] SW, vol. 6, 383.
[51] SW, vol. 6, 382.
[52] There is plenty of reason within Fichte's works and according to his actions to conclude that he thought Jews belonged to those who practiced "foreignness" and were thus not German. Not long after he delivered the *Reden*, Fichte joined the "Deutsche Tischgesellschaft" ("German Table Society," also "Christian-German Table Society"), founded in 1811, a group with anti-Semitism at its

In the *Reden*, Fichte defines the members of a nation first and foremost by their speaking of a common language; the physical borders of a nation also are determined by the language spoken within. He contends that "purity of descent" ("Reinheit der Abstammung") is less signifying for membership in the nation than language is.[53] But this monolingual fiction serves to advance an ethnically nationalist agenda. In a parallel to the Idealist philosophical move of identity being constituted by determining what it is not, the German nation is constituted by not being non-German, and specifically on not displaying "Ausländerei." That "Ausländerei" is marked by stereotypically non-European qualities, including a lack of "nobility," being non-Christian, and a supposed inability to perceive the depth behind surface appearances. Fichte engages rigorously with the question of how we can be sure that other minds exist and think as we do, in his philosophy, and concludes that we need the recognition of others to know ourselves.[54] And he asserts that we should not permit belief in an afterlife to divert us from solving problems—including those of the enslaved and imprisoned—here on earth. But he also argues that the enslaved and the colonized are responsible for their subjugation, following his own philosophy of morally correct action: "Cowardice is the *laziness* (that prevents us from asserting our freedom and independence) *in interaction with others*" ("Feigheit ist die *Trägheit, in der Wechselwirkung mit anderen unsere Freiheit und Selbstständigkeit zu behaupten*"). This is "the only explanation for slavery among human beings, both physical and moral" ("Nur so ist die Sklaverei unter den Menschen, die physische sowohl als die moralische, zu erklären").[55] In the essay fragments entitled *Republik der Deutschen* of 1807, which envision Germany in the twenty-second century, Fichte allows that non-Europeans may be living within Germany's

---

programmatic core and whose anti-Napoleonic fervor was in part motivated by Napoleon's emancipatory measures for Jews. Contemporaries already criticized Fichte's anti-Semitism: the author and journalist Saul Ascher focused on Fichte in an 1815 essay entitled *Die Germanomanie. Skizze zu einem Zeitgemälde*, which has been published in *Ascher. Flugschriften*, ed. André Thiele (Mainz: VAT, 2011).

[53] SW, vol. 6, 314. Abizadeh presents a detailed argument about the relation between Fichte's linguistic and ethnic nationalism in "Was Fichte an Ethnic Nationalist?", esp. 341–5.

[54] Robert R. Williams explicates this aspect of Fichte's philosophy in detail in "The Question of the Other in Fichte's Thought," in *Fichte: Historical Contexts, Contemporary Controversies*, ed. Daniel Breazeale and Tom Rockmore (Atlantic Highlands, NJ: Humanities Press, 1997), 142–57.

[55] Fichte, *System der Sittenlehre nach den Principien der Wissenschaftslehre* (*System of Ethics, According to the Principles of the Science of Knowledge*), SW, vol. 4, 1–365, here 202.

(considerably expanded) borders in that future time.[56] However, "Negroes" ("Neger") wear different colors from Europeans, whose clothing should be "brownish-gray" ("bräunlich-grau").[57] In Fichte's future, equality would demand separation.

In the introduction to this volume, I referred to Edward Said's psychoanalytically informed argument that "identity cannot be thought or worked through itself alone; it cannot constitute or even imagine itself without that radical originary break or flaw which will not be repressed."[58] Psychoanalysis here echoes Idealism, and specifically Friedrich Hölderlin's contention in 1795 that that "judgment is in the highest and strictest sense the original division between subject and object, which are intimately unified in intellectual intuition, the only separation, through which subject and object become possible" ("Urtheil ist im höchsten und strengsten Sinne die ursprüngliche Trennung des in der intellectualen Anschauung innigst vereinigten Objects und Subjects, diejenige Trennung, wodurch erst Object und Subject möglich wird").[59] Instead of beginning with the self, identity begins with the other, with what the self is not. This understanding only initially seems at odds with Fichte's insistence in the *Wissenschaftslehre* of 1794 that "the 'I' posits itself" ("das Ich *setzt sich selbst*").[60] For soon thereafter, in the *Grundlage des Naturrechts* of 1797, Fichte concludes that it is only through others, through our realization of their existence, that we can be conscious of ourselves, and therefore "posit" ourselves. Just a few years earlier, Moritz's *Magazin zur Erfahrungsseelenkunde* and other texts of empirical psychology had noted that our subjectivity is constituted in part by observing others and by being observed. Fichte's later interest in magnetism, a "science" that was based not only on the laying on of hands, but, perhaps even more crucially, on painstaking and lengthy observation of symptoms, was in some respects a continuation of his

---

[56] Helmut Walser Smith has created a map based on Fichte's projected description of Germany in the twenty-second century, noting that Fichte "brought in Königsberg and East Prussia [. . .], and extended Germany's northeast borders to the Memel, while describing the Vistula and the Warthe as the country's eastern extensions. [. . .] [The] small countries have been extirpated." See *Germany: A Nation in Its Time*, 173.
[57] GA, vol. 2, no. 10, 424.
[58] Edward Said, *Freud and the Non-European* (2003), cited in *The Selected Works of Edward Said, 1966–2006*, ed. Moustafa Bayoumi and Andrew Rubin, 2nd ed. (New York: Vintage, 2019), 494–517, here 517.
[59] Friedrich Hölderlin, *Urtheil und Seyn*, cited here in Manfred Frank, *Selbstbewusstseinstheorien von Fichte bis Sartre* (Frankfurt am Main: Suhrkamp, 1991), 26–7. Translation mine.
[60] SW, vol. 10, 83–238, here 96.

earlier interest in empirical psychology and its injunction to observe, and thus know, yourself. Fichte relentlessly defined Germany, Germans, and himself according to what it, they, and he were not. But throughout his career, his xenophobia and reactionary nationalism did not quite extinguish—or, could not quite repress—a radical originary break, that first leap of judgment enabled by the other, something "outside."

In the letter likely written to Jens Baggesen in 1795, Fichte bemoans the lack of time he has for writing, because of all his teaching responsibilities. He says that if he could he would devote his entire career just to working out the philosophical system of the *Wissenschaftslehre*.[61] Of course, in 1799 he was divested of his teaching responsibilities. But his return to the world of the university, to making concrete plans for new universities, and to arguing for the need *for* universities as havens of presence, spaces where the spoken word was indispensable despite the availability of print—that return indicates that teaching mattered for writing after all, that teaching was not a hindrance, but a necessary companion to writing and for doing philosophy. Fichte may have wished for solitude, but he needed the outside.

Works Cited

Abizadeh, Arash. "Was Fichte an Ethnic Nationalist? On Cultural Nationalism and Its Double," *History of Political Thought*, vol. 26, no. 2 (2005): 334–59.

Baumann, Bettina. "Two Brothers, One Exhibition: 'Wilhelm and Alexander von Humboldt' at the German Historical Museum," *Deutsche Welle*, November 21, 2019, dw.com/en/two-brothers-one-exhibition-wilhelm-and-alexander-von-humboldt-at-the-german-historical-museum/a-51349167.

Bayoumi, Moustafa, and Andrew Rubin, eds. *The Selected Works of Edward Said, 1966–2006*, 2nd ed. (New York: Vintage, 2019).

Beiser, Frederick C. *German Idealism: The Struggle Against Subjectivism, 1781–1801* (Cambridge, MA: Harvard University Press, 2008).

Bergner, Dieter. "Die Deutsche Demokratische Republik würdigt Johann Gottlieb Fichte (zu seinem 200. Geburtstag am 19. Mai 1962)," *Deutsche Zeitschrift für Philosophie*, vol. 10, no. 4 (1962): 417–28.

Breazeale, Daniel. "Fichte's 'Aenesidemus' Review and the Transformation of German Idealism," *Review of Metaphysics*, vol. 34 (1980–1): 545–68.

Breazeale, Daniel, and Tom Rockmore, eds. *Fichte: Historical Contexts, Contemporary Controversies* (Atlantic Highlands, NJ: Humanities Press, 1997).

Fichte, Johann Gottlieb. *Sämmtliche Werke und Nachlaß*, ed. Immanuel Hermann Fichte (Berlin: Veit & Co., 1845–6). Abbreviated as SW.

Fichte, Johann Gottlieb. *Gesamtausgabe der Bayerischen Akademie der Wissenschaften*, ed. Reinhard Lauth and Hans Gliwitzky (Stuttgart-Bad Cannstatt: Frommann, 1962–2012). Abbreviated as GA.

---

[61] GA, vol. 3, no. 2, 298, letter no. 282a.

Frank, Manfred. *Selbstbewusstseinstheorien von Fichte bis Sartre* (Frankfurt am Main: Suhrkamp, 1991).

Frank, Manfred. *"Unendliche Annäherung." Die Anfänge der philosophischen Frühromantik* (Frankfurt am Main: Suhrkamp, 1997).

Franzel, Sean. "Branding Berlin: The Humboldt University celebrates its Founding," *Germanic Review*, vol. 85, no. 3 (2010): 250–6.

Hohendahl, Peter Uwe. "Humboldt Revisited: Liberal Education, University Reform, and Opposition to the Neoliberal University," *New German Critique*, vol. 38, no. 2 (2011): 159–96.

Humboldt, Wilhelm von. *Schriften zur Bildung*, ed. Gerhard Lauer (Stuttgart: Philipp Reclam, 2017).

James, David. "Fichte on the Vocation of the Scholar and the (Mis)use of History," *Review of Metaphysics*, vol. 63, no. 3 (2010): 539–66.

James, David, and Günter Zöller, eds. *The Cambridge Companion to Fichte* (Cambridge: Cambridge University Press, 2016).

Johnson, Laurie Ruth. *Aesthetic Anxiety: Uncanny Symptoms in German Literature and Culture* (Amsterdam: Rodopi, 2010).

Krupp, Anthony. "Other Relations: The Pre-History of *le moi* and *(das) Ich* in Jean-Jacques Rousseau, Karl Philipp Moritz, and Johann Gottlieb Fichte," *Goethe Yearbook*, vol. 11 (2002): 111–31.

LaVopa, Anthony J. "The Revelatory Moment: Fichte and the French Revolution," *Central European History*, vol. 22, no. 2 (1989): 130–59.

Nakhimovsky, Isaac. *The Closed Commercial State: Perpetual Peace and Commercial Society from Rousseau to Fichte* (Princeton, NJ: Princeton University Press, 2011).

Nolte, Dorothee. "Im Hause des Sklavenhändlers. Alexander von Humboldt und der Kolonialismus," *Der Tagesspiegel*, August 27, 2019, tagesspiegel.de/wissen/alexander-von-humboldt-und-der-kolonialismus-im-hause-des-sklavenhaendlers/24947632.html.

Reitter, Paul, and Chad Wellmon. *Permanent Crisis: The Humanities in a Disenchanted Age* (Chicago: University of Chicago Press, 2021).

Schmidt, Alexander. Presentation at the Work-in-Progress seminar series at the Centre for Research in the Arts, Social Sciences and Humanities (CRASSH), Cambridge, UK, June 6, 2011.

Smith, Helmut Walser. *Germany: A Nation in Its Time: Before, During, and After Nationalism, 1500–2000* (New York: W.W. Norton, 2020).

Thiele, André, ed. *Ascher. Flugschriften* (Mainz: VAT, 2011).

Four Rewriting German Literary History from the Outside in: J. M. Coetzee's *Elizabeth Costello*

David D. Kim

I

Early on in J. M. Coetzee's 2003 novel *Elizabeth Costello*, the female protagonist gives a lecture at a small liberal arts college in the United States. This institution has bestowed upon her a prestigious literary prize and, in exchange, the world-renowned Australian writer is asked, as is customary, to deliver an acceptance speech. Yet, something curious happens in this public appearance. Costello summarizes Franz Kafka's *Ein Bericht für eine Akademie* (*A Report for an Academy*) before explaining that, like Rotpeter, she feels completely out of place. This analogy perplexes the audience. After all, Costello is the author of "nine novels" ("neun Romane"), as well as "two books of poems, a book on bird life, and a body of journalism" ("zwei Gedichtbände, ein Vogelbuch und eine Vielzahl journalistischer Arbeiten").[1] Not only is she the recipient of numerous literary prizes, but there is "even an Elizabeth Costello Society, based in Albuquerque, New Mexico, which puts out a quarterly Elizabeth Costello Newsletter" ("sogar eine Elizabeth-Costello-Gesellschaft, ansässig in Albuquerque, New Mexico, die ein vierteljährliches Elizabeth-Costello-Blatt herausgibt").[2] Her most famous work is *The*

---

[1] See *Elizabeth Costello* (New York: Viking, 2003), 1, and *Elizabeth Costello. Acht Lehrstücke*, trans. Reinhild Böhnke (Frankfurt am Main: Fischer, 2004), 7. In the following pages, I will quote from the English original and the German translation. This bilingual, translational attentiveness is integral to my argument concerning the possibility of rewriting German literary history from the outside in. All translations are mine unless otherwise stated.

[2] *Elizabeth Costello* (English) 1–2, (German) 8.

House on Eccles Street, a "path-breaking" ("bahnbrechende") novel published in 1969 and telling the fictive story of Marion (Molly) Bloom, the wife of Leopold Bloom in James Joyce's *Ulysses*.[3] It describes how Molly, who is herself a writer, feels incarcerated at home by her husband and lover, and by Joyce himself who has invented her. What the novel seeks to restore in imagination is freedom for this subaltern female character. As readers also find out, the novel has garnered world literary fame since its publication at the height of student protest movements. Now, it is taught at colleges and universities around the globe, with Costello's character embodying, in spite of being a fictive creation, women's emancipation from the clutches of "marriage and domesticity" ("der Ehe und des häuslichen Lebens") in patriarchal society.[4] So again: why does Costello compare herself with Kafka's talking ape to articulate such a profound sense of alienation?

Elizabeth Costello makes crucial references to Kafka's story for reasons that are not fully graspable simply on the basis of analyzing both texts. Readers need to examine them carefully side by side, but even close reading won't suffice to explain why Rotpeter's fate resonates so strongly with Costello's acute self-understanding. For this comprehension, readers must navigate cogently between different historical, political, and literary contexts: on the one hand, the Austrian imperial milieu in which Kafka writes as a German-speaking Jew; on the other hand, the contemporary postcoloniality in which Coetzee gives voice to an elderly female writer struggling with her identity. Perhaps, an even greater challenge involves working through Coetzee's characteristic allegorical writing.[5] Its open-ended, philosophical, and historically decontextualized elements call for a thoughtful negotiation between literality and universality. To put it another way, the contrast between Kafka's "minor literature" and Costello's world literary stature could not be more stark, but as Costello suggests, what binds them together is a shared sense of survival, of having escaped death, after building "a bridge" ("eine Brücke") in their own ways "to the far bank" ("ans

---

[3] *Elizabeth Costello* (English) 12, (German) 20.
[4] *Elizabeth Costello* (English) 13, (German) 22. This part of Costello's life story is loosely based on Judith Kitchen, the distinguished American poet and author of *The House on Eccles Road* (2002). This novel focuses on a single day in the lives of Molly Bluhm and her husband Leo in Dublin, Ohio, some eight years after the tragic death of their beloved son. *Elizabeth Costello* draws inspiration from this novel to tell a different story of postcolonial female authorship.
[5] Derek Attridge, "Against Allegory: *Waiting for the Barbarians, Life & Times of Michael K.* and the Question of Literary Reading," in *J.M. Coetzee and the Idea of the Public Intellectual*, ed. Jane Poyner (Athens: Ohio University Press, 2006), 63–83, here 63.

andere Ufer").[6] This insight makes sense only when the two texts are brought in relation to each other as cumulative aesthetic, linguistic, and ethical interrogations of self-knowledge and alienation in modernity. Their kinship rests on Coetzee's interpretation and reworking of Kafka's short story.

As this synopsis suggests, what interests me is the fictive template that *Elizabeth Costello* offers for redirecting the historical trajectory of German-language literatures from the outside in. How can we rethink the ossified genre of German literary history on this textual basis? How does the work of a South African writer now living in Australia and deeply attuned to literary criticism and Western philosophy provide scholars of German with a compelling point of departure for a new literary historiography, one that no longer contains the history of German literature in monolingual and national terms? As Jeannine Blackwell explains, German studies has staked its claim as an interdisciplinary field interrogating, among others, German literary history as a chronological and androcentric narrative of national consciousness in the dual institution of literature and history (Blackwell 2003)[7]. By increasingly focusing on the works of women writers, writers of non-German descent, and from the former German Democratic Republic, the discipline has generated alternative approaches to the study of German-language literatures informed by deterritorialization from Germany and invested in transatlantic cosmopolitanism. My goal is to extend this disciplinary transformation to the prospect of transnational literary history, which veers away from reading texts in an "encaged" chronological, national or monolingual framework and accounts for risky, locally specific, and historically particular encounters in world literature.[8] What

---

[6] *Elizabeth Costello* (English) 1, (German) 7. Gilles Deleuze and Félix Guattari evaluate Kafka's writing as an intervention in the dominant, state-centric conception of territory. To delineate how "minor literature" changes the landscape of language politics as such, they identify "a rhizome, a net, a spider's web" as models for a collectivity that takes new strategic positions within a larger polity: Gilles Deleuze and Félix Guattari, "Towards a Minor Literature: The Components of Expression," trans. Marie Maclean, *New Literary History*, vol. 16, no. 3 (Spring 1985): 591–608, here 592.

[7] Jeannine Blackwell, "German Literary History and the Canon in the United States," in *German Studies in the United States: A Historical Handbook*, ed. Peter Uwe Hohendahl (New York: Modern Language Association of America, 2003), 143–74.

[8] By "encagement," I mean in accordance with Michael Mann's sense of this term the violent process whereby powerful centers take over and incorporate smaller polities until they form together a larger imperial or national system: Michael Mann, *Sources of Social Power*, vol. 1 (Cambridge: Cambridge University Press, 1986). The same goes for literary texts. Although their local or historical context is discernable, literary history in its traditional sense erases this specificity by upholding a dominant teleological national framework.

happens when we read *Elizabeth Costello* in German translation—or in Rebecca Walkowitz's words, as a "born translated" novel—with a view to German-language writers and their works?[9] As Coetzee makes clear, his books "are not rooted in the English language," and he feels increasingly like a foreigner in this tongue. That explains why "the English" he writes "is so easily translatable," and he even considers "the versions [his] translators produce [. . .] in no way inferior to the original."[10] So how does *Elizabeth Costello* reorient literary historical narratives by undoing hegemonic norms and practices in literary production and reception, and by pushing back against myopic anxieties that stymy cosmopolitan approaches to German literary studies?

Since my inquiry makes little sense without revisiting at least briefly the role of literary history in *Germanistik*, I wish to proceed with an outline of the stakes here. Afterward, I will return to Coetzee's text in order to explore how German literary history might be reconceptualized on this critical and creative basis. Although Coetzee states on numerous occasions that his fiction is influenced by a wide range of modernist writers and thinkers working in different languages, the following investigation focuses on his adaptation of works by Franz Kafka and Hugo von Hofmannsthal for two reasons: first, because they figure centrally in *Elizabeth Costello*; second, because I want to investigate a promising example of a methodology for reframing the history of German-language literatures in cosmopolitan, postcolonial, and transnational terms.[11] Non-German writers such as Daniel Defoe, Nadine Gordimer, and Judith Kitchen are important for interpreting the book more comprehensively, just as comparative analyses of *The Lives of Animals* are helpful for evaluating Coetzee's deep understanding of writerly responsibility.[12] Due to the specific focus of this volume, though, I

---

[9] Rebecca Walkowitz, *Born Translated: The Contemporary Novel in an Age of World Literature* (New York: Columbia University Press, 2015).

[10] J. M. Coetzee, "On the Problem with English," *Financial Times*, February 17, 2018, podcast, www.ft.com/content/aa32c78b-d8e9-4da4-89aa-0685b53cfcb3.

[11] In addition to many interviews and literary reviews, three collections of critical essays written by Coetzee highlight the many different writers and critics who have shaped his oeuvres over the years. They include Samuel Beckett, Walter Benjamin, Jorge Luis Borges, Breyten Breytenbach, A. S. Byatt Paul Celan, Fyodor Dostoevsky, William Faulkner, Nadine Gordimer, Robert Musil, Jean-Jacques Rousseau, Salman Rushdie, W. G. Sebald, Italo Svevo, Leo Tolstoy, and Walt Whitman. For more information, see *Doubling the Point* (1992), *Stranger Shores* (2001), and *Inner Workings* (2007).

[12] James Meffan explains the immense influence that Defoe and Gordimer exert on Coetzee's ethical conception of writing in "Elizabeth Costello (2003)," in *A Companion to the Works of J.M. Coetzee*, ed. Tim Mehigan (Rochester, NY: Camden

shall restrict my investigation to rethinking German literary history on the basis of Coetzee's explicit allusions to Kafka and Hofmannsthal in *Elizabeth Costello*.

II

Along with the literary canon and philology, literary history constituted an essential genealogical pillar of *Germanistik* in the nineteenth century.[13] Even before the birth of the German nation, it contributed to the institutionalization of the discipline at reformed universities by engendering national imaginaries and cultivating "filiative" relationships among scholars and students.[14] Philologists and literary historians passed their knowledge of the German language and German-language texts onto younger generations, thereby solidifying their scholarly practices, norms, and orientations on the basis of what they deemed to be noteworthy literary and linguistic accomplishments. Around 1900, the reverential quality of literary history waned with the rise of literary theory and only in recent years has the genre seen a second life with scholars both in German Studies and in *Germanistik* taking account of

---

House, 2011), 172–91. What he does not point out in his otherwise thoughtful interpretation of *Elizabeth Costello* is that the protagonist's novel *The House on Eccles Street* is another hidden allusion to Judith Kitchen's *The House on Eccles Road* (2002). Published a year before the revised version of the first lesson in Coetzee's book, this novel tells the story of Molly Bluhm and her husband Leo who live in Dublin, Ohio, after the tragic death of their young son Arjay at the age of four. It is not an imaginary retelling of Molly Bloom's life story, but an even more creative and distant work of translation from a contemporary feminist perspective.

[13] According to Hans Ulrich Gumbrecht, literary history took root in Germany at the beginning of the nineteenth century, as historians and philologists sought to reconcile their emerging normative national identity marked by inequality and unfreedom with everyday experiences; see Hans Ulrich Gumbrecht, "Shall we continue to write Histories of Literature?" *New Literary History* vol. 39, no. 3 (2008): 519–32, here 520–1. The same bourgeois horizon did not arise in France where a *science de l'homme* in its Enlightenment universalism foreclosed this epistemological, self-reflexive possibility after the French Revolution: "'Un Souffle d'Allemagne ayant passé': Friedrich Diez, Gaston Paris, and the Genesis of National Philologies," *Romance Philology*, vol. 40, no. 1 (August 1986): 1–37. Once established, though, the teaching and learning of literary history began to form a "filiative" relationship between teacher and student in literary studies; see Edward Said, *The World, the Text, and the Critic* (Cambridge, MA: Harvard University Press, 1983), 16. It reinforced a seemingly natural *sensus communis* within the field. Edward Said differentiated this mode of relationship from "affiliation," which involved a deliberate crossing of cultural, linguistic, literary, and historical boundaries (16).

[14] Said, *The World*, 16.

multilingual and transnational connections in literary production, dissemination, and reception.[15] Taking inspiration from debates in comparative literature (on world literature), history (on global and transnational histories), digital humanities (on distant reading), and postcolonial studies (on contrapuntal readings), new possibilities for literary historiography have become visible.

This literary historical reorientation originates in a collaborative, experimental, and transformative spirit. Its newness is apparent when we recall Hans Ulrich Gumbrecht's reference to literary history as late as in 2008. In an article titled "Shall we continue to write Histories of Literature?" he offers several reasons why literary history, as it has been written in the past two centuries, no longer amounts to a meaningful scholarly pursuit. He explains that, under the contemporary historical condition, literary history does not lend itself to a deeper understanding of "different national identities"; nor does it operate with a shared normative conception of literature.[16] This dramatic "epistemological transformation," whose trajectory spans from nineteenth-century historicism and the rise of literary theory to New Historicism during the last quarter of the twentieth century, makes it impossible for literary critics to accept the validity of a "referential truth" or the possibility of a "great narrative" incorporating many different historical perspectives on the nation.[17] The idea that literary history is capable of facilitating national imagination in a teleological, self-reflexive, and streamlined way is no longer tenable in the twenty-first century. Finally, Gumbrecht argues that this development has changed our attitude toward the future. It is not an "open horizon of expectations" anymore, as Hans Robert Jauss describes it, but an "inaccessible" and "tendentiously unappealing" weight resting heavily on the living.[18] Therefore, writes Gumbrecht, "we have endlessly developed our technological and artisanal capabilities of preserving and reproducing artifacts from the past" and we "immerse ourselves, in a very material sense, into worlds that preceded our own" as opposed to "constantly 'leaving the past behind ourselves.'"[19] Gumbrecht illuminates why literary history in its original variant has shifted away from being a towering monument canonizing primarily male authors and celebrating the nation's mythical pasts to posing a mongrel genre.

---

[15] Büttner and Kim 2022; Kontje 2018; Mani 2017; Richter 2017; Tautz 2018; Wellbery et al. 2005.
[16] Gumbrecht, "Shall we continue to write," 525.
[17] Gumbrecht, "Shall we continue to write," 527.
[18] Gumbrecht, "Shall we continue to write," 528.
[19] Gumbrecht, "Shall we continue to write," 528.

Nevertheless, I do not share Gumbrecht's pessimism. My vision is more closely aligned with the tradition of German Studies as opposed to *Germanistik*, and it is guided by what has recently been possible and what remains to be rewritten in the near future. No longer chained to the national paradigm of the world, literary history is moving now between several different scales—local, national, and global—to include the works of women writers, writers of color, immigrants, and exiles. By the nature of its narrative construction, the principle of a chronological unfolding remains mostly in place without claiming to be comprehensive, but rather than conceive of literary history as a fulsome historical narrative of national literature written and read by right-bearing citizens of German descent with German-language mastery, whatever these essentializing categories mean, a new literary history is reconstructing the genre with a view to intercultural, transnational, and multilingual connections between different stakeholders of German-language books. Of particular importance are the lessons of postcolonial, German Jewish, gender, migration, medieval, and Renaissance studies and, more recently, book histories and inquiries into world literature. Instead of operating with a universal notion of language, nation, literature, or history, they document the messy diversity and cosmopolitanism of literary engagements in the German language well beyond modern, state-centric, Christian frameworks.

Such a prospect is both urgent and exciting not least because humanity, as we know it, depends on the humanities and their ethical or moral insights into nationalism or cosmopolitanism.[20] I am fully aware of the challenges and uncertainties that such a broad statement brings up for discussion, but it does not seem far-fetched to surmise that human nature will be fundamentally changed if we ever reach a point where we abandon the creative and critical works of the humanities. As far as our anthropological knowledge goes, human beings have undertaken these activities since their documented beginnings, and even though they do not matter for our survival in a way that air, food, and sleep do, we depend on them to try to make sense of ourselves and others in the world phenomenologically. "To survive," Martin Hägglund writes in this regard, "is to live on in a temporal process of alteration, where one is always becoming other than oneself."[21] Driven by all-too-human desires not just for survival, but for happiness or self-fulfillment, self-reflection and knowledge of the other draw upon humanistic inquiries

---

[20] David D. Kim, "German Studies and Cosmopolitanism," *German Quarterly*, vol. 94, no. 4 (Fall 2021): 427–43.

[21] Martin Hägglund, *Dying for Time: Proust, Woolf, Nabokov* (Cambridge, MA: Harvard University Press, 2012), 8.

into temporality, language, attachment, detachment, pain, joy, evil, and beauty to represent bodily and cognitive experiences in the continuously changing world. A transnational history of German-language literatures has the potential to shed light on such enduring, soul-searching, planetary conversations.[22]

III

The sort of literary historiography that responds to this conjecture is not out of sync with Coetzee's mode of writing. As he observes in *Doubling the Point*, fiction and criticism are not necessarily separate engagements with literature; they can go hand in hand. In addition, Kafka's writing presents for him "moments of analytic intensity," after which he feels better prepared to interrogate in writing what remains to be said about violence, alienation, the binary opposition between the West and the Rest, the expected duty of postcolonial writers to represent historical and political processes in realist terms, or the possibility of inventing history in terms that are not dictated by an authoritarian government.[23] If the dominant political order exerts control over its population by "stopping or even turning back the clock" or speeding up certain developments in time, writing can serve as an anachronistic mode of resistance whereby the burden of life is more tolerable without muting countervoices in oneself or others.[24]

In order to clarify this key argument, let us return to my initial question about Costello's connection to Rotpeter. In Kafka's short story, Rotpeter was captured along the west coast of Africa by hunters who were supplying wild animals to the Hagenbeck Zoo.[25] In captivity, he came to the realization that the only way out of his state of stupefying cruelty was to imitate human beings and acquire human speech. Without

---

[22] I explain elsewhere why the "contemporary cosmopolitanism talk should not be mistaken for a consensus either on the value or on the meaning of this ostensibly positive concept": *Cosmopolitan Parables: Trauma and Responsibility in Contemporary Germany* (Evanston, IL: Northwestern University Press, 2017), 31. Still, I concur with Kwame Anthony Appiah that "conversation" in cosmopolitanism is necessary for exchanging cross-cultural, transnational stories and for interrogating one's "habits" along with the underlying values; see Kwame Anthony Appiah, *Cosmopolitanism: Ethics in a World of Strangers* (New York: W. W. Norton, 2006), 85, 77.

[23] Coetzee, *Doubling the Point: Essays and Interviews*, ed. David Attwell (Cambridge, MA: Harvard University Press, 1992), 199.

[24] Coetzee, *Doubling the Point*, 209.

[25] For information about the Hagenbeck Zoo and Kafka's Rotpeter within the Austrian fin-de-siècle context, see David D. Kim, "The Task of the Loving Translator: Translation, *Völkerschauen*, and Colonial Ambivalence in Peter Altenberg's *Ashantee* (1897)," *TRANSIT*, vol. 2, no. 1 (2006): 1–21, here 5–7.

violating his animal nature, he saw no hope for freedom. Hence, he learned to talk, smoke, and drink alcohol. He performed tricks in front of astonished audiences. In return, he was spared life in a cage and was given a female ape as a companion. Now, after several years of survival under such alienating, yet physically less oppressive conditions, a scientific academy has asked him to give a report on the process of his own denaturation "in the human world" ("in der Menschenwelt").[26] The expectations are high. His public lecture is supposed to be "a depiction of the origin of his becoming-human" ("eine Darstellung des Ursprungs seiner Menschwerdung") and solve, once and for all, Darwin's secret of human evolution, as if Rotpeter were "a philosopher of culture" ("ein Kulturphilosoph") capable of reflecting on his own "metamorphosis" ("Verwandlung") from apedom into humanness.[27] Yet, the lecture does not deliver what the academy wants. As Rotpeter states, his human behavior is all mimicry and his transformation nothing other than an "evolution whipped forwards" ("vorwärts gepeitscht[e] Entwicklung").[28] Instead of becoming human, Rotpeter claims that he has simply put on a show—an act, so to speak—to escape from survival and death in the zoo.

Costello identifies with Rotpeter because she, too, believes that she cannot meet the expectations of her listeners. The audience is not unreasonable in wanting to see some gratitude from her and listen to her self-assessment in world literature. "The time has arrived for her to show her paces" ("Zeit für sie, zu zeigen, was sie kann"), as her adult son John says right before the acceptance speech.[29] Yet, Costello ruminates instead on the "transience of fame" ("Vergänglichkeit des Ruhms"), speculating in roundabout ways that her place in literary history is far from being guaranteed.[30] She may be of world literary stature now, but the recognition she has received won't secure any lasting prominence. At an earlier point in life, she mentions, she used to do everything possible to publish books that could be found in the British Museum, at the British Library or at the Library of Congress, but now she understands that even such venerable institutions will not be around forever. People tend to look for hope by turning their attention to classics, but even monumental institutions will eventually "crumble

---

[26] Franz Kafka, *Ein Landarzt und andere Drucke zu Lebzeiten* (Frankfurt am Main: Fischer, 2008), 235.
[27] Gerhard Neumann, *Verfehlte Anfänge und offenes Ende* (Munich: Carl Friedrich von Siemens Stiftung, 2011), 34.
[28] Kafka, *Ein Landarzt*, 235.
[29] Coetzee, *Elizabeth Costello* (English) 16, (German) 25.
[30] Coetzee, *Elizabeth Costello* (English) 17, (German) 27.

and decay" ("baufällig werden und verrotten"), just like the books therein, which will "turn to powder" ("zu Staub verfallen").[31] Repeated in Costello's private conversations with others and at other public events, these insights show how uncertain the author is about her literary legacy.

In a second lecture, Costello refers again to Kafka's short story. This time, she does so to redefine the aesthetic-philosophical concept of realism. She observes that *Ein Bericht für eine Akademie* is a prime example of this literary style because it depicts in a detailed, factual manner the brutality of human crimes against animals. In a third lecture, she builds upon this argument to protest against industrial farming and animal research. She speaks out against cruel mistreatments of animals in contemporary capitalist society and she goes so far as to compare the slaughter of animals in scientific experiments and on factory farms with the horrors of Nazi concentration camps during World War II. These comparisons may look superficial, obscene or nonsensical, but what they illustrate is the role that literature plays for Costello in recording hidden political and socioeconomic crises. Rotpeter's alienation in the human world touches her in a very personal way, although most human beings hardly care about the lives and deaths of animals. As these episodes show, Kafka's story allows Costello to condemn human cruelty towards animals in the current consumption- and profit-oriented society. More often than not, colonial, National Socialist, and post-industrial systems of oppression are treated as distinct problems of xenophobia, oppression or violence. Relating them is rejected as an overly global, toothless moralism—one that minimizes the suffering of human beings. Costello is not afraid of crossing this line because she is discontent with living in a world unfree for women, people of color, and animals.

This worldly ecological referentiality in recognition of humans and animals as equal members of planet earth is illustrated in several discussions about the concept of realism. This term has several meanings, which are not easy to separate from one another, reconcile or define in a concrete language, but the first definition is posited by Costello's son in a monologue. John insists that the term denotes a modern literary style. It is associated with showing details as opposed to abstract ideas. He mentions Daniel Defoe's classic colonial novel *Robinson Crusoe* as the earliest example of realism and points to his mother's writing as a similarly realist engagement with the world. She can be "cruel" ("grausam") in her writing; it is capable of "shaking" ("erschüttert") readers with deep insights into human emotions.[32] Yet, John does not

---

[31] Coetzee, *Elizabeth Costello* (English) 17, (German) 27.
[32] Coetzee, *Elizabeth Costello* (English) 5, (German) 12.

think that, with such criticism, she intends to be malicious or hopeless; rather, her goal is to represent the world through concrete "situations" ("Situationen") such as "walks in the countryside, conversations" ("Spaziergänge auf dem Land, Gespräche") where competing ideas are proposed and debated.[33] The characters in her writings are *"embodying"* ("verkörpern") these ideas and they come into view in relation to counterarguments.[34]

Although John is right about the dialogic nature of his mother's fiction, she makes clear that she does not agree with this assessment. When she takes up the topic herself in her speech, she claims that realism does not suggest a clear perception of the world in its reality; instead, it is a modern form of literary history with which one is able to interrogate dominant epistemologies and ontologies, including the idea of a unified subject. In order to support her position, she summarizes *Ein Bericht für eine Akademie* before raising questions, which contradict her son's definition of realism implicitly or explicitly. For example, she discusses the impossibility of knowing "what is really going on in this story" ("was wirklich in dieser Erzählung geschieht"):[35]

> For all we know, the speaker may not "really" be an ape, may be simply a human being like ourselves deluded into thinking himself an ape, or a human being presenting himself, with heavy irony, for rhetorical purposes, as an ape. Equally well, the audience may consist not, as we may imagine, of bewhiskered, red-faced gents who have put aside their bushjackets and topis for evening dress, but of fellow apes, trained, if not to the level of our speaker, who can mouth complicated sentences in German, then at least to sit still and listen; or, if not trained to that pitch, then chained to their seats and trained not to jabber and pick fleas and relieve themselves openly.

> [Nach allem, was wir wissen, ist der Affe vielleicht kein "wirklicher" Affe, er ist vielleicht einfach ein Mensch wie wir auch, der sich fälschlich für einen Affen hält, oder ein Mensch, der sich mit starker Ironie aus rhetorischen Gründen für einen Affen ausgibt. Genauso gut besteht die Zuhörerschaft vielleicht nicht, wie wir glauben, aus schnurrbärtigen, rotgesichtigen Herren, die ihre Safarijacken und Tropenhelme gegen den Abendanzug getauscht haben, sondern aus Mit-Affen, dressiert, wenn nicht bis

---

[33] Coetzee, *Elizabeth Costello* (English) 9, (German) 16.
[34] Coetzee, *Elizabeth Costello* (English) 9, (German) 16.
[35] Coetzee, *Elizabeth Costello* (English) 19, (German) 28.

zum Niveau unseres Redners, der komplizierte Sätze in deutscher Sprache bewältigt, dann zumindest dazu, still zu sitzen und zuzuhören; oder wenn ihre Dressur nicht soweit reicht, sind sie an ihre Stühle gekettet und so abgerichtet, dass sie nicht schnattern, sich flöhen und sich öffentlich erleichtern.][36]

As these different scenarios illustrate, realism unsettles any sense of certainty in reality. It exercises the readers' imagination of different possibilities in another language. According to Costello, Kafka's story shows how, in the modern world, the "word-mirror is broken, irreparably" ("Wort-Spiegel des Textes ist zerbrochen [. . .] irreparabel"), and, for this reason, she contends that she no longer knows who she really is. Nobody can speak on this issue unequivocally:[37]

> There used to be a time, we believe, when we could say who we were. Now we are just performers speaking our parts. The bottom has dropped out. We could think of this as a tragic turn of events, were it not that it is hard to have respect for whatever was the bottom that dropped out—it looks to us like an illusion now, one of those illusions sustained only by the concentrated gaze of everyone in the room. Remove your gaze for but an instant, and the mirror falls to the floor and shatters.

> [Wir glauben, dass es eine Zeit gegeben hat, als wir sagen konnten, wer wir sind. Jetzt sind wir nur Darsteller, die unsere Rollen sprechen. Wir haben den Boden unter den Füßen verloren. Wir könnten das für eine tragische Entwicklung halten, wenn es nicht schwer wäre, Respekt für das zu haben, was einst der Boden unter unseren Füßen war—uns erscheint das jetzt als Illusion, als eine der Illusionen, die nur durch den konzentrierten Blick aller im Raum Anwesenden aufrecht erhalten wird. Wenn man den Blick nur für einen kurzen Moment abwendet, fällt der Spiegel zu Boden und zersplittert.][38]

In the future, then, people won't remember her books, even the ones for which she has received prizes. That is not a bad thing, though, because there has to be a boundary between the past and the present for the sake of alleviating posterity's burden of memory. A common foundation has also been demythologized through literary language, and writers

---

[36] Coetzee, *Elizabeth Costello* (English) 18–19, (German) 28.
[37] Coetzee, *Elizabeth Costello* (English) 19, (German) 29.
[38] Coetzee, *Elizabeth Costello* (English) 19–20, (German) 29–30.

should continue to oppose their own literary tradition and be inventive of their own instead of "parasitizing the classics forever" ("die Klassiker [. . .] ewig ausbeuten").[39]

As Costello's explanation suggests, she is diametrically opposed to the Eurocentric conception of realism. For her, this terminology is associated with nineteenth-century literary history, including its imperial dimension and national context. She also calls for a subversive writing process, which introduces a self-critical, daring break with tradition, such that literature remains relevant for the latest generation of writers and readers in the postcolonial world. Costello does not want her literary legacy to be passed on from one generation to another uncritically. Following this idea, she seeks to determine for herself who is unjustly neglected or what is left out in literary history, and how she in a critical, creative spirit is capable as a writer of shedding light on this blind spot. This sort of writing is what she has learned from reading Kafka, and her first novel attends to whom Joyce treats dishonestly or unfairly in his magnum opus.

As a result of the aforementioned comparison between Nazi crimes against humanity and the exploitation of animals in neoliberal capitalism, Costello is invited a year later to give a lecture on the "the age-old problem of evil" ("das uralte Problem des Bösen") at a conference in Amsterdam.[40] On this occasion, she decides to criticize the work of a German writer by the name of Paul West. He has published a book, titled *The very Rich Hours of Count von Stauffenberg* (even the German translation gives this title in English) and describing in great detail the execution of the resistance fighters in July 1944. Costello argues that this realistic, yet ultimately fabricated illustration is arrogant, immoral, and *"obscene"* (*"obszön"*), since the author pretends to have a unique access to the suffering of those men.[41] That is wrong in Costello's view. Such terrible experiences cannot be portrayed morally. Death is "a private matter" ("eine private Sache") and "the artist should not invade the deaths of others" ("der Künstler sollte sich nicht in den Tod anderer Menschen hineindrängen").[42] West is guilty of perverse voyeurism. He has failed to practice the sort of vigilance necessary for writing fiction. For readers who are familiar with Susan Sontag's *Regarding the Pain of Others*, Costello's statement rings true. One should not circulate or take pictures of human suffering.

---

[39] Coetzee, *Elizabeth Costello* (English) 14, (German) 23.
[40] Coetzee, *Elizabeth Costello* (English) 156, (German) 198.
[41] Coetzee, *Elizabeth Costello* (English) 158–9, (German) 212.
[42] Coetzee, *Elizabeth Costello* (English) 174, (German) 219.

These contradictory, provocative, relational positions are at the core of the book's eight chapters, called "lessons" in the English original and "Lehrstücke" in the German rendition. They form a loose collection of vignettes, which can be read separately, but represent in essence different variations of the same dialogic encounter between Costello and another person in today's heterogeneous, conflict-ridden, postcolonial world.[43] Although the title of the book refers to a singular, untranslatable name, namely Elizabeth Costello, the chapters themselves do not add up to a wholesome picture of the main protagonist; instead, they explore the social value of literature in redressing ethical dilemmas, political deadlocks, and cultural prejudices, as Costello confronts family members, academics, and other writers who hold different positions. Their contentious exchanges, along with inward-looking reflections, shed light on various uses and abuses of literature in postcoloniality.

IV

Carrol Clarkson has pointed out that Coetzee's responses to other writers and thinkers contribute actively to the contemporary literary and philosophical debates. Both his fiction and nonfiction are responsive and responsible. In this dual sense, they are profoundly ethical writings.[44] While Clarkson is referring to Coetzee's emphasis on "authorial consciousness" as a way of refining Bakhtin's conception of dialogism, it is equally informative to consider the notion of "contrapuntal reading" in transnational literary historiography because the shift from author to reader places the onus on the critic as a central figure in reconceptualizing the genre of literary history from the outside in.[45] This term was coined by Edward Said in the early 1990s and the guiding idea was that the voices of those who had been oppressed by colonial infrastructures could be heard again through literary texts, although they tended to be drowned out by the colonizer's dominant discourse.[46] Said explained that the reason for this silencing had to do with European literary histories being told in national terms, although upon closer examination they were inseparable from supranational, imperial or

---

[43] Only in the English version do readers find out that six of the stories have been published previously in various literary volumes and magazines, the likely reason for this difference being that German readers have not had access to those chapters in translation prior to the publication of the book: *Stranger Shores: Literary Essays 1986–1999* (New York: Viking, 2001).

[44] Carrol Clarkson, "Coetzee's Criticism," in *A Companion to the Works of J.M. Coetzee*, ed. Tim Mehigan (Rochester, NY: Camden House, 2011), 222–34.

[45] Clarkson, "Coetzee's Criticism," 228.

[46] Edward Said, *Culture and Imperialism* (New York: Vintage Books, 1993), xxv.

colonial histories.[47] To recover these "intertwined and overlapping histories" from nineteenth-century British literature, Said argued that contrapuntal reading was necessary.[48] It involved listening to the "polyphony" of forgotten or neglected voices in literary texts and making them audible again.[49]

For Said, Erich Auerbach's *Mimesis* served as a model for contrapuntal, comparative literary historiography, but it could no longer be imitated as such. This scholarly masterpiece had been written based on the premise that history and literature corresponded with each other in a coherent way, a presupposition that the previous generation of multilingual comparatists such as Auerbach, Ernst Curtius, Leo Spitzer, and Karl Vossler had held, but was deemed, as Gumbrecht explained, no longer valid. In Auerbach's case, the experience of exile had also been decisive in writing a monumental history of European literature as world literature. Following his traumatic dislocation from Germany, he sought to resist hegemonic value systems to advocate for universal humanist ideas instead. Similar to what Deleuze and Guattari had claimed about Kafka's minor literature, Said contended that Auerbach had written *Mimesis* not as a scholarly attempt to escape from historical reality, but as a world literary mode of survival in Istanbul.

One should not ignore the fact that Auerbach had access to excellent libraries in the cosmopolitan metropolis.[50] He was not completely cut off from Western cultural and literary traditions. For Said, though, Auerbach's study of realism, which began with an analysis of Homer's *Odyssey* and ended with Virginia Woolf's *To the Lighthouse*, represented human relationships, as well as world literary encounters, as combinations of cultural "affiliation" and non-cultural "filiation."[51] As Said mentioned, there was a strong tendency in literary studies to privilege filiative structures and devalue affiliative connections because disciplines specialized in certain concepts, discourses, and methodologies and occupied specific areas within academic institutions. The study of a literary canon, which had been authorized across generations in a discipline-specific manner and handed down as the bearer of a national culture and a national language, contributed to the affirmation of uniform collectives. The introduction of students to respective cultural and literary histories preserved these hegemonic knowledge structures and

---

[47] Said, *Culture*, 51.
[48] Said, *Culture*, 18.
[49] Said, *Culture*, 32.
[50] Kader Konuk, *East West Mimesis: Auerbach in Turkey* (Stanford, CA: Stanford University Press, 2010), 135, 137–43.
[51] Said, *The World*, 19–20.

their associated practices. In light of this challenge, Said wrote that the knowledge of world literature was critical, but that universities could not teach it anymore even in departments of comparative literature. Hence, literary critics needed to work contrapuntally and exercise "secular criticism" by crossing borders, interrogating demarcations, and paying close attention to erasures or silences.[52] They needed to demonstrate a "secular critical consciousness."[53] With this strategic term, Said also questioned the lack of political and ethical commitments in the humanities, which had been shaped by Eurocentric concepts, discourses, methodologies, and values. In his opinion, literary and cultural studies had moved away from worldly concerns and political problems. They hardly paid any attention to historical contexts in which texts were written and they presented interpretations that seemed detached from cultural or political premises.

I do not wish to speculate whether *Elizabeth Costello* is Coetzee's literary meditation on Said's notion of contrapuntal reading. However, it seems fair to say that the novel qualifies for an aesthetic analogue to this distinctly postcolonial mode of inquiry. Readers come across the same skepticism toward the humanities in the fifth lesson from Costello's life story. This chapter depicts the contentious relationship between Costello and her sister Blanche, publicly known as Sister Bridget. The two siblings grew up Catholic in Australia, but Elizabeth turned away from the Church while attending college, whereas Blanche moved in the opposite direction. She studied classical philology before switching to medicine and becoming a nun in Zululand. Since then, she has served as the director of an internationally respected hospital for HIV/AIDS patients, where indigenous healers also get to work.

The story begins with Sister Bridget inviting the younger sister to a special occasion: an award ceremony where the former is scheduled to receive for her lifelong humanitarian work an honorary degree from a South African university. Despite their long-standing sibling rivalry, Elizabeth decides to fly to South Africa and take part in the celebration. However, Sister Bridget's acceptance speech surprises Elizabeth. Instead of talking about herself or her work, the internationally famous nun engages in a blatant critique of the humanities for having turned their back since the early modern period on biblical interpretations and for having given priority to Greek Hellenism. She takes issue with the secularization of modern society whose institutions, unlike their non-Western counterparts, have failed to alleviate the suffering of the poor or the sick. As Sister Bridget concludes, the humanities are hardly needed

---

[52] Said, *The World*, 24.
[53] Said, *The World*, 24.

anymore in life and even less so in death. Similar to Said, she argues that the gap between art and the public has become difficult to close in the contemporary world. Nonetheless, Elizabeth goes on to defend literature—more specifically, her own work—by conceiving of fiction and nonfiction as contrapuntal modes of writing in opposition to gender inequality, animal abuse, racial violence, and economic exploitation.

In the last lesson of the book, this worldview is upheld again with a new reference to Kafka. This story is titled "At the Gate" ("Vor dem Tor") in reference to Kafka's parable "Before the Law" ("Vor dem Gesetz"), and Costello, like the man from the country, reaches an unknown place with a gate. Yet, her precarious, uncanny situation is unique in important ways. Reminiscent of Dante's *Divina Commedia*, Costello finds the timeless place to be similar to a gulag in the Soviet Union or a concentration camp in Nazi Europe. She also discovers that, in order to go through the gate, she needs to submit a report on her "belief" ("Überzeugung") as a writer.[54] Again, she contends that writers should be more conscious of their own literary tradition, be creative in their own terms, and reflect more critically on the current world, but her two attempts to explain these convictions are rejected by the anonymous judges. The lesson ends without her passage through the gate, potentially indicating a ceaseless struggle until the end of her life.

At the end of the novel, Costello's contrapuntal reading and writing are staged one last time in the "postscript" ("Nachtrag"). Here, Costello appears as "Elizabeth C.," the wife of Lord Chandos in Hofmannsthal's *Ein Brief*. In an ecstatic letter to Francis Bacon dated September 11, 1603, she describes how her husband is suffering from a language crisis. He believes, she writes, that they are living in a world "where words give way beneath [their] feet like rotting boards" ("wo Worte unter den Füßen nachgeben wie morsche Bretter").[55] Therefore, he is waiting for a non-human "revelation" ("Offenbarung") in which "*not Latin nor English nor Spanish nor Italian*" ("weder die lateinische noch die englische, noch die spanische oder italienische Sprache") makes the world comprehensible again, but "rats and dogs and beetles" ("Ratten und Hunde und Käfer"), as well as "fleas" ("Flöhe"), somehow communicate with him in their terms.[56] For him, these animals are mystical vessels of revelation, whereas human words no longer represent concrete realities. Elizabeth C. goes on to write that she cannot live like this any longer. She cannot bear anymore his linguistic-philosophical mistreatment of animals. Hence, the honorable recipient of her letter should write to

---

[54] Coetzee, *Elizabeth Costello* (English) 194, (German) 242.
[55] Coetzee, *Elizabeth Costello* (English) 228, (German) 283.
[56] Coetzee, *Elizabeth Costello* (English) 229–30, (German) 284–5.

him as quickly as possible, explaining that "the time is not yet come, the time of the giants, the time of the angels" ("die Zeit noch nicht gekommen ist, die Zeit der Giganten, die Zeit der Engel"), which is to say, there is no redemption yet in sight.[57]

Coetzee creates this intertextual allegory not only to track past debates on the limits of language and realist representations, but also to expose the predicaments of a postcolonial Australian writer who is wrestling with ethical, historical, political, and intellectual legacies of European literature, criticism, and philosophy. Instead of identifying with Lord Chandos, she appears as his wife articulating her own despair over the failures of language, the limits of innovation, and the challenges of the foreseeable future. The problems remain, but the solutions have yet to be generated in postmodernity.

V

In cultural and literary studies, we continue to adopt binary oppositions, dualistic hierarchies, and fixed containers in order to weave together literatures and histories in accordance with predetermined, state-centric concepts and relations. As such, history and literature neatly reflect each other and present historical trends, organize literary works accordingly, and integrate author biographies therein. Such normative organizations are integral to national literary histories. However, scholars of German have been reconceptualizing for the past twenty years or so how literary history can be retold in multilingual, international, and transcultural terms. In recognition of the fact that German-language literatures have undergone various processes of localization and globalization across the Atlantic, they have proposed innovative models for examining them beyond monolingual, state-centric paradigms. Nina Berman's contrapuntal analysis of Hofmannsthal in North Africa is eye-opening in this regard. It tracks the political and economic interests of the Habsburg monarchy in the Middle East and North Africa. A more expansive case in point would be Axel Dunker's application of Said's contrapuntal reading to nineteenth-century German-language literatures. In reference to canonical writers such as Heinrich von Kleist, E. T. A. Hoffmann, Joseph von Eichendorff, Adalbert Stifter, Gottfried Keller, Wilhelm Raabe, Theodor Fontane, and Franz Kafka, Dunker shows how colonial impulses are equally detectable "in the German language realm, not only in Prussia and the other German states, but also in Austria and Switzerland" ("im deutschen

---

[57] Coetzee, *Elizabeth Costello* (English) 229, (German) 284.

Sprachraum, nicht nur in Preußen und den anderen deutschen Staaten, sondern auch in Österreich oder der Schweiz").[58]

In *Elizabeth Costello*, we find a striking example of contrapuntal reading and writing, one whose analysis gives rise to a new horizon of literary interpretation and historical understanding. It provides scholars and students of German-language literatures with a creative and critical point of departure for deterritorializing German literary history and reconstructing a literary historical interpretation that crosses cultural, linguistic, and national borders. Both available in English and in German, it challenges readers to read literature with situated cultural, linguistic, historical, and political sensibilities without prioritizing the original text in the form of separate essays or as a novel over the translation and without ignoring cross-cultural, multilingual, planetary matters of concern. It experiments with a feminist postcolonial perspective on redressing the violence committed against women and animals and it does so by referring to the works of Kafka and Hofmannsthal. It offers a renewed evaluation of the humanities in contemporary secular society, which remains deeply embedded within Christian norms and values. This reimagined postcolonial authorship opens the door for a multilingual, intercultural, and transnational combination of literature and history, one that refutes the dualistic hierarchy between the West and the Rest and transgresses an anthropocentric or Eurocentric set of relations. It offers a poetic template for rewriting German literary history from the outside in.

Works Cited

Appiah, Kwame Anthony. *Cosmopolitanism: Ethics in a World of Strangers* (New York: W. W. Norton, 2006).

Attridge, Derek. "Against Allegory: *Waiting for the Barbarians, Life & Times of Michael K.* and the Question of Literary Reading," in *J.M. Coetzee and the Idea of the Public Intellectual*, ed. Jane Poyner (Athens: Ohio University Press, 2006), 63–83.

Berman, Nina. "K. u. K. Colonialism: Hofmannsthal in North Africa," *New German Critique*, vol. 75 (1998): 3–27.

Blackwell, Jeannine. "German Literary History and the Canon in the United States," in *German Studies in the United States: A Historical Handbook*, ed. Peter Uwe Hohendahl (New York: Modern Language Association of America, 2003), 143–74.

Büttner, Urs, and David D. Kim. *Globalgeschichten der deutschen Literatur. Methoden–Ansätze–Probleme* (Berlin: J. B. Metzler, 2022).

Casanova, Pascale. *The World Republic of Letters*, trans. Malcolm DeBevoise (Cambridge, MA: Harvard University Press, 2007).

---

[58] Axel Dunker, *Kontrapunktische Lektüren. Koloniale Strukturen in der deutschsprachigen Literatur des 19. Jahrhunderts* (Munich: Wilhelm Fink, 2008), 8.

Clarkson, Carrol. "Coetzee's Criticism," in *A Companion to the Works of J.M. Coetzee*, ed. Tim Mehigan (Rochester, NY: Camden House, 2011), 222–34.

Coetzee, J. M. *Doubling the Point: Essays and Interviews*, ed. David Attwell (Cambridge, MA: Harvard University Press, 1992).

Coetzee, J. M. *The Lives of Animals* (Princeton, NJ: Princeton University Press, 1999).

Coetzee, J. M. *Stranger Shores: Literary Essays 1986–1999* (New York: Viking, 2001).

Coetzee, J. M. *Elizabeth Costello* (New York: Viking, 2003).

Coetzee, J. M. *Elizabeth Costello: Acht Lehrstücke* trans. Reinhild Böhnke (Frankfurt am Main: Fischer, 2004).

Coetzee, J. M. *Inner Workings: Literary Essays 2000–2005* (London: Harvill Secker, 2007).

Coetzee, J. M. "On the Problem with English," *Financial Times*, February 17, 2018, www.ft.com/content/aa32c78b-d8e9-4da4-89aa-0685b53cfcb3.

Deleuze, Gilles, and Félix Guattari. "Towards a Minor Literature: The Components of Expression," trans. Marie Maclean, *New Literary History*, vol. 16, no. 3 (Spring 1985): 591–608.

Dunker, Axel. *Kontrapunktische Lektüren. Koloniale Strukturen in der deutschsprachigen Literatur des 19. Jahrhunderts* (Munich: Wilhelm Fink, 2008).

Gumbrecht, Hans Ulrich. "'Un Souffle d'Allemagne ayant passé': Friedrich Diez, Gaston Paris, and the Genesis of National Philologies," *Romance Philology*, vol. 40, no. 1 (August 1986): 1–37.

Gumbrecht, Hans Ulrich. "Shall We Continue to Write Histories of Literature?" *New Literary History*, vol. 39, no. 3 (2008): 519–32.

Hägglund, Martin. *Dying for Time: Proust, Woolf, Nabokov* (Cambridge, MA: Harvard University Press, 2012).

Kafka, Franz. *Ein Landarzt und andere Drucke zu Lebzeiten* (Frankfurt am Main: Fischer, 2008).

Kim, David D. "The Task of the Loving Translator: Translation, *Völkerschauen*, and Colonial Ambivalence in Peter Altenberg's *Ashantee* (1897)," *TRANSIT*, vol. 2, no. 1 (2006): 1–21.

Kim, David D. *Cosmopolitan Parables: Trauma and Responsibility in Contemporary Germany* (Evanston, IL: Northwestern University Press, 2017).

Kitchen, Judith. *The House on Eccles Road: A Novel* (Minneapolis: Graywolf Press, 2002).

Kontje, Todd. *Imperial Fictions: German Literature Before and Beyond the Nation-State* (Ann Arbor: University of Michigan Press, 2018).

Konuk, Kader. *East West Mimesis: Auerbach in Turkey* (Stanford, CA: Stanford University Press, 2010).

Mani, B. Venkat. *Recoding World Literature: Libraries, Print Culture, and Germany's Pact with Books* (New York: Fordham University Press, 2017).

Mann, Michael. *Sources of Social Power*, vol. 1 (Cambridge: Cambridge University Press, 1986).

Meffan, James. "Elizabeth Costello (2003)," in *A Companion to the Works of J.M. Coetzee*, ed. Tim Mehigan (Rochester, NY: Camden House, 2011), 172–91.

Neumann, Gerhard. *Verfehlte Anfänge und offenes Ende* (Munich: Carl Friedrich von Siemens Stiftung, 2011).

Richter, Sandra. *Eine Weltgeschichte der deutschsprachigen Literatur* (Munich: C. Bertelsmann, 2017).

Said, Edward. *The World, the Text, and the Critic* (Cambridge, MA: Harvard University Press, 1983).

Said, Edward. *Culture and Imperialism* (New York: Vintage Books, 1993).

Tautz, Birgit. *Translating the World: Toward a New History of German Literature around 1800* (College Park: Pennsylvania State University Press, 2018).
Walkowitz, Rebecca. *Born Translated: The Contemporary Novel in an Age of World Literature* (New York: Columbia University Press, 2015).
Wellbery, David E. et al., eds. *A New History of German Literature* (Cambridge: Belknap, 2005).

II Stories of Expulsion, Exile, and Displacement

Five Looking for Heinrich Heine with Nâzım Hikmet and E. S. Özdamar

Azade Seyhan

> *that which i love unconditionally*
> *which is my second home*
> *which gave me more confidence*
> *which gave me more security*
> *which gave me more than those*
> *who supposedly speak it . . .*
> *it gave me lessing and heine*
> *it gave me schiller and brecht*
> *it gave me leibnitz and feuerbach*
> *it gave me hegel and marx . . .*
>
> *[die ich vorbehaltlos liebe*
> *die meine zweite heimat ist*
> *die mir mehr zuversicht*
> *die mir mehr geborgenheit*
> *die mir mehr gab als die*
> *die sie angeblich sprechen . . .*
> *sie gab mir lessing und heine*
> *sie gab mir schiller und brecht*
> *sie gab mir leibnitz und feuerbach*
> *sie gab mir hegel und marx . . .]*
>
> —Pazarkaya, "deutsche sprache"[7]

Much contemporary scholarship on Turkish-German literature interprets it as sharing in the narrative of the traumatic German past with a nod to an equally troubled recent Turkish history. While this approach, where meaning becomes material history, provides a seemingly equalizing critical framework of bilateral agreement, it overlooks the inherently universal character of literature as multiply connected and referential. In the wake of ever-growing debates on what counts as world literature—or transnational literature, although this may differ both in position and conception from the former—the paradigm of "touching tales"[1] needs a touch-up. A more expansive understanding of multidirectional writing traces the refractive influences of writers and writing over time and geography.

For Yüksel Pazarkaya, a first-generation Turkish-born poet of German letters, German language gave him a home, which he shares with Lessing, Heine, Schiller, and other greats of German literature and philosophy. In the same poem, he asserts that the German language does not belong to whoever speaks it like a curse to damn those not belonging to Germany: "die in ihr ein werkzeug der erniedrigung / die in ihr ein werkzeug der ausbeutung sehn / sie sind nicht in ihr sie nicht" ("those who find in it a means of humiliation / those who find in it a means of exploitation / they are not in it, they are not").[2] Pazarkaya's defiance raises the question of to whom language—and, by extension, culture—belong: those who abuse it and turn it into hate speech or those who adopt and enrich it by bringing two or more cultures into conversation? The latter are often writers and artists, who are first-generation émigrés or their children, among them, Pazarkaya, Emine Sevgi Özdamar, Zafer Şenocak, Navid Kermani, Feridun Zaimoğlu, Terézia Mora, or Ilija Trojanow, whose connection to the language and culture of home remains relatively undiminished by time. However, in no way does such connection imply a problematic allegiance to home, nation, or roots but rather points to the availability of a more inclusive archive of memory. Even this statement can be contested, as archives are constructs, and memories are shaped by the present rather than the past. Thus, in accord with my above statement about the multiple connections of literature, I cross-reference the work of three selected writers, who are separated by time and place yet share the common destiny of exiles and find the several languages they astonishingly make real to the reader.

Transnational Literature/World Literature(s)

The last few decades have been marked by a growing consciousness of the "transnational turn" in the German literary domain. German

---

[1] Leslie Adelson, "Touching Tales of Turks, Germans, and Jews: Cultural Alterity, Historical Narrative, and Literary Riddles for the 1990s," *New German Critique*, vol. 80 (Spring–Summer 2000): 93–124, here 93.

[2] Yüksel Pazarkaya, "deutsche sprache," in *Der Babylonbus*, vol.7 (Frankfurt am Main: Dag˘yeli Verlag, 1998). My translation.

transnational literature, which appeared in the title of many theses and dissertations and as the topic of graduate and undergraduate seminars, symposia, and conferences, was the product of writers of the first and second generations, who were non-German by birth or heritage. In *Writing Outside the Nation*, I defined this genre as a mode of writing that operates outside the national literary canon, is often composed not in the writer's own language but in that of the host nation, addresses issues of voluntarily or involuntarily displaced subjects, and becomes the expression of many in "'paranational' communities or alliances."[3] In time, I also used the term to include the work of writers who did not necessarily write elsewhere, and wrote in their native language, but whose work, nevertheless, revealed a transcultural and even translingual imagination. Among these, I count Orhan Pamuk, Ahmet Hamdi Tanpınar, Mahmoud Dowlatabati, Nawal el Saadawi, Sten Nadolny, and Robert Menasse. While their works may technically belong to a national literary canon, they also claim a place on the world literary map.

The academic discourse on transnational literature has more recently shifted toward the more global concept of world literature(s), perhaps in tandem with the awareness of living in an increasingly globalized world. While contemporary viewpoints in the debate about membership in world literature are legion and have traveled temporally and geographically far from Goethe's proclamation of the coming age of *Weltliteratur*, they agree on such common premises as replacing the calcified category of literary nationality by trajectory, stressing the importance of temporal mobility and loosening the concept of period, and questioning the problem of beginnings or firsts by seeing the text as already a product of many origins. The era of late liberal modernity has given rise to the question of what counts as world literature, which, with few exceptions and perhaps inadvertently, often omits literary texts produced beyond the borders of the West. I contend that while features and definitions of transnational or world literature are not stable, we can read works of world literary distinction in dialogue across time and space. These works share themes and topics of universal interest, such as human agency and its limitations, language and its constraints, cultural memory and amnesia, or resistance to oppression, but are also situated in the specificity of their history, territory, language, and culture.

In keeping with the above-mentioned catalogue of themes, I analyze how the respective voices of Heinrich Heine (1797–1856), one of Germany's greatest poets, and Nâzım Hikmet (1902–63), arguably the most

---

[3] Azade Seyhan, *Writing Outside the Nation* (Princeton, NJ: Princeton University Press, 2001), 10.

renowned Turkish poet of the twentieth century, are echoed in various modalities in the work of Emine Sevgi Özdamar, a contemporary Turkish-German author, playwright, and actress. While Heine, Hikmet, and Özdamar all belong to the broad category of writer in exile, Özdamar's work is aligned most closely with transnational literature, as defined above. Like many voluntarily or forcibly exiled and/or hyphenated authors of the late twentieth and early twenty-first centuries, such as Pazarkaya, Serbian-American Aleksandar Hemon, Korean-American Chang-Rae-Lee, Romanian-German Carmen-Francesca Banciu, and another Romanian-German, Herta Müller, a Nobel laureate, Özdamar writes primarily in the language of the host land. Her exilic as well as hyphenated writer status differs greatly from Heine's and Hikmet's position as national writers in exile. Both Heine and Hikmet were already well-known poets and virtuosos of German and Turkish, respectively, before being forced into exile. Their renown, identity, and livelihood all rested on their mother tongue, which continued to nourish them in exile. That they did not write in the language of the host country was not a matter of choice or resistance. On the other hand, most hyphenated writers, "writing outside the nation," were not established or well-known in the countries they left. In fact, almost all started writing in the host land and its language after arriving at their destination. Many well-known writers of different lands and eras, such as Victor Hugo, Bertolt Brecht, Pablo Neruda, Stefan Zweig, or Aleksandr Solzhenitsyn, who were forced into exile, continued to write and publish in their native languages, and their works were readily translated in the lands of their exile. In any study of exile literatures and exiled writers, it is important to point out this difference between writers of international reputation, who enjoyed the privilege of having their works translated, and the transnational writer, writing between languages and self-translating.

Heine in and out of Germany

In *Heinrich Heine and the World Literary Map: Redressing the Canon*,[4] I took my cue not only from Adorno in imagining Heine as the iconic poet of what György Lukács had called the "transcendental homelessness" ("transzendetale Heimatlosigkeit") of the modern individual, but also from Willi Goetschel and the Hegelian philosopher Terry Pinkard. In reassessing the critical solidity of Heine's work, in particular, *Zur Geschichte der Religion und Philosophie in Deutschland* (*On the History of Religion and Philosophy in Germany*), Pinkard notes that "there is a serious

---

[4] Azade Seyhan, *Heinrich Heine and the World Literary Map: Redressing the Canon* (Singapore: Palgrave Macmillan, 2019).

thesis at work; indeed, the seriousness of the thesis could perhaps be only made manifest by the ironic wit, with which it is presented."⁵ However, the broader claim of my own reassessment of Heine's work was based on its world literary stature, which is validated by the voices of many thinkers and writers, who reference, translate, and consciously or coincidentally reaffirm his vision of our troubled modernity.

In times of transition and crisis, writers, whose work crosses territorial, temporal, and conceptual borders, foreground the role of literature as both critique and the condition for the possibility of change or correction. In the ongoing trials of modernity, the rumble of revolutions, oppression of "others," or the displacement of masses, the voice of Heinrich Heine, "a brave soldier in the war of human emancipation" (as he often regarded himself), echoes across time and geography. Recent Heine scholarship has repositioned the poet's work beyond his poetic oeuvre to tease out not only its liberatory voice but also Heine's prescience in relation to the foundational ideas of Critical Theory associated with the Frankfurt School thinkers Theodor Adorno and Walter Benjamin. In *Heine and Critical Theory*, Goetschel moves Heine's writing beyond "the canon of philology" and situates it in the history of Critical Theory to highlight "the critical significance of literature as a form of critique that boldly reimagines modernity as the site for literary, social, and political renegotiation of culture and society."⁶ While Goetschel follows in the tradition of many Heine scholars, who maintain that the Jewish experience has been a catalyst in the formation of the modern Jewish intellectual, he greatly enhances this view by illustrating how Heine, as both a poet and a critic, demonstrates that his Jewish difference, rather than becoming a deterrent to modernity, inspired and energized him to imagine modernity with a difference.⁷

A little over a century after his death, in a world traumatized by two world wars and the persecution and displacement of millions of people by their own governments, Heine's fate became a reference for many exiled writers and intellectuals. In Adorno's variously and contradictorily assessed essay, "Die Wunde Heine" ("The wound that is Heine"), the poet becomes the iconic figure of those disowned and displaced by history. Adorno, who was forced into exile after the Nazis took the reins of power, darkly reflects that Heine's stereotypical theme of hopeless

---

5   Terry Pinkard, "Introduction," in Heinrich Heine, *On the History of Religion and Philosophy in Germany and Other Writings*, trans. Howard Pollack-Milgate, ed. Terry Pinkard (Cambridge: Cambridge University Press, 2007), vi–xxxii, here xvi.
6   Willi Goetschel, *Heine and Critical Theory* (London and New York: Bloomsbury Academic, 2019), 22.
7   Goetschel, *Heine* 4.

love is an "allegory" ("Gleichnis") of homelessness. He concludes that after the fate Heine had experienced was literally realized in the present, it has become the homelessness of all, who are damaged in nature and language like the banished poet. There will never be a *Heimat* anymore, except in a truly liberated world of humanity, from which no one will be banished. Only in such a world can the wound that is Heine heal.[8] In a world faced with one of the worst refugee crises since World War II, exacerbated by the worst pandemic since the end of World War I, Heine's wound still bleeds.

However, in different times and places during periods of oppression, tyranny, and defeat, it is not Heine's wound that people remember but rather his words that are conjured for both consolation and confrontation. His oft quoted lines from the play *Almansor*, "where they burn books / they will in the end burn people" ("dort wo man Bücher / Verbrennt, verbrennt man auch am Ende Menschen"),[9] have proven eerily prescient. His long poem *Vitzliputzli* became part of Mexico's fight for identity, as it resisted subjugation to the colonial imperialism of both Europe and the United States. While true to character, Heine sided with the underdog in this poetic rendering of the Conquest of Mexico, he did not romanticize the Aztecs in their confrontation with the Conquistadores, since he did not shy away from revealing the cruelty of Aztec rituals.[10] In implicit agreement with the Mexican Nobel laureate Octavio Paz, who saw Mexico born of a double violence, that of the Aztecs and of the Spaniards, Heine illustrates not merely an anticolonialist sentiment but also depicts a history of barbarity without any transcendent human benevolence. After Spain's defeat in 1898 in the Spanish-American War, which stripped the country of the last vestiges of its imperial status, the Generation of 1898, a group of intellectuals, among them Miguel de Unamuno, one of the great philosophers of the twentieth century, engaged in an intense self-reflection on the destiny of their country. For Unamuno, Heine's philosophical work became a reference for cultural rejuvenation and a model for his own nonsectarian humanism. Unamuno's admiration of Heine was to no small extent based on the poet's philosophical bent of mind, which energized his revolutionary voice and bound it to readers by transforming the power of dialogue with them into rebellious prose.

---

[8] Theodor W. Adorno, "Die Wunde Heine," in *Noten zur Literatur*, vol. I (Frankfurt am Main: Suhrkamp, 1958), 146–54, here 154.

[9] Heinrich Heine, *Almansor*, in *Historisch-kritische Gesamtausgabe der Werke* (DHA), vol. 5, ed. Manfred Windfuhr (Hamburg: Campe, 1973–97), 7–68, here 16.

[10] Heine, "Vitzliputzli," in DHA, vol. 3, 56–75, here 71–5.

Closer to home, the critically savvy first-generation Turkish-German writers like Özdamar and Pazarkaya reference Heine as an inspiration for their work as writers in and of exile. At the same time, Nâzım Hikmet Ran, commonly known as Nâzım Hikmet or Nâzım, may be the single most important muse of Turkish academics, poets, and novelists, writing in various geographies of exile, such as Zafer Şenocak in Berlin, Nedim Gürsel in Paris, and Mutlu Konuk Blasing at Brown University, among many others. Hikmet, who is almost always affiliated with the well-known world writers of varying communist sympathies like Pablo Neruda and Bertolt Brecht, bears a lesser known yet striking family resemblance to Heine. While the conspicuous parallels in the life and work of these two poets go unnoticed in critical literature, the diverse scales of transnational writing offer the conditions for the realization of a dialogue between such exilic voices as those of Heine, Hikmet, Özdamar, Walter Benjamin, or, more distantly, many exiled Iranian writers like Shahriar Mandanipour, thus mapping ways in which these writers deepen our understanding of the power of language against censorship, persecution, and human mortality. If we accept the universal character of literature as multiply and cross- and interculturally referenced, then there is no imperative to establish a direct influence among writers separated by history and geography but united in similar quests. Nevertheless, it behooves the critic to reflect on how the related quests of these writers are shaped by the specificities of their place, time, and value systems.

While many Turkish-German writers, even the auteur filmmaker Fatih Akın, whose 2020 short film, *Exile Poem*, is a reading of Nâzım Hikmet's "The Most Beautiful Sea" ("En güzel deniz"), often draw on Hikmet's poetic legacy and find aesthetic and political inspiration in the work of Heine and Hikmet, they do not necessarily draw parallels between the two poets. However, the crossed destinies of Heine and Hikmet become visible in the palimpsestic textures of Turkish-German literature and art. In other words, writers and artists of Turkish heritage in Germany do not necessarily read Hikmet against the legacy of Heine or Schiller but by drawing on the inheritance from both Turkish and German cultures, their own works become a catalyst for a deeper understanding not only of the multiply connected nature of literature as a verbal medium, but also of poetics as an intermedial form. In the following, I trail the trajectory of the respective lives and works of Heine and Hikmet and show how the legacy of each poet is explicitly and implicitly cross-referenced in Özdamar's work. I do not attempt to retrofit either Hikmet or Özdamar into a Heinean mold but rather seek to show how the bi- and multilingual 'non-German' writers of German, whose works are still not read as part of the German literary canon, foreground the world literary stature of exemplary writers of their two or more languages and cultures.

From a critical interpretive viewpoint, Heine's *Deutschland, ein Wintermärchen* (*Germany, a Winter Tale*) and Hikmet's *Memleketimden İnsan Manzaraları* (*Human Landscapes from my Country*) speak to citizens and inhabitants of all lands, who face political repression, the wounds of war, and displacement, irrespective of language, culture, or creed. Since Özdamar's bilingually titled *Karagöz in Alamania / Schwarzauge in Deutschland* (*Blackeye in Germany*), a tragicomic dramatic story about persecution and migration, coincidentally mimics Heine's satirical epic *Atta Troll. Ein Sommernachtstraum* (*Atta Troll, a Midsummer Night's Dream*), I intend to illustrate, not in the abstract notion of "touching tales" but in more concrete terms her mediating position between German and Turkish literary traditions. Not only Özdamar's work, but that of many other modern writers, such as Milan Kundera, Carlos Cerda, or more recently, Aslı Erdoğan—a Turkish author and physicist in German exile since June 2017—who were forced into exile because of war, censorship, and persecution, bears an uncanny resemblance to Heine's. Through mocking accounts of injustice and oppression in their own countries, they continue the time-honored literary practice of resisting oppression with barbs.

The Legacy of Two Poets beyond Borders

While best known for his poetry and voluminous poetic output, Nâzım Hikmet, who died in Russian exile in 1963 at the age of sixty-one, was also the author of novels, translations, short stories, children's books, and plays. Although his works have been translated into more than fifty languages, none were published in Turkey during his lifetime. More than half of his life was spent in prison and forced exile, separated from family, home, only child, and beloved mother tongue. Like his mother, he was also a gifted painter and became a master weaver in prison, supporting his family through this craft and translations. Despite persecution, imprisonment, and torture, all heaped upon his ailing body because of the implied communist sympathies in his poetry, his voice remained strong and defiant, thwarting and almost mocking those who tried to silence him. Like Heine, he used the language from which he was exiled, in multiple poetic forms, to register loss and nostalgia but also the power of art to battle injustice and human suffering. The sorrow of missing his beloved Turkish in print grieved him endlessly and became a tragic marker of his exile. Heine, too, suffered from not reaching his German readers directly and yearned for the comforting intimacy of German in his French exile. Both poets carried with them the only treasure they could smuggle out of their respective countries: an archive of world cultural goods stored in their minds. Hikmet's poetry is not so much about privation suffered in his own land as it is about people, famous or nameless, oppressed and persecuted by their rulers.

He writes an ode to an unknown fallen soldier in the Spanish Civil War, memorializes the tears of a refugee mother, or sheds tears for Nicola Sacco and Bartolomeo Vanzetti, two Italian immigrant workers, who were wrongfully executed in 1927 on suspicion of murdering a guard and a paymaster during an armed robbery of a shoe factory in Massachusetts. As anti-Italian and anti-immigrant sentiment seemed to play a role in their unjust conviction, they became actors in one of the greatest *causes célèbres* in modern history. Hikmet calls them "these two sergeants of the revolution" ("bu iki ihtilâl neferi"), who were not murderers but victims of murder and sacrificed to the "justice in the service of the dollar" ("doların emrindeki adalet").[11]

While Hikmet may not be considered one of the greats of the world literary pantheon, his work attests to an imaginative gaze that moved on the world map from real to imaginary cities, from stations of rest to those of unrest, from homelands forsaken to safe harbors yet uncharted. He commanded a liberating poetic imagination that traversed the world geographically and historically. Not only in creative imagination, but also in real life during his exile in Moscow, he traveled widely as a member of the administrative board of the World Peace Council. After thirteen years in prison, he was restless and eager to move constantly during his years in exile. His travels took him through several stations and cities in Europe and beyond, from Moscow to Berlin, Rome, Paris, Havana, Peking, and Tanganyika, all the while stripped of his Turkish citizenship. Though a multilingual and prolific translator, he saw himself first and foremost as a poet of Turkish, and his creative work, like that of Heine, was almost exclusively in his beloved mother tongue. Unlike Heine, however, Hikmet composed in a language not widely known or spoken, yet despite that hindrance his poetry spoke directly to the "transcendental homelessness" of the exiled. In the words of his prominent translator Mutlu Konuk Blasing,

> [. . .] the precariousness of the present in his exploding temporal and spatial world may also be understood in terms of the tension between nationalist, internationalist, and global models of modernism. While folk forms often voiced the wanderings of displaced, troubadour poets, their forms, for Nâzım and his Turkish readers, would carry a sense of "home"—a local, native poetic ground. But his run-on free forms speed through global

---

[11] Nâzım Hikmet, "Sakko ile Vanzetti" ("Sacco and Vanzetti"), in *Bütün Sˌiirleri* (Istanbul: Yapı Kredi Yayınları [YKY], 2007), 2077–8, here 2078.

spaces and times and project a different kind of homelessness, on a different scale.[12]

For both Heine and Hikmet, homelessness is registered in the wear and tear of the physical and the corporeal, be these the body, shirts, or shoes, which have sustained memories of a home that is fast fading into oblivion. In the first stanza of "Sterbende" from *Romanzero*, his third volume of poems, Heine writes, "You flew toward sun and happiness / You came back naked and forlorn / German loyalty, German shirts / Are worn out in foreign lands" ("Flogest aus nach Sonn' und Glück / Nackt und schlecht kommst du zurück / Deutsche Treue, deutsche Hemde / Die verschleißt man in der Fremde").[13] Likewise, in "My Country," Hikmet laments that the last shirt from his country on his back is in tatters, and now all that remains from the homeland "is in the gray of my hair / in the infarct of my heart / in the wrinkles of my face."[14]

Perhaps the most suitable medium for political engagement in Heine's and Hikmet's works happened to be the epic poem, which both employed as a kind of poetic historiography. Heine considered *Deutschland. Ein Wintermärchen*, an epic of 54,000 lines, the longest poem ever written. Hikmet's epic novel in *Human Landscapes from my Country* reaches the finish line at 17,000. There is no evidence that Hikmet had read *Deutschland*, but, as a devoted reader of other poets and a frequent visitor to East Berlin, it is quite likely that he was familiar with Heine. In any case, I take the liberty of imagining *Human Landscapes* not as a fantastic commentary on Heine's epic poem but as an expanded version of its ideas and concerns, poetically resituated in the context of a different time and place.

Deutschland represents the pinnacle of political poetry of the *Vormärz* before the March Revolution of 1848. Following the Napoleonic Wars, the old European order was restored at the Congress of Vienna under the leadership of the Austrian Chancellor Prince Klemens von Metternich. He returned all the German princes to their thrones and ushered in a winter of censorship, repression, and persecution, erasing the dream of a free and democratic Germany from the realm of possibility. Heine left Germany shortly after the July Revolution of 1830 in France,

---

[12] Mutlu Konuk Blasing, "Nâzım Hikmet: The Forms of Exile," in *A Chapbook of 2nd Annual Nâzım Hikmet Poetry Festival* (Cary, NC: Page Walker Art and History Center, 2010) 11–20, here 14.
[13] Heine, "Sterbende," in the Lazarus cycle of poems in *Romanzero* in DHA vol. 3/1, 105–22, here 108. My translation.
[14] Hikmet, "Yine Memleketim Üstüne Söylenmiştir" ("Again on My Country"), in *Bütün Şiirleri*, 1639. My translation.

which heralded for him the possibility of intellectual liberty. After a thirteen-year absence, he returned in "the sad month of November" ("im traurigen Monath November")¹⁵ to Germany to see his beloved aging mother and to visit his publisher Campe. However, this trip rather than acting as a balm for his homesickness intensified his sorrow for a lost homeland held in Metternich's dark and wintry grip. The versified epic, which has become part of the official educational curriculum in Germany and alternately assumes the form of a travelogue, a song of lament, a political satire, encounters with real and mythic figures, and a magical history tour, takes the poet through sites and cities associated in the poet's mind with specific aspects of a socially and morally stagnant Germany. The epic was published in 1844, and before the year was out, the book was banned in Prussia. In December 1844, King Friedrich Wilhelm IV of Prussia issued a warrant for Heine's arrest.

In an age of massive displacements of human populations and acts of violence born of nationalist sentiments, this verse-epic exerts a great deal of attraction for the "outsider," as it raises a wider concern with nationalism and narrow concepts of German identity. Perhaps in the most profound sense, it resounds with the sorrows of the exiled. The poet's melancholy persona, by keeping the personal so close to the poetic membrane, pulls the reader into an intimate understanding of the vicissitudes of persecution, displacement, exile, and the loss or impoverishment of once sustaining myths. The recurring apostrophic references in dreams to iconic or historical figures, such as an anthropomorphized father Rhine, Barbarossa slumbering in a cave in Thuringia, or Harmonia, the guardian goddess of Hamburg, endow these with an uncanny sense of being present, thus often overpowering the poet's ubiquitous satirical voice.

Like *Deutschland*, Hikmet's *Human Landscapes* is voiced by a myriad of characters, victimized by wars and war profiteers, forced exile, and constant migrations. This epic, or what Hikmet referred to as a novel composed of poetry and prose, unfolds both elliptically and sequentially on a vast field of intersections of the life of the imprisoned poet and the contemporary Turkish and European histories. Just as in *Wintermärchen*, Heine's characters are composite figures, so in *Human Landscapes*, while war and exile are the central themes of the epic, "the composite warrior [is] its hero."¹⁶ In *Französische Zustände* (*Conditions in*

---

¹⁵ Heine, *Deutschland. Ein Wintermärchen*, in DHA, vol. 4, 89–157, here 91.
¹⁶ Konuk Blasing, "Introduction," in Nâzım Hikmet, *Human Landscapes from my Country*, trans. Randy Blasing and Mutlu Konuk (New York: Persea Books, 2002), ix–xv, here xi.

France), Heine also emphasizes that the age in which the acts of the individual, a ruler, a warrior, or a savior shone is now over. People, parties, and masses are the composite heroes of the modern age.[17] In *Human Landscapes*, myriad stories about real or invented characters from all walks of life during ongoing wars are rendered in dialogue, thereby offering the reader a landscape in narrative "technicolor." The conversations take place between real historical persons or composites of real characters. The rarely interrupted dialogue format, similar to that of *Wintermärchen*, imagines the reader as a spectator of a dramatic play. In both epics, every event condenses many others and subjects them to a timed release, as the stories migrate through history.

A Turkish Scheherazade goes West

Özdamar, writer, playwright, stage actress and director, came of age in the 1960s in Turkey amidst the turmoil of a post-military coup, on and off military rule, persecution of leftist individuals, and the increasingly visible rift between secular and sectarian groups. At the same time, due to a relaxation of censorship, the book market was quickly filled with translations of Karl Marx, Friedrich Engels, Karl Liebknecht, Antonio Gramsci, Herbert Marcuse, Pablo Neruda, and Bertolt Brecht. Hikmet's poetry was also finally published at this time in his own country. Özdamar, schooled in this philosophical and literary tradition, naturally sympathized with the revolutionary ideals of her activist friends and, along with them, often faced police harassment. Her testimonies of the tortures her compatriots had faced in Turkish prisons are written with the passion and pathos characteristic of Hikmet's prison poems but lack his faith in human transcendence in the face of suffering and incarceration, as the last lines of his much-quoted poem "Angina Pectoris" show: "I look at the night through the bars, / and despite the weight on my chest / my heart still beats with the most distant stars."[18] Her self-avowedly favorite novel, *Das Leben ist eine Karawanserei* (*Life is a Caravansary*), is like Hikmet's *Human Landscapes* a saga of an era, the decade 1950–60, Turkey's first failed experiment with democracy, as told through the lives of the working classes. Although this semi-autobiographical novel reflects a distinctly Turkish perspective, Özdamar reveals a keen knowledge of German literary history in the next two novels of the trilogy: *Die Brücke vom Goldenen Horn* (*The Bridge on the Golden Horn*) and *Seltsame Sterne starren zur Erde* (*Strange Stars stare at the Earth*). While her works are informed by an autobiographical

---

[17] Heine, *Französische Zustände*, in DHA, vol. 12/1, 63–226, here 185.
[18] Nâzım Hikmet, *Selected Poetry*, trans. Randy Blasing and Mutlu Konuk (New York: Persea Books, 1986), 101.

tenor, they also focus, in seriously reflective and cunningly satirical ways, on themes of nation, exile, history, and myth.

Although Özdamar initially came to Germany as a guest worker, her aspiration was to become an actress. Trained at the Berliner Ensemble and later at the Comédie Française in Paris, Özdamar has proven to be an astute student of theater and is likely familiar with Heine's and Hikmet's lesser-known plays. In addition to her work on the stage, she had prominent roles in German films, including *Yasemin* (1988) by Hark Bohm and *Happy Birthday Türke* (1992) by Dorris Dörrie. However, she ended up being one of the most highly regarded exile writers in Germany. Her acting experience translated well into writing for the stage. Before *Das Leben*, which earned her the 1991 Ingeborg Bachmann Prize, given for the first time to a writer of non-German birth and heritage, writing in German, Özdamar published four short stories in a collection entitled *Mutterzunge* (*Mother Tongue*). These pieces display such an ingenious use of dialogue that each could easily have been translated into a play. In fact, Özdamar based *Karagöz in Alamania/Schwarzauge in Deutschland* on a play she had written and staged in 1986 at the Schauspielhaus Frankfurt. As in *Human Landscapes* and *Deutschland*, dialogue, conversation, and various speech acts form the motor of the text and become a mode of transportation in the metaphorical representation of escape and exile. However, more than either of those epics, *Karagöz* treads the same fantastical path as Heine's other epic poem *Atta Troll*. In *Karagöz*, Özdamar also tells an epic story of displacement, exile, and memory, where Hikmet's human landscapes are etched on Turkish and German backgrounds and peopled with Heine's harlequins and scoundrels.

Heine considered *Atta Troll* an unfinished work and a farewell to his time as a Romantic manqué. It takes more liberties with historical, mythical, and invented characters than *Deutschland* does. The story is about the narrator's trip to the Pyrenean town of Cauterets, where a dancing bear by the name of Atta Troll escapes from the bear master and goes home to his children and addresses them in a series of political emancipatory speeches. A hunt for the bear at large begins, and the animal is lured into a trap by the witch Uraka and killed by her son Laskaro. The final form the heroic bear takes on is a bearskin rug in the Paris apartment of the poet-narrator's love interest Juliette. Laskaro's motive for killing the bear remains unclear, for he is neither the bear owner nor a bear hunter by trade. However, after killing the bear he is honored for freeing France and Spain from this political provocateur. The mother and son—the narrator believes that the son may actually be a dead man—materialize out of nowhere like two evil characters from central casting. The bear seems to represent both tendentious poetry, Heine's pet peeve, and the noble hero, who dies but is immortalized in the poet's song.

Upon the "martyrdom" of the bear, the narrator drops the bear's story, and his journey takes him through real and invented "human landscapes" and histories and myths. It is the wild hunt on St. John's Eve that sets the stage for the unearthly encounter of long-gone poets like Goethe and Shakespeare and mythical figures like the Roman goddess of the hunt, Diana, the fairy Abunde, and the Jewess Herodias. The hunters of the celebratory wild hunt are from different zones and different times; next to Nimrod of Assyria rides Karl X. Goethe, who in life was damned by the theologian Hengstenberg and could, therefore, not rest in his grave, joins in the pleasure of the hunt. Next to Shakespeare rides Franz Horn, a German literary critic and Shakespeare scholar, who in life interpreted the Bard, but must now ride on a donkey at his side in the tumult of the wild hunt. But when Shakespeare gallops, he looks scornfully at the poor critic, who follows at the donkey's pace. Of course, this sarcastic arrow is aimed at all academic pedants, who are parasites living off the host, the poet and the artist.

Özdamar's *Karagöz* is similarly a tale of travel through real and imaginary events, and its "real-life" protagonist, the poor farmer, is a modern-day representation of the main character in the popular Ottoman shadow play of the same name, based on the mythical figures of Karagöz and Hacivat. According to legend, they were two construction workers on a mosque in Bursa, sometime in the fourteenth century. Their silly pranks amused the other workers so much that the construction was slowed down, which angered the Sultan, who had them executed. Their martyrdom became cause for their immortalization as the prankster puppets that to this day entertain Turkish audiences. Özdamar's portrayal of Karagöz, the farmer, is closer to this version of the legend than others, since the farmer is a tragic figure who is forced to emigrate to Germany as a "guest worker" ("Gastarbeiter") to pay his debt to a landlord. Özdamar learned about the real-life farmer from a letter she found on a train that transported guest workers. When she looked for him to invite him to the premiere of her play, she found out that he had passed away. The political undercurrent of the story is hard to miss, since Karagöz's father negotiated with the landlord to give him his son as an indentured servant to pay for the few apples Karagöz had stolen from the landlord's orchard. Then a usurer comes by and suggests that the father send his son to Germany, where 1 Mark (German currency) equals 25 Lira (Turkish currency), thus, one son will be worth twenty-five sons, and twenty-five sons worth twenty-five fields. The lender pays the father the travel money for his son in return for the poor father's only piece of land. And Karagöz gets on the road with his Camel-smoking, Marx-quoting donkey.

There is a further political motivation in the choice of the shadow play theme. Karagöz puppet theater played an important role as a medium of political resistance during the Ottoman reign. Since the play was not written, it was improvised by the puppeteers, who could easily ridicule the rulers or the palace for their crimes and misdemeanors. This popular street show was a staple during the month of Ramadan, when people usually spent the night hours after breaking fast on the street. The cast of characters in any given play was drawn from the multiple religious and ethnic groups populating the empire—Christians, Jews, Greeks, Armenians, Albanians, Arabs, and Laz, among others—and the puppeteer had to speak in the various colorful accents of these characters. His puppetry was a censor-defying performance, since what was said could neither be recorded, nor attributed to the puppeteer. Furthermore, the play thrived on hilarious double entendres, which Özdamar's characters also employ. In the shadow play, Hacivat is an educated, suave, urban type, who speaks high Ottoman. Karagöz is the less educated, coarse, streetwise smart aleck, who continuously subverts or purposefully mishears Hacivat's speech. Özdamar's choice to portray the donkey as a pretentious intellectual Hacivat-type outdoes even the satirical edge of the original shadow play.

While Özdamar's orientation to the German theatrical archive figures prominently in German and American scholarship, the presence of Turkish and Middle Eastern forms of non-traditional theater in her dramatic work has gone largely unnoticed. It is perhaps worth observing that Özdamar's choice of using a shadow play could have been motivated by Brecht's use of East Asian, particularly Chinese, dramatic forms, which were instrumental in the development of his technique of *gestus*. Just as the Brechtian actor relies on a canon of gestures that captures particular moments or attitudes rather than emotions, the puppets of the shadow play, handled by the puppeteer, do not and cannot emote but represent an outlook, manner, or a position. Shadow puppetry, which originated in the Han dynasty (206 BCE–220 CE) but continued to grow in popularity in China (in the Song and Ming dynasties), eventually arrived in Persia and the Ottoman Empire. Brecht drew on many and eclectic performance forms in the service of his epic theater. Not only Brecht's interest in shadow theater but also his political stance is reflected in the Berliner Ensemble-trained Özdamar's choice of using a major figure of the Ottoman Turkish shadow play as the protagonist of *Karagöz in Alamania*.

Although Özdamar's story displays the sharp political edges of Brecht's theater, her use of satire and parody is more Heinesque than Brechtian. As in the shadow play, Özdamar's motley crew speaks in different tongues, switching and transferring codes:

> Then the translator came [. . .] Spoke to the boss. You can't get child credit or such. None. No residency permit either. Immigration

police isn't giving it. The housing office also says no. The employment office isn't giving permission, either.

[Sonra Dolmetscher geldi. Meisterle konuştu [...] Kindergeld falan alamazsın. Yok. Aufenthalt da yok. Fremdpolizei vermiyor. Wohnungsamt da yok diyor. Arbeitsamt da Erlaubnis vermedi.][19]

The object of Özdamar's relentless parody is capitalism's ruthless exploitation of human labor and resources. The indentured laborers are not only alienated from their work in the Marxist sense, but also from their origins, languages, and families. The dramatic story or story as drama proceeds to the tempo of an eerie tango between various borders. Through this simultaneously macabre and humorous choreography, Özdamar shows how regimes of power can be rattled in linguistic space by disrupting dominant idioms.

While the bleak circumstances of Karagöz's troubled journey are reminiscent of *Deutschland*'s increasingly gloomy itinerary, the non sequitur incidents of the dramatic story are right out of the *Atta Troll* playbook. In a series of ten scenes and twenty-seven cantos, respectively, *Karagöz in Alamania* and *Atta Troll* move between borders and landscapes, encounter real or imagined characters, and fantastic and actual events. Every event is charged on several levels, chasing the next episode, moving at varying speeds, and affects are displaced, catapulting in all directions. These events don't conform to a structure; rather, they form a mode of movement. The farmer and his donkey shuttle back and forth between Turkish and German borders; they are later joined by the farmer's wife and his growing brood. On the endless back-and-forth trips, they encounter a motley of characters, among them, a lion, drinking rakı (a popular Turkish alcoholic drink); testy border officials; a *Gastarbeiter*, impersonating a Fenerbahçe (a famous Turkish soccer team) footballer; a Mabuse-like treasure hunter; and animated Rekord and Caravan models of the Opel car brand. Finally, when Karagöz returns home after many years as a guest worker, he encounters his doppelgänger (double), an image of his young self, on the apple tree. The donkey has to be called in as witness to determine who the real Karagöz is.

The donkey is eerily reminiscent of the bear Atta Troll. These two anthropomorphized animals are also highly politicized figures. While Atta Troll breaks his chains from the master and flees home to lecture his children about emancipation, the donkey tells his owner that he is in

---

[19] Emine Sevgi Özdamar, *Karagöz in Alamania / Schwarzauge in Deutschland*, in *Mutterzunge* (Berlin: Rotbuch, 1990), 47–101, here 75. My translation.

the left movement: "Ich stehe in linker Bewegung."[20] Donkeys are animals of labor in the Turkish hinterland, but since our Karagöz's donkey is unemployed in exile, he becomes an ardent reader of Marx and lectures his master and other workers on Marxist thought. In one Heinesque scene, he comforts Karagöz with Marx's words: "In effect, the realm of freedom begins, only where work that is determined by need and expediency, ends" ("Das Reich der Freiheit beginnt in der Tat erst da, wo das Arbeiten, das durch Not und äußere Zweckmäßigkeit bestimmt ist, aufhört").[21] In *Karagöz*, as in *Atta Troll*, pedantic academics are ridiculed. "The Enlightened One" ("Der Erleuchtete"), who has situated himself at the German border, sits in a bathtub with his typewriter and interviews Turks leaving Germany. This character, though not given a name, is an allusion to the Jacobin leader Jean-Paul Marat, a scientist and radical defender of the sans-culottes, who was one of the important figures of the French Revolution. Because of a skin disease, he is known to have spent many hours in the bathtub, where he was stabbed to death by Charlotte Corday, a royalist sympathizer. In *Karagöz*, this Marat-like character is knocked down by a karate blow from an eighteen-year-old Turkish youth, who is separated from his legal resident parents and kicked out of Germany, since he is no longer a dependent child. The knocked-down intellectual pleads for compassion for the Turkish workers suffering from culture shock and begins a long soliloquy about the discontents of cultural identity.

While Heine was never regarded as a model of compassion due to his sharp tongue, in Canto XV of *Atta Troll*, there is a scene which speaks volumes about the condition of millions of persecuted others today. Although Adorno had presciently seen the significance of Heine's "wound" for today's exiled and homeless peoples, I am not aware of any critical commentary on Heine's lament for the persecution suffered by the Cagots, an unjustly condemned minority in the Basque country. Although of Christian faith, they are only allowed to sneak into the church through a small lattice door, because every entrance is closed to them, as they are considered polluted. The narrator calls this hatred that still festers in the hearts of the Basques, a gloomy legacy from a gloomy age of belief. He visits a Cagot's home, calls the father his brother, and kisses his child.[22] The narrator's show of affection for the "outsider" is unambiguously expressed without any false sentiment and testifies to Heine's empathy for those excluded from the social order. This is a rare moment, where Heine's ubiquitous irony stops,

---

[20] Özdamar, *Karagöz in Alamania*, 70.
[21] Özdamar, *Karagöz in Alamania*, 80. My translation.
[22] Heine, *Atta Troll*, in DHA, vol. 4, 7–87, here 47.

rendering more directly and piercingly his criticism of social and political inequity.

Özdamar, on the other hand, never lowers the satirical tone through a different use of language. In the story, as in the play, double entendres and the frequent use of "talking over the other's head" ("Aneinandervorbeireden"), typical of the Karagöz shadow play, take aim at every exploitative aspect of labor migration. While both *Atta Troll* and *Karagöz*, from time to time, engage in complex maneuvers of storytelling, *Karagöz*, as it is so strongly dialogic, shows how dramatic language that bursts at the seams can challenge regimes of power. In the Ottoman shadow play, the characters speak with different yet recognizable ethnic accents. In Özdamar's story of the farmer and the donkey, the guest workers mix broken or high German with Anatolian dialects and standard Istanbul Turkish, thus registering a polyphony of voices on different social planes, which cannot be subsumed by a single authorial voice. The plurality of languages in the traditional Karagöz shadow play and in Özdamar's *Karagöz* consciously oppose the literary language. In Mikhail Bakhtin's view, such a heteroglossia, where the outward (centrifugal) and inward (centripetal) moving forces of a language collide, resists the controlling power of linguistic systems by parody and polemical aim at official languages of its time; thus, heteroglossia itself becomes "dialogized."[23]. By drawing on a selective archive of two or more languages and cultures, Özdamar integrates the political tenor of Heine and Brecht and the compassionate politics of Nâzım Hikmet that embraced the downtrodden of the world.

Since definitions of transnational literature or new world literature shift as I write, it is crucial for the reader to look at a work of art, literature, or culture with an awareness of their multiple references and sources. Distant reading, a current sophisticated buzzword for a world literary act of reading, or the old-fashioned notion of close reading are mere words if we cannot see the wood for the trees. The works of exiled writers, writers between languages and cultures, who are both in and out of national habitats, dare to separate literary and cultural currents and memories from entrenched sources of belonging and synthesize them as new forms of cognition and recognition. While no totalizing nomenclature will do justice to such writers and artists or the literature and art they create, we can be sure of one thing. They do not suffer from an anxiety of influence but rather create a confluence of influences, which reciprocally reflect and illuminate each other across time and borders.

---

[23] M. M. Bakhtin, *The Dialogic Imagination*, trans. Caryl Emerson and Michael Holquist, ed. Michael Holquist (Austin: University of Texas Press, 1981), 273.

Works Cited

Adelson, Leslie. "Touching Tales of Turks, Germans, and Jews: Cultural Alterity, Historical Narrative, and Literary Riddles for the 1990s," *New German Critique*, vol. 80 (Spring–Summer 2000): 93–124.

Adorno, Theodor W. "Die Wunde Heine," in *Noten zur Literatur*, vol. I (Frankfurt am Main: Suhrkamp, 1958), 146–54.

Akın, Fatih. *Exile Poem* (film), dir. Fatih Akın (USA: Strand Releasing, 2020).

Bakhtin, M. M. *The Dialogic Imagination*, trans. Caryl Emerson and Michael Holquist, ed. Michael Holquist (Austin: University of Texas Press, 1981).

Goetschel, Willi. *Heine and Critical Theory* (London and New York: Bloomsbury Academic, 2019).

Heine, Heinrich. *Historisch-kritische Gesamtausgabe der Werke* (Düsseldorfer Ausgabe, DHA), ed. Manfred Windfuhr (Hamburg: Campe, 1973–97).

Heine, Heinrich. *On the History of Religion and Philosophy in Germany and Other Writings*, trans. Howard Pollack-Milgate, ed. Terry Pinkard (Cambridge: Cambridge University Press, 2007).

Hikmet, Nâzım. "Yine Memleketim Üstüne Söylenmiştir" (Again on My Country), in *Bütün Şiirleri*, 1639.

Hikmet, Nâzım. *Selected Poetry*, trans. Randy Blasing and Mutlu Konuk (New York: Persea Books, 1986).

Hikmet, Nâzım. *Human Landscapes from my Country*, trans. Randy Blasing and Mutlu Konuk (New York: Persea Books, 2002).

Hikmet, Nâzım. "Sakko ile Vanzetti" (Sacco and Vanzetti), in *Bütün Şiirleri* (Complete Poems) (Istanbul: Yapı Kredi Yayınları [YKY], 2007), 2077–8.

Konuk Blasing, Mutlu. "Introduction," in Nâzım Hikmet, *Human Landscapes from my Country* (New York: Persea Books, 2002), ix–xv.

Konuk Blasing, Mutlu. "Nâzım Hikmet: The Forms of Exile," in *A Chapbook of 2nd Annual Nâzım Hikmet Poetry Festival* (Cary, NC: Page Walker Art and History Center, 2010), 11–20.

Özdamar, Emine Sevgi. *Karagöz in Alamania/Schwarzauge in Deutschland*, in *Mutterzunge* (Berlin: Rotbuch, 1990), 47–101.

Özdamar, Emine Sevgi. *Die Brücke vom Goldenen Horn* (Cologne: Kiepenheuer & Witsch, 1998).

Özdamar, Emine Sevgi. *Das Leben ist eine Karawanswerei—hat zwei Türen—Aus einer kam ich rein—aus der anderen ging ich raus. Roman* (Cologne: Kiepenheuer & Witsch, 2002).

Özdamar, Emine Sevgi. *Seltsame Sterne starren zur Erde* (Cologne: Kiepenheuer & Witsch, 2003).

Pazarkaya, Yüksel. "deutsche sprache," in *Der Babylonbus*, vol. 7 (Frankfurt am Main: Dağyeli Verlag, 1998), 7.

Pinkard, Terry. "Introduction," in Heinrich Heine, *On the History of Religion and Philosophy in Germany and other Writings*, trans. Howard Pollack-Milgate, ed. Terry Pinkard (Cambridge: Cambridge University Press, 2007), vi–xxxii.

Seyhan, Azade. *Writing Outside the Nation* (Princeton, NJ: Princeton University Press, 2001).

Seyhan, Azade. *Heinrich Heine and the World Literary Map: Redressing the Canon* (Singapore: Palgrave Macmillan, 2019).

Six Between Times and Places: Mobility and National Identity in Albert Vigoleis Thelen's Refugee Memoirs from Spain and Portugal (August 31– September 1, 1939)

Carl Niekerk

Albert Vigoleis Thelen (1903, Süchteln am Niederrhein–1989, Dülken am Niederrhein) is one of those literary figures who is hard to categorize and who, in general, is left out of histories of German literature. Thomas Mann, with whom Thelen corresponded, was under the impression that he was a Dutch author.[1] Thelen was born in Süchteln, close to the Dutch–German border, but on the German side. After dropping out of high school (*Gymnasium*), he initially trained to become a locksmith, worked as a technical draftsman, and attended a *Textilfachschule* before enrolling at the University of Cologne as a student of German, philosophy, and art history (1925–31). In 1931, Thelen spent six months in the Netherlands. From 1931 to 1936 he and his fiancée and, later, wife, Beatrice Bruckner, lived on Mallorca. From 1936 to 1939 they lived in Auressio, close to Locarno, Switzerland, from where, on August 29, 1939, they left for Portugal. In Portugal, Thelen worked as a private secretary for the poet and count Teixeira de Pascoaes (1877–1952), and he and Beatrice stayed there until 1947, at which point they

---

[1] See Léon Hanssen, "'Bald kann Menno seine Reise nach Europa antreten'— Albert Vigoleis Thelen en Menno ter Braak," in *Albert Vigoleis Thelen*, ed. Jattie Enklaar and Hans Ester (Amsterdam: Rodopi, 1988), 20–39, here 37, n. 26 (in his diaries Mann refers repeatedly to Thelen as a Dutch author).

returned to the Netherlands. Focusing on this part of Thelen's biography, his early years, it is no exaggeration to say that exile dominated his and his wife's lives. Vigoleis was a staunch opponent of Nazism, which is why he and Beatrice left Germany for the Netherlands and Mallorca relatively early (neither of them was Jewish, nor did they have political reasons to leave Germany). His flight from Mallorca, in 1936, was triggered by the beginnings of the Spanish Civil War (which led the authorities to force foreigners to leave the island). The Thelens left Switzerland in 1939 because they did not feel safe there, and their decision to leave Portugal, in 1947, is linked to the increasingly autocratic actions of its dictator, António de Oliveira Salazar (1889–1970).

Most of Thelen's texts are autobiographical, and they are situated in what could be called—borrowing a term from postcolonial studies—contact zones or border areas. Thelen's first and most successful novel, *Die Insel des zweiten Gesichts* (*The Island of Second Sight*, 1953), is based on his and Beatrice's life on Mallorca between 1931 and 1936. Mallorca, at the time, was a place in between many places. It was a destination for German(-Jewish) refugees, but also home to a sizeable Nazi presence. It was popular among tourists from Germany and Austria as well as a favorite destination for travelers from England. And writers and intellectuals from all over Europe spent time on Mallorca. The novel shows how the histories, life stories, and identities of these people clash, but also are constantly negotiated and renegotiated. Mallorca may in fact have been one of the few places in the mid-1930s where something resembling a dialogue between opponents and defenders of Hitler's Germany was still possible. Mallorca is a world in which mobility is the rule, not the exception. It allows us to study the many different shapes mobility can take on (and the novel does not downplay the rather dire conditions in which some exiles lived). The novel documents a sense of Germanness that is interrogated and constantly questioned, but also perpetually reconstituted. An important insight the novel offers is that one's identity is always, at least in part, shaped by the outside world—it depends on how one is perceived by others. At times these perceptions can be completely wrong. For example, the narrator's partner, Beatrice Bruckner, is of Swiss and native South American descent, but is frequently perceived as Jewish. In contradiction to such assigned identities, the narrator situates himself as a translator and cultural mediator, holding on to transculturation as a dynamic process—to the idea that a dialogue between people is possible.[2]

---

[2] See my essay "Literatures of the Contact Zone: Hans Keilson, Nico Rost, Albert Vigoleis Thelen, and the Literary Spaces of the Late 1940s and Early 1950s," in *On Margins and Contact Zones: 500 Years of Dutch-German Cultural Interaction*, ed. Carl Niekerk and Simon Richter, *Journal of Dutch Literature*, special issue, vol. 9, no. 1 (2018): 112–27, esp. 117–22.

Thelen's second novel, *Der schwarze Herr Bahßetup* (*Black Mr. Bahssetup*, 1956), is situated in Amsterdam and The Hague in 1951 and narrates the events surrounding the visit of a Brazilian law professor on a (somewhat unclear) diplomatic mission in the Netherlands. This professor, José Alvaro da Silva Ponto, based on a real person (Manuel Francisco Pinto Pereira, 1889–1956), for whom Thelen indeed worked, is Black—something many of his Dutch interlocutors did not expect. Their attitudes mirror that of a society that sees itself as progressive, open-minded, and tolerant, and yet, or precisely for that reason, is entirely unprepared to understand difference when confronted with it (a phenomenon that the Dutch Afro-Surinamese anthropologist Gloria Wekker has termed "white innocence").[3] At least in part, this can be explained by the fact that the Netherlands of the early 1950s was still a very homogeneous society, preoccupied with the loss of its most important colony, Indonesia (a loss it perceived as unfair), and with the aftermath of World War II (the idea of victimhood in this conflict was important to Dutch national identity). In *Der schwarze Herr Bahßetup*, identity is also something that is largely, although not exclusively, determined by the outside world. For the narrator, Vigoleis, his friendship with da Silva Ponto is a kind of learning experience.

In the following, however, I am interested in one of Thelen's other and little-known autobiographical projects, on which he presumably worked in the 1970s and 1980s—a project that remained unfinished and of which only fragments have been published.[4] For this project too, Thelen chose a transitional setting: at the beginning of the series of fragments, we find Beatrice and Vigoleis traveling through Spain in the hope of reaching Portugal, where the poet and mystic Teixeira de Pascoaes has invited Vigoleis to work as his private secretary (and where Vigoleis and Beatrice will indeed live through 1947). The temporal

---

[3] Gloria Wekker, *White Innocence: Paradoxes of Colonialism and Race* (Durham, NC: Duke University Press, 2016). I analyze Thelen's novel with Wekker's framework in my essay "Toleranz, Kolonialismus und die 'Unschuld der Weißen'. Zur Triangulierung der interkulturellen Kommunikation in *Der schwarze Herr Bahßetup*," in *Albert Vigoleis Thelen—ein moderner Tragelaph. Perspektiven auf ein vielgestaltiges Werk*, ed. Moritz Wagner and Magnus Wieland (Dusseldorf: Aisthesis Verlag, 2019), 135–56.

[4] I am particularly interested in the texts "Der Hirtenbrief," "Grenzstein der Freiheit," and "Die Gottlosigkeit Gottes oder Das Gesicht der Zweiten Insel," in *Poetische Märzkälbereien. Gesammelte Prosa*, ed. Werner Jung (Monchengladbach: Juni-Verlag, 1990), 12–120; and "Ankunft in Porto. 'Angewandte Erinnerungen'— Aus dem portugiesischen Erzählkreis," in *Lauter Vigoleisiaden oder Der zweite Blick auf Albert Vigoleis Thelen*, ed. Jürgen Pütz, *die horen, Zeitschrift für Literatur, Kunst und Kritik*, special issue, vol. 45.3, no. 199 (2000): 123–36.

frame of these texts is interesting as well. The first text starts on August 31, 1939, eight days after the Molotov–Ribbentrop Pact was signed and the day before the night during which Hitler invaded Poland. Thelen's notes end on September 1, the day they arrive at Pascoaes's estate.[5] We are not only between spaces (between Nazi Germany and the safe haven of neutral Portugal) but also on the brink of World War II. Vigoleis and Beatrice do not find out about the beginning of the war until their arrival in Porto, around three o'clock in the afternoon of September 1, 1939, when they buy newspapers in front of the train station.[6] Vigoleis and Beatrice are refugees in Francoist Spain—a country that in 1939 was perceived and often acted as an ally of Nazi Germany, although it chose to remain neutral during the war.

In all of Thelen's writings, identity is linked to mobility—he is nowhere at home, but always on the move from one place to another, and he is highly skeptical of those who idealize a certain place as home. This nexus of mobility and identity means for Thelen that identity (national or otherwise) is something that has become unstable and needs to be questioned. I am interested in Thelen's perception of his own identity as something that is always, at least to some extent, determined by the outside world. In part this has to do with material conditions: on their trip to Portugal, Vigoleis and Beatrice are dependent on the availability of transportation, on their ability to pay for it, and on the goodwill of those in positions of authority (train conductors, soldiers and policemen, cab drivers, and customs officials). But even these material conditions are linked to the way in which Vigoleis and Beatrice are perceived. In other words, one's identity is, at least in part, constructed by the look of the other at oneself, by the perception of the other.

Thelen's texts stage this battle over identity in a historically specific situation—with Vigoleis and Beatrice fleeing from the threats of Nazi Germany through a country on friendly terms with the Nazis, a country whose language and culture Thelen knew well, and that had earlier, in 1936, forced Vigoleis and Beatrice to leave Mallorca. It is interesting to note how in Thelen's memoirs, visual, linguistic, and cultural registers come together in this battle over one's (national) identity. Thelen's texts communicate a highly sophisticated notion of identity—one that is aware of the philosophical criticism of a self-conscious and autonomous subject, as well as of the fact that identity is always constructed and staged and the product of interaction with images and text from the surrounding environment. What intrigues me is that Thelen shows identity

---

[5] See Thelen, "Die Gottlosigkeit Gotttes," 119: "an diesem denkwürdigen ersten September des Jahres 1939."
[6] Thelen, "Ankunft in Porto," 123.

as dependent on "trans- or pre-subjective foundational powers,"[7] in line with the kind of criticism of modernity developed by thinkers such as Nietzsche, Freud, Heidegger, and members of the Frankfurt School. In particular, the threat of violence in Thelen's memoirs functions as a catalyst for its narrator, Vigoleis, to reflect on issues of belonging and exclusion, nationalism and xenophobia, not unlike how 1920s Germany brought Walter Benjamin to conceive the notion of "Gewalt," in its double meaning of both "violence" and "power," as a force that both interrupts reality and creates the law, into one of the cornerstones of his thinking.[8]

In spite of the roots of Thelen's thinking in German intellectual discourse at the time, I want to develop my approach to his texts from a somewhat different point of view, focusing on the spatial and temporal dynamics surrounding someone who is seen and sees himself as exiled and, therefore, as an outsider. Thelen narrates from the perspective of someone on the run, someone who has no home and has had to learn to accept and maybe even embrace a sense of homelessness. I am intrigued by the link in Thelen's autobiographical texts between national identity, itself closely tied to linguistic and cultural identities, and the accompanying implication of an in- and outside, a boundary between a place that is supposed to be constitutive for one's identity and a world outside of it that is seen as alien. In an essay entitled "Secular Criticism," Edward Said reads the history of nineteenth-century thought, of the age in which nationalism emerged all over Europe, from the perspective of the creation of such mechanisms of in- and exclusion, based on fundamental discriminations "between what is fitting for us and what is fitting for them, the former designated as inside, in place, common, belonging, in a word *above*, the latter, who are designated as outside, excluded, aberrant, inferior, in a word *below*."[9] To be an in- or an outsider is more than just a matter of the place one chooses or is assigned;

---

[7] Although Thelen rarely quotes philosophers or cultural theorists, he shows a familiarity with Freud and Nietzsche (and was on friendly terms with Menno ter Braak, who knew the German intellectual landscape of the time very well). I borrow the term used here ("trans- oder vor-subjektive Ursprungsmächte") from Manfred Frank, *Die Unhintergehbarkeit von Individualität. Reflexionen über Subjekt, Person und Individuum aus Anlaß ihrer 'postmodernen' Toterklärung* (Frankfurt: Suhrkamp, 1986), 12.

[8] See Walter Benjamin, "Zur Kritik der Gewalt," in *Sprache und Geschichte. Philosophische Essays*, ed. Rolf Tiedemann (Stuttgart: Reclam, 1992), 104–31, here 123 and 125.

[9] Edward W. Said, "Introduction: Secular Criticism," in *The World, the Text, and the Critic* (Cambridge, MA: Harvard University Press, 1983), 1–30, quotation on 13–14.

it is linked to a sense of hierarchy. Commenting on the case of Erich Auerbach, a German-Jewish intellectual and university professor who survived World War II in exile in Turkey, Said points out that the notion of culture can be linked to "an aggressive sense of nation, home, community, and belonging."[10] It is precisely the experience of exile that leads Said to investigate and question how culture functions as a conduit for the nation and its power to include or exclude, especially where this is not explicitly articulated.[11]

For Said, this insight is not limited to the specific historical and political realities that forced Auerbach into exile. Rather, Auerbach's experience points to something broader. On a fundamental level, it complicates the understanding of the role of culture in our relationship to the nation. Culture is an integral part of the creation of an in- and outside:

> To be for and in culture is to be in and for a State in a compellingly loyal way. With this assimilation of culture to the authority and exterior framework of the State go as well such things as assurance, confidence, the majority sense, the entire matrix of meanings we associate with "home," belonging and community. Outside this range of meanings—for it is the outside that partially defines the inside in this case—stand anarchy, the culturally disfranchised, those elements opposed to culture and State: the homeless, in short.[12]

The dynamics between the in- and outside of a (national) culture are here given an almost psychological interpretation: to be part of a culture comes with authority, security, and the tools to make sense of the world. To be outside means to lose these certainties, to be disenfranchised and confronted with chaos and anarchy. Yet this in- and outside are mutually dependent; the inside defines itself at least partially through what the outside has created. This is a dynamic, the creation of in- and outsiders, that can easily be and frequently is exploited by those in power. But Said also wants us to remember that cultures are never homogenous. In Said's diagnosis, culture has always been accompanied by a movement of resistance that "has come from individuals or

---

[10] Said, "Secular Criticism," 12.
[11] The term *culture* is characterized by an interesting ambiguity in Said's work. On the one hand, it refers to the literary and artistic canon; on the other hand, it encompasses the discursive patterns of specific communities (among them nations). The underlying (and perhaps not entirely unproblematic) premise is that we can learn about a community through its (elite) cultural achievements.
[12] Said, "Secular Criticism," 11.

groups declared out of bounds or inferior by the culture"—a group that may include intellectuals whose activities "transcend and deliberately interfere with the collective weight imposed by the nation-state and the national culture."[13] While (willingly or not) complicit in the enforcement of a notion of belonging and a concomitant sense of security, someone who writes can use her/his writing to express what it means to be on the outside.

In the following I will argue that Said's introduction of the terms *outside/inside* as a way of understanding national identity allows for an original and complex consideration of how our cultural background determines our identity when autocratic regimes use linguistic and cultural means to colonize our life world. In the case of Thelen's work, these terms help us understand the paradox and often highly ambiguous modes through which the author relates to his German background. While Thomas Mann, in an interview with the *New York Times* on February 22, 1938, could claim, "Where I am, there is Germany,"[14] suggesting that he could take Germany with him, for Thelen to make such a claim would have been preposterous. Thelen's memoirs of his flight to Portugal explore, on the eve of World War II, the tensions accompanying his relationship to Germany and its culture. On the one hand, his texts trace the impact of national, linguistic, and cultural identities on a person, and what happens when one loses the sense of security they offer. On the other hand, Thelen's texts resist being taken in by a sense of belonging to a (national) culture and explore the anarchy of being on the "outside." In spite of their subject-critical views and their frequent pessimism, Thelen's texts emphasize the importance of holding on to notions of agency and the resistance that comes with it—of insisting on deciding one's own fate, even when living through difficult circumstances. Precisely the importance of this notion of agency would make one expect him to embrace a realist poetics, but that is not what happens. In all of his texts, Thelen works with a decisively modernist poetics. This also goes for the texts discussed here. As realistic as these refugee memoirs may seem, Vigoleis's, Beatrice's, and the readers' perceptions of the world are always at stake, and, as we will see, Vigoleis often reflects on the (in)adequacy of his perception of reality. Thelen's

---

[13] Said, "Secular Criticism," 14.
[14] See "Mann finds U.S. Sole Peace Hope," *New York Times*, February 22, 1938, www.nytimes.com/1938/02/22/archives/mann-finds-u-s-sole-peace-hope-german-writer-here-holds-it-is-lone.html. The meaning and contexts of this statement are discussed by Tobias Boes, *Thomas Mann's War: Literature, Politics, and the World Republic of Letters* (Ithaca, NY: Cornell University Press, 2020), 3, 5, 7, 10–11, 188–93.

texts are part of a tradition that links modernism[15] and mobility in a highly original way, exploring the critical perspective the combination of both allows.

The Looks of the Refugee (Images)

Identity and the perception of identity, national and otherwise, are central in Thelen's memoirs, which he characterizes as "Fluchtkapitel" ("Flight Chapters").[16] Identity in these texts is shaped by mobility: the experience of what it means to be a refugee at a specific time and place. One idea steering Thelen's narrative is that identity as a refugee is communicated especially through one's appearance, placing it in the realm of the visual, as the early pages of Thelen's memoirs, in particular, show.

On August 31, 1939, Vigoleis and Beatrice arrive at the station of Medina del Campo, in Spain, having traveled there from Bordeaux (where they had hoped to take a ship, to avoid traveling through Spain) and through Irun, on the border between France and Spain. In total, their trip will last sixty-five hours.[17] The two of them hope to reach Porto, but are told in Medina del Campo that in order to do so they need to switch trains. They and the other travelers, however, are barred from entering the train to Porto by men in uniform (military police), who do not respond to protests, requests, or screaming (16–17), until an older Portuguese man speaks up on behalf of the stranded travelers and suddenly and unexpectedly "a kind of social contract" ("eine Art Gesellschaftsvertrag") (18) is established that will allow the travelers to use the corridors of the "sleeper cars" ("Schlafwagen") (18–19). But Vigoleis, Beatrice, and one other traveler are separated from the group, not allowed to board the train, and are put under arrest. Earlier, we learn, Vigoleis had alienated a representative of Franco's secret police on the train by refusing to give the Nazi salute, showing that Vigoleis and Beatrice do not identify with the new German regime and its Spanish sympathizers—"we refused to greet and honor the idols Hitler and Franco by word and arm" ("[wir weigerten uns], den Abgöttern Hitler

---

[15] Moritz Wagner and Magnus Wieland make the very valid point that Thelen's modernism is generally overlooked; see their "Einleitung. Albert Vigoleis Thelen—ein moderner Tragelaph," in Wagner and Wieland, *Albert Vigoleis Thelen*, 7–20, esp. 11–16.

[16] Thelen, "Der Hirtenbrief," 12. Parenthetical page numbers in the following refer to this text.

[17] See Thelen's report in a letter to his mother written from Portugal on September 2, 1939, in Albert Vigoleis Thelen, *Meine Heimat bin ich selbst. Briefe 1929–1953*, ed. Ulrich Faure and Jürgen Pütz (Cologne: Dumont, 2010), 108.

und Franco Gruß und Ehre zu erweisen mit Wort und Arm") (12–13). It is this unwillingness (the clearly visible refusal to fit in) that frames the first two chapters of Thelen's memoirs: "Pastoral Letter" ("Der Hirtenbrief") and "Border Stone of Freedom" ("Grenzstein der Freiheit").

What follows is a detailed description of the station in Medina del Campo and the people it hosts. What is remarkable about Thelen's text is its strong visual orientation—something that I would interpret as an attempt to invent a language that speaks to readers' imagination both within and beyond specific cultural affiliations. This is clear, for instance, in the description of "a military clergyman" ("Feldgeistlicher") with a "colorfully wrapped-up child" ("bunt eingewickelten Kinde"), looking for the parents of this "lost little sheep" ("verlorenen Schäfleins") (19). This last image, with its clear biblical connotations (Matthew 18.12–14; Luke 15.3–7), is very much part of a Christian tradition. But the image is used here in such a way that its meaning is also clear without realizing the cultural allusion: it expresses separation (the child has become an outsider to the community), but with it the expectation that the lost child will quickly be reunited with its family, making its outsider status only a temporary misunderstanding.

Elsewhere, too, Thelen's visual language seeks to capture this sense of being an outsider, and in a way that is highly coded, but with the imagery of the outsider as a sort of "countertype" to the social norm in German (and European) culture in mind.[18] As a refugee, the text tells us, one looks a certain way—the other traveler singled out with Vigoleis and Beatrice

> [. . .] was a slight man, from the south, unshaven, like many others, poorly dressed, like few others—judging by his pack a vagabond or wayfarer, judging by his facial expression an intellectual, he probably had TBC, caved-in chest, poorly nourished—on balance we had some things in common.
>
> [war ein schmächtiger Mann, Südländer, unrasiert, wie übrigens viele, schlecht gekleidet, wie übrigens wenige,—nach dem Bündel zu schließen ein Vagabund oder fahrender Geselle, dem Gesichtsausdruck nach zu schließen ein Intellektueller, vermutlich war er auch tuberkulös, eingesunkener Brustkorb, schlechter Futterzustand,—alles in allem hatten wir einiges gemeinsam.]
> (21)

---

[18] On the role of the outsider and the imagery of masculinity in nationalist ideologies, see George L. Mosse, *The Image of Man: The Creation of Modern Masculinity* (Oxford: Oxford University Press, 1996), 56–76. Mosse in particular emphasizes the visual component in the construction of the outsider or counterfigure.

Precisely this look, although in a rather vague way, determines that their companion is perceived as a refugee and also an intellectual. He, too, is a clear outsider. But this does not only concern him. Vigoleis realizes that he and Beatrice are in the same category, and the implication is that this visible status as an outsider may very well explain why the three of them are singled out.

This third traveler stays with them throughout their time in Medina del Campo; it turns out that he is a Mexican anarchist who fought in the Spanish Civil War and then fled to France and is now on his way back to Mexico. Vigoleis elaborates further on how this man is perceived later on in the text. There is something else about his looks that makes him a target, we learn later. He looks "racially alienated" ("rassenverfremdet") Thelen notes, and "any Nazi would have burned the stamp of death into his skin" ("jeder Nazi hätte ihm den Todesstempel in die Haut gebrannt") (66). Something similar goes for Beatrice, who is Swiss but also of South American heritage, and "as a consequence of her in part Native American blood did not at all look Aryan and by many, caught up in the racial madness of a madman, bluntly was labeled a Jewish pig" ("zufolge ihrer indianischen Blutbeimischung gar nicht arisch aussah und von vielen, im Rassenwahn eines Wahnsinnigen befangen, rundheraus als Judensau abgestempelt wurde") (66). The terms Thelen uses here—"rassenverfremdet," "Blutbeimischung," and "Judensau"—tell us several things. In imagining how others look at the Mexican man and Beatrice, he makes clear that the general perception is coded by racist ideology—in this case, the anti-Semitic ideology of the Third Reich. It is an anti-Semitism that Hitler legitimated by evoking a Christian heritage, as Thelen reminds his readers elsewhere, through a direct citation from Hitler's *Mein Kampf*: "By resisting the Jew, I fight for the work of the Lord" ("Indem ich mich des Juden wehre, kämpfe ich für das Werk des Herrn") (40), one of the most frequently quoted passages of Hitler's text at the time.[19] It also shows that the Third Reich's racism by 1939 had moved well beyond Nazi Germany and had succeeded in becoming part of a more general European frame of reference.

Of Words, Letters, and Passes (Texts)

The fact that Vigoleis and Beatrice have valid, albeit temporary, papers at the station of Medina del Campo (22) is nullified by their looks and

---

[19] See *Mein Kampf. Eine kritische Edition*, ed. Christian Hartmann a.o. (Munich and Berlin: Institut für Zeitgeschichte, 2016), 231; Thelen's quotation slightly modifies the original: "*Indem ich mich des Juden erwehre, kämpfe ich für das Werk des Herrn.*" Regarding the observation that this sentence belongs to the most cited from the text, see the editors' footnote, 228. Elsewhere Thelen also speaks of a "christliche Scheinkultur" (113).

by the impressions they make on those in positions of authority. National identity is of course a matter of administrative and sometimes political convention (one either owns a passport or not), but the mechanism at work here is quite different. Regardless of one's papers or passport, one's identity is ultimately determined visually. As a construction, identity is dependent on time and space, and embedded in material conditions. For the Spanish secret police, if one does not give the Nazi salute, one cannot be German.

When Vigoleis threatens with a legal complaint against his and Beatrice's detention, he is met with laughter (22). He, Beatrice, and the anonymous third person are told by the representative of Franco's secret police "that we had to stand in front of/next to/along/against[20] the wall" ("daß wir uns an die Mauer stellen mußten"), something that "was probably meant metaphorically, since the horse-faced man did not let the order be followed by the command to shoot us; furthermore this grand wordplay does not exist in Spanish" ("war wohl sinnbildlich gemeint, denn der Pferdegesichtige ließ der Order nicht den Befehl folgen, uns zu erschießen; obendrein gibt es im Spanischen dieses erhabene Wortspiel nicht") (24). Here, too, the text reflects on an image in relation to language—the image places the three protagonists of this scene in some kind of relation to a wall: the order "sich an die Mauer zu stellen" in German suggests that the suspect will be shot; in Spanish, however, Vigoleis thinks, the expression does not have this connotation.[21] Being able to figure out a linguistic question like this presupposes an ability to move between languages, and a high degree of proficiency in each. Thelen is in possession of such linguistic knowledge, and at times fetishizes it.[22] In these memoirs, however, he emphasizes that his linguistic versatility was necessitated by his being a refugee.[23]

---

[20] Since there is not one correct translation of "an" in "sich an die Wand stellen," I suggest a range of possible translations of the preposition here.

[21] In semiotic terms we are dealing with the difference between the denotative and connotative meaning of the expression "an die Wand stellen"; see Roland Barthes, *Elemente der Semiologie*, trans. Eva Moldenhauer (Frankfurt: Suhrkamp, 1983), 75–6.

[22] See my essay "Schreiben außerhalb der Nation und die niederländisch-deutsche Kontaktzone: Hans Keilson, Nico Rost und Albert Vigoleis Thelen," in *Im Abseits der Gruppe 47. Albert Vigoleis Thelen und andere "Unzeitgemäße" im Literaturbetrieb der 1950er und 1960er Jahre*, ed. Heinz Eickmans, Jürgen Pütz, and Werner Jung (Dusseldorf: Universitätsverlag Rhein-Ruhr, 2019), 125–43, esp. 136–7.

[23] Thelen, "Ankunft in Porto," 123. Interlingualism, code switching, and conscious code mixing may be strengths, as Seyhan suggests in *Writing Outside the Nation* (Princeton, NJ: Princeton University Press, 2001), 106–9, but also come at a price, as Thelen's text makes clear.

The scene Thelen describes at the station in Medina del Campo is likely the source of the rumor circulating that Vigoleis and Beatrice have been shot—something that everyone in Porto assumes to be true, as they will find out the day after their arrival there.[24] What Thelen's memoirs establish here is a close link between language, assigned identity, and the potential for violence, in a historical situation in which these links are constantly evoked without it necessarily being clear that violence will be used. Thelen also problematizes, however, his own desire to be obedient and to internalize this given identity, even if it has negative connotations. Once the man from the secret police has left with the train, the suggestion is made, by a worker who happens to be present, that they enter the station's inn for a cup of coffee. Vigoleis initially rejects this more or less intuitively, but then he starts to question his response: "Was his corpse bent on obedience? Had the limping secret gnome [member of the secret police], himself a lamentable creature of his leader, strangled his drive for freedom?" ("War sein Kadaver auf Gehorsam aus? Hatte der hinkende Geheimwicht, der selbst ein Jämmerling seines Führers war, in ihm den Drang nach Freiheit abgewürgt?") (36). Vigoleis notices a tendency in himself to mimic the discipline of the policeman he is confronted with and in doing so to internalize the rules and hierarchies of Franco's regime, while a better strategy would be to act according to his own insights. The soldiers do, however, let Vigoleis and Beatrice enter the station's restaurant; soon a bedroom is prepared for them, and the situation does not look entirely as dire as it initially had.

To get out of the deadlock in which they find themselves—Vigoleis and Beatrice are arrested; the man responsible for their arrest, the member of the secret police, has left with the train they were scheduled to take, and the remaining soldiers do not really know what to do with them—Vigoleis, suffering from something resembling a panic attack, proposes that they ask for permission to take a taxi to the Spanish–Portuguese border (46, 48). For that, however, they will first need permission to leave and to obtain written documents permitting them to travel by car. In this context, identity is something that is officially sanctioned, in the form of a document that certifies who they are. The officials look with suspicion at their German passes, to which Vigoleis had earlier referred as "limited transit papers (the at the time still life-endangering *laisser-passer* documents)" ("beschränkte Geleitpapiere (die damals noch lebensgefährdenden *salvoconductos*)") (22). Vigoleis and Beatrice have temporary German passes, which we later learn were issued in Switzerland (61). These passes are valid for only three months,

---

[24] Thelen, "Ankunft in Porto," 128, 131.

something that makes border-patrol agents suspicious, because it makes clear that they are enemies of the Nazis (39). What he needs, ideally, is an additional document certifying to the Spanish authorities his identity and his intentions.

Earlier, at the station's hotel, Thelen had shown an awareness that his Catholic background might be helpful and had referred to himself as a "Catholic German [...]; in the higher circles around Franco that was a recommendation" ("aléman catolico [...]; in den hohen Franco-Kreisen war das eine Empfehlung") (36). This is another indication that, as a somewhat flexible cultural construction, national identity can be fashioned according to one's momentary needs. When seeking permission to drive to Portugal by car, Thelen claims to be on a special mission of peace on behalf of the Catholic Church. To prove this, he shows a handwritten petition in Latin (from 1931), written by Thelen's uncle, who is a Catholic bishop in Münster, and countersigned by the Archbishop of Mallorca, requesting that Thelen be given permission to consult all Catholic archives and libraries (53–54).[25] Thelen suggests that a local military cleric be called to the office to translate the document (54–55). He is working under the assumption that the clergyman's Latin will not be sufficient to do so, but also because Church Latin is quite different from the kind of Latin one learns in school (57). This indeed turns out to be correct: the priest confirms that Thelen has "*no bad intentions toward his fellow human beings*" ("*nec vere fecit proximo suo malum*") (60), and the officer gives them the necessary stamps and lets them go. The officer, who is suspicious of the knowledge of his cleric, and perhaps with good reason, makes clear that he is not necessarily convinced by their story—according to Vigoleis's account, he says "in whatever matter you may be traveling" ("[i]n welcher Angelegenheit auch immer Sie unterwegs sein mögen") (61)—but there is a moment of real communication between the two when he asks Thelen whether he thinks it will come to war (62).

"Gewalt" as Power and Violence (Beyond Image and Text)

In the above I have shown how in Thelen's flight memoirs, images and texts play key roles in shaping the way Thelen and Beatrice are perceived by their environment. To some extent this perception is shaped by Thelen himself, but much of it is coded by the ideologies of his interlocutors. Thelen's text also analyzes in great detail how violence interacts with the images and texts shaping his identity, but also develops its own dynamics under an autocratic regime like that of Franco. Violence

---

[25] The same letter helped get Vigoleis and Beatrice out of Mallorca in 1936; see *Die Insel des zweiten Gesichts* (Berlin: List, 2014), 873, 875, 900.

follows and reinforces the hierarchies and conventions of society, but it may also disrupt those with a randomness that threatens vulnerable people, like Vigoleis and Beatrice. And it may force new rules and conventions. It is possible to read Thelen's texts, then, as a treatise on violence.

In an exemplary way, Thelen's memoirs illustrate how the two semantic dimensions of the term *Gewalt* (which can mean both "power" and "violence")[26] collude. Violence may be used instrumentally in the service of power, but not necessarily in the service of the law. Sometimes it only serves the greed of individuals. This kind of instrumentalization of violence is highlighted by Thelen in the opening pages of his text, when he points to Göring having people executed in order to obtain a particular work of art, or to a family on Mallorca who were buried alive in a dry well for a pair of gloves (13).[27] Thelen plays here with a long philosophical and political tradition that interprets violence as instrumental in nature, as a means to an end.[28] The excerpt from his text suggests that power and violence, in spite of their seeming randomness, have a clear goal: to take possession of something material. Hermann Göring (1893–1946) helped establish and was in charge of the Einsatzstab Reichsleiter Rosenberg (ERR), which, with the assistance of the Gestapo, confiscated art collections in occupied Europe (often those owned by Jews or in the possession of Jewish art dealers). Here, Thelen problematizes the viewing of culture as an object to be collected and exhibited, as well as the accompanying disregard for its owners.

That power and violence are tied to society's hierarchies and that such hierarchies can easily be abused is also clear at other moments in the narrative. Walking around on the platform of the station in Medina del Campo, Thelen attracts the attention of the authorities, and realizes that to move around freely can be dangerous under a regime "that lives from violence and the rule of the strongest alone" ("aus der Gewalt lebt und einzig vom Faustrecht") (44). Vigoleis and Beatrice's mobility and outsider status do not fit into any frame of reference for the authorities.

---

[26] On this ambiguity, see Beatrice Hanssen's interpretation of Walter Benjamin's "Kritik der Gewalt" in *Critique of Violence: Between Poststructuralism and Critical Theory* (London: Routledge, 2000), 3, 8.

[27] Anne Rothfeld, "Nazi Looted Art," *Prologue Magazine*, vol. 34, no. 2 (2002), www.archives.gov/publications/prologue/2002/summer/nazi-looted-art-1.html. Thelen may be thinking in particular of Göring's activities in the Netherlands (Lynn H. Nicholas, *The Rape of Europe: The Fate of Europe's Treasures in the Third Reich and the Second World War* (New York: Alfred A. Knopf, 1994), 81–114), where Göring was already quite active acquiring art before the outbreak of World War II.

[28] See Beatrice Hanssen, *Critique of Violence*, 18–19.

Thelen's observation is reminiscent of a comment by Walter Benjamin, who observes that the police are supposed to exert their power or violence for the purpose of the law, yet simultaneously they are able to stipulate within broad parameters what the law is.[29] As outsiders (who are also, therefore, outside the law), Vigoleis and Thelen are easy prey for any authority figure in this autocratic country: every policeman is now potentially "an executioner with an arrest warrant and a license to kill" ("ein Henker mit Haftbefehl und Mordpatent") (45). The potential for random acts of violence is always there: "A blow on a horn, a whistle, and the shooting starts" ("Ein Stoß ins Horn, ein Pfiff, und los geht die Knallerei") (45). But Vigoleis and Beatrice are not entirely without power. To resolve their predicament, Vigoleis and Beatrice seek to make existing power structures work for them, something that is possible because the Spanish officials they are dealing with do not trust one another (27). The officer in charge at the station of Medina del Campo has an adversarial relationship with the member of Franco's secret police who has barred them from taking the train to the Portuguese–Spanish border. In the end, this officer decides to act against the secret agent's orders and lets them go.

After quite a bit of trouble, Vigoleis and Beatrice find a chauffeur willing to transport them in his luxury cab from Medina del Campo to Fuentes de Oñoro, at the Spanish–Portuguese border, for 400 pesetas, which, despite being rather a lot of money for the time, is presented as a special deal in the name of both of their "Führer," as the chauffeur states (62). Once they arrive at the border, the driver suddenly acts angrily, throwing their suitcases out of the trunk, cursing them as enemies of God, Franco, Mussolini, Hitler, the Pope, and fatherland (75), and demanding 1,000 pesetas, something that greatly upsets Vigoleis. Beatrice disagrees and tells him to give the Spaniard the money since they are entirely in his power (77). It is unclear what motivates the driver—greed, certainly, but it is also clear that he sees himself as on the side of those in power; he is an opportunist who is willing to transport people fleeing from the Nazis for financial gain, but he also does everything he can to abuse their powerlessness. In his case, too, power and the ability to inflict violence are identical; there is no recourse to the law.

Precisely because of the visual spectacle of their treatment in front of soldiers and other officials present at the Fuentes de Oñoro station, Vigoleis and Beatrice fear being arrested (78). They again need their papers stamped to be able to cross the border, and there is a real danger that they will face arrest. Here, too, the border functions as a zone "of perpetual motion, confrontation, and translation," a place of constant

---

[29] See Benjamin, "Zur Kritik der Gewalt," 115.

transition.[30] However, when Vigoleis is sent to a group of card-playing officers he is asked whether he is German, something he confirms (92, 95). This impresses the officers and leads to the follow-up question of whether he is also an officer—something Vigoleis, against all truth, also confirms, adding that he is an artillery captain (96) and that he is on a secret diplomatic mission to Portugal (97). The effect of this answer is dramatic; nobody is interested in Vigoleis's papers anymore (98). Because of Thelen's presumed diplomatic status, it is illegal for soldiers to remove items from his and Beatrice's suitcases. This goes against diplomatic protocol, is "a mockery of the law of nations; [...] an interference with my extraterritoriality" ("eine Verhöhnung des Völkerrechts; [...] ein Eingriff in meine Exterritorialität"), and is therefore legally inappropriate (99). "Exterritorialität" refers to the long-standing principle in international law that diplomats are exempt from the civil and criminal laws and, more generally, the authority of a country in which they serve.[31] The soldiers' action is quickly reversed. The train, from which Vigoleis and Beatrice had been removed earlier, is stopped. Vigoleis and Beatrice are treated with great respect, a first-class compartment is cleared, and all the passengers, including the secret agent, who had earlier seen Vigoleis and Beatrice being forced to leave the train, now see them board with an honor guard of representatives of the Spanish military (101–02).

Vigoleis realizes, however, that in order to play the role of a German army captain convincingly, he will need to give the Nazi salute—something that he deeply resents (102). At an earlier point in the journey, Thelen's unwillingness to give the Nazi salute on the train had led to the incident with the representative of Franco's secret police that got them sidelined in Medina del Campo. At this point, though, the stakes are very different. Not giving the Nazi salute would effectively contradict the role he has constructed for himself—one that protected his status as an outsider—and it would betray his real intentions. Vigoleis therefore "*raises* his arm" ("*hebt* den Arm") (103). He does so in order not to give up his role. Had the soldiers taken the time to check his papers, his elaborate act would have been exposed immediately (103). But even after this, Thelen is not finished. As the train is preparing to leave, Vigoleis watches from his compartment the military salute on the platform, and he cannot help himself:

---

[30] See Seyhan, *Writing Outside the Nation*, 115.
[31] See, for instance, Ernst Beling, *Die strafrechtliche Bedeutung der Exterritorialität nach Völkerrecht. Beiträge zum Völkerrecht und zum Strafrecht* (Breslau: Schletter, 1896), 3–4.

But what is that? I felt a force in my own arm—was it the Faustian hellish force, more powerful than gold and shotguns? Invisible threads pulled my arm up again, drew it fully out of the window, until it hung immovable in the air. I heard Vigoleis say with a firm voice, "General, sir, and all you captains, thousands of thanks! I will report to my Führer what in a great and perhaps the final hour in Fuentes de Oñoro was done for a great brother nation."

[Aber da, was ist das? Ich verspürte einen Zwang im eigenen Arm,—war es der faustische Höllenzwang, der mächtiger ist als Gold und Flinten? Unsichtbare Schnüre zogen ihn wieder hoch, rückten ihn zum Fenster ganz hinaus, bis er unbeweglich in der Schwebe stand. Ich hörte Vigoleis sagen, mit fester Stimme: "Herr General, ihr Hauptleute alle, tausend Dank! Ich werde meinem Führer berichten, was man in Fuentes de Oñoro in großer, und, vielleicht letzter Stunde für ein großes Brudervolk getan."]
(105–06)

After this ordeal, Vigoleis and Beatrice both feel dead, but once they have crossed the border the conductor tells them they are free and there is no more need to "play theater" ("Theater zu spielen") (107) and pretend to be something they are not. On the one hand, this is in line with Vigoleis's own views: he, too, refers to the theatrical aspect of his behavior (it is nothing but an act). On the other hand, the involuntary nature of the second Nazi salute to some extent contradicts this. It appears that Vigoleis is no longer in control of his actions. The text does not resolve this, other than referring to a Faustian element in this compulsion. It confirms a more general element of Thelen's view of humans: that in their action they are at least in part propelled by motives beyond their rational control.

Literature, Counter-Memory, and Life in Common

In the end, Vigoleis and Beatrice are able to outsmart those in positions of authority using their language skills and what they know (or suspect) about the expectations of the people they are dealing with. The text also clearly communicates their awareness that they are in a privileged position, because they have seen something of the world, have the language skills to make themselves understood, and have money. Strolling around the station in Medina del Campo, having for a moment left Beatrice in the restaurant, Vigoleis imagines how the locals look at him: as someone endangering "the so strenuously reached peace" ("den so mühsam erkämpften Frieden"), even though there is no certainty about where their daily bread will come from, something that no dictatorship can provide (45). What his thought demonstrates is empathy: he is able to imagine how others see him, to be an out- and an insider simultaneously.

But this ability to navigate intercultural encounters (and outsmart one's enemies in the process) is not entirely the message or ideology of these memoirs. Once Vigoleis and Beatrice have reached freedom, they are driven to Teixeira de Pascoaes's estate—a house that still shows the traces of being set on fire by French troops led by General Jean-de-Dieu Soult in 1812–13. Angelo Cesar, Pascoaes's lawyer and assistant, who has brought them to his estate, calls them "the first refugees" ("die ersten Flüchtlinge") of the new war (117). Pascoaes, who, like many others, had assumed that they were dead, welcomes them with the words that man is only present and alive "in the tears shed because of his absence" ("in den Tränen, die um seine Abwesenheit vergossen werden") (118). It is a reference to one of his own aphorisms translated by Thelen.[32] What intrigues me about this comment is the link between emotion, the values associated with a person's humanity, and that person's absence. Pascoaes alludes to the ability to be empathic and feel compassion because of a person's absence. It is a call for a form of memory—or, better: counter-memory—that illustrates the potential of literature. Memory, in a sense, erases the border between the outsider and insider: it brings someone inside from the outside.

This form of memory is closely linked to what I earlier called the visual dimension in Thelen's text. As a "visual text," Thelen's memoirs contribute to a memory archive. At the end of the chapter "Der Hirtenbrief," when Vigoleis and Beatrice are about to leave the station in Medina del Campo, we find a detailed description of a war victim, a former soldier who has lost his right hand. When Thelen gives him a coin, he immediately checks with the help of a rock whether it is real (70–1). Leaving town, Vigoleis and Beatrice see the silhouette of a man with a long walking stick, a donkey, a woman, and child. It is an image that, Vigoleis notes, has existed for thousands of years. It is also an image that Vigoleis immediately decodes as the "legend-turned-into-image" ("bildgewordene Legende") of the flight to Egypt (71). Vigoleis wants to read it as some kind of prophecy, a sign, but Beatrice disagrees and emphasizes their own responsibility in shaping their future (71–2). The image thus resists fixation; it rather emphasizes a mobility that is not ideological and cannot be used to build community.

---

[32] See Teixeira de Pascoaes, *Das dunkle Wort*, trans. Albert Vigoleis Thelen (Zurich: Rascher, 1949), 77. In the remainder of the aphorism, Pascoaes speaks of pain and love: "Der Schmerz und die Liebe sind das Fleisch und Blut seines wesenlosen und göttlichen Leibes, der vor Gott erscheint." Humans live through their emotions.

At the conclusion of his essay on "Secular Criticism," Edward Said refers to "noncoercive knowledge produced in the interests of human freedom" as a social goal, a form of living in common that is inclusive and that actively fosters difference.[33] One of the characteristics of the diasporic, wandering, and cosmopolitan destinies in which Said is interested throughout his work is the ability of a person to think of themselves as "both inside and outside his or her community."[34] But can something still be a community if it is non-coercive? Is it possible to think about a community without borders? And what establishes commonality if not a shared set of images and texts? Vigoleis Thelen, like Edward Said, has written extensively about figures in exile, and yet his memoirs also offer a vision of a non-coercive community (one that, like Said's, is informed by the traumatic history of displacement and forced exclusion in the twentieth century). One of the forgotten people, one of the people who remain absent at the memoirs' end, is the anonymous Mexican anarchist, who, despite playing a marginal role in the plot, in many respects functions as a key figure in these memoirs. At the station in Medina del Campo, Vigoleis and Beatrice propose that he share their cab to the Portuguese border without having to pay anything, since they know that he has no money (64), but the man politely declines. He saw Vigoleis refuse to give the Nazi salute and is afraid that they will evoke suspicion when traveling as a group—"are you willing to raise your arm," he asks Vigoleis, "when the sturdy fellows stop the car?" ("sind Sie gewillt, den Arm zu heben, wenn die fixen Kerle den Wagen anhalten?") (65). He declines accompanying them because he does not want to endanger Beatrice's life, although he may also suspect that she is Jewish, something that would, in turn, endanger him (66). He is arrested in the train station of Medina del Campo before Vigoleis and Beatrice leave (68).

What the Mexican anarchist, who has remained nameless throughout the text and whose fate will remain unknown to author and reader, shows is an ability to look at himself and others from both the outside and inside, as well as an ability to act on that knowledge. In part he is

---

[33] See Said, "Secular Criticism," 29; compare also Said, "Traveling Theory," in *The World, the Text, and the Critic* (Cambridge, MA: Harvard University Press, 1983), 226–47, here 247. I borrow the term "life in common" from Tzvetan Todorov, *Life in Common: An Essay in General Anthropology*, trans. Katherine and Lucy Golsan (Lincoln: University of Nebraska Press, 2001), in which Todorov seeks to reread the history of Western thought searching for traces of non-conventional communal thinking.

[34] The specific characterization here concerns Freud. See Edward Said, "Freud and the Non-European," in *The Selected Words of Edward Said, 1966–2006* (New York: Vintage, 2019), 494–517, here 516.

concerned with his own survival, but he also thinks of Beatrice and Vigoleis—likewise, they are worried about him, which is why they offer him a ride to the border. What the text articulates here is a higher ethics that acknowledges a form of commonality: the ability to make decisions in the interest of others, even though doing so may not be in one's own interest. The anonymous Mexican anarchist is the embodiment of this type of ethics, and it is Thelen's text that reminds us of his existence.

Works Cited

Barthes, Roland. *Elemente der Semiologie*, trans. Eva Moldenhauer (Frankfurt am Main: Suhrkamp, 1983).

Beling, Ernst. *Die strafrechtliche Bedeutung der Exterritorialität nach Völkerrecht. Beiträge zum Völkerrecht und zum Strafrecht* (Breslau: Schletter, 1896).

Benjamin, Walter. "Zur Kritik der Gewalt," in *Sprache und Geschichte. Philosophische Essays*, ed. Rolf Tiedemann (Stuttgart: Reclam, 1992), 104–31.

Boes, Tobias. *Thomas Mann's War: Literature, Politics, and the World Republic of Letters* (Ithaca, NY: Cornell University Press, 2020).

Frank, Manfred. *Die Unhintergehbarkeit von Individualität. Reflexionen über Subjekt, Person und Individuum aus Anlaß ihrer "postmodernen" Toterklärung* (Frankfurt: Suhrkamp, 1986).

Hanssen, Beatrice. *Critique of Violence: Between Poststructuralism and Critical Theory* (London: Routledge, 2000).

Hanssen, Léon. "'Bald kann Menno seine Reise nach Europa antreten'—Albert Vigoleis Thelen en Menno ter Braak," in *Albert Vigoleis Thelen*, ed. Jattie Enklaar and Hans Ester (Amsterdam: Rodopi, 1988), 20–39.

Hitler, Adolf. *Mein Kampf. Eine kritische Edition*, ed. Christian Hartmann a.o. (Munich and Berlin: Institut für Zeitgeschichte, 2016).

Mosse, George L. *The Image of Man: The Creation of Modern Masculinity* (Oxford: Oxford University Press, 1996).

Niekerk, Carl. "Literatures of the Contact Zone: Hans Keilson, Nico Rost, Albert Vigoleis Thelen, and the Literary Spaces of the Late 1940s and Early 1950s," in *On Margins and Contact Zones: 500 Years of Dutch-German Cultural Interaction*, ed. Carl Niekerk and Simon Richter, *Journal of Dutch Literature*, special issue, vol. 9, no. 1 (2018), 112–27.

Niekerk, Carl. "Schreiben außerhalb der Nation und die niederländisch-deutsche Kontaktzone. Hans Keilson, Nico Rost und Albert Vigoleis Thelen," in *Im Abseits der Gruppe 47. Albert Vigoleis Thelen und andere "Unzeitgemäße" im Literaturbetrieb der 1950er und 1960er Jahre*, ed. Heinz Eickmans, Jürgen Pütz, and Werner Jung (Dusseldorf: Universitätsverlag Rhein-Ruhr, 2019), 125–43.

Niekerk, Carl. "Toleranz, Kolonialismus und die 'Unschuld der Weißen'. Zur Triangulierung der interkulturellen Kommunikation in *Der schwarze Herr Bahßetup*," in *Albert Vigoleis Thelen—ein moderner Tragelaph. Perspektiven auf ein vielgestaltiges Werk*, ed. Moritz Wagner and Magnus Wieland (Dusseldorf: Aisthesis Verlag, 2019), 135–56.

Pascoaes, Teixeira de. *Das dunkle Wort*, trans. Albert Vigoleis Thelen (Zurich: Rascher, 1949).

Rothfeld, Anne. "Nazi Looted Art," *Prologue Magazine*, vol. 34, no. 2 (2002), www.archives.gov/publications/prologue/2002/summer/nazi-looted-art-1.html.

Said, Edward W. "Introduction: Secular Criticism," in *The World, the Text, and the Critic* (Cambridge, MA: Harvard University Press, 1983), 1–30.
Said, Edward W. "Traveling Theory," in *The World, the Text, and the Critic* (Cambridge, MA: Harvard University Press, 1983), 226–47.
Said, Edward W. "Freud and the Non-European," in *The Selected Words of Edward Said, 1966–2006* (New York: Vintage, 2019), 494–517.
Seyhan, Azade. *Writing outside the Nation* (Princeton, NJ: Princeton University Press, 2001).
Thelen, Albert Vigoleis. "Der Hirtenbrief," in *Poetische Märzkälbereien. Gesammelte Prosa*, ed. Werner Jung (Mönchengladbach: Juni-Verlag, 1990), 12–73.
Thelen, Albert Vigoleis. "Die Gottlosigkeit Gottes oder Das Gesicht der Zweiten Insel," in *Poetische Märzkälbereien. Gesammelte Prosa*, ed. Werner Jung (Mönchengladbach: Juni-Verlag, 1990), 108–20.
Thelen, Albert Vigoleis. "Grenzstein der Freiheit," in *Poetische Märzkälbereien. Gesammelte Prosa*, ed. Werner Jung (Mönchengladbach: Juni-Verlag, 1990), 74–107.
Thelen, Albert Vigoleis. *Poetische Märzkälbereien. Gesammelte Prosa*, ed. Werner Jung (Mönchengladbach: Juni-Verlag, 1990).
Thelen, Albert Vigoleis. "Ankunft in Porto. 'Angewandte Erinnerungen'—Aus dem portugiesischen Erzählkreis," in *Lauter Vigoleisiaden oder Der zweite Blick auf Albert Vigoleis Thelen*, ed. Jürgen Pütz, die horen, Zeitschrift für Literatur, Kunst und Kritik, special issue, vol. 45.3, no. 199 (2000): 123–36.
Thelen, Albert Vigoleis. *Meine Heimat bin ich selbst. Briefe 1929–1953*, ed. Ulrich Faure and Jürgen Pütz (Cologne: Dumont, 2010).
Thelen, Albert Vigoleis. *Die Insel des zweiten Gesichts* (Berlin: List, 2014).
Todorov, Tzvetan. *Life in Common: An Essay in General Anthropology*, trans. Katherine and Lucy Golsan (Lincoln: University of Nebraska Press, 2001).
Wagner, Moritz, and Magnus Wieland. "Einleitung. Albert Vigoleis Thelen—ein moderner Tragelaph," in *Albert Vigoleis Thelen—ein moderner Tragelaph. Perspektiven auf ein vielgestaltiges Werk*, ed. Moritz Wagner and Magnus Wieland (Dusseldorf: Aisthesis Verlag, 2019), 7–20.
Wekker, Gloria. *White Innocence: Paradoxes of Colonialism and Race* (Durham, NC: Duke University Press, 2016).

Seven Writing Germany with Brazil: Julia Mann's Memoir

Veronika Fuechtner

This chapter explores the work of a writer who is usually not perceived to be writing "Germany from the Outside," but who seems solidly connected to the very inside of the German-language canon. Julia Mann (née da Silva Bruhns, 1851–1923) was the matriarch of a large and influential family of writers, which includes most famously her sons Heinrich and Thomas Mann. Julia Mann did write from Brazil, but not geographically: she wrote in Germany in the German language, but assumed the voice of a Brazilian, or what she thought to be a Brazilian. Her memoir, *Aus Dodos Kindheit* (*From Dodô's Childhood*), traces her traumatic migration to Germany in the mid-nineteenth century and her process of becoming German in a Lubeck boarding school. It also presents an important commentary on what it meant to be German in the Wilhelmine era, and what it meant to write an autobiography in the context of literary modernism—that is, in the context of a family that came to represent it in so many ways. Julia Mann's writing belongs to the often fragmentary and elusive archives of migration. These archives can also be traced in the very center of the seemingly monolithic and permanent libraries of the canon. Thus, they have the potential to unsettle any clear notion of belonging, any division between inside and outside.

Today, Julia Mann is mostly known for her role as mother, and even in that role, her person and influence have been given short shrift. While innumerous biographies have been written about most Mann family members, as well as many of their friends and interlocutors, the first biography of Julia Mann was only published in 2018. As biographer Dagmar von Gersdorff has pointed out in her effort to finally change the narrative about Julia Mann, it was even possible for a recent book about the women in Thomas Mann's life to exclude his mother.¹ Mann was an accomplished writer and musician in her own right, who read widely and wrote fluently in several languages. She grew up in Paraty, a small coastal town south of the Brazilian imperial capital Rio de Janeiro. Her father, Johann Ludwig Hermann Bruhns (1821–93), had emigrated as a young man to Brazil from Lubeck. He grew and exported sugar and coffee, he had strong connections with the Brazilian imperial court, and he spent most of his adult life in Brazil. He became a Brazilian citizen and called himself João Luiz Germano Bruhns.²

Bruhns's first wife, Julia Mann's mother, Maria Luiza da Silva, was the daughter of a wealthy neighboring Brazilian plantation owner. Much of the scholarship on the Mann family follows a particular narrative proposed by the family itself and emphasizes the Portuguese descent of the da Silva family. Thus, Julia Mann is subtly constructed as Southern, yet European. But this narrative is easily unsettled by considering that after four generations of living in Brazil no one simply remained Portuguese in any sense that one might be inclined to read this category, be it nationally, racially, or culturally. Maria Luiza da Silva died in childbirth at age twenty-six, a few months before Julia Mann's fifth birthday. In her memoir, Mann describes the dread she felt seeing

---

[1] Dagmar von Gersdorff, *Julia Mann, die Mutter von Heinrich und Thomas Mann. Eine Biographie* (Berlin: Insel, 2018), 9. This is also true for other biographical literature on the Mann family; for example, a book on the women around Heinrich Mann includes a chapter on his sister Carla but none on his mother, and a book about the women in the Mann family extensively discusses Thomas Mann's mother-in-law but not his mother. There has been important scholarly literature on Julia Mann in German and Portuguese, and I included more extensive treatments in the "Works Cited." Dieter Strauss has provided detailed biographical accounts in the 1999 catalogue he co-edited for the seminal Goethe-Institute exhibition about Julia Mann, as well as more recently in 2019 in the important volume edited by Ulrike Leutheusser. Together with the 2009 volume co-edited by Kuschel, Mann, and Soethe, and an MA thesis by Christina Weise, these scholarly interventions and their implications for how the work of the Manns could be reread are just starting to register, and as Strauss writes, even many "Germanisten" don't know about the Brazilian origins of the Mann family. See Dieter Strauss, "Julia Mann—'Du bist eben eine Brasilianerin!'" in Ulrike Leutheusser, *Julia Mann und ihre Kinder* (Munich: Allitera, 2019), 14. In addition, two Portuguese-language novels deal with the Brazilian history of the Mann family: João Silvério Trevisan's *Ana em Veneza* (1994), which was translated into German, and Teolinda Gersão's *O Regresso de Júlia Mann a Paraty* (2021).

[2] For more information on Bruhns's biography, see Maria Sene, "Johann Ludwig Hermann Bruhns," in *Julia Mann. Brasilien-Lübeck-München* (Lubeck: Dräger Druck, 1999), 99–128. As I elaborate in my forthcoming book, Bruhns applied for Brazilian citizenship in 1889 on behalf of his nephew, Carlos Luiz Bruhns, citing his own Brazilian citizenship.

her mother's pale dead body with the stillborn baby placed on her chest.[3] After his wife's death, João Luiz Germano Bruhns decided to bring his five children to Germany. The family traveled across the Atlantic accompanied by the children's nanny, an enslaved woman from Mozambique named Anna. Bruhns enrolled his children in boarding schools in Lubeck and then returned to Brazil with Anna. Julia Mann was barely seven years old when her father left her in a foreign country with a foreign culture, a foreign language, and a foreign religion. She would never see her beloved nanny and Brazilian grandparents again. For a few years, she could still visit with her three brothers on weekends, but they all returned to Brazil at the end of their schooling, and only she and her older sister Mana remained in Germany. In 1869, at age seventeen, Julia was married off to the wealthy merchant and politician Thomas Johann Heinrich Mann and her father came from Brazil for the occasion.[4] Bruhns remarried, with the widow of his brother Eduard, Emma Bruhns, four years later. Julia was chagrined by her father's remarriage and described it as the loss of yet another mother figure. In an uncanny repetition of family history, Bruhns enrolled Emma's older daughters, that is, his nieces, in the same Lubeck boarding school his daughters Julia and Mana had attended. He took Emma and her youngest son back to Brazil. He had four more children with his second wife there and later in Italy. After many decades abroad, Bruhns retired in Kassel, where Julia Mann visited him shortly before his death and where she returned to attend his funeral. As she writes in her memoir, his death affected her deeply. Less than two years earlier, her own husband had died from bladder cancer. In his testament, he had expressed doubts about his wife's ability to guide her children in practical matters.[5] She was not allowed to control the family assets and was forced to sell the family home. In this time of great instability, she lost her father and with him one of the most significant connections to her Brazilian past. Given the turmoil of this time, it is not surprising that her memoir from a decade later focuses on the love for her father. Her feelings for her husband find no mention.

Julia Mann wrote her memoir in 1903 in Munich. She had moved there with her children after her husband's death to escape the confines of what she felt to be a rigid Lubeck society. In Munich she blossomed: she performed music, she wrote, and she was able to be part of artistic

---

[3] Julia Mann, *Ich spreche so gern mit meinen Kindern* (Berlin: Aufbau, 1994), 19.
[4] Marianne Krüll, *Im Netz der Zauberer. Eine andere Geschichte der Familie Mann* (Frankfurt: Fischer, 2011), 31.
[5] Krüll, *Im Netz der Zauberer*, 89.

circles.⁶ And over the years she could stay close to her children and grandchildren, many of whom remained in Munich. She was to experience other significant losses: the death of Therese Bousset, the boarding school director who raised her when she came from Brazil; the death of her sister Mana; and, most tragically, the suicide of her daughter Carla. The emotional pain that was part of Julia Mann's life since losing her mother as a young child is probably best expressed in the words that she wrote after her daughter's suicide in 1910: "my existence is like a constant nightmare; a piece of my heart is missing, and it has been violently ripped away" ("mein Sein ist wie in beständigem bösem Traum; mir fehlt ein Stück meines Herzens, und es ist ihm gewaltsam abgerissen").⁷ She was spared the knowledge that her older daughter Lula would also commit suicide. She died in 1923 after bidding farewell to her three sons, Heinrich, Thomas, and Viktor, and her two daughters-in-law, Mimi and Nelly.⁸

As I mentioned earlier, Julia Mann wrote *Aus Dodos Kindheit* in 1903, but it was only posthumously published in 1958. The memoir is often taken as a truthful historical representation of life in Brazil at the time, and it is rarely discussed as a literary work—or, in the words of Sander Gilman and Cathy Gelbin, as "a fantasy world of Brazilian colonialism and slavery."⁹ There are several contexts that are significant for this memoir. First, it narrates Mann's life as a string of experiences of loss: the loss of her mother and all subsequent mother figures, and the distance from and then loss of her father. Second, it was written for Mann's children and in conversation with them. Her son Thomas wrote about the importance of her childhood memories for their relationship and

---

[6] Mann's son Thomas stayed in Lubeck to complete boarding school and moved to Munich more than one year later. André Banuls, "Leben und Persönlichkeit," in *Thomas Mann Handbuch*, ed. Helmut Koopmann (Frankfurt: Fischer, 2005), 3. For an account of Julia Mann's life in Munich, see Dieter Strauss, "Julia Mann. Ein Leben im Spannungsfeld zwischen Brasilien und Deutschland," in *Julia Mann. Brasilien—Lübeck—München*, ed. Dieter Strauss and Maria A. Sene (Lubeck: Dräger Druck, 1999), 17–79. See also Gersdorff, *Julia Mann*, 113–42.

[7] My translation. Gersdorff, *Julia Mann*, 250.

[8] Viktor Mann provides a vivid account of her death in his own memoir. Viktor Mann, *Wir waren fünf. Bildnis der Familie Mann* (Konstanz: Südverlag, 2017), 487–92. In this case, Nelly refers to Viktor's wife, not Heinrich Mann's second wife, whose nickname was also Nelly. At this point in time, Heinrich Mann was still married to the Czech actress Maria Kanová (Mimi), the mother of his only child, Leonie Mann. Mann and Kanová divorced in 1930 and Mann went into exile with his second wife, Nelly Kröger. Kanová died in 1947 from the effects of her years of imprisonment in Theresienstadt.

[9] Cathy Gelbin and Sander L. Gilman, *Cosmopolitanisms and the Jews* (Ann Arbor: University of Michigan Press, 2017), 175.

that "she couldn't tell me enough of the magic beauty of her homeland."[10] Her memoir is one version of these constant retellings, the story of her trauma, the expulsion from a childhood paradise, which proliferated in many versions in the family throughout generations. Third, the memoir could be read as the touchstone of many Mann family fictions, most importantly Thomas Mann's 1901 family saga *Buddenbrooks*, Heinrich Mann's 1907 novel *Zwischen den Rassen* (*Between the Races*), and what could be read as Thomas Mann's response to his brother's reworking of their mother's memoir—his novel *Königliche Hoheit* (*Royal Highness*) of 1909.[11] Julia Mann was consulted on these novels and took an active role in her children's literary production. The memoir is also an assertion of Julia Mann's own claim to authorship—it stands at the beginning of a series of short stories and vignettes that she was to write over the next two decades. Finally, her memoir provides a blueprint for the Mann family narrative on race and German culture. It narrates Julia Mann's process of becoming German—from her painful struggles with German grammar and German dogmatism to her enthusiastic embrace of German music and literature. While providing a blueprint, it also follows one: that of narratives of Jewish assimilation in the nineteenth century, many of which also posit Schubert and Goethe as the apex of this process of becoming German.[12] And this is also a narration of becoming modern, and in Julia Mann's case of simultaneously asserting Brazilian modernity—that is, a decidedly European Brazilian modernity—over images of Brazilian primitivity, extra-European primitivity. This primitivity is also articulated in racial terms. The text attempts to Europeanize and whiten Julia Mann's origins, but also provides the blueprint for the exoticizing language around them. In this textual tension the threat of miscegenation and anxiety around it

---

[10] Strauss, "Julia Mann," 77. Frido Mann, who partly grew up with his grandfather Thomas Mann, mentions that he spoke often to him of his great-grandmother's Brazilian memories. Interview with Frido Mann, Munich, August 2, 2017.

[11] Other narratives include Heinrich Mann's first novel, *In einer Familie* (*In a Family*; its printing was financed by his mother), or Thomas Mann's short story *Der Wille zum Glück* (*The Will to Happiness*) or his seminal novella *Tonio Kröger*. Frido Mann's 1999 Brazil novel, *Brasa*, explicitly pays homage to Julia Mann's memoir.

[12] There are many such narratives: for example, Ludwig Geiger's or Rahel Varnhagen's writings on Goethe. Hannah Arendt has stated that Goethe came to be Varnhagen's "friend" and her "great mediator" between two worlds. This description resonates with Julia Mann's adoration of Goethe and her practice of excerpting from and commenting on his works. Her daughter Carla Mann also collected her favorite literary quotes from the German-language canon. Hannah Arendt and Haun Saussy, "Rahel Varnhagen and Goethe," *Critical Inquiry*, vol. 40, no. 1 (2013): 15–19, here 17.

becomes legible, and it is therefore not entirely surprising that Thomas Mann opposed its publication during his lifetime.[13] In the following, I will focus on this last point, Julia Mann's narrative of modernity, race, and culture, with an emphasis on the theme of loss and the conversations this book evokes between people and between fictions.

Aus Dodos Kindheit begins with a long excerpt from Ernst Moritz Arndt's 1824 poem "An das Vaterland" ("For the Fatherland"). The poem asserts that the birthplace is the place of belonging, the location of the fatherland: "And may there be bare rocks and bleak islands, and may poverty and travails live with you, you have to love this land forever" ("Und seien es kahle Felsen und öde Inseln, und wohne Armut und Mühe dort mit dir, du mußt das Land ewig liebhaben").[14] While Arndt might have evoked the German Baltic coast in this description, Julia Mann uses this language to claim the Brazilian Costa Verde as her fatherland. However, in stark contrast to Arndt's "bleak islands," that part of the Brazilian coast is lush and green. The hardship of Mann's fatherland lies not in its geography, but in the process of leaving it behind and recovering it from the austere landscape of traumatic memory. Mann subscribed to a conservative German patriotism, and it may be a surprising move to deploy a nineteenth-century German nationalist writer to make the point that her homeland was not Germany but Brazil.[15] She implies here that it is her birthplace that matters for her sense of belonging, not her parentage—that is, her German father. Her use of Arndt's language thus also uncouples the idea of the homeland from citizenship, which in the German Empire was based on the *ius sanguinis*. While she claims Brazil as her homeland, the fact that she mobilizes this poem simultaneously signals her education and dexterity regarding the German-language literary canon. In this way her citation does enact her German cultural patriotism while simultaneously unsettling geography and bloodline as the basis of Germanness.

This memoir begins with thoughts on the fatherland and it ends with thoughts of the father. Bruhns's letters to his daughter are included in the last pages of the text. Mann's relationship to him clearly is

---

[13] Yahya Elsaghe, *Thomas Mann und die kleinen Unterschiede. Zur erzählerischen Imagination des "Anderen"* (Cologne: Böhlau, 2004), 285. Viktor Mann lobbied to publish his mother's memoir, but he died in 1949—before its eventual publication.

[14] My translation. This poem is sometimes confused with the more famous 1813 poem, "Des Deutschen Vaterland" ("The German's Fatherland"). Mann, *Ich spreche so gern mit meinen Kindern*, 11.

[15] In the conflict between the brothers Thomas and Heinrich Mann around the politics of World War I, Julia Mann expressed her support for the German Empire against its "enemies." Mann, *Ich spreche so gern mit meinen Kindern*, 241.

layered into what fatherland means to her. Her father writes in German but also in Portuguese, and Mann translates her father's words into German, demonstrating her ability to mediate this language. The inclusion of the letters also makes the point that João Luiz Germano Bruhns ceased to be German along the way and that her intimate family relationships are Brazilian—her father remains "pai" to her even after they switch to German. As in the case of the father's letters, other materials are pasted into the narrative, at times even literally into the manuscript. The insertion of these materials and voices set up this memoir as a polyvocal text. They interrupt a narrative that otherwise is in the third person. This allows for affective distance between author and narrator, and it inhibits an easy identification of the reader with the subject position the text enacts. It could be read as a form of modernist ethnography, an ethnographic collage, in which authenticity is signaled through the included materials, but which already carries the doubt that these materials might elude authenticity. Mann's use of the third-person point of view also signals the potential for a reading of the text as fiction.

The memoir is not only polyvocal but also multilingual, as it also includes other languages such as Italian and French, or the Lubeck dialect of Julia Mann's grandmother. Moreover, the reader follows Mann's acquisition of the German language. Her text recreates the sense of alienation that accompanies such language learning: the slow grasping of these strange foreign sounds as in the name "Therese," which the narrator keeps repeating in disbelief that someone could answer to such a foreign-sounding name. The reactions to this process of coming into the language are also mirrored, for example, when the German grandmother grows irritated that she is called "vovó," Portuguese for grandmother, and believes for a moment that her grandchildren call her a dog, "wauwau."[16] If indeed we read the text as an ethnography, as I have already suggested, it could be described in Mary-Louise Pratt's terms as a form of autoethnography, in which Julia Mann writes against the prejudice she encountered in Lubeck, yet simultaneously reasserts racist typologies.[17]

The influence of Anna, the Mozambican woman who raised Julia Mann, looms large in the memoir and, with it, the history of Brazilian slavery and slave culture. Mann relates how she grew up playing with "white," "yellow," and "brown" children, mostly children of the enslaved men and women on her father's and grandfather's estates.[18]

---

[16] Mann, *Ich spreche so gern mit meinen Kindern*, 22.
[17] Mary Louise Pratt, *Imperial Eyes: Travel Writing and Transculturation* (New York: Routledge, 1992), 9.
[18] Mann, *Ich spreche so gern mit meinen Kindern*, 16.

In fact, her nickname, "Dodô," is a common Afro-Brazilian term of endearment, meaning "small" or "loveable." Mann describes how Anna curled her hair to make it look just like hers, and how she and the other enslaved workers taught her songs, which Mann considers in hindsight to be "very inferior" ("sehr minderwertig").[19] The Brazilian writer João Silvério Trevisan has pointed out the emotional significance of the song "Molequinho do meu Pai," which Mann frequently sang to her children and grandchildren.[20] In this song, a young girl mourns the death of her mother. She is buried alive by her stepmother, and finally rescued by her father. This song certainly must have resonated with Mann, whose mother died, whose father left her alone in Lubeck, and who had to accept her aunt as her stepmother. Moreover, I would argue, this song points to illegitimate sibling relationships as part of plantation life in nineteenth-century Brazil and might have carried additional emotional significance for Mann for that reason (albeit not necessarily consciously). In this song the singer is addressing a "molequinho do meu pai." The term "molequinho" has many meanings—it refers to a boy who is unruly in one or more than one way, a mischievous child, and possibly an illegitimate child. The word derives from the African language Kimbundu, where it means small child. In mid-nineteenth-century Brazil it was used, often pejoratively, to describe a boy of African origin.[21] Mann translates it as "my father's negro boy" ("Negerknabe meines Vaters").[22] She thus describes him as an enslaved errand boy—this boy is considered to be the property of the girl's father. However, the ambiguity of the term allows for another sense of belonging, namely that of illegitimate kinship. In 1855, at age twenty-nine, Julia Mann's nanny Anna gave birth to a daughter named Lucianna. Bruhns's slave inventory describes her as racially mixed.[23] Mann mentions this younger childhood companion in her memoir as the "mulatto child Luizianna" ("Mulattenkind Luizianna").[24] It is noteworthy that Mann's version of the name conflates the mother's name, Anna, with Bruhns's Brazilian name, Luiz. There is some historical evidence that supports the

---

[19] Mann, *Ich spreche so gern mit meinen Kindern*, 30.
[20] João Silvério Trevisan, *Ana em Veneza* (Rio de Janeiro: Editora Record, 1998), 132. See also Angela Pawlik and Henrick Stahr, "Die produktive Rezeption von Thomas Mann im Roman 'Ana em Veneza' von João Silvério Trevisan (1994)," *Pandaemonium Germanicum*, vol. 3, no. 1 (1999): 85–107, here 89.
[21] António Morais da Silva, *Diccionário da Lingua Portugueza*, Lisbon, 1789, www.cepese.pt/portal/en/databases/dicionario-de-morais/m.
[22] Mann, *Ich spreche so gern mit meinen Kindern*, 30.
[23] *Inventário, 1856*. Maria Senhora da Silva Bruhns. Acervo do Poder Judiciário do Estado do Rio de Janeiro, CX 794 A, Cod. 7055.
[24] Mann, *Ich spreche so gern mit meinen Kindern*, 14.

possibility that Bruhns fathered a child with Anna.[25] Regardless of the exact nature of Bruhns's relationship to Anna, we know enough about her to make the point that Anna and, with her, the complex negotiation of intimacy and subjugation inherent in slaveholding were an integral part of the Bruhns' family life. We also know that Julia Mann's view of race was shaped by an experience of deep intimacy coupled with a sense of racial superiority. The slaveholding system was inextricably linked to violence, threatened or actualized. Those who were owned were separated from those who owned them by racial prejudice, including ideas that Africans and Afro-Brazilians were like children or animals. These ideas also are clearly present in *Aus Dodos Kindheit*, for example in the specific way it mentions a "negro" on the voyage to Germany who entertained the children by acting like a monkey.[26]

Mann's memoir contains many observations that provide further insight into the racial politics of her upbringing. For example, it makes a point of describing the generational (and gender) differences in the way enslaved people are treated. While Mann's maternal grandmother enforced a strict separation from slaves, her mother personally tended to a critically injured enslaved man in her living room. Mann herself emphasizes that she liked to eat their food with them.[27] The presentation of changing generational attitudes towards slavery re-enacts the historical movement towards abolition. This 1903 narrative is clearly also a narrative of Brazil's progress and entry into modernity, written after Brazil became a republic, after it abolished slavery, and two years

---

[25] It is possible that Bruhns was Lucianna's father, given that Anna's social interactions would have been closely monitored and that she would not have lived in the slave quarters since she was the main carer for Bruhns's children. As the Brazilian historian Emilia Viotti da Costa has shown, a large "mestizo" population emerged out of forced or consensual unions between slaveholders and enslaved women: Emilia Viotti da Costa, *The Brazilian Empire, Myths and Histories* (Chapel Hill: University of North Carolina Press, 2000),136. Slaveholders would enslave their own children, siblings, or in some instances even mothers in order to avoid acknowledging a blood relationship or to avoid enslavement of their relatives by other masters. Starting in the 1820s, there were proposals for a law that would free an enslaved woman who gave birth to her master's child, but the implied public acknowledgment of extra-marital relationships contained in such a law prevented its implementation. In light of these discussions, it seems significant that after Anna's daughter was born, Bruhns promised Anna her freedom on the condition that she was to work another five years for him. Sene, "Johann Ludwig Hermann Bruhns,"107. While gratitude might have been a factor, as some of the literature on Bruhns claims, his motives might also have been more complex.

[26] Mann, *Ich spreche so gern mit meinen Kindern*, 20.

[27] Mann, *Ich spreche so gern mit meinen Kindern*, 14.

after the Brazilian aviator Alberto Santos-Dumont circled the Eiffel tower in a self-designed airship signaling the technological and industrial prowess of the country at the beginning of the new century.[28] Here, Julia Mann is writing as a mediator of Brazilian modernity, a distinctly white modernity, to her children and her German readers.

It is thus fitting that this memoir registers with a certain sense of discomfiture, that the carefully calibrated mechanism of intimacy and distance to slaves in Paraty based on Brazilian nineteenth-century constructions of whiteness as linked to social status did not translate to nineteenth-century Germany. Mann remarks that a relative in Lubeck thought of her and her siblings as "Ludwig's little black kids" ("Ludwig sin lütten Swatten").[29] And while this sense of blackness is portrayed as an exotic spectacle for mid-nineteenth-century Lubeck, the dominance of scientifically framed racial theories by the late nineteenth century created a different paradigm for the way Mann and her family had to negotiate their race in 1903. *Aus Dodos Kindheit* thus undertakes the work of shifting the perception of difference from race to culture. A key element of this shift is the trope of "in-betweenness." In the memoir, Bruhns tells his daughter that she was born in the middle of a move from one family estate to another, in the jungle "among monkeys and parrots" ("[u]nter Affen und Papageien").[30] Up to this day, this image still serves to emphasize the exotic nature, the animality, the wildness, and the homelessness of Julia Mann.[31] The characteristics assigned to Black slaves threatened to shape her own image, and the text enacts the very anxiety it attempts to quell: the fear of contagion of racial primitivity. The notion that Mann needed to be "civilized" infuses her own account of her schooling in Lubeck, which was to eliminate the effects of what is described as her "negro education" ("Negererziehung").[32] This included beliefs connected to Brazilian Catholicism and Afro-Brazilian or indigenous religions, particularly superstition and apparitions. For example, the text narrates how the young child hears a loud

---

[28] Alberto Santos-Dumont built his first airship in Paris in 1898 and "became a pop culture icon and flyboy hero." The iconic image of his blimp circling the Eiffel Tower is said to depict his 1901 flight, but in fact, the image is difficult to date. Peter Soppelsa and Blair Stein, "Santos-Dumont's Blimp Passes the Eiffel Tower," *Technology and Culture*, vol. 54, no. 4 (October 2013): 942–6, here 944.

[29] Mann, *Ich spreche so gern mit meinen Kindern*, 21.

[30] Mann, *Ich spreche so gern mit meinen Kindern*, 11.

[31] For example, in her biography of Julia Mann's granddaughter, Erika Mann, Viola Roggenkamp uses the term "jungle beauty" to describe Julia Mann: Viola Roggenkamp, *Erika Mann. Eine jüdische Tochter* (Zurich: Arche, 2005), 13. Other frequently used terms include "exotic," "foreign," "Southern," "Latin," "Romanic," or "creole."

[32] Mann, *Ich spreche so gern mit meinen Kindern*, 23.

knocking in the garden of her German grandmother and believes she hears the devil. When she screams in loud panic, her uncle Eduard proceeds to beat her. This "hard procedure" ("harte Prozedur")—as it is called in hindsight—supposedly rids her forever of superstition.[33] This language evokes the violence of an exorcism, a ritual associated with Catholicism and also Afro-Brazilian religions. Here, the text presents a sort of Northern German Protestant exorcism, rather than describing an ostensibly non-violent Protestant moral education and the psychological violence that could be associated with that type of schooling, as depicted in many narratives ranging from Helene Lange's urgent call for educational reform, *Die höhere Mädchenschule und ihre Bestimmung* (*The Girls' Finishing School and its Purpose*) in 1887, to Michael Haneke's harrowing film *Das weiße Band* (*The White Ribbon*) in 2009. The belief in the devil is exorcised through physical pain, which forever imprints a new relationship to the past onto the narrator's body and memory, though on old and familiar terms. Mann's text thus subtly turns the ethnographic gaze around—the civilizing process is just more of the same, and it is not perceived as different from what it seeks to eradicate.

The very form of the memoir manuscript, its handwriting, and its corrections also reflect the forcefulness of this German Protestant re-education effort: from a distance, it grasps for the language of childhood, and after almost half a century emerges the Portuguese of a child that was not yet formally schooled in her mother tongue. Moreover, the European languages of her musical education, Spanish and Italian, are layered over her Brazilian Portuguese. She writes "madre di dio" rather than "mãe de deus" ("mother of God") or "diabolo" rather than "diabo" ("devil").[34] In other instances, Julia Mann researches and corrects her writing and adds explanations in the manuscript, for example adding the name of the dried meat she frequently ate with the slaves, "carne seca."[35] In this context it is significant that some of the words that Julia Mann

---

[33] Mann, *Ich spreche so gern mit meinen Kindern*, 23.
[34] Manuscript "Aus Dodos Kindheit," 8. Archiv der Akademie der Künste Berlin, Heinrich Mann Sammlung 5245.
[35] It is noteworthy that the German edition of 1991 makes some corrections to the manuscript, for example Mann's "Makako" ("monkey") becomes "Macao," like the city, which makes the text unintelligible. This edition also manages to diminish the emotion expressed in the writing: the majority of Mann's underlining, emphases, and exclamation marks are omitted. The result is a text that comes across as less dramatic than the manuscript. The argument for these editorial decisions is an alignment with contemporary grammar and punctuation. However, considering the image (and perceived problem) of excessive "Southern" emotionality that Julia Mann herself (and subsequently her children) narrated as part of her Brazilian story, these corrections unwittingly help to reinforce this image.

insisted on writing in their original language are not actually Portuguese words but came from indigenous languages, for example "mengão" (correct: mingau) for porridge, a Tupi word, which was a language spoken in the area where Mann grew up. The memoir is multilingual beyond Europe. As the language Tupi found its way into the Portuguese language, many elements of indigenous spiritual life made their way into Brazilian Catholicism, the religion into which Julia Mann was initiated: the belief in a spirit-nature, the idea of rebirth, or the notion that dreams were predictive of the future. And Brazil's syncretic religious festivals left a deep impression on Julia Mann, among them most memorably Rio's street carnival. The memoir describes the young child watching it from inside the house, separated from this world not just by age but also by class. She registers a colorfully-dressed lady, whose movements seem to have "nothing ladylike" ("gar nichts Damenhaftes").[36] She then realizes that some of the dancers are crossdressing. This revelation and the inappropriateness of the movements clearly stuck with the narrator, and while the scene is presented as an aside, it stands at the beginning of the expulsion from the childhood paradise—the move to Rio de Janeiro after her mother's death and the emigration to Lubeck. As in the biblical story of Adam and Eve, the attainment of sexual knowledge precipitates the loss of paradise. In Mann's framing, it marks the transition from a world of innocence to a world of loss and disillusionment.

Besides the linguistic and visual traces that Brazilian indigenous and African cultures and languages left in Mann's narrative, there are also auditory traces. The memoir registers the sounds of many different types of musical instruments, for example the loud piercing sound of the indigenous conch. Mann would have heard other Tupi instruments, and also instruments of African origin, such as the reco-reco from Angola, already a crucial component of samba music by the mid-nineteenth century. Her upbringing was fundamentally shaped by a syncretic Brazilian culture and not solely by its European elements (which in Brazil would also have included a strong connection to France).

It is important to note that, besides perpetuating racial stereotypes, Mann's text also creates a positively connoted narrative of "Southernness" and musicality. In fact, her "negro education" stands at the origin of Mann's later successes as a musical performer. Mann reconstructed the melody of the already discussed slave song "Molequinho do meu pai," pasted it into the manuscript, and then continued: "They [Julia and her sister Mana] sang in the nasal way they had adopted from the negroes, but they held tone and pace firmly; and later they counted among the

---

[36] Mann, *Ich spreche so gern mit meinen Kindern*, 18.

musically most sure in the choir" ("Sie sangen in der von den Negern angeeigneten näselnden Art, aber fest im Ton und Takt; und später beim Chorsingen zählten sie zu den musikalisch Sichersten").[37] The theme of musicality as a passion fueled by emotional and linguistic "primitivity" while simultaneously providing access to the higher echelons of bourgeois education not only resonates in the scholarly language about Julia Mann's musical talent, but also becomes in different ways a paradigm for her children's writing on music. For example, Thomas Mann's novel *Doktor Faustus* critiques the evolutionary frame of protagonist Adrian Leverkühn's composition. Leverkühn's oratory "Apocalypsis" depicts the "life history of music" ("Lebensgeschichte der Musik"), ranging from the "pre-musical, magical-rhythmic elementary states" ("vor-musikalischen, magisch-rhythmischen Elementar-Zuständen") such as "magical-fanatical-negro-like drumming" ("magisch-fanatisch-negerhaftes Trommeln") to the "highest music" ("höchste[r] Musik"), that is, its "most complex perfection" ("komplizierteste Vollendung").[38]

In reading Mann's memoir, it is important not only to consider the visible traces but also what remains invisible and is left unspoken about Paraty: it was a childhood paradise built on a geography of violence. Bruhns's ascent from young immigrant to established plantation owner and slaveholder is an important example of German involvement in the transatlantic slave trade. Heike Raphael-Hernandez and Pia Wiegmink have argued that it shaped "German cultural memory and identity to a larger extent than has been illustrated and admitted so far."[39] Mann benefited from a system that exploited and subjugated the very people she was most intimate with, particularly her nanny Anna. But as the family moved to Europe, Mann remained not only a participant in perpetuating racial prejudice; she herself also became its object as she was not seen as strictly white. In reaction to this prejudice, *Aus Dodos Kindheit* attempts to write Julia Mann as white and frames her "re-education" as successful. However, its language still transports the anxiety around an

---

[37] Mann, *Ich spreche so gern mit meinen Kindern*, 30.
[38] My translation. (Thomas Mann's first translator, Helen Lowe-Porter, omitted his reference to race in 1948.) Thomas Mann, *Doktor Faustus*, Grosse Kommentierte Frankfurter Ausgabe, vol. 10, no. 1 (Frankfurt: S. Fischer, 2007), 542. Hans Vaget has emphasized the influence of Julia Mann's music tastes and education with regard to Thomas Mann's passion for music: Hans Vaget, *Seelenzauber. Thomas Mann und die Musik* (Frankfurt: Fischer, 2006), 59. See also Volker Mertens's essay about the "mother's voice" as a key metaphor of Thomas Mann's literary construction of the eternally feminine, and the erotic basis of Mann's personal and intellectual relationship to music.
[39] Heike Raphael-Hernandez and Pia Wiegmink, "German Entanglements in Transatlantic Slavery: An Introduction," *Atlantic Studies*, vol. 14, no. 4 (2017): 419–35, here 422.

assumed immutability of race. For example, when Mann describes how Anna curled her hair "after her taste" ("nach ihrem Geschmack"), she emphasizes that she was originally blonde as a child, just like her German father.[40] As I argue in my forthcoming book, this violence resurges as an uncanny presence in the writings of Mann's family that were inspired by this memoir. Fictions such as Thomas Mann's *Der Wille zum Glück* (*The Will to Happiness*) and *Königliche Hoheit* (*Royal Highness*), and Heinrich Mann's *In einer Familie* (*In a Family*) and *Zwischen den Rassen* (*Between the Races*) even directly evoke the language and scenes from *Aus Dodos Kindheit*.[41] For example, in *Zwischen den Rassen*, the description of the childhood of protagonist Lola Gabriel very closely follows Julia Mann's memoir. At the moment when Lola Gabriel is brought to Germany and experiences foreignness, she identifies with the sufferance of the men who were enslaved by her grandfather. The night before her father and her nanny Anna leave her in the care of her German grandmother and return to Brazil, she dreams that a Black man she knows and likes is being brutally beaten by a guard. As she hears his "whimpering" ("Winseln"), she herself starts to cry and awakes in sobs. The crying of the beaten man continues in the "wailing" ("Schluchzen") of Anna, who crouches over her bed to say goodbye to her.[42] Later, in her intense loneliness and desperation, Lola imagines becoming sick

---

[40] Mann, *Ich spreche so gern mit meinen Kindern*, 12.

[41] The way in which race operates in some of these narratives as a "symbol," a "poetics of stigmatization," a politics of difference, or a shifting marker of "imperial imagination," particularly in connection to Jewishness, has been analyzed by other scholars, for example Jacques Darmaun, Heinrich Detering, Yahya Elsaghe, Ruth Klüger, and Todd Kontje. Other scholars have more explicitly connected Thomas Mann's preoccupation with degeneracy and the marginality of artistic existence with his Brazilian family background. Richard Miskolci conceives of Mann as a "mestiço artist," and Paolo Soethe extensively documents fictional clues of "mnemonic alterity" in Heinrich and Thomas Mann's works.

[42] Heinrich Mann, *Zwischen den Rassen* (Munich: Albert Langen, 1907), 17. For more extensive discussions of the role of Julia Mann's biography and of race and exoticism in Heinrich Mann's *Zwischen den Rassen*, see Manfred Eickhölter, "Nähe und Distanz—Heinrich Mann und seine Mutter Julia," in *Julia Mann und ihre Kinder*, ed. Ulrike Leutheusser (Munich: Allitera, 2019), 41–68, and Gabriele Dürbeck, "Rassismus und Kosmopolitanismus in Heinrich Manns *Zwischen den Rassen*," *Heinrich Mann-Jahrbuch*, vol. 25 (2007): 9–30. Heinrich Mann most certainly also drew from his time of engagement to the Argentinian Inés Schmied. See Ariane Martin, "Faszination und Ressentiment. Heinrich Mann's Freundin Inés Schmied," in *"Luftschifferinnen, die man nicht landen läßt". Frauen im Umfeld der Familie Mann*, ed. Hans Wißkirchen (Lubeck: Dräger, 1996), 89–111; and Anke Lindemann-Stark, "Heinrich Manns Nena. Biographisches zu Ines Schmied," *Heinrich Mann-Jahrbuch*, vol. 19 (2001): 7–28.

without being able to point to the source of her pain and screaming "like the negro, who had a hole in his stomach, screamed back then" ("wie damals der Neger schrie, der ein Loch im Magen hatte").[43] Lola Gabriel's pain over the loss of her family, her nanny, and homeland, and her inner torment over the differences between her German and her Brazilian heritages drive the novel. She is unable to choose between two men, who each represent different poles of a racially inflected spectrum of North and South, of bourgeoisie and *bohème*. In particular, Lola Gabriel's relationship to her Brazilian mother (who like Lola Gabriel herself also features many of Julia Mann's traits) is framed in terms of a sexualized and incestuous "Southern" degeneracy. Certainly, this was a common literary trope of the time, but it resonated deeply with the Manns on a biographical level as they used it to rewrite again and again their mother's story. Underneath the surface impression of Julia Mann's memoir and the idealization of the childhood paradise, the horror of the adult hell of those who had been enslaved by her family lingered. In *Zwischen den Rassen*, the child's identification with enslaved men and women simultaneously reads as empathy and appropriation, as intimate and inappropriate, as recognition and abjection. The suffering of the artist and the cultural foreigner that became so paradigmatic for the literature of Heinrich and Thomas Mann explicitly connected with Julia Mann's Brazilian world and the screams it had transported across the ocean.

Many losses are narrated in *Aus Dodos Kindheit*, including the trauma of the early death of the mother. This trauma also finds its way into the opening of Thomas Mann's *Der Zauberberg* (*The Magic Mountain*), where Hans Castorp's mother dies suddenly at the end of a pregnancy—the first of several significant losses for the novel's protagonist.[44] Hans Castorp is the same age as Julia Mann was when her mother died in childbirth. The image of a young child watching a beloved relative lying in repose, which *Aus Dodos Kindheit* so powerfully narrates, is also present here as well as in many other Mann family narratives. In *Der Zauberberg* it is used to full effect to emphasize the conflict between the impressions of transcendent beauty and nauseating decay that death evokes in the protagonist. It also prefigures the constant threat of death due to a lung ailment, which will pervade the novel from that point onwards. Julia Mann's narration of her Brazilian childhood, her constant retellings as well as her written memoir, sets up a fictional blueprint that many Mann family narrations subsequently draw on. The negotiation

---

[43] Heinrich Mann, *Zwischen den Rassen*, 32.
[44] Thomas Mann, *Der Zauberberg*, Grosse Kommentierte Frankfurter Ausgabe, vol. 5, no. 2 (Frankfurt: S. Fischer, 2002), 34.

of race and of cultural difference in *Aus Dodos Kindheit*, its narrative of the process of *Bildung*, and its mediation of trauma become points of reference that are perpetuated or contended with. Understanding the way in which Julia Mann wrote Germany with Brazil is crucial to understanding the investment with which the Mann family wrote Germany. They wrote Germany from inside and outside, literally, from within Germany and later in exile from fascism, but also metaphorically, following the narrative of an outsider, who ultimately made them more German.

Works Cited

Arendt, Hannah, and Haun Saussy. "Rahel Varnhagen and Goethe," *Critical Inquiry*, vol. 40, no. 1 (2013): 15–24.

Banuls, André. "Leben und Persönlichkeit," in *Thomas Mann Handbuch*, ed. Helmut Koopmann (Frankfurt: Fischer, 2005), 1–17.

Darmaun, Jacques. *Thomas Mann, Deutschland und die Juden* (Tübingen: Max Niemeyer, 2003).

Detering, Heinrich. *"Juden, Frauen und Litteraten." Zu einer Denkfigur beim jungen Thomas Mann* (Frankfurt: Fischer, 2005).

Dürbeck, Gabriele. "Rassismus und Kosmopolitanismus in Heinrich Manns *Zwischen den Rassen*," *Heinrich Mann-Jahrbuch*, vol. 25 (2007): 9–30.

Elsaghe, Yahya. *Die imaginäre Nation. Thomas Mann und das "Deutsche"* (Munich: Wilhelm Fink, 2000).

Elsaghe, Yahya. *Thomas Mann und die kleinen Unterschiede. Zur erzählerischen Imagination des "Anderen"* (Cologne: Böhlau, 2004).

Gelbin, Cathy, and Sander L. Gilman. *Cosmopolitanisms and the Jews* (Ann Arbor: University of Michigan Press, 2017).

Gersão, Teolinda. *O Regresso de Júlia Mann a Paraty* (Porto: Porto Editora, 2021).

Gersdorff, Dagmar von. *Julia Mann, die Mutter von Heinrich und Thomas Mann. Eine Biographie* (Berlin: Insel, 2018).

Klüger, Ruth (also Angress-Klüger). "Jewish Characters in Thomas Mann's Fiction," in *Horizonte*, ed. Hannelore Mundt, Egon Schwarz, and William J. Lillyman (Tübingen: Max Niemeyer, 1990), 161–72.

Kontje, Todd. *Thomas Mann's World: Empire, Race and the Jewish Question* (Ann Arbor: University of Michigan Press, 2011).

Krüll, Marianne. *Im Netz der Zauberer. Eine andere Geschichte der Familie Mann* (Frankfurt: Fischer, 2011).

Kuschel, Karl-Josef, Frido Mann, and Paul Soethe, eds. *Mutterland. Die Familie Mann und Brasilien* (Dusseldorf: Artemis & Winkler, 2009).

Leutheusser, Ulrike, ed. *Julia Mann und ihre Kinder* (Munich: Allitera, 2019).

Mann, Frido. *Brasa* (Munich: Nymphenburger, 1999).

Mann, Frido. Interview with Frido Mann. Munich, August 2, 2017.

Mann, Heinrich. *Zwischen den Rassen* (Munich: Albert Langen, 1907).

Mann, Julia. *Aus Dodos Kindheit* (Konstanz: Rosgarten, 1958).

Mann, Julia. *Aus Dodos Kindheit* (Manuscript). Heinrich Mann Sammlung 5245, Akademie der Künste Berlin.

Mann, Julia. *Ich spreche so gern mit meinen Kindern* (Berlin: Aufbau, 1994).

Mann, Thomas. *Der Zauberberg*. Grosse Kommentierte Frankfurter Ausgabe, vol. 5, no. 2 (Frankfurt: S. Fischer, 2002).

Mann, Thomas. *Doktor Faustus*. Grosse Kommentierte Frankfurter Ausgabe, vol. 10, no. 1 (Frankfurt: S. Fischer, 2007).
Mann, Viktor. *Wir waren fünf. Bildnis der Familie Mann* (Konstanz: Südverlag, 2017).
Mertens, Volker. *Die Stimme der Mutter. Thomas Mann und die Musik* (London: Institute of Modern Language Research, University of London School of Advanced Study, 2015).
Miskolci, Richard. *O Artista Mestiço* (Sao Paulo: Annablume Editora, 2003).
Paulino, Sibele, and Paulo Soethe. "Thomas Mann e a cena intelectual no Brasil: encontros e desencontros," *Pandaemonium Germanicum*, vol. 14 (2009): 28–53.
Pawlik, Angela, and Henrick Stahr. "Die produktive Rezeption von Thomas Mann im Roman *Ana em Veneza* von João Silvério Trevisan (1994)," *Pandaemonium Germanicum*, vol. 3, no. 1 (1999): 85–107.
Pratt, Mary Louise. *Imperial Eyes: Travel Writing and Transculturation* (London and New York: Routledge, 1992).
Raphael-Hernandez, Heike, and Pia Wiegmink. "German Entanglements in Transatlantic Slavery: An Introduction," *Atlantic Studies*, vol. 14, no. 4 (2017): 419–35.
Roggenkamp, Viola. *Erika Mann. Eine jüdische Tochter* (Hamburg: Arche, 2005).
Sene, Maria. "Johann Ludwig Hermann Bruhns," in *Julia Mann. Brasilien—Lübeck—München* (Lübeck: Dräger Druck, 1999), 99–128.
Soethe, Paulo. "Deutsch, Italienisch, Brasilianisch. Heinrich Mann 'Zwischen den Rassen,'" *Estudios Filológicos Alemanes*, vol. 12 (2006): 413–28.
Soppelsa, Peter, and Blair Stein. "Santos-Dumont's Blimp Passes the Eiffel Tower," *Technology and Culture*, vol. 54, no. 4 (October 2013): 942–6.
Strauss, Dieter, and Maria Sene, eds. *Julia Mann. Brasilien-Lübeck-München* (Lubeck: Dräger Druck, 1999).
Trevisan, João Silvério. *Ana em Veneza* (Rio de Janeiro: Editora Record, 1998).
Vaget, Hans. *Seelenzauber. Thomas Mann und die Musik* (Frankfurt: Fischer, 2006).
Viotti da Costa, Emilia. *The Brazilian Empire: Myths and Histories* (Chapel Hill: University of North Carolina Press, 2000).
Weise, Christina. *Thomas Mann und Brasilien. Untersuchungen zur Produktion und Rezeption*, MA thesis, University of Cologne, 2012.

Eight From Vienna to the Midwest: Austrian Refugees and Quaker Rescue Efforts after 1938

Bettina Brandt

When the US Seventh Armored Division landed on the beaches of Normandy in August 1944, thirty-three-year-old Sergeant Rudolph J. Schreck found himself on European soil for the first time in five years. His division engaged in heavy fighting, first on the Western front, including the Battle of the Bulge, and later as far east as the German city of Lubeck on the Baltic Sea. The German-speaking Jewish refugee from Vienna had been eager to fight the Nazis and, a year later, had earned five "Battle Participation Stars." In a letter from August 1945 addressed to the American Friends Service Committee (AFSC) in Philadelphia, Schreck briefly outlined his wartime experiences to the Quaker humanitarian aid organization. Without going into detail, since what he was doing was secret, he mentioned that he had been working as a military intelligence officer gathering strategic information through interrogating German prisoners. In the months leading up to the end of what for him had also been an intensely personal war, he had seen so many "horrible things, just from the human point of view" that he "could write a book about it." He particularly mentioned "convoys of thousands of displaced Russians and Poles," as well as "the devastation of Kassel and Magdeburg," cities that had been heavily bombed by the Allies.[1]

---

[1] United States Holocaust Museum (USHMM) (2002), 296, Box 73, AFSC refugee case file 2112. This chapter was made possible thanks to the author's tenure as an Edith Milman Memorial Fellow at the Jack, Joseph and Morton Mandel Center for Advanced Holocaust Studies, United States Holocaust Memorial Museum. I also would like to thank my friend Günther Marx, a Jewish refugee from Remscheid, who has been living in New York City since fleeing Germany, for his thoughtful feedback on this article.

While Schreck made sure to keep the AFSC up to date with news from recently liberated Germany, his main reason for writing to the offices in Philadelphia had been to ask for help in a personal matter. Could the aid organization help him locate his mother? Schreck had last heard from her in 1941. Since then, the only news that had reached him was that his mother—as well as several of his maternal aunts—had been "deported" to "an unknown destination, probably Poland," the next year. Now that the war had ended, Schreck wondered, might the AFSC be able to tell him how to find "these unfortunate people," who had likely since then "been dragged around by the Nazis?"[2]

Rudolph Schreck had been communicating with the Quakers for years. He first established contact with them through their International Friends Center in Vienna in the summer of 1939. At that time, the Quakers had provided help to get him out of the Third Reich. On March 13, 1938, at the time of the *Anschluss*—Hitler's annexation of Austria—the city of Vienna was home to some 185,000 Jews, or about 10 percent of the city's population. Including converted Jews, the total number of people with a Jewish family background was about 206,000. In the *Ostmark*, as Austria under Nazi control now was called, daily life for Jews progressively worsened. In 1938 alone, more than 100 anti-Semitic laws and bans had gone into effect, including the infamous Nuremberg Laws of 1935, retroactively extended to Austria. These laws and bans left most Jewish families without an income, robbed them of their assets, and increasingly isolated them socially. In response to the relentless Nazi persecution and the pressure put on Jews to leave as quickly as possible—weekly emigration quotas had been put in place and the Jewish community in Vienna, now under Nazi control, was put in charge of filling them—many Jewish families planned to emigrate.[3] To expedite and systematize Jewish emigration, Adolf Eichmann had established a Central Office of Jewish Emigration in August 1938. At this office the financial and administrative emigration-related paperwork of those about to move away was examined for Nazi compliance purposes. If none of the myriad of required documents were missing, or had expired since they first had been issued, and if all outstanding anti-Semitic and other emigration-related taxes had been paid, an exit permit was issued, and a passport, stamped with a "J" to make clear that the passport holder was Jewish, was validated.

---

[2] AFSC refugee case file 2112.

[3] Pressuring Jews to emigrate from Vienna started as early as two weeks after the *Anschluss*, when Hermann Goering organized a rally at which he declared that "all Jews must quit Austria." See the *New York Times*, March 27, 1938, 1 and 6.

From Vienna to the Midwest 171

Getting cleared for emigration from Nazi Vienna was, however, only half the problem. Locating a country to which the increasingly destitute refugees could immigrate, and finding the means to get there, was the other. A number of organizations provided emigration-related aid to Jews fleeing from Vienna. The Israelitische Kultusgemeinde (IKG) helped only religious Jews. The Swedish Mission, Svenska Israelmissionen, helped Jews who had converted to Protestantism and Jews who were married to Protestants, while the Archepiscopal Office for non-Aryan Catholics in theory was the place to go for Jews who had converted to Catholicism, though this organization did very little in terms of emigration aid.[4] Nuremberg Law Jews, as well as those who had been let down by the other aid organizations because they "did not fit in anywhere," came to the offices of the International Friends Center on the third floor of Singerstrasse 16, behind St. Stephen's Cathedral, in the heart of Vienna.[5] There, British Quakers (via the Friends Service Council) and Quakers from the United States (through the AFSC) had been working together on alleviating Vienna's social problems ever since the first decades of the newly formed Republic of Austria. The Center provided food for tens of thousands of starving children daily.[6] After the *Anschluss*, the Quakers in Vienna benefitted from their nonpartisanship, their previous experience in relief work, and their long-established connections both locally and internationally. Supported by funds from England and the United States, the Quakers at the International Center in Vienna now worked under tremendous strain to accommodate the renewed and growing demand for their services.[7] While the Center continued to offer assistance through food pantries, soup kitchens, and the distribution of clothes, the offices at the Singerstrasse now also started offering emigration-related aid.[8] By the early fall of 1938,

---

[4] For the role of the IKG, see Doron Rabinovici, *Eichmann's Jews: The Jewish Administration of Holocaust Vienna, 1938–1945*, trans. Nick Somers (Cambridge: Polity Press, 2011). See Traude Litzka on the role of the churches, in *The Church's Help for Persecuted Jews in Nazi Vienna*, trans. Gerda Joseph (Vienna: LIT, 2019), here 91.

[5] AFSC refugee case file 2112.

[6] The AFSC was founded in 1917 in response to the United States' entry into World War I. Its immediate purpose was to give conscientious objectors a way to serve their country through assisting civilian victims of this war. After 1918, the AFSC opened several Friends Centers in critical European countries to continue helping the war-ravaged communities. The Centers in Berlin and Vienna remained open until the summer of 1941.

[7] AFSC annual report, 1938, 9.

[8] Hans Schmitt, *Quakers and Nazis: Inner Light in Outer Darkness* (Columbia and London: University of Missouri Press, 1997), 137.

the Center was handling 500 interviews a week.⁹ Tirelessly conducting interviews, writing cables and letters on behalf of all potential refugees, those at the Center cooperated closely with other refugee agencies, different consulates, several banks, and numerous travel companies.¹⁰

During the orchestrated anti-Semitic pogrom that took place on November 9, 1938, almost all of Vienna's synagogues and small prayer houses were burned to the ground. A total of 6,547 Austrian Jews were arrested, 3,700 of whom were deported to the Dachau concentration camp, outside of Munich.¹¹ This particularly brutal event left no doubt, even in the minds of the most hopeful, that for Jews there was no future in the Third Reich. It also made clear to the world at large that a refugee crisis was brewing, and more international help was needed, but not much more help was forthcoming. Still, in response, the AFSC, which so far had been offering ad hoc help only, set up a Refugee Division to increase and systemize Quaker aid to the persecuted in urgent need of getting out of Nazi Europe. By the time the Friends Center in Vienna was forced to shut down, at the end of June 1941, the Quakers had helped to bring between 2,408 and 4,500 persecuted Austrians out of Nazi Europe.¹²

For each potential refugee, the AFSC created a file. Of the 22,000 files produced, some 20,000 have survived. Some files hold but a few pages; others are over 100 pages long. Large files may contain notes from initial and follow-up interviews with the applicant, an applicant's CV, a passport-size photograph of the applicant, summaries of educational degrees, letters of recommendation from former employers, copies of extensive correspondence that AFSC workers produced on behalf of their applicant, letters from other refugee organizations that were approached for help, correspondence from consular officials as well as the State Department regarding the applicant's emigration plans, and personal letters from the applicant addressing the ever-changing circumstances. Finally, files often contain cross references to other files, thus laying bare networks of family and friends in need, as well as the successful and failed attempts to get would-be immigrants out of Nazi Europe. The contents of an AFSC refugee case file are the elements out of which researchers can attempt to create what Valentina Glajar, in a

---

[9] AFSC annual report, 1938.
[10] AFSC annual report, 1939, 16.
[11] Rabinovici, *Eichmann's Jews*, 58.
[12] Schmitt, *Quakers and Nazis* 139–40, and Sheila Spielhofer. *Stemming the Dark Tide: Quakers in Vienna 1919–1942* (York, UK: William Sessions, 2001), 115.

different context, has called "a file story."[13] By connecting the dots while also looking for the silences and absences in a case file, a "precarious and polyphonic collage" (Glajar) can be brought to life: a compelling narrative about one particular (would-be) immigrant's life story.

Situated at the intersection of Refugee Studies and Holocaust Studies, AFSC refugee case files offer an outside view on refugee applicants from Nazi Germany. They challenge mainstream narratives of Jewish emigration by shifting the perspective to the margins of Jewish experiences—to those who fell between the cracks of other aid organizations—thus underlining the diversity of forced Jewish emigration from Europe in this period. This chapter shows how the Quaker network stretched from Central Europe to the American Midwest and how it assumed different functions at each stage: from helping Jews escape Nazi Vienna to assimilating them in Iowa. At different stages along these routes, the Quakers worked to overcome political and administrative barriers to moving refugees away from the center of oppression.

I first came across Rudolph Schreck's name while translating a transatlantic post-*Anschluss* German family correspondence between a Jewish widow, Nelly Lehnert, left behind in Vienna, and her forty-some-year-old daughter who had fled from Vienna to the United States, where she and her husband and their two daughters arrived in late November 1939.[14] In her three-year-long weekly correspondence with her daughter, Nelly's main topic is the progress she was making toward emigration to the United States. Equally important, however, was Nelly's weekly chatter about the lives of family, friends, and acquaintances, a group of about 120 people, who made up Nelly's present and former Viennese microcosm, which overlapped with that of her daughter. With patience, through an eventual understanding of the code that Nelly used to protect the identity of those, who, like herself, were still endangered in Vienna, through research in American, Austrian, British, and German archives, and with a bit of luck, I was able to identify about 100 relatives, friends, and acquaintances. Two-thirds survived in exile, many in the USA; the remaining third, mostly the elderly, including Nelly herself, perished in the Holocaust. Rudolph and his mother Dora Schreck, who had worked as a clerk for the law firm of Nelly's husband

---

[13] Valentina Glajar, "The File Story of the Securitate Officer Samuel Feld," in *Cold War Spy Stories from Eastern Europe*, ed. Valentina Glajar, Alison Lewis, and Corina L. Petrescu (Lincoln: University of Nebraska Press, 2019), 30–1. I altered Glajar's definition slightly to make it applicable to AFSC refugee case files.

[14] See Bettina Brandt, "Trudie and Nelly: Deciphering a Transatlantic Family Holocaust Correspondence," in *On Being Adjacent to Historical Violence*, ed. Irene Kacandes (Boston: De Gruyter, 2021), 315–22.

and who was of great support to Nelly after most of the widow's relatives had emigrated, are two of the people in Nelly's network.

The refugee case file consists of three distinct storylines. The first file story is an AFSC success story about emigration and assimilation. This narrative shows how Rudolph was able to leave Vienna and traces his path to New York City. It then takes a close look at his experiences in the United States, including in three small towns in Iowa to which he initially had been sent (the AFSC had just opened a hostel for European refugees in West Branch). This narrative highlights the different ways in which Americans in the Midwest reacted to the presence of German refugees like Rudolph and how Quaker volunteers and others helped Rudolph overcome initial difficulties and supported him throughout his ordeals. It also draws attention to how the AFSC collaborated with other refugee organizations to help the new immigrants resettle while initiating a public awareness campaign to counter anti-Semitic and xenophobic prejudices that were rampant in the United States at that time.

The second file story is one of administrative and human failure. It reveals that once Rudolph finds himself in safety in the United States, he turns again to the AFSC for help in rescuing his loved ones left behind in fascist Europe. This narrative makes clear what these laborious and painstaking rescue efforts were up against in the fall of 1940, when immigrant visas were barely being issued anymore. This left thousands of (often elderly) Jews in Nazi Germany in a hopeless situation, including Rudolph's mother and several other relatives. This second file story shows not only how "difficult it was to cheer up these downhearted people"—as the Head of the AFSC's Relief and Refugee Services wrote to the head of the Friends' Center in Vienna concerning Rudolph's relatives still in Austria—but also how, after a certain moment in time, the American Quakers could do little else for the persecuted trapped in Nazi Europe. The third file story, with which this chapter opened, shows Rudolph gathering intelligence for the US army in postwar Europe while looking for relatives who had been deported years earlier.

Schreck's basic biographical information can be quickly summarized. Born in Vienna in 1911 with three Jewish grandparents (his mother's parents as well as his father's mother), Rudolph Schreck was classified as Jewish according to the Nuremberg Laws. He self-identified as Catholic. His mother, Dora (Dorothea) Springer (born in 1879) was the youngest child of a large Viennese Jewish family. When Dora married Franz Schreck (1875–1919), who was Catholic, she converted. Unlike in Prussia, where each partner retained his or her original religion, in Austria, entering a mixed marriage "meant that one of the partners had to list himself or herself as *konfessionslos* (without religion) or adopt the religion of the fiancé(e), an option that almost always meant baptism for the Jewish intended."[15] Franz and Dora raised Rudolph in the Catholic faith. When Franz died, Dora and her then eight-year-old son moved in with Dora's oldest sister Clementine (born in 1868), who had never married. In the 1930s, Rudolph, Dora, and Clementine lived in Vienna's Ninth district. His work experience shows that Rudolph Schreck was willing to take whatever job was available. From age fifteen to age twenty-seven he worked for a company that manufactured Turkish hats, face caps, berets, and blankets. When asked to do so, he had relocated for a few years in the early 1930s to the company's subsidiary in Silesia, now in Poland. After the *Anschluss*, much to their regret but "due to the new circumstances," the Viennese firm had to dismiss this dutiful bookkeeper and cost accountant.[16]

By the end of July 1938, 40,000 Austrian Jews had registered at the American Consulate in Vienna.[17] Six months later that number had doubled. Since the persecuted hoping to emigrate were simply lumped in with the ordinary American immigration system, which had been working with immigration quotas based on national origins since the 1920s, it was difficult to migrate to the United States, and became increasingly more so over time. Moreover, the total number of immigrants worldwide allowed to enter the United States yearly was limited to a maximum of 153,000 people. While each nationality "could make a claim to a proportion of the total based on two percent of its population in the United States in 1890," the quotas were understood as maximums, not as targets to be reached.[18] The immigration quota for Austria was only 1,413, but after the *Anschluss*, President Roosevelt combined the quota numbers for Germany and Austria for a total of 27,370, improving the chances for Austrian Jews. Between 1933 and 1941, about 110,000 Jews were able to emigrate from Nazi-occupied Europe to the United States. Hundreds of thousands of others seeking refuge registered with American consulates as well but were placed on the waiting list and never stood a chance.

Rudolph Schreck had registered with the American consulate in Vienna on July 20, 1938, and was placed on the waiting list as number 35293. One year and three months later, Rudolph was requested to

---

[15] See Charles S. Maier, "Christianity and Conviction: Gustav Mahler and the Meanings of Jewish Conversion in Central Europe," *Simon Dubnow Institute Yearbook*, vol. 11 (2012): 127–47, here 138.
[16] AFSC refugee case file 2112.
[17] Alan M. Kraut, Richard Breitman, and Thomas W. Imhoof, "The State Department, the Labor Department and German Jewish Immigration, 1930–1940," *Journal of American Ethnic History*, vol. 3, no. 2 (Spring 1984): 5–38, here 19.
[18] David A. Gerber, *American Immigration: A Very Short Introduction* (New York: Oxford University Press, 2011), 43.

appear for an interview. Being called up for an interview meant not only that one's turn on the waiting list had come up, but also that all the necessary paperwork now had arrived at the consulate, including the so-called "affidavit." This all-important document, in which an American citizen, acting as a sponsor for the would-be immigrant, disclosed his financial situation to make clear that the new immigrant would not become a public charge, or burden on the state, once he or she had landed in the United States, could make or break one's chances of getting out of Austria. If the affidavit was considered strong enough—since no guidelines had been issued, the final decision rested in the hands of the particular consul who ended up conducting the interview with the potential immigrant—and, if all other aspects of the interview went well, a visa was issued.

Looking for help in obtaining all the necessary emigration-related documents, Rudolph turned to a number of refugee aid organizations, also called committees, including the Catholic Committee for Refugees from Germany in New York City. As a memorandum in his case file makes clear, however, the Catholic organization's most recent letter, which dated back to January 1939, "had been discouraging."[19] In early July 1939, while waiting for his quota number to come up, Schreck was interviewed at the International Center in Vienna by J(uliane) R. Perry.[20] Pleased with the ease with which the twenty-seven-year-old interacted with others, his sense of humor, and his "more than average intelligence," this interviewer concluded, "I believe this young man would be a good risk. He is not the type to sit down and wait for someone to help him but will be able to help himself if he gets half a chance."[21]

Giving Rudolph Schreck half a chance meant that the British and American Quakers in Vienna now activated their extensive network abroad on his behalf. The day after his interview, Ethel Houghton, a British relief worker at the Vienna Center, sent a letter to the AFSC headquarters asking for help in securing an affidavit for Rudolph. In response to such a request, the offices in Philadelphia would reach out to Friends meetings across the United States. These Friends, in turn, would then approach their members who, if necessary, made connections with total strangers to secure the necessary papers for a European refugee. Thus, the AFSC was able to attain thousands of affidavits for the persecuted stuck in Nazi Europe. Case file 2112 does not reveal whether the two affidavits from New York City that Rudolph eventually

---

[19] AFSC refugee case file 2112.
[20] Perry is listed as traveling commissioner and field staff member in the AFSC's annual report of 1939.
[21] AFSC refugee case file 2112.

received had been provided with the help of the AFSC or through some other organization or connection. What we do know is that on September 26, 1939, the American Consulate issued an immigration visa to Rudolph J. Schreck under the German quota: number QIV7176. His was one of the 27,370 visas (the maximum under the quota law) that were issued to Germans that year.[22]

Two weeks later, on Wednesday, October 11, Schreck deregistered from the city of Vienna. He had listed the United States of America as his destination.[23] But even with the right visa stamps in one's passport and a ship ticket in one's pocket, getting to America was still a perilous undertaking. On October 12, Rudolph found himself at the port of Genoa on board the *Conte di Savoia*. On schedule, the Italian ocean liner arrived in the New York Harbor ten days later. But something had happened underway. The *Morning Tribune* reported that after the ocean liner left Naples "a French seaplane flew over her and signaled her to put into Algiers to which she was conducted by a French destroyer" and that there, sixty German men were taken off the boat and put "in concentration camps for the duration of the war."[24] The *Jewish Telegraphic Agency News*, which reported about the incident two days later, added that most of these men were Jewish refugees, and that their wives and children had been allowed to stay on the ship bound for New York City.[25] A note in his file from the National Refugee Service (by Cecilia Razovsky) makes clear that Rudolph was one of these German Jewish refugees, and that more than a month later the French had still not released him.[26] The file offers no information about how much time and with the help of whom he was set free. What we do know is that Schreck finally arrived in New York City on December 23, 1939.

---

[22] Richard Breitman and Alan M. Kraut, *American Refugee Policy and American Jewry, 1933–1945* (Bloomington and Indianapolis: Indiana University Press, 1987), 112.

[23] MA8-B-MEW-177451-2021, author's correspondence with the city of Vienna, February 22, 2021.

[24] "France Detains German Emigrants," *Morning Tribune*, October 23, 1939, eresources.nlb.gov.sg/newspapers/Digitised/Article/morningtribune19391023-1.2.64.

[25] *Jewish Telegraphic News*, vol. 6, no. 67, Wednesday, October 25, 1939, pdfs.jta.org/1939/1939-10-25_067.pdf?_ga=2.30230843.544602390.1616342417-1151408973.1607610102.

[26] Razovksy was the Director of the Migration Department of the National Refugee Service.

For Jews from Germany and Austria, the United States of America was the most popular destination, and most arrived in New York City.[27] There, an array of organizations helped the newly arrived get started. In a report from 1939, the recently landed are portrayed as follows:

> They sit nervously in the waiting room, stand up, bow, click heels when someone speaks to them. They are still far from being American. In broken English they tell their stories—lawyers, doctors, merchants, innkeepers, teachers, candymakers, jewelry designers, cooks. If America wants what they have, it is comparatively easy; otherwise, they must develop painfully what America wants. Some will succeed quickly: a few never will—but that is true of any human adjustment.[28]

Like their counterparts in Europe, each organization focused on a particular group of refugees. Yet, they also worked together and helped one another. Six days after arriving in New York City, Schreck was interviewed by Jean Reynolds from the Refugee Division of the AFSC. Reynolds recorded in her notes that Schreck was staying at 601 West 151st Street, just south of Washington Heights, a popular Manhattan area for German Jews to settle.[29] She also wrote down his previous employment history, noted his pleasant personality, that he was intelligent, and that the New York-based Catholic Committee for Refugees from Germany was helping him financially while "trying to get him established in this country."[30]

More than two-thirds of all immigrants settled on the eastern seaboard.[31] The National Refugee Service, which until the summer of 1939 had been known as the National Coordination Committee for Aid to Refugees and Emigrants coming from Germany, had been promoting resettlement away from the East Coast since 1936, for instance in the Midwest or California, where comparatively few refugees had settled.[32]

---

[27] A total of 308 German-Jewish refugees arrived in New York City with the assistance of the AFSC in January of 1940 alone. See Allan W. Austin, *Quaker Brotherhood: Interracial Activism and the American Friends Service Committee, 1917–1950* (Champaign: University of Illinois Press, 2012), 116.

[28] AFSC annual report 1939, 16.

[29] For more about Washington Heights, see www.lbi.org/exhibitions/refuge-heights-german-jews-washington-heights/.

[30] AFSC refugee case file 2112.

[31] *Refugees at Work*, compiled by Sophia M. Robinson with a prefatory note by Eleanor Roosevelt, The Committee for Selected Social Studies (New York: King's Crown Press, 1942), 4.

[32] Haim Genizi, *American Apathy: The Plight of Christian Refugees from Nazism* (Tel Aviv: Bar-Ilan University Press, 1983), 173–214.

Reynolds, who was responsible for choosing potential candidates for a new AFSC refugee hostel located in rural Iowa, brought up the idea with Schreck in his initial interview. Schreck expressed interest; the Catholic Committee for Refugees from Germany, which did not have its own resettlement project, was open to the idea as well.[33] After a month of unsuccessfully pursuing job leads in New York City, Rudolph submitted an application for Scattergood, the AFSC's new refugee hostel in Iowa. The Catholic Committee cosigned the application, agreeing to contribute five dollars weekly for Rudolph's lodging and board, plus two dollars a week for incidentals. In return, the Committee expected that the staff at Scattergood would help Rudolph resettle in the Midwest and, most importantly, find him an acceptable job. This cooperation between the Catholic Committee for Refugees from Germany and the AFSC's most successful hostel shows that while the Quakers had initiated and implemented a number of refugee hostels, including Scattergood, the money and most of the refugees (or "guests" as they were called at Scattergood) came from other committees and agencies.

A former Quaker boarding school from 1890 that had closed its doors in 1931, Scattergood had been turned into a temporary hostel for European refugees in the spring of 1939.[34] After necessary renovations, the hostel welcomed its first guests in April of that year. When Scattergood closed four year later, at the end of March 1943—when no more refugees were escaping from Nazi Europe—the hostel had taken in a total of 185 refugees. Refugees typically stayed at Scattergood between three and four months.

To further their assimilation and to Americanize the refugees—about thirty lived at the hostel at any given time—the new immigrants resided with young volunteers, both East Coast Quakers and local Quaker farmers, in a makeshift commune on the Iowa prairie. Although none of the volunteers were trained in refugee or social work, all were enthusiastic and idealistic. Some refugees had been in concentration camps, and most had to leave behind close relatives about whom they were deeply concerned and whom they attempted to rescue. The volunteers expressed their empathy and offered practical advice for a new life in the United States. Some were college students, helping out for the summer only, but most lived and worked at Scattergood for a year or longer. Both volunteers and local Iowa professors offered classes at Scattergood

---

[33] Haim Genizi, "New York is big—America is bigger: The Resettlement of Refugees from Nazism, 1936–1945," *Jewish Social Studies*, vol. 46 (Winter 1984): 61–72, here 67.

[34] Michael Luick-Thrams, ed., *Far from Hitler: The Scattergood Hostel for European Refugees, 1939–1943* (Waukee: Iowa Jewish Historical Society, 2001), 11.

on topics ranging from English phonetics to courses on American government and culture. Several of the Americans who assisted the European refugees at Scattergood continued to stay in touch with individual refugees for decades.[35] Rudolph Schreck arrived at Scattergood on February 25, 1940 and stayed three months. Later, he would refer to this ad hoc community, where he found a home that offered him consolation and support, as "a place of peace in a world of war, a haven amidst a world of hatred."[36]

Twenty-five-year-old Giles Zimmerman was of particular importance to Scattergood refugees hoping to land their first job in the United States. As Scattergood's placement director he was responsible for establishing and maintaining work contacts, and for following up with the refugees in their new jobs.[37] Zimmerman and the various refugee committees were well aware of strong public resistance to immigration in the late 1930s. Three factors contributed to the negative public opinion about refugees: significant unemployment, nativistic nationalism, and widespread anti-Semitism. The American Jewish Congress, therefore, began a campaign in 1939 to "create a healthier attitude to the refugee problem" through clarifying "misconceptions regarding the impact of refugees."[38] Under the auspices of the AFSC but in collaboration with twenty-one committees—including the American Jewish Joint Distribution Committee, the Hebrew Sheltering and Immigrant Aid Society, the International Migration Service, and the Committee for Catholic Refugees from Germany—the Quakers published 25,000 copies of a twenty-four-page report called *Refugee Facts: A Study of the German Refugee in America*.[39] This booklet hoped to contribute to the realization that the acceptance of refugees did not present a danger but rather an opportunity for enriching American life, both economically and culturally.

When the Low Countries and France fell to Germany in a matter of weeks during the early summer of 1940, American anti-foreigner sentiment climbed to an all-time high. Fear of the presence of a "fifth column" then took hold in the popular imagination. A Roper poll from

---

[35] Michael Luick-Thrams, *Out of Hitler's Reach: The Scattergood Hostel for European Refugees 1939–43* (Des Moines: Iowa Community Action Coalition, 1996), 146.
[36] Luick-Thrams, *Out of Hitler's Reach*, vi.
[37] Austin, *Quaker Brotherhood*, 136.
[38] Haim Genizi, "American Interfaith Cooperation on Behalf of Refugees from Nazism, 1933–1945," *American Jewish History*, vol. 70, no. 3 (March 1981): 347–61, here 351.
[39] American Friends Service Committee, *Refugee Facts: A Study of the German Refugee in America* (Philadelphia: American Friends Service Committee, 1939).

July 1940 found that an astonishing 71 percent of respondents were concerned that a significant percentage of German refugees were likely in the United States as spies working for the Nazis, with their relatives abroad being held as hostages, thus forcing the refugees into this role.[40] By the summer of 1940, Americans were concerned not only that refugees might push them out of their jobs; they thought of refugees as a threat to national security as well.[41]

AFSC refugee case file 2112 picks up again in May 1940 and records Schreck's entrance into the American job market. This part of the file first shows twenty-nine-year-old Rudolph working in Marshalltown, a city in rural Iowa currently with a little over 27,000 inhabitants. Zimmerman apparently reported Schreck's initial job placement to the Catholic Committee in New York City without going into any details. In a note from June 3, 1940, Father Joseph D. Osterman acknowledged the placement but also re-emphasized that the Catholic Committee was hoping for a more suitable job for this refugee: "We are grateful for your report concerning the case of Rudolph Schreck. Incidentally, we hope that he is not going about from house to house selling Fuller Brushes."[42] Working as a Fuller Brush man, however, was exactly what this refugee from Vienna was doing in his first job in the Midwest.

Eking out a living as a peddler has always been difficult. This was especially true for German refugees in the summer of 1940. Knocking on the doors of American homes in the hopes of selling their wares, these refugees, speaking with a strong German accent, gained firsthand experience of America's prevailing attitudes towards the newcomers. A Columbia University report from 1942 entitled *Refugees at Work* notes that Americans thought that the "refugee canvasser" presented "a persistent and annoying problem."[43] But the report was eager to point out that this issue would resolve itself quickly. Only the poorest refugees from Europe fell back on working as Fuller Brush Men, typically "former salesmen and small manufacturers" who had been lured to this job through "numerous newspapers advertisements" that had sold "tales of fabulous success." It was understandable that, like their American competitors, these refugee peddlers wanted to "try their hands and feet at the canvassing game." Yet, they too, the report concluded, gave up as soon as they "found other opportunities for making a living."[44] Rudolph, three weeks into his job, found his situation

---

[40] Breitman and Kraut, *American Refugee Policy*, 117.
[41] David S. Wyman, *Paper Walls: America and the Refugee Crisis 1938–1941* (New York: Pantheon, 1985), 184–205.
[42] AFSC refugee case file 2112.
[43] *Refugees at Work*, 60.
[44] *Refugees at Work*, 60.

challenging. In a letter to Scattergood he explained that he had been assigned the poorest part of Marshalltown where "nobody has the money to buy a lot of high-priced Fuller-Products."[45] He also imparted that he now had personally experienced how suspicious many locals indeed were of European refugees. He writes that "somebody told him, that the other Fuller-Brush-Man in town (that's me) is said to be a German spy. [. . .] I had noticed that some people asked me quite strange questions. [. . .] I am going around here now as if I would still be in Vienna, always with the feeling that the other person, to which I am speaking, thinks me to be her enemy."[46] At the end of his letter, Rudolph conveys that the work is not only demoralizing because of the "fifth column" fear, but that it also doesn't allow him to earn a living, pay off his debts, or save for his mother's passage out of Nazi-occupied Europe.

As it happened, the Scattergood hostel had just received a job advert for a hotel porter/clerk in Corning, Iowa, a town of 2,000 people located three and half hours west of the hostel. In need of an "honest and reliable night porter," the Hotel Bacon had turned to Scattergood's cheap labor pool to recruit a new employee.[47] The future worker would be provided with room and board and earn wages of $30 a month, plus tips if any. Zimmerman brought up this new opening to Schreck in a letter dated June 20, 1940. While he described the combination of night porter and day clerk job in realistic terms ("it would be hard work"), he also made it sound attractive ("you would practically have no expenses at all, and most likely could save all of your earnings"). Schreck applied and a week later was offered the job.[48] Initially, the relationship between the Williams family, the hotel owners, and Rudolph, their most recent hire, was anything but smooth. As the new porter/clerk soon discovered, no fewer than fourteen men had held his position in the two months prior to Rudolph's arrival. Due to the strenuous working conditions, and Mr. Williams's difficult character, none of them had lasted longer than a few days. Before long, Rudolph was ready to throw in the towel as well. The job left him exhausted and always hungry. Relations with the hotel owners improved over time but remained quite strained. At the hotel, Rudolph once again was exposed to the public fear that Jewish refugees in the United States were actually Nazi spies. The particular way in which this thought manifested, in the imagination of those at the Hotel Bacon, was in a fear of Rudolph's mail. In a letter to Zimmerman, Rudolph expressed his frustration about the negative commentary that his mail produced and how it impacted his private

---

[45] AFSC refugee case file 2112.
[46] AFSC refugee case file 2112.
[47] AFSC refugee case file 2112.
[48] AFSC refugee case file 2112.

life: "Mr. Williams won't even bring me my mail together with the other mail anymore. I write too many letters, I get too many letters, I get too many German letters (from my mother only) etc. etc. ad infinitum [. . .]."[49] In the six months during which he was employed at the hotel, Rudolph indeed wrote a lot of letters, especially to his mother Dora in Vienna. But he also regularly corresponded with the AFSC, prodding the Quakers for practical advice on how to rescue a dozen of his relatives still in Europe.

Like Rudolph, Dora and Clementine Schreck had registered with the US Consulate in Vienna on June 20, 1938. From the moment Rudolph landed in the United States, his focus had been on procuring the necessary documents to bring over his "parents," as he thought of Dora and Clementine, since both women had raised him after his father had died. While still in New York City, Schreck had convinced Mr. Katz and Mr. Scadron, the two men who had provided affidavits for him, to draw up affidavits for his mother and aunt as well. After three months at the Hotel Bacon, Schreck had managed to save enough money for his mother's voyage, proof of which was necessary to be granted an interview at the American Consulate in Vienna. Since Dora Schreck and Clementine Springer had registered more than two years earlier and all their paperwork had arrived in Vienna, their turn for an interview at the American Consulate would be coming up shortly. The Quakers in Vienna and in Philadelphia had been in constant contact with the US Consulate since the *Anschluss*. The last American Director of the Friends Center in Vienna, Margaret E. Jones, who returned to the USA in September 1940, occasionally had worked with the consular staff at the visa division in Vienna when they were short-handed.

In the months before her departure from Vienna, Jones had started to notice a disconcerting trend: an astonishingly high percentage of visa applicants were being turned down after their final interview. In a letter to Clarence Pickett, executive head of the AFSC from 1929 to 1953, Jones wondered whether a new policy had been put in place that the State Department had not yet made official. Jones's assumption was correct: the fear of fifth columnists, a fear Rudolph had experienced in both jobs in the Midwest, had begun to have a direct impact on the United States' immigration policy. By the end of June 1940, the State Department had informed all consuls abroad—but not the general public—that an immigration visa should not be issued if there was "any doubt whatsoever" concerning the alien, particularly if the applicant was currently residing in Germany, reasoning that their

---

[49] AFSC refugee case file 2112.

presence in the United States might endanger national security.[50] This unspoken policy, driven by the desire to put an end to inadvertently importing Nazi spies, practically stopped immigration from the Third Reich.[51]

Intuiting a policy shift but ignorant about the particulars, the Quakers were quite concerned about Dora Schreck and Clementine Springer's chances of obtaining an immigration visa. Yet, they also expressed cautious optimism, since Jones had personally met both women in August 1940 and found them to be in good health. She also felt reasonably confident that their paperwork could pass muster. When, on November 16, 1940, a few days after having been interviewed at the American Consulate in Vienna, Dora and Clementine received a form letter from the Consulate notifying them that "their application for an immigration visa for the United States of America had to be rejected," all were distressed.[52] With that one sentence and without any further explanation provided, an emigration process that had been set in motion two and a half years earlier and to which many had contributed had come to an abrupt end.

Direct communication between Vienna and the United States had always been difficult. Those living under Nazi control were hampered in expressing their thoughts in writing. All their letters were scrutinized (external censorship); parents also did not want their children in exile—who had plenty of challenges of their own—to worry about the older generation (internal censorship). Quakers were important messengers between Nazi refugees in the United States and their relatives still in Europe. On the day that Dora Schreck received the consular rejection, she shared the news with Käthe Neumeyer, who had succeeded Jones as Director of the International Friends Center.[53] Neumeyer immediately brought the information to the attention of the Quakers in Philadelphia, adding that Mrs. Schreck had been "very much depressed," and now thought it very "questionable" that she would "ever see her son again."[54] Was there anything the AFSC could do in this case, Neumeyer wondered.

---

[50] Breitman and Kraut, *American Refugee Policy*, 120.
[51] The State Department now gave preference to qualified applicants already outside of Germany, particularly to those who had found temporary refuge in England, the Netherlands, Belgium, France, Spain, or Portugal.
[52] AFSC refugee case file 2112. The letter from the consulate was dated November 13, 1940.
[53] Leonard S. Kenworthy characterizes Neumeyer as "an ardent catholic, an astute business manager, and a fearless individual" in *Another Dimension of the Holocaust: An American Quaker inside Nazi-Germany* (Kennett Square, PA: World Affairs Materials, 1982), 35.
[54] AFSC refugee case file 2112.

Once the news reached Rudolph Schreck, he, too, contacted the AFSC in Philadelphia, asking the Quakers for an honest update about daily life for Jews in Vienna. How exactly was "the Jewish situation," Schreck inquired, and was there "any danger" for "these persons" in Vienna right now?[55] Margaret Jones, who had recently returned from Vienna to Philadelphia, answered his letter in early December 1940:

> When I saw your mother and aunt last summer [. . .] they both seemed to be quite well, but naturally awfully worried and quite unhappy. I do not believe that at the time there was any danger for the Jewish people in Vienna. Of course, the police are constantly checking with individuals to ask them if they are continuing to make plans to leave the country.[56]

Jones also touched on problems that Jews would be facing in the coming winter months: a shortage of fuel and a lack of appropriate clothes ("a serious situation because Jews do not have clothing cards"). Most importantly, perhaps, food continued to be a problem. While Jews did receive food ration cards, they were allowed only to shop during certain hours when "most of the supplies in the shops" had already "been exhausted."[57] Still, she reassured Schreck that the Friends Center, the Swedish Mission, and the IKG all were endeavoring to distribute clothing.[58] The aid organizations had set up soup kitchens as well. Schreck thanked Jones for having painted "such a good picture of the whole situation."[59]

Like most of the refugees who had spent their first few months at the Quaker hostel in Iowa, Schreck returned to Scattergood for the December holidays. In early 1941, he moved to Buffalo, New York, where he had found a better job in the "refugee industry."[60] From there, he wrote to Jones again: did the AFSC consider it advisable to "send a petition to the Department of State" to appeal the visa rejections?[61] Prompted by Schreck's inquiry, Jones sent a letter to the Chief of the Visa Division at the State Department, Avra Warren, asking for clarification about the visa rejection of Schreck's relatives. Jones, appealing to Warren as a humanitarian, made it clear that the Quakers had been supporting the

---

[55] AFSC refugee case file 2112, letter dated November 19, 1940.
[56] AFSC refugee case file 2112, letter dated December 9, 1940.
[57] AFSC refugee case file 2112.
[58] Gertrude Schneider recalls that the allotted hours were from 11 am to 4 pm. See *Exile and Destruction: The Fate of Austrian Jews, 1938–1945* (Westport, CT, and London: Praeger, 1995), 54.
[59] AFSC refugee case file 2112, letter dated December 16, 1940.
[60] AFSC refugee case file 2112.
[61] AFSC refugee case file 2112, letter dated January 12, 1941.

emigration process of these two women for years. "In so far as it was the hope of the State Department to reunite families," Jones further argued, attention ought to be given to these two women. Jones asked Warren for a full report and added:

> Passage money has been provided for these two women, and their affidavits of support have been filed with the United States Consulate for some time. Our Vienna Center, as well as the Philadelphia Office, has been keeping in close touch with this case [. . .].
>
> We have every reason to believe that these two women, who were, when I left Vienna, in vigorous health—active and well able to do housework—will not become public charges in this country.[62]

Though Warren promised to inquire in Vienna and let Jones know, no further correspondence with the State Department has survived.[63] The National Catholic Welfare Council's Bureau of Immigration also got active in this case and wrote to Vienna on behalf of Rudolph Schreck's relatives. More details emerged in March, when Schreck learned that both visas had been withheld on the very grounds that Jones had stressed were not applicable: the likelihood of becoming a public charge. The consulate now recommended that Schreck himself submit an additional affidavit for his mother and aunt. A letter from his employer stating his salary was also needed.[64] The National Catholic Welfare Council also offered advice on how to counter the fifth column anxiety, suggesting that Schreck obtain additional affidavits from American friends stating that they had "personal knowledge of the backgrounds" of Dora Schreck's "past political affiliations."[65]

One of the characteristics of the unannounced shift in immigration policy was a tactic of endless delay. A clash between the State Department, intent on closing the door to immigration from Europe, and humanitarians such as the Quakers, intent on getting as many as possible of the persecuted into the United States and out of danger, had

---

[62] AFSC refugee case file 2112, letter dated January 28, 1941.
[63] AFSC refugee case file 2112, letter dated February 13, 1941. The National Archives and Records Administration (NARA) holds a record locator, an index card, for Dora Schreck's visa case (VD 811.111); however, the file itself no longer exits. As a rule, the State Department considered all immigration records of this type as non-permanent and discarded them.
[64] AFSC refugee case file 2112, letter from Schreck to Jones dated March 3, 1941.
[65] AFSC refugee case file 2112, letter from Schreck to Zimmerman dated January 19, 1941.

been brewing for some time. Jones voiced her exasperation to Clarence Pickett in an undated letter from this period:

> Perhaps I feel too strongly about this—but I know only too well what the life of the Jew in Vienna is today. I know of the terror and despair, and of the unbelievable difficulties each man and woman endures, and tries to solve, in connection with obtaining the US visa. [. . .] it seems to me that if the US wants to make a new ruling due to the war, etc., that it must make it openly and give the reasons. We cannot continue to let these tragic people go on hoping that if they comply with every requirement, if they get all the special documents required [. . .], they <u>may</u> just possibly be the lucky ones to get visas, when we know that practically no-one is granted visas in Germany today.[66]

The ongoing danger, which Schreck mentioned to Jones in his November 1940 letter, was, of course, the risk of deportation. After the pogrom of November 9, 1938, thousands of Jews were deported from Vienna to Dachau. The majority were released again from the camp due to having emigration papers in hand, or the clear imminent promise thereof. By February 1941, mass deportations from Vienna were again underway. The Quakers in Vienna and Philadelphia were well informed about this escalating situation.[67] Having the promise of a visa, or in its absence, simply proof of passage by ship, the Quakers still thought might be a means "to stave off the chances of deportation."[68] Between January and June of 1941, when 5,000 Jews from Vienna were already being deported to rural towns in the Lublin district of occupied Poland, a total of 429 Viennese Jews were still able to emigrate to the United States.[69]

In June 1941, all American consulates in Europe closed. In November, one month before the Unites States entered World War II, emigration from the Third Reich became illegal. Rudolph Schreck last heard from Dora Schreck and Clementine Springer in December 1941. Documents in Schreck's refugee case file regarding the following three war years are scant. The file provides a bit more information about Rudolph's job in Buffalo, where he had found work at a company that produced headwear. It also tells us that in 1943 Schreck married Rachel Nelson and that he enlisted in the US Army in March.

This returns us to the moment at which GI Schreck, in postwar Germany, wrote to the AFSC in Philadelphia asking for assistance in

---

[66] Spielhofer, *Stemming the Dark Tide*, 142.
[67] Kenworthy, *Another Dimension of the Holocaust*, 36.
[68] AFSC refugee case file 2112, letter from Jones to Schreck dated March 1941.
[69] Rabinovici, *Eichmann's Jews*, 136.

locating his mother and aunt. Schreck immediately followed the AFSC's suggestion to list his missing relatives in the Central Location Index (CLI). In the last AFSC letter to Schreck from August 20, 1945, the Quakers remarked that perhaps "it wasn't surprising that he had not heard from his relatives yet" given that the process of seeking missing people in Europe "was slow and uncertain," and that, therefore, there might be an "indefinite wait for the desired news."[70]

Of the 67,962 Jews deported from Vienna to ghettos and camps, only 1,747 survived. Dora Schreck was deported from Vienna on August 17, 1942 to Maly Trostinets, near Minsk, where she was murdered upon arrival. Her oldest sister Clementine was deported from Vienna to Theresienstadt on July 22, 1942, and from there to the Treblinka extermination camp, where she was murdered upon arrival on September 26, 1942.[71] Rudolph had brought half a dozen other close family members, who were in danger in Nazi Europe, to the attention of the AFSC as well, including his aunt Rosa Schück, née Springer, in Vienna, and his aunt Gisela Springer, a celebrated concert pianist in Berlin. These two maternal aunts did not survive the war either.[72]

Schreck's file stories offer an outside perspective on American relief workers' responses to the misery of Austrian Jews after March 1938. Their view is not passive, nor do they serve as eyewitnesses only. Rather, their shock motivates them to rescue and integrate Austrian Jews into a suspicious America. To the extent that Schreck's file stories trace his repeated efforts to rescue older family members still in Vienna, the archive also reveals an implicit distinction made by all administrative institutions: young adults were favored over the elderly, giving them a better chance to survive. Rudolph's 1945 letter to the AFSC asking about his mother and aunts brings the process full circle. His Army uniform positions him ostensibly as another American outsider. While he was once a refugee and then an alienated immigrant, he writes in 1945 with the voice of an American returned to Europe—from one American institution (US Army) to another (AFSC), thus completing a circuit, but too late.

---

[70] AFSC refugee case file 2112.

[71] On March 15, 1965, Dora Schreck was officially declared dead: author's correspondence with the city of Vienna MA 8-B-MEW-416548-2016. The information regarding the deportations of Rudolph's mother Dora Schreck, her oldest sister Clementine Springer, and two of her other sisters, Rosa Schück and Gisela Springer, was obtained from the online Arolsen Archives (previously known as ITS).

[72] On September 21, 1942, Rosa Schück was deported from Theresienstadt to Treblinka, where she was murdered. Gisela Springer was deported from Berlin to the Lodz ghetto on October 18, 1941. From there, she was deported to Chelmno, where she was murdered on May 9, 1942.

Works Cited

American Friends Service Committee. *Refugee Facts: A Study of the German Refugee in America* (Philadelphia: American Friends Service Committee, 1939).

Austin, Allan W. *Quaker Brotherhood: Interracial Activism and the American Friends Service Committee, 1917–1950* (Champaign: University of Illinois Press, 2012).

Brandt, Bettina. "Trudie and Nelly: Deciphering a Transatlantic Family Holocaust Correspondence," in *On Being Adjacent to Historical Violence*, ed. Irene Kacandes (Boston: De Gruyter, 2021), 315–22.

Breitman, Richard, and Alan M. Kraut, *American Refugee Policy and American Jewry, 1933–1945* (Bloomington and Indianapolis: Indiana University Press, 1987).

Genizi, Haim. "American Interfaith Cooperation on Behalf of Refugees from Nazism, 1933–1945," *American Jewish History*, vol. 70, no. 3 (March 1981): 347–61.

Genizi, Haim. *American Apathy: The Plight of Christian Refugees from Nazism* (Tel Aviv: Bar-Ilan University Press, 1983).

Genizi, Haim. "New York is big—America is bigger: The Resettlement of Refugees from Nazism, 1936–1945," *Jewish Social Studies*, vol. 46 (Winter 1984): 61–72.

Gerber, David. *American Immigration: A Very Short Introduction* (New York: Oxford University Press, 2011).

Glajar, Valentina. "The File Story of the Securitate Officer Samuel Feld," in *Cold War Spy Stories from Eastern Europe*, ed. Valentina Glajar, Alison Lewis, and Corina L. Petrescu (Lincoln: University of Nebraska Press, 2019).

Kenworthy, Leonhard S. *Another Dimension of the Holocaust: An American Quaker inside Nazi-Germany* (Kennett Square, PA: World Affairs Materials, 1982).

Kraut, Alan M., Richard Breitman, and Thomas W. Imhoof. "The State Department, the Labor Department and German Jewish Immigration, 1930–1940," *Journal of American Ethnic History*, vol. 3, no. 2 (Spring 1984): 5–38.

Litzka, Traude. *The Church's Help for Persecuted Jews in Nazi Vienna*, trans. Gerda Joseph (Vienna: LIT, 2019).

Luick-Thrams, Michael. *Out of Hitler's Reach: The Scattergood Hostel for European Refugees 1939–43* (Des Moines: Iowa Community Action Coalition, 1996).

Luick-Thrams, Michael, ed. *Far from Hitler: The Scattergood Hostel for European Refugees, 1939–1943* (Waukee: Iowa Jewish Historical Society, 2001).

Maier, Charles. "Christianity and Conviction: Gustav Mahler and the Meanings of Jewish Conversion in Central Europe," *Simon Dubnow Institute Yearbook*, vol. 11 (2012): 127–47.

Rabinovici, Doron. *Eichmann's Jews: The Jewish Administration of Holocaust Vienna, 1938–1945*, trans. Nick Somers (Cambridge: Polity Press, 2011).

Schmitt, Hans. *Quakers and Nazis: Inner Light in Outer Darkness* (Columbia and London: University of Missouri Press, 1997).

Schneider, Gertrude. *Exile and Destruction: The Fate of Austrian Jews, 1938–1945* (Westport, CT, and London: Praeger, 1995).

Spielhofer, Sheila. *Stemming the Dark Tide: Quakers in Vienna 1919–1942* (York, UK: William Sessions, 2001).

Wyman, David S. *Paper Walls: America and the Refugee Crisis 1938–1941* (New York: Pantheon, 1985).

Nine Keeping Time: Trauma as Intimate Alienation in Hans Keilson's Writing

Anna M. Parkinson

The involuntary exile turned into the voluntary diaspora [. . .]. Yes, they remained "outside" and continue to write—in spite of it all?—in German.

[Das unfreiwillige Exil wurde zur freiwilligen Diaspora [. . .]. Ja, sie sind "draußen" geblieben und schreiben—trotzdem?—immer noch Deutsch.][1]

The title of this volume, *Germany from the Outside*, implies distance or alterity, whether literal or figurative. Germany, the nation state and all else gathered in this portmanteau, is not an a priori entity. "Germany" from this place, "outside," is an object of observation, potentially by a critical gaze of alterity, the constitutive relief against which it first gains contour. In this chapter I consider how the Jewish German-born author, psychoanalyst, and survivor Hans Keilson navigated the suture binding his traumatic memories of the Nazi regime and subsequent exile to a complex—even paradoxical—condition of nonetheless belonging to Germany. The question remains, however: to which Germany? Through the fractured lens of what I call intimate alienation we can see how an "involuntary exile" metamorphoses into a "voluntary" self-recognition as a member of the Jewish diaspora. Keilson may have lived most of his life outside of Germany, but it would be difficult to argue that Germany remained exterior to him.

---

[1] All translations are my own unless otherwise stated. Hans Keilson, "Vorwort [zu *Ach, Sie schreiben deutsch?*]," in *Werke in Zwei Bänden, Gedichte und Essays*, vol. 2, ed. Heinrich Detering and Gerhard Kurz (Frankfurt am Main: Fischer Verlag, 2005), 386–94, here 388.

Hans Keilson's writings about his life in Weimar Germany depict a prelapsarian existence of sorts: his fond memories of his childhood in Freienwalde an der Oder, his lively performances in bands, and the publication of his first novel in 1934 while at the same time completing his medical studies in Berlin. After Hitler's takeover, Keilson's life becomes perilous: he becomes aware of virulent anti-Semitic persecution, and in 1936 emigrates to the Netherlands. While in hiding there during the German occupation of the Netherlands, his future is uncertain, and he is tormented by the indelible knowledge of his inability to save his parents from deportation and murder in 1943, which led to his becoming a Dutch citizen.

It should come as no surprise that in his fictional and non-fictional writings alike, Keilson paints a picture of his relationship to Germany that is colored by the antimony of alienation and intimacy. The word "intimacy" is constituted by a hermeneutical paradox. According to the Oxford English Dictionary, as an adjective "intimate" means "close in acquaintance or association; closely connected by friendship or personal knowledge; very familiar" and "pertaining to or dealing with such close personal relations"; likewise, in its transitive verb form "intimate" means "to communicate (knowledge)" and "to imply, to suggest, to hint at." Simultaneously, implying a close relationship or a communication between people, the word "intimate" can also signify the exact opposite tendency to that of intersubjective proximity, designating something "closely personal" and "proceeding from, concerning, or affecting one's inmost self."[2] Not quite evincing the plasticity of the Freudian "uncanny," with the Gordian Knot tied between that which is strange and that which is intimately familiar, "intimate" nonetheless refers both to intersubjective proximity in personal relations as well as to that which is deeply private and known to one's self alone. However, the overt dialectical hermeneutics of the term "intimate" only goes part of the way towards capturing the ambivalence and fascination that characterize Keilson's complex relationship to Germany after 1936. In order to calibrate the affective, historical, and socio-political complexity of this relationship—Germany from the outside by dint of the ill-fated historical conjunction of fascism and Jewish identity (also from the outside)—I propose that we trace his relationship to "Germany" in his psychoanalytical and autobiographical writings as one of "intimate alienation." Although Keilson never returned to live in Germany after 1936, his writing, thinking, and psychoanalytical practice embodied his earlier

---

[2] "intimate, *adj.* and *n.*," OED Online, Oxford University Press, oed.com, lemma "intimate."

formative experiences in German institutions of learning and culture production—a Germany "inside" from the "outside," if you will.

Da: Here/There, Home and Away

Even a cursory glance at the titles of Keilson's essays and poems exhibits his self-reflective awareness of his ambivalent and evolving relationship to Germany. The imprimatur of his German Humboldtian university education, his *Bildung* (quite literally that which forms him), is fundamental to this thought, as evidenced in his psychoanalytic and poetic writings. Take, for example, his response in 1986 to an invitation to write an article as a naturalized Dutch citizen to mark the occasion of the 150th anniversary of the Dutch cultural magazine *De Gids*. Keilson's non-indigeneity was the reason for their invitation, however Keilson proudly displays his fluency in Dutch culture and language. Writing in Dutch, his quotidian language after 1936, he peppers his contribution with amusing and astute observations on Dutch culture, such as quirky quotidian expressions, and his enthusiastic embrace of the Dutch football team.

His most sustained autobiographical text up to this point, his contribution bears the deceptively simple title "Lieber Holland als Heimweh . . ."[3] On closer examination of the German translation, this nominal sentence is anything but straightforward, depending where the emphasis falls in the title. In the German translation of the title, "Holland" might represent Keilson's preferred choice ("lieber") rather than ("als") homesickness ("Heimweh"). Alternatively, the alliteration of the nouns "Holland" and "Heimweh," separated by the conjunction "als," which can be translated as either "than" or "as," is less hermeneutically conclusive. Translated as "as," "als" equates Holland with homesickness. Any residual doubts about the ambiguity of the title are dispelled by the concluding ellipses in the title. Used as a literary device earlier in his novels, deictic ellipses compound interpretative equivocation, purposively suspending interpretative closure.[4]

---

[3] Hans Keilson, "Lieber Holland als Heimweh," in *Werke in Zwei Bänden, Gedichte und Essays, Bd.* 2, ed. Heinrich Detering and Gerhard Kurz (Frankfurt am Main: Fischer Verlag, 2005), 150–9; first published as "Vijftig jaar in Holland. Liever Holland dan heimwee," *De Gids*, vol. 150 (1987): 115–20, dbnl.org/tekst/_gid001198701_01/_gid001198701_01_0023.php.

[4] For an interesting essay on the role of silence and deictic ellipses in Hans Keilson's fiction, see Heinrich Detering, "Wortlosigkeit. Zur Figur der deiktischen Ellipse in Hans Keilsons Erzählungen," in *"die vergangene Zeit bleibt die erlittene Zeit." Untersuchungen zum Werk von Hans Keilson*, ed. Simone Schröder, Ulrike Weymann, and Andreas Martin Widmann (Würzburg: Königshausen & Neumann, 2013), 127–44.

Another essay characterized by a pronounced dialectical tension between distance and proximity, alienation and intimacy, is Keilson's contribution to the German essay volume *Psychoanalyse in Selbstdarstellungen* (*Psychoanalysis in Self-portrayal*) (1992). Titled "In der Fremde zuhause" ("At Home in a Foreign Place"), the essay proclaims an external vantage point, "outside" ("draußen") of Germany, yet simultaneously declares an allegiance to a diasporic community of German-language authors, perhaps not unlike members of the PEN Centre of German-Speaking Writers Abroad (PEN-Zentrum deutschsprachiger Autoren im Ausland), for which Keilson held the office of President from 1985 to 1988.[5] Less ambiguous than paradoxical, the title suggests that one can feel at home ("zuhause") in a foreign place ("In der Fremde"). Keilson's essay is a sustained meditation on how psychoanalysis both reveals and veils aspects of the self, particularly in intersubjective encounters through language and in psychoanalytical practice, despite the German language's contamination by fascist ideology, once again returning us to the topos of the intimate and the alien in his writing. He declares his affective tie to the Germany of his childhood: "One cannot hate the landscape where one was born and grew up. It appears once again in dreams" ("Die Landschaft, in der man geboren und aufgewachsen ist, kann man nicht hassen. Sie erscheint wieder in Träumen").[6] However, the ambivalence determined by the flux between intimacy and alienation in relation to Germany persists as caustic negativity: "My life and memories are corroded by the swathes of destruction" ("Mein Leben und Erinnerungen sind geätzt von den Schwaden der Zerstörung").[7]

Keilson charts his life over almost the entirety of the twentieth century in this essay, focusing in particular on his years in the Netherlands from 1936 onwards:

> In these years of emigration the evolution of that diffuse mixture of discontinuity, survival, threatening destructivity, and attempts at rebuilding, discovery, and preservation of that which perhaps can be understood as the substance of a human being began; that personal intermixture of perceptions which, only in retrospect, in the contemplation of the self-portrayal, do I once again perceive as my own.

---

[5] Hans Keilson, "In der Fremde zuhause," in *Werke*, Bd. 2, 214–52. For a summary of Keilson's biography, see "Zeittafel," in Hans Keilson, *Kein Plädoyer für eine Luftschaukel. Essays, Reden, Gespräche*, ed. Heinrich Detering (Frankfurt am Main: Fischer Verlag, 2011), 157–60.
[6] Keilson, "In der Fremde," 215.
[7] Keilson, "In der Fremde," 217.

[In diesen Jahren der Emigration begann sich jene diffuse Mischung aus Abbruch, Überleben, drohender Zerstörung und Versuchen des Wiederaufbaus, des Entdeckens und Bewahrens dessen, was man vielleicht unter der Substanz eines Menschen verstehen kann, herauszubilden, jene persönliche Mischung von Empfindungen, die ich erst in der Rückschau, in der Betrachtung der Selbstdarstellung, als mir zugehörig wieder empfinde.][8]

That the construction of the self is a process characterized by contingency rather than teleology is axiomatic in psychoanalysis. However, what is at stake in this instance is the individual's survival of a world fixated on one's extermination. Even more difficult is the attempt after the disaster to discover an adequate common language through which to convey extreme experiences, one that would account for the particular significance of a survivor's experiences.

By citing a stanza from his poem "Sprachwurzellos" (a neologism suggesting language unmoored or without roots) written in 1963, Keilson alludes to a painful process of deracination, whereby German language in the diaspora gains a life independent of the German nation state. His perennial return to this poem suggests that it holds some of the truth of his experience of "residing" in a language, when all other connections to the homeland are irreparably severed:

> struggling to master the secrets
> of the subjunctive
> —the time of the colorful balls—
> in vain
> by the canals
> greeting the new friends
> and they call me mijnheer
>
> [um die geheimnisse
> des konjunktivs
> —die zeit der bunten bälle—
> mühte ich mich
> vergebens
> an den grachten
> die neuen freunde grüßend
> und sie nennen mich mijnheer][9]

---

[8] Keilson, "In der Fremde," 225.
[9] Hans Keilson, "Sprachwurzellos," in *Werke, Bd. 2*, 32.

Abandoning the capitalization of nouns particular to the German language, and threading Dutch words into the weave of German, emphasizes the poet's shifting relationship with his mother tongue. His anguished attempts to maintain a relationship with German through the intricate moods of the language contrast starkly with the welcoming Dutch friends and their respectful address of him as "mijnheer" (Dutch for sir or mister). Despite its quality of openness, inhabiting the Dutch language initially feels foreign and requires application: "also lernte ich *ihre* sprache" ("so I learned *their* language," emphasis mine). The poem's concluding lines convey Keilson's painful relationship with Germany through the self-reflexive trope of language, intermingling loss with deracination in the titular "sprachwurzellos." Despite his best intentions, and seemingly against his own will, he continues to be fascinated by German with its "ecstasy / of withered letters" ("in der wollust / verdorrter schriftzeichen"), at the same time arousing an intimate sense of abasement ("I know myself to be humiliated"). To a large extent, Keilson's relationship with Germany remained that of a self-determined outsider, despite his deeply pleasurable memories of youthful immersion in the culture of Weimar Germany. His attachment to German denied the conflation of the nation state with the language.[10] He continued to write fiction and non-fiction in German, such that when his collected writings were published in 2005, his writings in German filled two capacious volumes.

Perhaps due to his flair for storytelling, Keilson's writings over the years are characterized more by continuity than rupture—so much so, that his writings in different genres came to resemble a dense intertextual web, mimicking the palimpsestic layering associated with processes of remembering.[11] This is especially evident in his final publication, *Da steht mein Haus* (*There / Here Stands my House*), a slender memoir with a final interview with editor Heinrich Detering, completed just before

---

[10] Carl Niekerk suggests that writing by Keilson and other exile authors might be understood as part of "contact or border zones [...] places where people with diverse national and cultural backgrounds [...] engage in dialogue [...] in-between national traditions." See "Literatures of the Contact Zone: Hans Keilson, Nico Rost, Albert Vigoleis Thelen, and the Literary Spaces of the Late 1940s and Early 1950s," *Journal of Dutch Literature*, vol. 9, no.1 (2018): 125, 114.

[11] For a comparative reading of Keilson's writing with other survivor autobiographies, see Andree Michaelis, "Nachbarn in der Fremde. Hans Keilsons *Da steht mein Haus* im Horizont kanonischer Erinnerungsbücher von Überlebenden der Shoah," in "*die vergangene Zeit bleibt die erlittene Zeit*," 223–38. See also in the same volume Marie-Christin Bugelnig, "'Schreiben, das ist für mich eine andere Möglichkeit spazieren zu gehen, in der Welt'. Topografien der Erinnerung. Zu Hans Keilsons Erinnerungsbuch *Da steht mein Haus*," 239–53.

his death in 2011.[12] In his "Erinnerungen" he cites verbatim from "In der Fremde zuhause" (1992), in which he in turn had quoted from his poem "Sprachwurzellos" (1963). The interplay between the earlier essay title and that of his memoir is significant, for the phrase "In der Fremde" ("In a foreign place") has been displaced by the confident deictic adverb "da" that can mean "here" or "there," depending on the context. The possessive pronoun and noun in the title ("mein Haus") offer a stability and solidity that varies from the more abstract, affective meaning of the adverb "zuhause," which describes a subjective perception rather than a specific physical location.

Ironically, Keilson appears to have come to feel at home precisely where language becomes deracinated ("sprachwurzellos"). His use of the past tense in response to a question asked by Detering in his final interview illustrates this: "But my own, my natural language was German. It was the language of my childhood. It was the language of my parents. It was my nature. . . . Yes, language was home" ("Aber meine eigene, meine natürliche Sprache war das Deutsche. Es war die Sprache meine Kindheit. Es war die Sprache meine Eltern. Es war meine Natur. . . . Ja, die Sprache war die Heimat").[13] Learning of his parents' murder in Birkenau after the war made it impossible for him to return to Germany or even identify as German: "I am Dutch. I was German. I am a Dutch doctor who publishes in German. When I heard of the death of my parents I ceased being German" ("Ich bin Holländer. Ich war Deutscher. Ich bin ein niederländischer Arzt, der auch auf Deutsch publiziert. Als ich vom Tod meiner Eltern gehört habe, habe ich aufgehört, ein Deutscher zu sein").[14] At the same time, his relationship to his more distant past, including his memories of his parents, are captured in the amber of German language. Writing from a deracinated linguistic position ("sprachwurzellos") allowed Keilson to find an alternative perspective on the catastrophic history of destruction and loss associated with Germany.

Keilson's inability to prevent the deportation and murder of his parents accompanied him for the rest of his life, prompting emotions of guilt, regret, and loss. His writing aspires to give form to memory through language: his poetry, fiction, and essays—and perhaps most of

---

[12] Heinrich Detering reflects on the process of developing the final book with Hans Keilson in Heinrich Detering, "Der Analytiker auf der Couch. Bemerkungen zur Entstehungsgeschichte von Hans Keilsons *Da steht mein Haus*," in *"die vergangene Zeit bleibt die erlittene Zeit,"* 273–8.

[13] "Hundert Jahre. Ein Gespräch mit Hans Keilson," in *Da steht mein Haus. Erinnerungen*, ed. Heinrich Detering (Frankfurt am Main: Fischer Verlag, 2012), 117.

[14] Detering, *Da steht mein Haus*, 112.

all, his psychoanalytical work on trauma. The act of practicing psychoanalysis, usually in Dutch in his sessions, but in German in his published research on trauma, with recently returned Jewish-Dutch orphans after World War II, restored both his patients and himself to their present moment in the Netherlands. His commitment to working with child survivors was complexly intertwined with his ongoing commitment to remembering his parents. Psychoanalysis, with its particular understanding of temporality as an agonistic space that one can (and also must) return to in the wake of traumatic events, offered some of the many children he worked with a path back to the present. Through the mediation of language and silence, they grappled with extreme events executed solely with the aim of their annihilation, for which nothing had prepared them. Existential prop and an immersive practice of working with the past alike, his work with child survivors provided what he called "traces of broken continuity" ("Spuren der gebrochenen Kontinuität") between his early fascination in Weimar Germany with Freudian psychoanalysis,[15] and his psychoanalytical practice in the Netherlands after the war.[16]

Time after Time: The *après-coup* of Trauma

The many unknown factors which surrounded the files like a massive wall of silence were an inherent part of the persecution situation experienced by the children in hiding. It was, after all, this silence to which they owed their lives.[17]

---

[15] Keilson often retold the tale of how as a young man he bought Sigmund Freud's *Vorlesungen* with prize money that he won in an essay contest for which he submitted an essay on Hermann Hesse's *Demian*. The slender leather volume by Freud somehow survived the discontinuities of exile. For example, Keilson, "All das Schöne, nicht den Abgrund. Aus einem Gespräch mit der niederländischen Zeitung *De Pers* (2010, gekürzt)," in Keilson, *Kein Plädoyer für eine Luftschaukel*, 151. See also in *Da steht mein Haus*: "Es war dieselbe Zeit, in der ich mit meinem Beitrag zu einem Schülerwettbewerb des Börsenvereins des deutschen Buchhandels, über Hermann Hesses *Demian*, den dritten Preis errang. Von dem so gewonnenen Betrag von dreißig Mark kaufte ich mich drei Bücher: ein Novellenbuch von Stephan Zweig, dann von Karl Plättner, einem Kumpan von Max Hoelz, den Band *Eros im Zuchthaus* (um meine Neugierde zu befriedigen) und schließlich die in Leder gebundenen, im Taschenbuchformat und Dünndruck erschienenen Vorlesungen von Sigmund Freud, eines der Bücher, die mein Exil überdauert und mein Leben bestimmt haben," in Keilson, *Da steht mein Haus*, 66.

[16] Keilson, "In der Fremde zuhause," in *Werke, Bd. 2*, 220.

[17] Hans Keilson, *Sequential Traumatization in Children: A Clinical and Statistical Follow-Up Study on the State of the Jewish War Orphans in the Netherlands*, together with Herman R. Sarphatie, trans. Yvonne Bearne, Hilary Coleman, and Deirdre Winter (Jerusalem: Magnes Press, 1992), 18.

What might it mean to consider your life's work with Holocaust child survivors a belated form of saying *kaddish*, a Jewish prayer of mourning, for one's murdered parents, as Keilson did? What repercussions are there for having been absent at the death of one's loved ones, to have been unable to save them from a violent and undignified death when most vulnerable? Hans Keilson's discovery of the circumstances of his parents' deaths is characterized by belatedness, in historical and psychological terms. One psychological danger of belatedness—of not being present for a traumatic event, failing to witness it, or missing it all together—is that the event may remain unassimilable in or exterior to the psychic life of a person.[18] In Keilson's case, the knowledge was quite literally delayed, in that he only learnt after the war about his parents' April 1943 deportation to the Dutch transit camp Westerbork and subsequent relocation to and murder in Birkenau six months later, in November 1943. In this sense, Keilson might be understood in some ways to have occupied a similar zone of belatedness (the Freudian *Nachträglichkeit*; Lacanian *après-coup*) alongside the Jewish Dutch orphans he counseled after their emergence from hiding or return from the concentration camps to Amsterdam.

Although already in his mid-thirties at the end of the war, Keilson nonetheless shared several key experiences with the much younger Jewish children and adolescents with whom he worked. He too was Jewish, had experienced anti-Semitic persecution, survived for the most part in hiding, and had lost both parents and his home(land) by the end of World War II. He writes of the Jewish children's home where he worked in the postwar period:

> I saw the children who had lost everything, as they emerged from their hiding places and returned from the camps, their parents, siblings, relatives—often sixty to seventy people—lost. I saw the destruction in us and in them during the day, when they were at play, and I heard them in their beds in the evenings crying, crying unrestrainedly. No one needed to feel ashamed, each child knew why another was crying, and we too, the adults in the home, knew it. We were all bound together in the same fate.
>
> [Ich sah die Kinder, die alles verloren hatten, als sie aus den Verstekken [sic] und aus den Lagern zurückkamen, verloren ihre

---

[18] The psychoanalytic temporality peculiar to missed events can be seen in trauma, where an overwhelming event occurs unexpectedly. On the temporal economy of trauma, see Freud's *Beyond the Pleasure Principle* (1920) and *Inhibitions, Symptoms and Anxiety* (1925).

Eltern, Geschwister, Angehörige, oft bis zu sechzig, siebzig Personen. Ich sah die Zerstörung in uns und in ihnen, tagsüber, wenn sie spielten, und ich hörte sie abends in ihren Betten weinen, ohne Zurückhaltung weinen. Niemand brauchte sich zu schämen, ein jedes Kind wußte, warum ein anderes weinte, und auch wir, Erwachsene im Heim, wußten es. Das Los verband uns alle.]¹⁹

Empathetically and through the prism of his own loss, Keilson recognized the common fate that bound him to the suffering of Jewish Dutch child survivors, even though their common "fate" diverged vastly in cultural, experiential, and developmental terms. Through his work with child survivors, he intuited important affective dimensions in their sometimes-dense silence in sessions; through them he learned the skill of attentive listening for the valences of silence of traumatic experience. Some of his initial failed therapeutic sessions with child patients, whose symptoms of trauma were far more extreme than analysts had yet encountered in psychiatric treatment anywhere,²⁰ helped him to understand the wall of silence surrounding them as an indication of the radical otherness that had defined their daily life in the camps, estranging them from the conventions of communication and their original communities.

His first consultation with a child survivor from a concentration camp was with a twelve-year-old boy, the sole survivor of an orthodox Jewish family, called "Esra" in his case study. Keilson's initially failed sessions with Esra, whom he compares to "a sleepwalker from 'another' world" ("ein Schlafwanderer aus einer 'anderen' Welt"), later became key for understanding the extent to which extreme traumatic experience destroys norms and creates a state of radical alterity in survivors, particularly in the developmental stages of childhood.²¹ When revisiting Esra's case file from November 1945 several decades later for his longitudinal study of trauma, Keilson notes how the everyday language conventions that a community takes for granted as the basis for communication had often been distorted to unrecognizability by the quotidian conventions of the camps. In their sessions, Keilson came to understand how semantic norms were radically reconfigured in the hostile camp

---

[19] Hans Keilson, "In der Fremde zuhause," in *Werke, Bd. 2*, 218.

[20] Keilson states, "In der kinderpsychiatrischen Praxis hat man Bilder in diesem Ausmaß und in dieser Intensität bisher noch nicht erlebt. Das Neuartige dieser Bilder war, dass sie das menschliche Vorstellungsvermögen übertrafen." Keilson, "Die fragmentierte Psychotherapie eines aus Bergen-Belsen zurückgekehrten Jungen," in *Werke, Bd. 2*, 279.

[21] This case study forms the basis for Keilson's essay, "Wohin die Sprache nicht reicht," first published in *Psyche* (1984). Keilson, "Wohin die Sprache nicht reicht," in *Werke, Bd. 2*, 145.

environment. For example, if Keilson said the word "bed," meaning that in which one sleeps, Esra understood it to mean something beneath which to hide while sleeping.²² In other words, Keilson could not presume that the most basic elements of quotidian language held the same affective and symbolic valence for Esra and the society to which he had returned. The space of communication in which experience and language create common meaning first needed to be re-established.

Many years after this experience, in a German-language essay written for a psychoanalytic readership in 1984 and titled "Wohin die Sprache nicht reicht" ("Where Language Falters"/"Where Language Falls Short"), Keilson analyzed Esra's case in more detail. His title is not a gesture towards a reified realm of "unspeakability"—a secular theological "beyond" of language—a now-familiar topos in Holocaust scholarship; nor is it a reference to the Lacanian psychoanalytical concept of the Real as that which exceeds and breaches the symbolic order.²³ Rather, it points to the fundamental ways in which massive traumatic experiences impacted the referential function of language for many of the children, initially completely alienating them from their former socio-linguistic community. Only later is Esra able to articulate his disturbing experiences in the Bergen-Belsen concentration camp, including having woken up one morning beside his mother's corpse. Over time, this quality of otherworldliness, ascribed to what passed for "everyday life" in the extraordinary world of the camps, has become a topos in autobiographical accounts by survivors and in fiction. But for decades after the war's end, this aspect of survivors' behavior was not widely understood or appreciated.²⁴

The geo-linguistic aspects of Keilson's writing enjoyed some scholarly attention, not least because he himself often foregrounded this in his writing.²⁵ In what follows, I would like to turn to the significance of

---

22   Keilson, "Wohin die Sprache nicht reicht," 145.
23   Keilson, "Die fragmentierte Psychotherapie eines aus Bergen-Belsen zurückgekehrten Jungen," in *Werke*, Bd. 2, 290.
24   Two well-known examples are David Rousset's term "the concentrationary universe" ("l'univers concentrationnaire"), which is also the title of his account of the Neuengamme and Buchenwald concentration camps: David Rousset, *L'univers concentrationnaire* (Paris: Éditions du Pavois, 1946); and Yehiel De-Nur (writing under the pen-name Ka-Tsetnik), known internationally for his Stalag novels, but in particular because of his dramatic testimony at the Eichmann trial (Jerusalem, 1961), during which he collapsed (Session No. 68). He opened his testimony as follows: "this is the history of planet Auschwitz. [...] the time there is not a concept as it is here, on our planet." Citations are transcribed from the original English translation in subtitles of the Hebrew testimony from a live recording of the trial. Session No. 68, 69, youtube.com/watch?v=m3-tXyYhd5U.
25   See notes 9 and 10.

temporality as a mode of alienated intimacy in Keilson's psychoanalytical writing about trauma. Pace Keilson, I wish to consider how he understood his work on trauma as a labor of mourning, a substitute for the kaddish for his murdered parents, following the dedication in his monograph. Among other factors, Keilson's remarkable longevity—he died in 2011 at the age of 101—allowed him at age seventy, after eleven years of research, to publish the scientific monograph for which he received his doctorate after having (re)trained as a psychiatrist and psychoanalyst in the Netherlands. Written in German and published in Germany in 1978,[26] it took more than a decade until an English translation entitled *Sequential Traumatization in Children: A Clinical and Statistical Follow-up Study on the Fate of the Jewish War Orphans in the Netherlands* was published by Magnes Press at the Hebrew University.[27]

Begun in 1967, the study provides a descriptive-clinical and a quantitative-statistical analysis of orphaned Jewish Dutch child survivors emerging from hiding and returning from the concentration camps in 1945. Keilson defined sequential traumatization as a confrontation with "life-threatening danger and a succession of extremely stressful events."[28] He frames this definition by hypothesizing that the children's persecution by the Nazi regime, and the effects of that persecution in their postwar environment, create cumulative and lasting traumatization. His work outlines a complex and multivalent understanding of the temporalities peculiar to persecution, as well as the political and social contexts in which historical events and their psychological aftereffects unfolded in the Netherlands, both during and after World War II.[29]

---

[26] Hans Keilson, *Sequentielle Traumatisierung bei Kindern. Untersuchung zum Schicksal jüdischer Kriegswaisen*, together with Herman R. Saphartie (Gießen: Psychosozial-Verlag, 1979).

[27] Keilson, *Sequential Traumatization*. Many thanks to Marita Keilson-Lauritz for an English copy of the book.

[28] Keilson, *Sequential Traumatization*, 4.

[29] Keilson, *Sequential Traumatization*, 48–9. Two organizations were engaged in what was at the time referred to as the "war orphan problem." Tension arose between the two agencies in relation to what each considered to be the most appropriate home for Jewish Dutch orphan child survivors. The government-implemented Commissie voor Oorlogspleegkinderen framed the issue as one of national identity, whereas the organization LeEsrat HaYeled, which had been established by remaining members of the Dutch Jewish community (and of which Keilson was a co-founder), saw the dire need to rescue the orphans' Jewish identities to ensure the continuity of their community. Keilson gently broaches this volatile history in his study (32–5). See also Joel S. Fishman, "The War Orphans Controversy in the Netherlands: Majority–Minority Relations," in *Proceedings of the Symposium on the History of the Jews in the Netherlands. November 28–December 3, 1982. Tel Aviv–Jerusalem*, ed. Jozef Michman and Tirtsah Levie (Jerusalem: Daf-Chen, 1984), 421–32.

By nature, trauma is untimely, and Keilson's pathbreaking study argued for a more nuanced understanding of trauma's temporality, conceiving of trauma as a sequence of life-threatening events arising again and again in the situation of ongoing persecution—up to and including later displacements. These culminate in what he called the *sequential traumatization* of the orphans. Some of his findings were surprising and significant: for example, depending on the developmental stage of the children, those who had experienced traumatic events under the Nazi regime might experience chronic stress in the postwar environment as equally, if not even more, traumatic than the initial separation from their family. Here, trauma is defined as a sequence of life events that are not unrelated to one another for an individual. It is possible that seemingly less traumatic events, such as the postwar placement of an orphaned survivor in a new family, might be exacerbated by earlier traumatic events. That is, the seemingly less extreme event triggers the manifestation of massive cumulative trauma that seems disproportionate to earlier reactions to life-threatening traumatic situations.

This interpretation challenges the more familiar psychoanalytical understanding of trauma as a single unexpected, overwhelming event. Instead, Keilson's study underscored the cumulative nature of a sequence of events called the "traumatic situation," which he associated with "chronic, extreme psychological stress."[30] For the purpose of the study he identified three phases of stress, or traumatic sequences: the first is defined by the onset of persecution, confinement, enforced isolation, and the destruction of the Jewish family unit, beginning with the invasion and occupation of the Netherlands by German troops. The second traumatic sequence began either with a child's deportation to a concentration camp or being forced into hiding, experienced as either being at the mercy of a hostile environment (hunger, illness, and privation) or as utter dependency on others and the necessary erasure of Jewish identity in the new family. The third and final traumatic sequence represents the shift from illegality to legally ordered and bureaucratically structured life in a completely altered world, which was often accompanied by an intensification of the traumatic situation through acknowledging the death of the parents as well as the question of guardianship.[31]

The study was based on case files of Dutch Jewish children and adolescents kept by two Dutch organizations active in the postwar years. The files recorded biographical details, guardianship decisions, and

---

[30] Keilson, *Sequential Traumatization*, 48–9.
[31] Keilson, *Sequential Traumatization*, 52–75.

partial trajectories of the postwar lives of 1,854 Jewish Dutch orphans who had been in hiding or had survived the Nazi concentration camps. One organization, LeEsrat HaYeled (to the help of the child), which Keilson helped found, was established after the war by survivors of the Jewish Dutch Community to administer care to orphans and remain attentive to their Jewish background. Up until 1970, Keilson lent LeEsrat HaYeled his pedagogical and medical expertise, skills the Dutch resistance had drawn on earlier to assist with behavioral disturbances in Jewish children in hiding.[32] The second source was the Oorlogspleegkinderen Office (Wartime Foster Children Office/OPK), a government commission established at the behest of the Dutch resistance to oversee the guardianship of the orphans.

Sequential Traumatization was the first longitudinal study to examine the effects of trauma that took the children's developmental stages into account. A study of this scope and ambition had never been attempted (or possible), and it contributed to concurrent research on the long-term damage inflicted on children through manmade disasters.[33] It provides both clinical-descriptive and statistical-quantitative analysis; the latter adhering to psychiatric statistical metrics, the former following the descriptive analysis of psychoanalytic case studies. Particularly striking are the results of Keilson's in-person, follow-up interviews twenty-five years later of 200 now-adult survivors in Europe and Israel, demonstrating his hope of providing better understanding of the "effects of the social-psychiatric and educational rehabilitation" of the survivors, both as children and adults.[34]

The interviews with the adults demonstrate the ongoing disruption wreaked by earlier traumatic sequences.[35] The unreconciled relationship between the present and the past, experienced by adult

---

[32] Keilson, "In der Fremde zuhause," 218–20.
[33] Keilson was not alone in his attempts to understand the effects of wartime trauma on children. For example, Anna Freud, living in exile in England, founded the Hampstead War Nurseries for foster children with single parents in 1940. Rebecca Clifford, *Survivors: Children's Lives After the Holocaust* (New Haven and London: Yale University Press, 2020).
[34] Keilson, *Sequential Traumatization*, 11.
[35] See, for example, the case studies of "Franz," a survivor of nine concentration camps, separated from his family at fifteen, who was forty-five years old at his interview in 1972 and suffered from paralyzing episodic breakdowns, alienation, an inability to hold a job, and early retirement due to his poor physical condition (*Sequential Traumatization*, 243–6). Another example is the case study "Carla," separated from her family just before her fifth birthday, who survived the occupation in hiding with a family, with legal guardianship given to a surviving uncle who allowed her to remain with the foster family; due to a conflict at age sixteen, she left her foster family, was taken to an Orthodox Jewish children's home, came into conflict with the home, became aggressive, was intensely

survivors as conflicts of loyalty, psychosomatic complaints, affective disturbances, breakdowns, or an inability to live or work in a place for a sustained length of time, are ongoing manifestations of the recurring deferred temporality of trauma. As mentioned above, one aspect of the articulation of traumatic experience is its dislocating temporality of belatedness, Freud's *Nachträglichkeit*, between the traumatic event and the unconscious manifestation or conscious articulation of the experience by the individual concerned.[36]

Significantly, the study emerges from an intimate interlacing of personal experience with postwar professional specialization in psychiatry and psychoanalysis. Keilson, too, had lost his parents to Nazi persecution, while he was able to survive the occupation in hiding or traveling with forged Dutch papers for the resistance organization "Vrije groepen Amsterdam" as a counsellor helping Jewish children manifesting dangerous behavioral problems while in homes or hiding.[37] In the brief preface to the 1978 publication, Keilson emphasizes the deeply personal roots of his scholarship:

> Despite the purely clinical design of the study, my double training as a physician and teacher in Germany and my sphere of work there until 1936, as well as my years of experience as adviser to the Jewish war orphans organization in the Netherlands after the end of the Second World War, meant that the concept of a follow-up study of children took on a personal significance which went beyond the thematic unity of psychiatric, social-psychological and pedagogical problems."[38]

---

interested in Jewish culture, and worked on a kibbutz in Israel for four years, where she met her husband. She was thirty-four years old at the time of the interview, in which she seemed tense and hunted, displayed conflicts of loyalty, suffered from physical ailments, hypomania, and feelings of resentment and guilt (*Sequential Traumatization*, 173–81).

[36] For an influential literary-psychoanalytical account of trauma, see Cathy Caruth, *Unclaimed Experience: Trauma, Narrative, and History* (Baltimore, MD: Johns Hopkins University Press, 1996). Caruth's argument draws heavily on late Freudian and Lacanian psychoanalysis for her understanding of trauma as that which sutures together the experience of the "missed encounter" with history, belatedness and the call for ethical recognition. For a critique of the universalism and European-centrism in much work on trauma, see Didier Fassin and Richard Rechtman, *The Empire of Trauma: An Inquiry into the Condition of Victimhood* (Princeton, NJ: Princeton University Press, 2009). These two publications represent important positions in recent discussions in this ever-expanding field of research.

[37] Keilson, "In der Fremde zuhause," 218–20.

[38] Keilson, *Sequential Traumatization*, xiii.

In this citation, Keilson takes pains to render visible the above-mentioned "traces of broken continuity" ("Spuren der gebrochenen Kontinuität") from his earlier life experiences. Thus, his clinical study is more than a scientific exercise: it also renders visible and thus helps to restore an interrupted arc of life experience. This experience encompasses his medical and pedagogical education and work with youth in Weimar Germany and his wartime activities as a therapist for disturbed Jewish children in hiding at the request of the Dutch resistance, culminating in his training as a psychiatrist and work as a psychoanalyst in the Netherlands after World War II. This also may well explain Keilson's choice of the word "destiny" ("Schicksal"), in his book's title, to describe the life events of the Jewish Dutch orphans.

Indeed, Keilson's late autobiographical writings and interviews demonstrate how his lived experience had the temporal quality of a "before" and "after," with the end of World War II acting as an affective as much as a temporal watershed in psychological terms: "On Liberation Day, with the end of World War Two, began the unceasing time of mourning" ("Mit dem Tag der Befreiung, dem Ende des Zweiten Weltkriegs, begann die Zeit der Trauer, die nie endet").[39] This citation is the final sentence in an essay published in 2005 in the *Neue Zürcher Zeitung*; significantly, the grammatical subject or agent for whom the time of mourning began remains unspecified. The tension between the specificity of historical dates and the indeterminate subject emphasizes how, like trauma, mourning is a state or feeling with its own temporality. Through his work, Keilson generated a communal space for mourning, while recognizing mourning to be temporally unpredictable and open-ended. The final stage of the above-mentioned three traumatic sequences was often the most challenging, for this is when an individual recognizes the end of a life-threatening period of persecution and, at the same time, the immense and irrevocable losses accrued over this time emerge most sharply. The survivors are now subject to the temporality of mourning, for better or for worse. Speaking of his relationship to his own losses in an interview he gave late in life, Keilson declared, "Mourning/grief is actually the substrate of my sense of life" ("Die Trauer ist eigentlich die Grundlage meines Lebensgefühls").[40] Perhaps the most persuasive proof of the personal significance of his work on trauma with child survivors, and the element that makes this work, as Keilson put it, "more than merely a scientific exercise,"[41] is the dedication that precedes the foreword to the monograph, a modest address of

---

[39] Keilson, "Die Zeit der Trauer (2005)," in *Kein Plädoyer für eine Luftschaukel*, 137.
[40] Keilson, "Hundert Jahre," in *Da steht mein Haus*, 103.
[41] Keilson, *Sequential Traumatization*, xiv.

mourning at the bottom of an otherwise blank page: "IN PLACE OF KADDISH."[42]

Keeping Time: Intimate Alienation

As suggested in the introduction to this chapter, the concept of intimate alienation captures the complex dialectical tension constitutive of Keilson's relationship to Germany from 1936 onwards. Psychoanalytical work on trauma directly thematizes the temporal registers of belatedness and retroactivity and asks how past suffering interrupts the subject's present. In his final autobiographical account, Keilson offers us the metaphor of the calendar, with its reassuring universality and cyclical rhythms, over and against which we might grasp the particular and untimely (out-of-joint) temporality of persecution:

> Whoever has lived and survived on the run in the middle of Europe as a Jew and a persecuted person is offered, in retrospect, only one single, unbroken continuity as the background of his existence: that of the calendar with its monotonous, recurring numbers of weeks and months, weekdays, Sundays, and holidays, printed in red ink and valid all over the world.
>
> [Wer als Jude und Verfolger auf der Flucht mitten in Europa gelebt und überlebt hat, dem bietet sich im Rückblick, als Hintergrund seines Daseins nur eine einzige, ungebrochene Kontinuität an: die des Kalenders mit seinen eintönig wiederkehrenden Zahlen der Wochen und Monate, Wochen- und Sonn- und Festtagen, mit roter Farbe gedruckt und gültig in aller Welt.][43]

Working with trauma entails understanding a concept of time that does not run according to calendrical time or the twenty-four-hour schedule through which we measure and calculate our days. In the therapeutic setting, the analyst is an interlocutor directly and intimately exposed to the alienation of others. In this sense, Keilson's psychoanalytical project and practice engaged the time of others through careful listening and the dialectic of empathy and alienation, navigating the affective storms and voids caused by the violence of one's erstwhile homeland. And all the while, in his sessions, he spoke Dutch with a German accent. As a mode of intimate alienation, psychotherapy itself is a practice of

---

[42] The dedication appears in emphatic capital letters in the English version. Keilson, *Sequential Traumatization*, n.p. In the German edition the dedication reads, "An Stelle eines Kaddisch," in Keilson, *Sequentielle Traumatisierung*, n.p.
[43] Keilson, *Da steht mein Haus*, 9.

maintaining affective proximity to a difficult past, a form of engaging the history of German persecution in its many lived dimensions, through empathetic encounters with survivors who had lost everything when they were at their most vulnerable.

In his desire to fully comprehend the suffering of the Jewish orphans in the Netherlands, Keilson gained an intimate understanding of the history of destruction wrought on the Jewish Dutch community, as well as Jewish German exiles seeking shelter in the Netherlands, throughout the Nazi occupation. His psychoanalytic study and practice from a location and perspective outside of Germany reveal his deep engagement with some of the most difficult aspects of Germany's fascist past and its afterlife. His decision to write his monograph in German, despite having conducted his sessions in Dutch with the majority of his patients, also speaks to this: "in addition to the psychological results, [I wanted to] describe the historical facts that had led to their being orphaned in the language of the perpetrators, which also was and still remains mine" ("[ich wollte] außer den psychologischen Ergebnissen die historischen Tatsachen, die zu der Verwaisung geführt hatten, in der Sprache der Täter beschreiben, die auch meine war und immer noch ist. In dieser gebrochenen Formulierung liegt auch mein Verhältnis zur deutschen Sprache, ein vielleicht gebrochenes Verhältnis, das gewiß nicht nur als ein Verlust betrachtet werden muß").[44] Keilson's own experience of intimate alienation as a former German and a Jewish Dutch citizen no doubt fostered his nuanced concept of "sequential traumatization," which was a valuable contribution to the psychoanalytical understanding of trauma long before it had become an acknowledged diagnostic tool and popularized term.[45]

By tracking the specific relationship between the events that produced trauma and the manifestation of psychosomatic or affective symptoms at discrete moments in these children's lives, by looking for specific patterns of loss and disruption, Keilson also addresses the spatial dislocation that so often appears as both a symptom and cause of trauma. This, in turn, demonstrates the ongoing relevance of the concept of trauma in relation to migration, forced exile, and other forms of deracinated existence pervasive also in the twenty-first century. Although Keilson never returned to Germany to live there, the consequences of its fascist history of destruction during the so-called Third Reich continued to occupy him in his home in the Netherlands. Ironically enough, we

---

[44] Hans Keilson, "Wohin die Sprache nicht reicht," in *Werke*, Bd. 2., 246.
[45] For an outline of a genealogy of the term "trauma" in the context of psychiatric/psychological epistemologies of the late nineteenth and twentieth centuries, as well as an analysis of the changing moral attitudes towards suffering and the attendant moral politics, see Fassin and Rechtman, *Empire of Trauma*, 1–39.

may have Keilson's experience of intimate alienation from Germany to thank for his singular production of psychoanalytical knowledge on trauma, the ongoing relevance and application of which exceeds national boundaries, for better or for worse.[46]

Works Cited

Becker, David, and Margarita Diaz. "The Social Process and the Transgenerational Transmission of Trauma in Chile," in *International Handbook of Multigenerational Legacies of Trauma*, ed. Yael Danieli (New York: Plenum Press, 1998), 435–45.

Bugelnig, Marie-Christin. "'Schreiben, das ist für mich eine andere Möglichkeit spazieren zu gehen, in der Welt': Topografien der Erinnerung. Zu Hans Keilsons Erinnerungsbuch *Da steht mein Haus*," in *"die vergangene Zeit bleibt die erlittene Zeit." Untersuchungen zum Werk von Hans Keilson*, ed. Simone Schröder, Ulrike Weymann, and Andreas Martin Widmann (Würzburg: Königshausen & Neumann, 2013), 239–53.

Caruth, Cathy. *Unclaimed Experience: Trauma, Narrative, and History* (Baltimore, MD: Johns Hopkins University Press, 1996).

Clifford, Rebecca. *Survivors: Children's Lives After the Holocaust* (New Haven and London: Yale University Press, 2020).

DeNur, Yehiel (Ka-tsetnik). Testimony given at the trial of Adolf Eichmann in Jesusalem, Israel, 1961. Session No. 68, 69, youtube.com/watch?v=m3-tXyYhd5U.

Detering, Heinrich. "Der Analytiker auf der Couch. Bemerkungen zur Entstehungsgeschichte von Hans Keilsons *Da steht mein Haus*," in *"die vergangene Zeit bleibt die erlittene Zeit." Untersuchungen zum Werk von Hans Keilson*, ed. Simone Schröder, Ulrike Weymann, and Andreas Martin Widmann (Würzburg: Königshausen & Neumann, 2013), 273–8.

Detering, Heinrich. "Wortlosigkeit. Zur Figur der deiktischen Ellipse in Hans Keilsons Erzählungen," in *"die vergangene Zeit bleibt die erlittene Zeit." Untersuchungen zum Werk von Hans Keilson*, ed. Simone Schröder, Ulrike Weymann, and Andreas Martin Widmann (Würzburg: Königshausen & Neumann, 2013), 127–44.

Fassin, Didier, and Richard Rechtman. *The Empire of Trauma: An Inquiry into the Condition of Victimhood* (Princeton, NJ: Princeton University Press, 2009).

---

[46] On the significance of Keilson's work on trauma, see Dierk Juelich, ed., *Geschichte als Trauma. Festschrift für Hans Keilson zu seinem 80. Geburtstag* (Frankfurt am Main: Nexus Verlag, 1991); Marianne Leuzinger-Bohleber and Wolfdietrich Schmied-Kowarsik, eds., *"Gedenk und vergiß—Im Abschaum der Geschichte ..." Trauma und Erinnern. Hans Keilson zu Ehren* (Tübingen: edition diskord, 2001). Reference to Keilson's work on trauma can be found in more recent publications on sequential traumatization in transnational contexts. See Dieter Nelles, Armin Nolzen, and Heinz Sunker, "Sequential Traumatization: The Living Conditions of Children of those Politically Persecuted under the Nazi Regime," *Taboo* (Fall–Winter 2005): 59–70, and David Becker and Margarita Diaz, "The Social Process and the Transgenerational Transmission of Trauma in Chile," in *International Handbook of Multigenerational Legacies of Trauma*, ed. Yael Danieli (New York: Plenum Press, 1998), 435–45.

Fishman, Joel S. "The War Orphans Controversy in the Netherlands: Majority–Minority Relations," in *Proceedings of the Symposium on the History of the Jews in the Netherlands. November 28–December 3, 1982. Tel Aviv–Jerusalem*, ed. Jozef Michman and Tirtsah Levie (Jerusalem: Daf-Chen, 1984), 421–32.

Freud, Sigmund. *Beyond the Pleasure Principle, Group Psychology and Other Works (1920–1922)*, in *The Standard Edition of the Complete Psychological Works of Sigmund Freud, Vol. 18*, trans. and ed. James Strachey together with Anna Freud, assisted by Alix Strachey and Alan Tyson (London: Hogarth Press and the Institute of Psychoanalysis, 1955).

Freud, Sigmund. *Inhibitions, Symptoms and Anxiety (1926 [1925])*, in *On Symptoms, Inhibitions, and Anxiety*, in *The Standard Edition of the Complete Psychological Works of Sigmund Freud, Vol. 20*, trans. and ed. James Strachey together with Anna Freud, assisted by Alix Strachey and Alan Tyson (London: Hogarth Press and the Institute of Psychoanalysis, 1959), 77–178.

Juelich, Dirk, ed. *Geschichte als Trauma. Festschrift für Hans Keilson zu seinem 80. Geburtstag* (Frankfurt am Main: Nexus Verlag, 1991).

Keilson, Hans. *Sequentielle Traumatisierung bei Kindern. Untersuchung zum Schicksal jüdischer Kriegswaisen*, together with Herman R. Saphartie (Gießen: Psychosozial-Verlag, 1979).

Keilson, Hans. *Sequential Traumatization in Children: A Clinical and Statistical Follow-Up Study on the State of the Jewish War Orphans in the Netherlands*, together with Herman R. Sarphatie, trans. Yvonne Bearne, Hilary Coleman, and Deirdre Winter (Jerusalem: Magnes Press, 1992).

Keilson, Hans. "*Das Leben geht weiter*—nach fünfzig Jahren," in *Werke in Zwei Bänden, Romanen und Erzählungen, Bd. 1*, ed. Heinrich Detering and Gerhard Kurz (Frankfurt am Main: Fischer Verlag, 2005), 581–6.

Keilson, Hans. "Die fragmentierte Psychotherapie eines aus Bergen-Belsen zurückgekehrten Jungen," in *Werke in Zwei Bänden, Gedichte und Essays, Bd. 2.*, ed. Heinrich Detering and Gerhard Kurz (Frankfurt am Main: Fischer Verlag, 2005), 273–90.

Keilson, Hans. "In der Fremde zuhause," in *Werke in Zwei Bänden, Gedichte und Essays, Bd. 2.*, ed. Heinrich Detering and Gerhard Kurz (Frankfurt am Main: Fischer Verlag, 2005), 214–52.

Keilson, Hans. "Lieber Holland als Heimweh," in *Werke in Zwei Bänden, Gedichte und Essays, Bd. 2.*, ed. Heinrich Detering and Gerhard Kurz (Frankfurt am Main: Fischer Verlag, 2005), 150–9.

Keilson, Hans. "Vorwort [zu *Ach, Sie schreiben deutsch?*] Ach, Sie schreiben deutsch?" in *Werke in Zwei Bänden, Gedichte und Essays, Bd. 2.*, ed. Heinrich Detering and Gerhard Kurz (Frankfurt am Main: Fischer Verlag, 2005), 386–94.

Keilson, Hans. "Wohin die Sprache nicht reicht," in *Werke in Zwei Bänden, Gedichte und Essays, Bd. 2.*, ed. Heinrich Detering and Gerhard Kurz (Frankfurt am Main: Fischer Verlag, 2005), 137–49.

Keilson, Hans. "Das Wirkliche erzählbar machen. Dankrede zur Verleihung der Moses-Mendelssohn-Medaille (2007)," in *Kein Plädoyer für eine Luftschaukel. Essays, Reden, Gespräche*, ed. Heinrich Detering (Frankfurt am Main: Fischer Verlag, 2011), 138–39.

Keilson, Hans. *Kein Plädoyer für eine Luftschaukel. Essays, Reden, Gespräche*, ed. Heinrich Detering (Frankfurt am Main: Fischer Verlag, 2011).

Keilson, Hans. *Da steht Mein Haus. Erinnerungen*, ed. Heinrich Detering (Frankfurt am Main: Fischer Verlag, 2012), 7–100.

Keilson, Hans, and Heinrich Detering. "Hundert Jahre. Ein Gespräch mit Hans Keilson," in *Da steht mein Haus. Erinnerungen*, ed. Heinrich Detering (Frankfurt am Main: Fischer Verlag, 2012), 103–26.

Leuzinger-Bohleber, Marianne, and Wolfdietrich Schmied-Kowarsik, eds. *"Gedenk und vergiß—Im Abschaum der Geschichte . . ." Trauma und Erinnern. Hans Keilson zu Ehren* (Tübingen: edition diskord, 2001).

Michaelis, Andree. "Nachbarn in der Fremde. Hans Keilsons Da steht mein Haus im Horizont kanonischer Erinnerungsbücher von Überlebenden der Shoah," in *"die vergangene Zeit bleibt die erlittene Zeit." Untersuchungen zum Werk von Hans Keilson*, ed. Simone Schröder, Ulrike Weymann, and Andreas Martin Widmann (Würzburg: Königshausen & Neumann, 2013), 223–38.

Nelles, Dieter, Armin Nolzen, and Heinz Sunker. "Sequential Traumatization: The Living Conditions of Children of those Politically Persecuted under the Nazi Regime," *Taboo* (Fall–Winter 2005): 59–70.

Niekerk, Carl. "Literatures of the Contact Zone: Hans Keilson, Nico Rost, Albert Vigoleis Thelen, and the Literary Spaces of the Late 1940s and Early 1950s," *Journal of Dutch Literature*, vol. 9, no.1 (2018): 112–27.

Rousset, David. *L'univers concentrationnaire* (Paris: Éditions du Pavois, 1946).

III Rewriting German Culture

Ten   Tracing the Continual Present: Yoko Tawada and Vilém Flusser[1]

Gizem Arslan

Introduction: The Past, Present, and Future of Writing

German-Japanese author Yoko Tawada and Czech-born, German-speaking media theorist Vilém Flusser have in common multilingual oeuvres that resist systematization, and for which an intense preoccupation with self-translation and the medium of writing are constitutive.[2] Yet they constitute an unlikely pair for a single analysis, particularly when one recalls their divergent approaches to comparative histories of writing. Tawada's most prominent theoretical interlocutor is not Flusser but Walter Benjamin, with whose texts—specifically those on language and translation—Tawada engages in a much more sustained fashion. Expressly dissimilar are the comparative treatments of writing in Flusser's speculatively periodized media history on the one hand and Tawada's numerous reflections on the writing systems of the world on the other. As Gundela Hachmann notes, to speak of literary texts in conjunction with Flusser's techno-imagination "runs contrary to what Flusser's media philosophy is so well known for: the end

---

[1] An alternate version of this contribution has been published in *German Quarterly* (94.3, August 2021). The author would like to thank Jocelyn Aksin, Aria Cabot, Daniele Forlino, Justin Germain, Lourdes Molina, Carl Niekerk, Lucas Riddle, and Didem Uca for their invaluable feedback on earlier drafts of this chapter.

[2] See Rainer Guldin, "Vilem Flusser's Practice of Multiple Self-Translation," in *Self-Translation: Brokering Originality in Hybrid Culture*, ed. Anthony Cordingley (New York and London: Bloomsbury Academic, 2013), 95–109; Sigrid Weigel, "Yoko Tawada's Poetics on the Threshold of Different Writing Systems," in *Tawada Yōko: On Writing and Rewriting*, ed. Douglas Slaymaker (Lanham, MD: Lexington Books, 2020), 49–59; and Madalina Meirosu, "Yoko Tawada's Überseezungen: Feminist Self-Translation and Creative Resistance," in *Tawada Yōko: On Writing and Rewriting*, 121–38.

of writing, and with it, the end of history."³ After all, Flusser's answers to the question *Does Writing Have a Future?* in numerous essays published in 1987 can be summed up as "no."⁴

Precisely this divergence on the question of writing renders a point of contact between the two speculative essayists particularly fruitful. One of many short prose works by Tawada that blend episodic autofiction with essayistic reflection, the fiction-essay "An der Spree" ("On the Spree River"), from the 2007 prose and poetry collection *Sprachpolizei und Spielpolyglotte* (*Language Police and Play Polyglot*), cites Flusser's essay "Letters of the Alphabet" from *Does Writing Have a Future?*⁵ Recalling Flusser's depiction of the Latin alphabet's imagistic roots, Tawada proceeds to rediscover and retrace written signs of all origins (letters of the Latin alphabet, Sino-Japanese logograms, Arabic numerals) in twenty-first-century Berlin. Tawada's text culminates in a moment in which the narrator traces the shape of the numeral 0 (zero) on a piece of paper, intermedially performing mathematical calculation, alphabetic writing, cartographic orientation, and gesturing towards binary code. This point of citational contact between Tawada and Flusser yields two key critical insights. First, Tawada illuminates and resists the Eurocentrism of Flusser's theory of writing in particular and of Western histories of writing more generally. Second, by suggesting that the written sign has to be traced and retraced in subsequent moments of writing, Tawada produces a continual present. This reconfiguration of the present poses at once an alternative to Flusser's linear-teleological understanding of writing and history, as well as to the common conception of our current age as one of simultaneity. As an increasingly significant minority voice in East and West, Tawada's brief engagement with Flusser illustrates the need for a broader effort to address interventions in the arts and literatures of migration in connection with our existing understanding of media.

---

[3] Gundela Hachmann, "Drafting the Techno-Imagination: A Future for Literary Writing?" *Flusser Studies*, vol. 18 (2018): 1–13, here 1.

[4] The German title of the collection is *Die Schrift. Hat Schreiben Zukunft?* Originally published in German in 1987, and republished in German in 2002. The complete English translation appeared in 2011 as *Does Writing Have a Future?*, ed. Mark Poster, trans, Nancy Ann Roth (Minneapolis: University of Minnesota Press, 2011). All subsequent citations will be provided from this latest English translation.

[5] See Yoko Tawada, "An Der Spree," in *Sprachpolizei und Spielpolyglotte* (Tübingen: Konkursbuch Verlag Claudia Gehrke, 2007), 11–23. All parenthetical page references in the following refer to this edition; all translations from Tawada are my own unless cited otherwise.

Yoko Tawada and Vilém Flusser on Time and the Medium of Writing

Yoko Tawada has been developing her œuvre simultaneously and independently in German and Japanese since 1987. Enduring points of fascination for her are the materiality of language experienced in translation (translation treated as an intensified mode of writing and reading) explored in the context of intensified global mobility (of people and texts), as Tawada explores in numerous works such as her novels *Das nackte Auge* (*The Naked Eye*, 2004) and *Schwager in Bordeaux* (*Brother-in-law in Bordeaux*, 2008), as well as collections of essays and short fictional works, such as *Talisman* (1996), *Verwandlungen* (*Transformations*, 1998), and *Überseezungen* (*Overseatongues*, 2002). Tawada's texts in German often feature a narrator loosely sketched as East Asian as she navigates a world equally loosely sketched as European, reflecting on cultural attitudes and perspectives in ways that question the givenness of identities and humorously subvert linguistic norms. Although most texts by Tawada foreground the materiality of the writing medium to some degree, the simultaneous engagement with the history of writing and digital media in "An der Spree" is echoed in fewer texts, among them most notably *Überseezungen* (2002). "An der Spree" is concerned in particular with the relationship between interlingual and intermedial contact on the one hand, and old and new media on the other. It subtly addresses Eurocentric debates surrounding the seemingly politically neutral disciplines of mathematics and informatics. It does so by addressing two of Tawada's common themes: orientation and legibility. Perhaps much more intensively than most other works by Tawada, however, it relates questions of orientation to contemporary modes of conveyance such as transportation and new media, as well as to the legibility of diverse modes of communication in a contemporary context. The temporal dimension inherent to the medium of writing comes in contact with comparative histories of the world's writing systems, as Tawada's narrator moves across Berlin in modern modes of transportation, ruminates on the history of Eastern and Western writing, and finally alludes to binary code and computation.

The interventions in "An der Spree" are illimitable to media-materiality in any limited sense. The text often extrapolates human–media interactions to intercultural and interlingual contact more broadly. In a series of autofictional episodes, an East Asian female narrator crosses paths with friends and strangers in Berlin. Their encounters often lead to exchanges about migration, translation, and travel. These conversations are juxtaposed in turn with the narrator's reflections on modes of conveyance (e.g., planes, Berlin's transportation system) and elements of the world's writing systems as she encounters them in Berlin's cityscape. Contrasts become visible in the narrator's verbal exchanges, on the one hand between the heterogeneity of languages, identities, and spaces in Berlin, and, on the other, enduring attitudes towards language and culture that construe them as homogeneous and originary. For example, the narrator stands by the open door of a church to enjoy the organ music issuing from inside, when an elderly passerby smiles and asks her, "How do you find our music?" ("Wie finden Sie unsere Musik?"). The narrator muses angrily to herself, "Why her music? I was appalled. She rudely called my Bach her music, only because she had probably been born in Saxony" ("Wieso ihre Musik? Ich war entsetzt. Sie nannte meinen Bach einfach ihre Musik, nur weil sie wahrscheinlich in Sachsen geboren war") (20). "An der Spree" prominently features the narrator's movements in Berlin and elsewhere in the world against the backdrop of a modern cityscape with billboards and street signs in various languages and writing systems. The narrator is attuned to the presence of Arabic numerals, the number zero, and Chinese logograms, both on surfaces typically intended for writing and those that are not.

If one can speak of a focal point in a text about these movements, conversations, and reflections of a *flâneuse*, then that focal point is the numeral zero. Two of Tawada's key literary strategies revolve around this written sign and are encapsulated in a conversation between the narrator and a friend. This friend misreads the title of the short story by Heinrich von Kleist "Die Marquise von O . . ." ("The Marquise of O . . .") as "Die Marquise von Null" ("The Marquise of Zero"). The narrator recognizes this as a misreading, but also notes that the zero marks the Marquise's loss of consciousness, the mnemonic void around which the entire text revolves. The first key literary strategy here is intermedial reading, that is, reading written signs at once as sound transcription, mathematical symbols, image, and concrete objects. The second strategy is paragrammatic misreading.[6] According to Leon Roudiez, this is "any reading that challenges the normative referential grammar of a text by forming "networks of signification not accessible through conventional reading habits."[7] "An der Spree" exploits these strategies in order to challenge Eurocentric notions of space and time and the writing employed to inscribe them.

In *Sprachpolizei und Spielpolyglotte* and elsewhere, Tawada's whimsical ruminations render strange the works of canonical German-speaking writers such as Johann Wolfgang von Goethe, Paul Celan, Heinrich von Kleist, Else Lasker-Schüler, and Walter Benjamin. In contrast to her

---

[6] Gizem Arslan, "Making Senses: Translation and the Materiality of Written Signs in Yoko Tawada," *Translation Studies*, vol. 12, no. 3 (Sept. 2019): 338–56, here 341.
[7] Cited in Craig Douglas Dworkin, *Reading the Illegible* (Evanston, IL: Northwestern University Press, 2003), xx.

sustained engagement with the works of these figures in other essays in *Sprachpolizei und Spielpolyglotte*, her reference to the media theorist Vilém Flusser in "An der Spree" is made in passing:

> I arrived on the Warsaw Express in the Zoologischer Garten station in Berlin and discovered a "B" in "Berlin," a "C" in "Zoologischen" and an "A" in "Garten." The alphabet reminded me of the Near East. Vilém Flusser wrote: "The letter A still shows the horns of the Syriac steer, B still the domes of the Semitic house, C (G) still the hump of the camel in the near eastern desert." One writes the alphabet in order to evoke the desert in language. The desert is reason, the soul of the mathematician.
>
> [Mit dem Warszawa-Express kam ich in "Berlin Zoologischer Garten" an und entdeckte in "Berlin" ein "B", im "Zoologischen" ein C und im "Garten" ein A. Das Alphabet erinnerte mich an den Nahen Osten. Vilém Flusser schrieb: "Das A zeigt noch immer die Hörner des syriakischen Stiers, das B noch immer die Kuppeln des semitischen Hauses, das C (G) noch immer den Buckel des Kamels in der vorderasiatischen Wüste". Man schreibt das Alphabet, um die Wüste in der Sprache wachzurufen. Die Wüste ist die Vernunft, der Geist eines Mathematikers. (12)][8]

In consequence of this apparent short shrift to Flusser, it would be as wrong to overstate Flusser's textual presence in Tawada as to understate the percolation of his theories of media and history in "An der Spree." Tawada cites Flusser sparsely and selectively. And yet, Flusser's media-historical milestones from images to writing to technical images appear in "An der Spree" as metaphorical stations in a text that treats travel and the material of media as major themes. Flusser's theories of writing in particular serve as the springboard—if not the ultimate object of analysis—of Tawada's double-pronged critique in this essay: of theories and histories of writing that treat the alphabet as superior to logographic writing, and, in an extended sense, of enduring Eurocentric attitudes regarding language and culture.

---

[8] The English version of the passage Tawada cites reads slightly differently in the published English translation of Flusser's *Does Writing Have a Future?*: "Letters belong to the oldest cultures we have. In the fifteen hundred years since their invention, their original form has changed repeatedly, and yet it remains recognizable: the two horns of the Semitic steer (Hebrew: *aleph*) in the A, the two domes of the Semitic house (Hebrew: *beth*) in the B, the hump of the Semitic camel (Hebrew: *gimul*) in the C" (29–30).

Tawada's and Flusser's biographies are both marked by itinerancy, while Flusser's multilingual oeuvre, like Tawada's, spans across multiple languages and genres. Flusser was born in Prague to a family of Jewish intellectuals and studied philosophy there. During World War II, he managed to escape to the UK and then to Brazil, but his entire family died in concentration camps. He lived the rest of his life first in Brazil, then in Tirol, Germany, and Aix-en-Provence. Given this biography, it should come as no surprise that he produced an oeuvre with a complex publication history scattered across five languages: German, Portuguese, English, French, Italian, and Czech.[9] Flusser would repeatedly translate his own texts and alter them significantly in the process. His reception and fame are additionally fragmented: distinct aspects of his thought are studied in more detail in certain countries than in others.[10] Despite the difficulty of categorizing his work, Flusser's thinking can be described broadly as a theory of cultural techniques based on phenomenological analyses of elementary gestures such as writing, calculating, building, and designing, among others. Flusser believed that our thinking, behavior, feelings, wishes, our very perception, and imagination were formed by the structure of the codes in which we experience the world and ourselves.[11] History, particularly cultural history is, for Flusser a cultural history of media (*Medienkulturgeschichte*).

Flusser's milestones in this history rely on a writing–image binary interlinked with a linear conceptualization of time. Flusser's insistence on the writing–image binary and writing's relationship to historical consciousness distinguishes him from some key thinkers on media, history, and media history. A prime example is Friedrich Kittler, who highlighted interlinks between, and even the co-presence of, writing and image. In contrast to Jacques Derrida's conception of writing as difference and deferral, Flusser sees writing as resistance to images. Flusser's binary also leads to a denaturalized temporality (moving away from cyclical nature towards linear progression through time). Flusser believed that writing engendered human awareness to events unfolding sequentially, an idea expounded at length in the posthumously edited collection of essays titled *Does Writing Have a Future*? Here,

---

[9] Gustavo Bernardo, Anke Finger, and Rainer Guldin, "Migration, Nomadism, Networks: A Biography," in *Vilém Flusser: An Introduction* (Minneapolis: University of Minnesota Press, 2011), 1–26; Guldin, "Vilem Flusser's Practice."

[10] Bernardo, Finger, and Guldin note that "Flusser was known only in parts: in Brazil, for his texts on art, language, and communication in Portuguese; in Germany, for his ideas on media theory, technical images, writing, and history in German; and for a few English- and French-speaking readers, for some of the numerous essays published in their languages in between" (xviii).

[11] Dieter Mersch, *Medientheorien zur Einführung* (Hamburg: Junius, 2006), 138.

Flusser reflects on the medium of writing as a period in a historical continuum that begins with images, continues with writing, and will culminate in what Flusser terms "technical images."[12] Flusser's conceptualization of this history can be summarized as follows:

> In the beginning humans experienced life in four dimensions situated in time and space. New forms of visual media came about that reduced the number of dimensions available through experience. This led to increasing abstraction. Sculpture reduced the number of dimensions to three: length, width, and height. Traditional images such as cave paintings further reduced the dimensions to two: length and width. The penultimate stage is marked by the advent of writing that reduced human experience to one dimension: the linearity of print. The final stage began with the photograph, the first "technical image," that reduced experience to zero dimensions where visual media consist of code.[13]

As the emphasis on human perception in this exposition demonstrates, Flusser's media history is phenomenological. It concerns itself little with the media in which history is stored and accessed, with media-material conditions, or the historical development of media as such. Rather, Flusser is interested in the perceptions and practices of literate humans who experience, understand, and evaluate the world in a linear becoming. The linearity with which Flusser associates writing applies indeed to his history of media, which progresses by stages from reflecting human experience in four dimensions towards zero dimensions. When juxtaposed with Flusser's views on writing, this view of media history reveals two key contradictions in Flusser's media theory that Tawada's brief contact with him reveals. First, despite Flusser's professed distaste for a view of history "as continuous growth and unchecked linear progress," his media history cannot entirely escape this linear view. Flusser privileges a linear consciousness that writing's linearity engenders in humans, which in turn prompts him to place European writing systems higher on a civilizational scale than "pictographic writing" associated with images.[14] Second, Flusser's phenomenological method, which seeks to liberate the thinker from his misconceptions, fails to

---

[12] Technical image: image produced by apparatuses such as camera and film, as distinct from images produced by artists.
[13] P. Schaefer, "Vilem Flusser's Philosophy of New Media History," *New Media & Society*, vol. 13, no. 8 (December 2011): 1389–95, here 1390.
[14] Anke Finger, *Vilém Flusser: An Introduction* (Minneapolis: University of Minnesota Press, 2011), 38.

liberate him from his Eurocentric biases as they apply to the history of writing. Flusser is in many ways a phenomenologist of media, applying Edmund Husserl's method of phenomenological reduction in order to examine "phenomena as they appear in consciousness before preconceptions can shape those perceptions."[15] This is a practice by means of which a phenomenologist can liberate himself from the captivation in which one is held by all that one accepts as being the case (all of one's existing knowledge, everyday experience, and preconceptions).[16] Flusser applies this method to a cultural history of media since before the inception of writing. His distinction between logographic and alphabetic writing, however, rests on a conceptualization of writing as distinct from images. Flusser excludes logographic writing from his analysis. For Flusser, the origin of writing is the image—that is, not pictograms or ideograms as prototypes for letters, but the gestures of writing's unfolding. Yet, he does align logograms with images. In agreement with some leading grammatologists of the twentieth century, he privileges phonographic over logographic writing:

> Ideograms are signs for ideas, for images seen with the inner eye. The preservation of images, however, was exactly what writing sought to avoid. Writing set out to explain images, to explain them away. Pictorial, fanciful, imaginative thinking was to yield to conceptual, discursive, critical thinking. It was necessary to write alphabetically rather than ideographically to be able to think iconoclastically. This is the reason for denoting the sounds of a language.
>
> (30–1)[17]

Although this passage is not cited in "An der Spree," it appears to be subtly critiqued in it. The primary object of Tawada's oblique critique is the questionable dichotomy Flusser posits here between text and image, and by extension, between alphabetic and logographic writing. Flusser conflates ideograms ("signs for ideas," in his words) with pictograms (written signs that suggest or convey visual images), and neglects to acknowledge the abundance of phonographic elements in logographic writing (logogram as the more commonly accepted umbrella term for written signs denoting units of utterance). More importantly, however, he relegates logographic writing by implication to a fanciful, backward

---

[15] Schaefer, "Vilem Flusser's Philosophy," 1390.
[16] John Cogan, "Phenomenological Reduction," in *The Internet Encyclopedia of Philosophy*, iep.utm.edu/phen-red/.
[17] Flusser, *Does Writing Have a Future?* 30–1.

era. This era is later overcome by the iconoclasm and critical thinking inherent to phonographic, alphabetic writing. Admittedly, in *Does Writing Have a Future?* Vilém Flusser acknowledges writing's origins through frequent references to the Arabic etymology of the number zero as well as to the origins of writing in today's Middle East.[18] As elaborated above, however, he is quick to distance alphabetic writing from non-linear and non-alphabetic systems of writing and insists on writing's unidirectionality. For Flusser, transforming images into writing is not a geometric undertaking (not unspooling an image into a linear continuum of its components), but rather a semantic one. Flusser believed that turning an image into text is a matter of turning imaginary relations into conceptual ones. It follows thus for Flusser that the triumph of writing over the image is the triumph of the conceptual over a magical or mythic consciousness. He holds that writing allowed the development of logic, philosophy, mathematics, and the other sciences.[19]

In his approach to alphabetic versus logographic writing, Flusser at once assumes a unique position in European media studies and represents common Eurocentric attitudes that permeated comparative histories of writing. Flusser is perhaps the media theorist who most closely linked the gesture of writing—setting written signs one after the other—with historical consciousness. He sees writing not simply as recorded language, but rather as a discrete system, a cultural schema, from which we have some of the greatest cultural attainments since the classical era. In this, he draws from the medial periodizations of the Canadian School that linked the linearity of alphanumeric code with Western thinking.[20] Flusser places heightened emphasis on the gesture of writing as discrete system and cultural schema in a panlogistic system in which alphabetic writing is calculation and critique. By contrast, logographic writing has been declared by grammatologists and media theorists as "cumbersome, imperfect, even primitive," even though it has been used continuously for over 3,000 years and "serves the longest uninterrupted literary tradition of all living languages."[21] One of the most significant proponents of such a view is Ignace Gelb, whose influential work *A Study of Writing* (1952) espouses a teleology of writing that tends towards full phonography, a linear evolution from logography to the alphabet. Gelb is both unequivocal and unapologetic in his conclusion:

---

[18] Flusser, *Does Writing Have a Future?* 29–30, 87.
[19] Mersch, *Medientheorien*, 143.
[20] Mersch, *Medientheorien*, 144.
[21] Florian Coulmas, *The Writing Systems of the World* (Oxford: Blackwell, 1989), 91.

[I]s writing progressing as it passes along the course of evolution marked by the logographic, syllabic, and alphabetic stages? I should say yes, it is progressing! Looking at writing from the broadest point of view I should say without hesitation that the alphabetic systems serve the aim of human intercommunication better than the logographic or logo-syllabic systems."[22]

Gelb's work represents "fundamental cultural attitudes toward what writing is and should be," and is joined by influential linguist and paleographer David Diringer, who subtitled his seminal work on the alphabet "A Key to the History of Mankind."[23] One of Flusser's uncited interlocutors, Walter Ong (1986) of the Canadian School of media theory, also went so far as to claim that the Latin alphabet will replace Chinese characters, deeming the following sacrifice necessary: "The loss to literature will be enormous, but not so enormous as a Chinese typewriter using over 40,000 characters."[24] Not unlike Flusser, Ong contrasted cyclic thought (associated with orality in Ong's case), with linear or historical or evolutionary thought (associated with writing and literality). Although Flusser did not subscribe to the Canadian School's cultural categorizations of orality, literality, and postliterarity, he too identified periods of cultural techniques that corresponded to particular media (image, writing, technical images). This conflation of images and logograms relegates logographic writing to a lower rung on a civilizational scale. It also glosses over "the contingency of perception" in readerly encounters with writing, in which writing is never entirely reducible to its phonographic dimension.[25]

Without directly addressing Flusser's conflation of logograms with pictograms, Tawada counters Flusser's disavowal of writing as image.

---

[22] Ignace J. Gelb, *A Study of Writing* (Chicago: University of Chicago Press, 1963), 239.
[23] David B. Lurie, "The Development of Writing in Japan," in *The Shape of Script: How and Why Writing Systems change*, ed. Stephen Houston (Santa Fe, NM: SAR Press, 2012), 182; David Diringer and Reinhold Regensburger, *The Alphabet: A Key to the History of Mankind* (London: Hutchinson, 1968).
[24] Walter J. Ong, *Orality and Literacy: The Technologizing of the Word* (New York and London: Routledge, 2002), 86.
[25] See Clive Scott, *Translating the Perception of Text: Literary Translation and Phenomenology* (Oxford: Legenda, 2012), 5. In this study on the phenomenology of reading, Scott emphasizes processes by means of which readers transform texts with which they come in contact. These transformations, according to Scott, can be elicited by "written signs, designs and dispositions." Scott emphasizes "a perceived excess of the signifier over the signified, a valorization of language as language (its acousticity, graphicity, parts of Speech, structures), in such a way that the imaginary is engaged" (8, 15).

This in turn produces a critique of writing's link with linear temporality. Tawada does so by referring to writing as a conjuring instead of critical practice. For Tawada, writing the alphabet is not a move from mythic to discursive thinking, as it is for Flusser. On the contrary, it is an almost magical attempt of "Wachrufen," an evocation of the Near Eastern deserts—particularly in Syria, Mesopotamia, and Egypt—where writing came into being, initially as complex pictographic writing such as Sumerian and Egyptian hieroglyphics and then the much simpler alphabet in the form of Old Canaanite and Linear Phoenician inscriptions.[26] In contrast to Flusser's conception of linear writing, which leads to historical consciousness and critical, abstract thinking, Tawada emphasizes its presence on billboards, in the structure of buildings, and even the form of the Ringbahn in Berlin—that is, in modes of conveyance understood in the broadest sense and in contexts where writing is not necessarily linear or unidirectional (12–13, 19). On billboards or signs, writing is often read (and indeed, sometimes needs to be read) intermedially, in unconventional directions, and based not solely on referential meaning but on visual or acoustic resemblance. In musing that "one writes the alphabet to awaken the desert in language" ("[m]an schreibt das Alphabet, um die Wüste in der Sprache wachzurufen"), Tawada traces concepts commonly associated with the Enlightenment such as "reason" ("Vernunft") and "spirit" ("Geist") to the Near Eastern desert. By suggesting that "the desert is reason, the spirit of a mathematician" ("[d]ie Wüste ist die Verunft, der Geist eines Mathematikers"), Tawada also recalls the origins of writing and of the number zero in India, as well as zero's subsequent promulgation by Arab merchants between the tenth and thirteenth centuries (12).[27] Tawada's engagement with media, in particular the medium of writing, thus becomes a prime locus of her resistance both to Eurocentrism and a unilinear temporal order epitomized by, but not limited to, Flusser's theories of writing. In short, Tawada exposes a "temporalized comparison" in Western theories of writing. These theories have admittedly been challenged in the intervening decades, but the cultural attitudes they represent have

---

[26] Frank Moore Cross, "The Invention and Development of the Alphabet," in *The Origins of Writing*, ed. Wayne M. Senner (Lincoln: University of Nebraska Press, 1989), 77–90, here 77–81.

[27] Brian Rotman, in *Signifying Nothing: The Semiotics of Zero* (New York: St. Martin's Press, 1987), 7. The number zero was initially greeted with anything but reason in Europe. Christian Europe initially refused it, thinking it incomprehensible and unnecessary. Zero was branded an "infidel symbol" because it designated nothingness. Rotman reasons that "zero, being somehow about 'nothing,' became therefore the object of hostility to 'nothing' already entrenched within Christian orthodoxy," 8.

proved intractable on the ground and permeate the interactions between Tawada's narrator and her interlocutors in Berlin. These attitudes can be summed up, in Natalie Melas's words, as holding to "a single civilizational scale where all the world's cultures had their place in an evolutionary hierarchy progressing from the simple or 'savage' to the complex and highly differentiated societies of 'civilization.'"[28] In "An der Spree," Tawada seeks to undermine the linearity and diachronicity of this civilizational scale, which Flusser associates with the linearity of alphabetic writing. In one particular moment of writing in "An der Spree," Tawada reveals that alphabetic writing is neither that Western nor that linear.

Rewriting Zero as Reorientation in Space and Time

As identified earlier, many of the literary strategies in "An der Spree" can be linked to the body of the numeral zero. Its simple, circular form is read intermedially and misread paradigmatically as numeral, prime meridian, and textual presentation of absence, and later as one digit of binary code. This alphanumeric character allows writing to be performed not only as the representation of spoken language, but also as the operative technique of calculation. This operative technique in turn allows reorientations, not only on paper as typo-topographic surface, but in an extended sense in the world. By linking writing and orientation, Tawada presents writing as cartography and intimates the status of *0* as prime meridian in "An der Spree." In doing so, she urges spatial and temporal reorientations that subvert existing power structures at the root of such designations as "the Far East" and "Europe." These reorientations appear in the following passage in the essay, in which the narrator decides to write a postcard to a friend and realizes that she still does not know her address. In fact, she knows neither her friend's whereabouts nor her own. It is at this point that she solves the problem on a piece of paper:

> If there is a zero here, then one knows that there's a free space. If there is no zero, then one overlooks the free space. That's why without zero, one can neither orient oneself nor calculate well. I drew a zero on the letter paper and wrote alongside it: "Look, the zero is India. The Far East is just as far away from point zero as Europe. The zero in the middle, to the left of it the Near East with

---

[28] Natalie Melas, *All the Difference in the World: Postcoloniality and the Ends of Comparison* (Stanford, CA: Stanford University Press, 2007), 15. Melas's object of analysis here is the field of comparative literature. However, her observations are applicable to comparative histories of writing as well.

its Europe, to the right the Far East: That is a symmetrical picture. I know now where I am."

[Steht hier eine Null, so weiß man, dass es einen leeren Platz gibt. Steht hier keine Null, übersieht man den freien Platz. Deshalb kann man ohne die Null weder sich orientieren noch gut rechnen. Ich zeichnete auf einem Briefpapier eine Null und schrieb dazu: "Schau, die Null ist Indien. Der Ferne Osten ist genauso weit entfernt von Punkt Null wie Europa. Die Null in der Mitte, links der Nahe Osten mit seinem Europa, rechts der Ferne Osten: Das ist ein symmetrisches Bild. Ich weiß jetzt, wo ich bin".]

(22)

The card containing the cited passage appears to be directed just as much to the narrator herself as to her interlocutor. In short, whether the postcards have in fact communicated with their addressee remains unclear, while the writing featured here appears to have resolved the problem of orientation. This is orientation achieved not with reference to fixed points such as street signs or place names, but dynamically, through play with deixis—in the narrator's use of the words I, here, and now—and importantly for this particular moment of writing, through acts of reading and writing performed continually.

This moment of intermedial writing captures the etymological roots of "cartography," as writing (*graphein*) on leafs of paper (*carta* or *charta*). The circular zero that aids orientation by marking the middle of the world is, in form and function, a meridian. Indeed, it is Tawada's prime meridian, and one that differs in significant ways from the prime meridian that passes through Greenwich, England. Tawada's attitudes towards Eurocentric geographic conventions become perceptible in this moment, both in her placement of this circular form in South Asia and in echoing her humorous statements about world-orientation elsewhere in "An der Spree." To address the former, meridians and the equator are all imaginary lines, but there can be only one equator (a circle around the earth equidistant from the poles and perpendicular to the earth's axis), whereas the placement of the prime meridian is an arbitrary convention. Like the prime meridian in Greenwich, England, Tawada's line divides the world into hemispheres and, along with longitudes, aids in orientation. The Greenwich meridian is to be found in the middle of countless world maps, where Europe is printed at the center. Tawada's prime meridian, on the other hand, marks India as a "point zero" ("Nullpunkt"), as zero's birthplace. In the world depicted on Tawada's minimalistic map, the "East" is the center of the world with respect to which its readers need to reorient themselves. In contrast to the Greenwich meridian, Tawada's meridian passes not through the imperialist colonial power Great Britain but through the once-colonized India, challenging and subverting the enduring self-evidence of categories such as Europe and the West. In so doing, it responds to the narrator's earlier humorous skepticism regarding signifiers such as "Europe," and the "Far East," questioning the stability of their signifieds: "I am in Europe, I don't know where I am. One thing is certain: The Near East is really close to here. The place to which the Near East is really near is called Europe. When I was still living in the Far East, the Near East was really far" ("Ich bin in Europa, ich weiß nicht, wo ich bin. Eines ist sicher: der Nahe Osten ist von hier aus ganz nah. Der Ort, von dem aus der Nahe Osten ganz nah ist, heißt Europa. Als ich noch im Fernen Osten lebte, war der Nahe Osten ganz fern") (11). It is only through producing writing as orientation, and in moving from fixed-point orientation to dynamic orientation that she can revise this view of the world and finally declare that she knows where she is.

Tawada's meridian is not only a marker of space however, but also of time. Meridians are measured in degrees, minutes, and seconds, and indicate the exact local time in any given location in the world. This is not only historical time as discussed earlier with respect to Eastern and Western writing, but the interlinked times of writing, reading, and media (particularly the medium of writing) in Tawada. In reference to another text and tense, Leslie Adelson observes that Tawada's 2000 text "Zukunft ohne Herkunft" ("Future without Origin") conceives of the future as an act of reading. The title's oblique allusion to Walter Benjamin's concept of "origin" (Ursprung) in the same breath as the word "future" recalls the temporal aspect Benjamin accorded the concept of origin, which was for him "an event involving both singularity and repetition." Adelson notes that "Zukunft ohne Herkunft" continually presents textual production as serial, and the dimension of time as rhythmic and subject to repetition. This attention to repetition in time and seriality in textual production harmonizes with Tawada's critical focus on language's structures of repetition, both on the material level of repeatable signs and on the level of reading. Indeed, Adelson states that everything in the essay pivots on the implied reader.[29] In "Zukunft ohne Herkunft," but also in "An der Spree" and numerous other texts by Tawada, present and future readers are called upon to refashion and retranslate texts anew. In the moment of writing the zero as prime meridian in "An der Spree," Tawada produces just such a moment. In the very moment the sign is set to paper, time and belatedness are introduced into the writing practice: the earth keeps turning and we are

---

[29] Leslie A. Adelson, "The Future of Futurity: Alexander Kluge and Yoko Tawada," *Germanic Review*, vol. 86 (July 2011): 153–84, here 161–5.

already in the next moment, moving east.[30] The moment needs to be recreated again and again in subsequent acts of writing and reading. As distinct from the texts in Adelson's analysis that engage in creative acts of future-making, however, "An der Spree" is concerned primarily with present-making. Its zero as meridian produces and reproduces a continual present in serial moments. In doing so, the text counters prominent conceptualizations of our present as one of simultaneity and synchronization. Instead, it offers the possibility of a contemporaneity of difference.

In recent years, there has been growing scholarly attention to the contemporary as analytical construct, linked to a gradual shift in Western temporal consciousness, which Aleida Assmann has characterized as a shift away from the "modern time regime" that conceived of time as a linear continuum, in which the present was understood as a hiatus.[31] Gradual reconfigurations of temporal consciousness in the late twentieth century and early twenty-first century have been linked to the intensified flows of global capital, the emergence of digital media, and the changed status of futurity in the present. Since the modern temporal regime denied non-European subjects a shared present with their "civilized" European counterparts, the search for new ways of defining the present has also been linked to the project of working through the history of Western hegemony and of imagining postcolonial futures. Art historian Terry Smith's elaboration of the terms "present" and "contemporaneity" addresses this anti-hegemonic impulse. Contemporaneity, according to Smith,

> [...] consists precisely in the constant experience of radical disjunctures of perception, mismatching ways of seeing and valuing the same world, in the actual coincidence of asynchronous temporalities, in the jostling contingency of various cultural and social multiplicities, all thrown together in ways that highlight the fast-growing inequalities within and between them. This certainly looks like the world as it is now. No longer does it feel like "our time" because "our" cannot stretch to encompass its contrariness.[32]

---

[30] Many thanks to John Namjun Kim of UC Riverside for pointing out the text's play with belatedness in this scene.

[31] Aleida Assmann, *Is Time out of Joint? On the Rise and Fall of the Modern Time Regime*, trans. Sarah Clift (Ithaca, NY: Cornell University Press, 2020), 97.

[32] Terry Smith, "Contemporary Art and Contemporaneity," *Critical Inquiry*, vol. 32, no. 4 (2006): 681–707, here 703–4.

Smith reveals the temporal dimension that has remained underexamined in analyses of power structures, which emphasized their socio-economic, geographic, linguistic, and other dimensions. Smith's emphasis on the pronoun "our" and its deictic slipperiness highlights the destabilization of the very spatial and temporal contexts on which such deictic terms as "here," "now," and "we" depend. It also recalls that the referents of the term "our" in the modern temporal regime were more often than not Euro-American peoples and cultures. Indeed, art historian and theorist John Rajchman notes that the contemporary "is itself a deictic term; it means 'at the same time' as when one is speaking and that time itself shifts."[33] Critical attention to the shifting time of this speaking in the context of globalization raises the questions, "Who speaks to whom?"; "What is the temporal logic of this dialogic communication?"

A dialogic scene implies the sharing of space and time. Our global present as depicted by texts like "An der Spree" suggests an intensification of travel and encounter, intercultural and intersubjective contact, which juxtapose dialogic contact with shared time. "The speed of cultural, economic, migratory circulation inaugurates a generalized sharing of time" on a global scale, notes Marc Augé.[34] Sharing time on a global scale might imply mutual understanding and a sense of community in intercultural contact, but anthropological analyses of this contact suggest otherwise. Johannes Fabian observes "bad faith" dating back to the Enlightenment (which makes its presence known in "An der Spree" in the word "Vernunft"): knowledge that stems from personal and prolonged interaction with the other is disseminated in discourse "which construes the Other in terms of distance, spatial and temporal. The Other's empirical presence turns into his theoretical absence," with the ultimate result of keeping "the Other outside the Time of anthropology."[35] Taking up Fabian's terms for the analysis of visual and verbal arts, Pedro Erber observes the "contemporanization of diversity."[36] Through the work of the theorist of history and media Osamu Nishitani, Erber notes that anthropology as a discipline studied man in his cultural diversity, but cultural anthropology construed the difference between Europeans and their others in terms of temporal difference, that is, translating spatial difference into temporal difference, or what Johannes Fabian refers

---

[33] John Rajchman, "The Contemporary: A New Idea?", in *Aesthetics and Contemporary Art*, ed. Armen Avanessian and Luke Skrebowski (London: Sternberg Press, 2011), 126–44, here 127.

[34] Marc Augé, quoted in Pedro Erber, "Contemporaneity and Its Discontents," *Diacritics*, vol. 41, no. 1 (September 2013): 28–48, here 35.

[35] Johannes Fabian, *Time and the Other: How Anthropology Makes its Object* (New York: Columbia University Press, 2014), xxxix.

[36] Erber, "Contemporaneity," 36.

to as the "spatialization of time."[37] Here, the European self is construed as "new" while the "other" is historicized. The Western experts' self-placement in the "new" moment while relegating non-Western others to history aligns with "a progressive or teleological temporality" that undergirds anthropology as well as comparative literary method, and that produces such terms as "primitives" that one can then utilize as a "time machine" in order to gaze into "our" past.[38] Our present globalized sharing of time brought on by accelerated cultural, economic, and migratory movement urges new theoretical and artistic work open to multiple temporal and narrative orders and which revises unilinear, teleological, and totalizing theorizations of temporality.

Literary fiction's place in this theoretical and artistic terrain has enjoyed limited critical attention to date, compared to that accorded to visual, musical, and screen arts. This gives short shrift to the roles of narrative and narrative time, and the status of the print medium in history, historiography, and the concept of historical consciousness are neglected as well. Literary and theoretical interventions in "An der Spree," on the other hand, draw attention to the times of genre, dialogic exchange, and writing as medium: the genre of "An der Spree," as well as of many other similar short texts by Tawada, can best be described as fiction-essay, committing neither to narrative time nor to logical consistency. Instead, these texts open themselves up to multiple temporal orders. Thematically, "An der Spree" addresses dialogic exchange in time and about time, often between a non-Western narrator and her European interlocutors, and it questions the premises of parochial attitudes regarding the time and space that a non-Western subject can occupy in the Western capitol Berlin. In foregrounding the medium of writing in the age of digital media, the text questions biases in Western theories of writing regarding history and consciousness.

In terms of genre and narrative time, "An der Spree" does not lend itself to precise classifications. It consists of vignettes about daily encounters with friends and strangers in Berlin, as well as brief observations and reflections on Berlin's cityscape. The genre straddles fiction and non-fiction and can be best described as fiction-essay. Although the narrative structure is loose, the narrator does appear to move from a sense of being lost in Europe and perhaps even the world at large toward a moment of orientation. Indeed, the genre of "An der Spree" does not itself stage as forceful an intervention into the concepts of

---

[37] Osamu Nishitani, quoted in Erber, "Contemporaneity," 36; Fabian, *Time and the Other*, 111.
[38] Fabian, *Time and the Other*, 39.

temporality and contemporaneity as do these observations and moments of dialogue. As in many other works by Tawada, the narrative does not unfold in linear fashion, but is told in short vignettes that cannot be reconstructed along a timeline. Indeed, as Dan Fujiwara observes, there is a circular temporal structure and a multiplicity of narratives in Yoko Tawada's texts in general. As Fujiwara notes, Tawada's "spherical temporality" is something of which one could say that it "constructs a reading and narrative mode that questions the very foundations of an assumed linear temporality."[39] In contrast to the universality and completion suggested by the word "spherical," the preferred term with respect to "An der Spree" for this analysis remains "continual present." This term captures the seriality, repetition with a difference, and resistance to linear time in the text.[40] A non-linear, loose narrative structure and episodic scenes are admittedly not specific to "An der Spree." However, they do support the text's themes and its treatment of the print medium.

The genre of "An der Spree" buttresses the text's interventions, which are performed more pointedly in its interlinked play with deixis on the one hand, and thematic and textual-material emphases on movement on the other. "An der Spree" continually destabilizes any notion of space, time, and identity one might associate with the deictics "here," "now," and "I" or "we." Its playful and critical treatment of time surfaces in key moments in the text, such as the intermedial reading and paradigmatic misreading of the title "Marquise of O . . ." mentioned earlier. More frequently, however, the text refers to transportation and foregrounds modes of movement in space and time. Of particular importance are moments in which this movement is both the theme and setting for dialogic encounters between the narrator—who presumably looks non-Western—and her Western interlocutors.

Verbal exchanges in "An der Spree" between the narrator and her interlocutors betray, to various degrees, the interlocutors' inability to share the same time, space, or identity with the narrator. In so doing, the narrator's interlocutors deny what the anthropologist Johannes Fabian terms "coevalness," as "the temporality of dialogical interaction

---

[39] Dan Fujiwara, "Spherical Narrative Temporality in Tawada Yōko's Fiction," in *Tawada Yōko: On Writing and Rewriting*, ed. Douglas Slaymaker (Lanham, MD: Lexington Books, 2020), 145–62, here 146, 160–1. Dan Fujiwara writes about Yoko Tawada's texts in Japanese, but a similar phenomenon can be observed in her texts in German.

[40] Many thanks to Alexis Radisoglou of Durham University for drawing attention to the distinction between the terms "cyclical time" and "spherical" on the one hand and "continual present" on the other.

between human beings: time shared through action, interaction, and communication."⁴¹ In anthropological fieldwork, as Fabian observes, there is an original temporality of observation, which is coeval, oral, and dialogic, which later gets displaced to a later time of scientific writing and results in an aestheticization of the other. In Fabian's analysis, "distance based on a denial of the conditions of shared Time" is glorified as "empirical objectivity."⁴² "An der Spree" reverses this temporality and relationship: the dialogic moments are marked by a denial of coevalness. These moments are later recounted in writing by the presumably non-Western narrator. In one scene in "An der Spree," an elderly gentleman on a train platform claims, "In our country the train always arrives on schedule" ("Bei uns kommt der Zug immer pünktlich an") (14). The narrator immediately registers the othering gesture of this pronouncement, observing, "He surely thought that I belonged to another group of WE, at whose country no train arrives on schedule" ("[e]r dachte sicher, ich würde zu einer anderen Gruppe von WIR gehören, bei denen kein Zug pünktlich ankommt") (14). When another female passenger turns around to claim "[t]hat's not true. Our trains are always delayed" ("[d]as stimmt nicht. Unsere Züge haben immer Verspätungen") (14), this passenger negates the content of the elderly man's assertion, but not its underlying premises, according to which the narrator, loosely sketched as a non-German person, is excluded from the "we" and "our" that her fellow passengers apparently share (14).

The narrator is shut out of this conversation because she is excluded from the subjective and cultural referents understood by the pronouns in this context. She asks "Wo?", "Wo kommen sie pünktlich an und wo haben sie immer Verspätungen?" ("Where? Where are they on schedule and where are they always delayed?) (14). There is no answer, and the doors of the train close between her and her interlocutors. Although it is not her interlocutors who close these doors in her face, their inability or unwillingness to include the narrator in this conversation or to respond to her challenge to the premise of their assertions indicate their refusal to share with her pronouns and space, but also time, which is the topic of this conversation. By drawing links between the pronoun "wir" (we) and "unser" (our) on the one hand and either punctuality or belatedness on the other, the narrator's interlocutors relegate her not only to the pronoun "they" and "their," but also to another time. Whether the narrator's time is before or after that of her interlocutors, it is certainly not theirs.

---

41 Fabian, quoted in Erber, "Contemporaneity," 30.
42 Fabian, *Time and the Other*, 65.

Conclusion

The ubiquity and permanence of the medium of writing occlude the structures of power embedded in the comparative history of writing, as well as the established reading practices as presented in the text. Tawada's literary project in general, and "An der Spree" in particular, finds writing in materials and surfaces not commonly associated with text. Even as the fiction-essay remains intensely preoccupied with writing, it questions what grammatologists consider to be its fundamental characteristics: "1 it consists of artificial graphical marks on a durable surface; 2 its purpose is to communicate something; 3 this purpose is achieved by virtue of the marks' conventional relation to language."[43] The surfaces are often fleeting or on the move; the writing perceived by the narrator does not have communication as its primary purpose, and in fact disrupts its own conventional relation to language(s). By presenting writing not only as elements of Western alphabets but also as images, numerals, and concrete objects associated with numerous histories and geographies, Tawada reveals how histories associated with "Europe," "the West," or "the Far East" have anchored prevalent conceptions of writing and reading. In response, she performs modes of reading that break this anchor and forge new, unexpected connections that subvert the culturally determined hierarchies in which such terms are imbricated.

In addition to prying writing apart from loci of power, Tawada accords it a new temporality. Tawada's text remains cognizant of the history and intermediality of written signs, as evidenced by references to the media theorist Vilém Flusser's writings on the origins of the Latin alphabet. Tawada's fiction-essay deconstructs Flusser's approach to writing as unidirectional, unrepeatable, and a cultural inscription of time as progressive. This intervention is not limitable to Flusser's media philosophy, but is of broader relevance to Tawada scholarship as well as to what has been called the "temporal turn" in humanistic studies. Unlike many theorists of contemporaneity, Tawada does not overtly critique the time of global capital. Rather, her fiction-essay plays with the time of writing and reading a single alphanumeric character to explore our thinking about time, media, and mobility in an episodic, serial present. "An der Spree" and its readers are in a present moment, and are invited to reconstruct it sign by sign, as continual practice.

---

[43] Coulmas, *Writing Systems*, 17. Coulmas's description is also a distillation of definitions of writing by other prominent grammatologists such as Ignace Gelb, Johannes Friedrich, and Hans Jensen.

Works Cited

Adelson, Leslie A. "The Future of Futurity: Alexander Kluge and Yoko Tawada," *Germanic Review*, vol. 86 (July 2011): 153–84.

Arslan, Gizem. "Making Senses: Translation and the Materiality of Written Signs in Yoko Tawada," *Translation Studies*, vol. 12, no. 3 (September 2019): 338–56.

Assmann, Aleida. *Is Time out of Joint? On the Rise and Fall of the Modern Time Regime*, trans. Sarah Clift (Ithaca, NY: Cornell University Press, 2020).

Bernardo, Gustavo, Anke Finger, and Rainer Guldin. "Migration, Nomadism, Networks: A Biography," in *Vilém Flusser: An Introduction* (Minneapolis: University of Minnesota Press, 2011), 1–26.

Cogan, John. "Phenomenological Reduction," in *The Internet Encyclopedia of Philosophy*, https://iep.utm.edu/phen-red/.

Coulmas, Florian. *The Writing Systems of the World* (Oxford: Blackwell, 1989).

Cross, Frank Moore. "The Invention and Development of the Alphabet," in *The Origins of Writing*, ed. Wayne M. Senner (Lincoln: University of Nebraska Press, 1989), 77–90.

Diringer, David, and Reinhold Regensburger. *The Alphabet: A Key to the History of Mankind* (London: Hutchinson, 1968).

Dworkin, Craig Douglas. *Reading the Illegible* (Evanston: Northwestern University Press, 2003).

"Equator," in *Britannica Academic*, academic-eb-com.proxy.libraries.smu.edu/levels/collegiate/article/Equator/32837.

Erber, Pedro. "Contemporaneity and Its Discontents," *Diacritics*, vol. 41, no. 1 (September 2013): 28–48.

Fabian, Johannes. *Time and the Other: How Anthropology Makes Its Object* (New York: Columbia University Press, 2014).

Finger, Anke. *Vilém Flusser: An Introduction*. NED-New edition, vol. 34 (Minneapolis: University of Minnesota Press, 2011).

Flusser, Vilém. *Does Writing Have a Future?*, ed. Mark Poster, trans. Nancy Ann Roth (Minneapolis: University of Minnesota Press, 2011).

Fujiwara, Dan. "Spherical Narrative Temporality in Tawada Yōko's Fiction," in *Tawada Yōko: On Writing and Rewriting*, ed. Douglas Slaymaker (Lanham, MD: Lexington Books, 2020), 145–62.

Gelb, Ignace J. *A Study of Writing* (Chicago: University of Chicago Press, 1963).

Guldin, Rainer. "Vilem Flusser's Practice of Multiple Self-Translation," in *Self-Translation: Brokering Originality in Hybrid Culture*, ed. Anthony Cordingley (New York and London: Bloomsbury Academic, 2013), 95–109.

Hachmann, Gundela. "Drafting the Techno-Imagination: A Future for Literary Writing?" *Flusser Studies*, vol. 18 (November 2018): 1–13.

Lurie, David B. "The Development of Japanese Writing," in *The Shape of Script: How and Why Writing Systems Change*, ed. Stephen Houston (Santa Fe, NM: SAR Press, 2012), 159–86.

Meirosu, Madalina. "Yoko Tawada's *Überseezungen*: Feminist Self-Translation and Creative Resistance," in *Tawada Yōko: On Writing and Rewriting*, ed. Douglas Slaymaker (Lanham, MD: Lexington Books, 2020), 121–38.

Melas, Natalie. *All the Difference in the World: Postcoloniality and the Ends of Comparison* (Stanford, CA: Stanford University Press, 2007).

Mersch, Dieter. *Medientheorien zur Einführung* (Hamburg: Junius, 2006).

Ong, Walter J. *Orality and Literacy: The Technologizing of the Word* (New York and London: Routledge, 2002).

Rajchman, John. "The Contemporary: A New Idea?" in *Aesthetics and Contemporary Art*, ed. Armen Avanessian and Luke Skrebowski (London: Sternberg Press, 2011), 126–44.
Rotman, Brian. *Signifying Nothing: The Semiotics of Zero* (New York: St. Martin's Press, 1987).
Schaefer, P. "Vilem Flusser's Philosophy of New Media History," *New Media & Society*, vol. 13, no. 8 (December 201): 1389–95.
Scott, Clive. *Translating the Perception of Text: Literary Translation and Phenomenology* (Oxford: Legenda, 2012).
Smith, Terry. "Contemporary Art and Contemporaneity," *Critical Inquiry*, vol. 32, no. 4 (2006): 681–707.
Tawada, Yoko. "An der Spree," in *Sprachpolizei und Spielpolyglotte* (Tübingen: Konkursbuch Verlag Claudia Gehrke, 2007), 11–23.
Weigel, Sigrid. "Yoko Tawada's Poetics on the Threshold of Different Writing Systems," in *Tawada Yōko: On Writing and Rewriting*, ed. Douglas Slaymaker (Lanham, MD: Lexington Books, 2020), 49–59.

Eleven Mobilizing the Archive: Marica Bodrožić and Deniz Utlu's *Unterhaltungen deutscher Eingewanderten*

Claudia Breger

Questions of archives—or, more abstractly, the archive as institution and concept—have been at the center of scholarly interest since the 2000s, and perhaps particularly over the course of the last few years.[1] Surrounding conceptual discussions have focused in part on the violences inscribed in the archive, its gaps and distortions, but in part also on the productive capacities of alternative "counterarchives" and the ways in which archival pursuits may facilitate a "reframing of history" and rearranging of the value hierarchies imposed by dominant histories and aesthetics.[2] In this chapter, I look closely at the public presentation of one such archival pursuit, Marica Bodrožić and Deniz Utlu's web presentation *Unterhaltungen deutscher Eingewanderten* (*Conversations of German Immigrants*), and ask how it might contribute to this volume's project of rethinking the contours of the field of German Studies. The urgency of this larger endeavor unfolds at the intersection of several vectors. First, there is the long-standing crisis of the humanities produced by neoliberal budget pressures and now accelerated by a global

---

[1] On the so-called archival turn, see, e.g., Stephen Best, "Neither Lost nor Found: Slavery and the Visual Archive," *Representations*, vol. 113, no. 1 (2011): 150–63, here 158.

[2] Gayatri Gopinath, *Unruly Visions: The Aesthetic Practices of Queer Diaspora* (Durham, NC: Duke University Press, 2018), 10, 16. On violence, see, e.g., Saidiya Hartman, "Venus in Two Acts," *Small Axe* 26 (2008): 1–14; and below for detail. On archival resistance, see, more recently, Annika Orich, "Archival Resistance: Reading the New Right," *German Politics and Society*, vol. 38, no. 2 (2020): 1–34.

pandemic. Second, the contemporary resurgence of rampant nationalisms on both sides of the Atlantic meets, on the other side of the political spectrum, an increasingly forceful challenge to the very paradigm of a discipline initially constituted by nineteenth- and early twentieth-century nationalist and imperialist frameworks.[3] The intellectual answer to these challenges to which my reading of Bodrožić and Utlu's archival pursuit hopes to contribute is, in a nutshell, one that pushes back against disciplinary "globalization"—motivated by either budget constraints or the goal of a radical break with the institutional legacies of nationalism and settler colonialism—insofar as such globalization risks a neglect and potential loss of local, and especially alternative or minoritized, archives.[4] I hope to show that we can (non-militaristically) mobilize the archives of a nationally delineated field toward transnational investigations that programmatically open political and culturalist borders while attending to local, specific, presumably small, multilingual, and variously marginalized (or reductively appropriated) histories and texts.[5]

Unterhaltungen deutscher Eingewanderten was created by Bodrožić and Utlu as one of several thematic "audio/listening rooms" ("Hörräume") on dichterlesen.net, a web portal of the Literarisches Colloquium Berlin (LCB), in cooperation with the Literaturhäuser Basel and Stuttgart and the Deutsches Literaturarchiv Marbach. Online since 2015, the portal facilitates access to an audio archive of historical as well as contemporary literary readings. As part of this initiative, undertaken by major literary institutions in the German-speaking world to make their (dominant) archives publicly accessible, the "virtual thematic rooms" ("virtuellen Themenräume") are intended to showcase the "diversity" ("Vielfalt") of their holdings: there is, for example, also a queer audio room. As I argue in this chapter, however, the *Unterhaltungen deutscher Eingewanderten* web presentation does more than just showcase diversity. Bodrožić's and Utlu's pages also conceptually and artistically reassemble notions of the archive and literature in relation to "Migration" (migration which may be voluntary) and "Flucht" (forced

---

[3] See, e.g., the discussion forum (ed. by Carl Niekerk) "Does German Cultural Studies need the Nation-State Model?", *German Quarterly*, vol. 92, no. 4 (2019): 431–503; and Simone Pfleger and Carrie Smith (eds.), *Transverse Disciplines: Working Across and Beyond Academic Communities* (Toronto: University of Toronto Press, forthcoming).

[4] On this point, see Venkat Mani, *Recoding World Literature: Libraries, Print Culture, and Germany's Pact with Books* (New York: Fordham University Press, 2017), in particular 236–9.

[5] As implied here, I use the term *transnational* to designate specific flows across national borders usually smaller in scale than the whole globe.

migration)—hence the thematic designation of their audio room. To be more precise, they present two sets of artistic and conceptual "conversations" on these topics: arranged to the left and right sides of the opening page, respectively, Bodrožić and Utlu each put together their own "parcours" (journey, route, run) through overlapping but not identical materials. Their individual digital paths through—and encounters with—archival materials, framed and connected by commentary, are in some respects quite different. Entitled "The Infinity of Language" ("Die Unendlichkeit der Sprache"), Bodrožić's parcours repeatedly returns to a number of key authors in staging a sustained conversation about and multifaceted exploration of literature's aesthetic affordances, against the backdrop of exile and migration. Meanwhile, Utlu's "The Language of the Archive" ("Die Sprache des Archivs") assembles a broader network of authors and materials in explicitly probing the concept of the archive, and the aesthetics and politics of a "Literary Archive of Migration" ("Literarisches Archiv der Migration," his first section title) from different angles. Given my interests in this particular chapter, my own reading parcours in later sections primarily follows Utlu's, but I will also cross over onto Bodrožić's side of the web "room" to engage her contributions to the conversation in dialogue with his.

Utlu is perhaps best known to German literary audiences as the author of two novels, *Die Ungehaltenen* (*The Indignant Onesgeg*) (2014) and *Gegen Morgen* (*Toward Morning*) (2019), but he has also been active as an editor and organizer of a broad range of cultural events. After founding the *freitext. Kultur- und Gesellschaftsmagazin*, in 2003, he became affiliated with the "postmigrant" theater scene grouped around the Ballhaus Naunynstr, and, later, the Gorki Theater in Berlin-Mitte, not only writing for and adapting his own work to the stage but also hosting various literary series at both locations and beyond.[6] By disciplinary background, Utlu is, notably, not a scholar of literature, theater, or cultural studies but an economist who has developed a second professional profile and publication record as an expert on international human rights.[7] Bodrožić trained as a bookseller in addition to studying cultural anthropology, psychoanalysis, and Slavic studies. She has worked as a translator, critic, filmmaker, and guest professor of German literature and creative writing, in addition to assembling a substantial creative oeuvre across genres since her 2002 debut volume, *Tito ist tot*.[8]

---

[6] denizutlu.de/ich/. All translations from this website and other German-language publications are my own.
[7] www.institut-fuer-menschenrechte.de/das-institut/team; de.linkedin.com/in/deniz-utlu-9794aa80.
[8] *Erzählungen* (Frankfurt: Suhrkamp, 2002).

Bodrožić's and Utlu's multifaceted backgrounds clearly inform the assembly of their *Unterhaltungen deutscher Eingewanderten* audio room. Firstly, their parcours emerges and operates at the intersection of multiple media. In addition to the authors' expository writing and the featured archival sound recordings, their presentation includes visuals opening the different sections, along with smaller, icon-style photographs of each author, and, to introduce their oeuvres and lives, various scans of manuscripts, book pages or covers, letters, photos, collages, flyers, performance videos, and historical documents of exile, displacement, and immigration. As Utlu explains, some of these materials are from his own personal collection—that is, materials added to the LCB and its partners' archival resources. Curiously, the digital location of Bodrožić and Utlu's multimedia assemblies is thrown into relief by the counterpoint visual design of their audio room. Its background evokes the uneven texture and discoloration of aged paper, and the font used for the text throughout reminds me of the electronic typewriter on which I wrote in the 1980s. One of the visuals opening the first section of Utlu's parcours features an even older, non-electronic typewriter (see Figure 11.1).

Should we be tempted to suspect nostalgia, or even authorial reservations vis-à-vis the digital medium's soundness as an archival environment? German media theorist Wolfgang Ernst articulates a pronounced version of such reservations: for him, the emergence of digital multimedia archives equals the demise of the archive proper. "The archive," he proclaims, "is a given, well-defined lot; the Internet, on the contrary, is

Figure 11.1 Screenshot from *Unterhaltungen deutscher Eingewanderten*. Reprinted with permission from Deniz Utlu and Literarisches Colloquium Berlin/Dichterlesen.net, www.dichterlesen.net/unterhaltungen-deutscher-eingewanderten.

[. . .] an archive of sensory data for which no genuine archival culture has been developed."[9] As multimedia archives have "confused the clear-cut distinction between the (stored) past and (the illusion of) presence," memory operates at best "as a radical constructivism."[10] One illusion, to be sure, may be that such a clear-cut distinction ever existed. As Diana Taylor argues, "the archive" and "the repertoire"—that is, a body of "supposedly enduring materials (i.e., texts, documents, buildings, bones) and the so-called ephemeral" ensemble "of embodied practice/knowledge (i.e., spoken language, dance, sports, ritual)"—tend to operate "in a constant state of interaction," as two dimensions of cultural practices.[11] The sound recordings that form the basis for Bodrožić's and Utlu's performative intervention—again, their parcours—are a case in point: the archival source material documents oral performances of literary texts. *Unterhaltungen deutscher Eingewanderten*'s visual evocation of old media may be nostalgic, playful, or both. With its invitation to activate pre-digital memories, we may interpret the design of the web presentation as a reminder of "the actual materiality" of archival records, or a reverberation of the materialist commitments that have shaped contemporary returns to the archive far beyond Ernst's media archeology.[12] But this visual guidance of audience experience merely adds a layer to a complex digital intertwining of media and media resonances that I propose to read as an environment of proper archival creation rather than demise.

Where Ernst sees only digital "[d]ata trash,"[13] Bodrožić and Utlu performatively design, probe, and reflect on archival culture. Taylor's analysis of the fraught but influential distinction between the archive and the repertoire is useful for further characterizing the multifaceted interplay of absence and presence, event and tradition through which, I propose, *Unterhaltungen deutscher Eingewanderten* creatively activates or mobilizes the archive. Etymologically, Taylor spells out, the archive designates a "public building" but also, from *arkhe*, a "beginning" or the "government"; it is deployed to sustain identity, memory, and power "over time

---

[9] Ernst, Wolfgang, "Dis/continuities: Does the Archive Become Metaphorical in Multi-Media Space?" in *New Media-Old Media: A History and Theory Reader*, ed. Wendy Hui Kyong Chung and Thomas Keenan (New York: Routledge, 2006), 105–23, here 119.
[10] Ernst, "Dis/continuities," 119–20.
[11] Diana Taylor, *The Archive and the Repertoire: Performing Cultural Memory in the Americas* (Durham, NC: Duke University Press, 2003), 19, 21.
[12] The quotation is from Mani, *Recoding* 5; see Lauren F. Klein, "The Image of Absence: Archival Silence, Data Visualization, and James Hemings," *American Literature*, vol. 85, no. 4 (2013): 661–88.
[13] Ernst, "Dis/continuities," 120.

and space," more or less "immunized against alterity."[14] The repertoire, however, has been associated with the powers of "anti-hegemonic challenge" via "individual agency."[15] *Unterhaltungen deutscher Eingewanderten*, I argue, creatively reconfigures the archive through these latter powers (to be sure, I will qualify the notion of individual agency). The archive-vs.-repertoire distinction is further charged, and relevant, insofar as the repertoire, associated with orality, has tended to be relegated to "other" (pre-, post-, non-modern) times and cultures—that is, to some outside, per this volume's title.[16] If the thematic audio parcours on exile and migration hosted by some of Germany's major literary institutions were merely to showcase diversity, it would run the risk of confirming these asymmetric distinctions. As indicated, however, I read it, more forcefully, as a reassembly of the archive(s) of German literature as such—a reassembly that unfolds in a complex intertwining of movement vectors to create networks across borders rather than fortified inside–outside distinctions.

Exile, Immigration, and the Transnational Alchemy of Literary Tradition

Let me begin with the title of Bodrožić and Utlu's audio room. With its intertextual reference to Johann Wolfgang von Goethe's *Unterhaltungen deutscher Ausgewanderten*, *Unterhaltungen deutscher Eingewanderten* points to the very center of a traditionally understood German literary canon, in which Goethe reigns supreme.[17] To be sure, it may simultaneously index the contested margins of this canon and the processes of exclusion that accompany its regulation (or immobilization) insofar as Goethe philology has separated this particular text from the bulk of Goethe's oeuvre as "primarily popular literature written for entertainment" ("zuerst einmal Unterhaltungsliteratur").[18] Of course, a slightly closer look reveals the fraught character of the popular vs. "high" literature distinction, along with that of any attempt to put national in

---

[14] Taylor, *The Archive*, 19, with reference to Michel de Certeau, *Heterologies: Discourse on the Other*, trans. Brian Massumi (Minneapolis: University of Minnesota Press 1986), 216.
[15] Taylor, *The Archive*, 22, 20.
[16] Taylor, *The Archive*, 21.
[17] Johann Wolfgang von Goethe, "Unterhaltungen deutscher Ausgewanderten," in *Werke*, vol. 6 (Hamburger Ausgabe), ed. Erich Trunz and Benno v. Wiese (Munich: dtv, 1998), 125–241.
[18] Lothar Bluhm, "'In jenen unglücklichen Tagen ...': Goethes *Unterhaltungen deutscher Ausgewanderten* oder: Die Ambivalenz von Kunst und Gesellschaft," in *Erzählte Welt—Welt des Erzählens. Festschrift für Dietrich Weber*, ed. Rüdiger Zymner et al. (Cologne: edition chōra, 2000; Goethezeitportal, 2008) 1, publikationen. ub.uni-frankfurt.de/frontdoor/index/index/docId/9442.

contradistinction to transnational or world literature. In fact, Goethe's *Unterhaltungen deutscher Ausgewanderten* indicates the very creation of concepts and canons of national literature from transnational canons: while its narrative structure was inspired by two world literature classics, Giovanni Boccaccio's *The Decameron* and *One Thousand and One Nights*, the text contains diegetic discourse that moves toward delineating an emphatically German storytelling tradition. Thus, Miss Luise, a daughter of the text's aristocrat family turning to storytelling while exiled by French occupation, complains "that I don't love the stories that always force our imagination into foreign countries" ("daß ich die Geschichten nicht liebe, die unsre Einbildungskraft immer in fremde Länder nötigen") and asks for "domestic [. . .] family paintings" ("einheimische [. . .] Familiengemälde").[19] We may further note that the text unfolds the drama of delineating boundaries, borders, or en/closure, also in terms of form. With explicit negative reference to *One Thousand and One Nights*, Luise's mother, the baroness, articulates norms for narrative coherence: "I reprehend the attempt to make rhapsodic riddles of stories that ought to approach the unity of the poem" ("Ich tadle das Bestreben, aus Geschichten, die sich der Einheit des Gedichts nähern sollen, rhapsodische Rätsel zu machen").[20] However, this diegetic discourse unfolds within a loose frame story that never finds any kind of closure, unless one counts the frame narrative's displacement by one of the stories told—the fairy tale that effectively ends the text.[21]

To reiterate, the text's diegetic activity of delineating national culture unfolds at the site of emigration: among German aristocrats having fled the French revolutionary army. Bodrožić and Utlu's quotation of Goethe's title with a difference, *Unterhaltungen deutscher Eingewanderten*, reverses the movement vector, with the effect of further underscoring the inseparability of inside and outside, or the processes of creating, contesting, and reassembling both via multivectoral traffic across boundaries. If Bodrožić and Utlu's work on the archive intervenes "from the outside" insofar as socio-political realities of exclusion have shaped their first- and second-generation immigration experiences (Bodrožić was born in Dalmatia, and Utlu in Hannover), it simultaneously intervenes from the inside of a Germany that was only ever homogenous (at best/worst) in nationalist fiction alone. The linkage of *Flucht* and *(Im-)Migration*, emigration and immigration, performed by their audio room showcases how processes of migration have formed the nation and its cultural archive(s) across generations and time

---

[19] Goethe, "Unterhaltungen," 187.
[20] Goethe, "Unterhaltungen," 166.
[21] Goethe, "Unterhaltungen," 209–41.

periods. In performatively underscoring these processes at the center of the national archive, their web presentation can guide us toward reconceptualizing German literature as a tradition created and recreated through multivectoral, material, and virtual movements, or through human and bibliomigrancy, to use B. Venkat Mani's term.[22]

The linking and layering of *Einwanderung* and *Auswanderung* not only indexes the experiential imbrication of both processes in the life of anyone who has ever changed countries. In the assembly of Bodrožić und Utlu's parcours, it connects, more specifically, postwar labor immigration and the twenty-first-century movements of flight from war, poverty, and climate change, which have been at the center of today's debates on immigration, to longer-term histories and traditions of exile and diaspora, with an emphasis on the legacies of totalitarianism and the Holocaust. Utlu develops these touching tales (as Leslie Adelson might put it) by opening his web parcours with an "encounter" ("Treffen") with Elias Canetti—the word choice, of course, underlines the dialogic potential of the imagined in-person, live conversation.[23] Canetti, Utlu reminds us, was born in Bulgaria, emigrated to England, and lived in Austria and Switzerland. At the same time, he was perhaps "the first German-language author of Turkish descent" ("der erste türkischstämmige Schriftsteller deutscher Sprache")—or at least the first, Utlu qualifies carefully, in the twentieth century. Most Sephardic Jews, Utlu elaborates, had remained Turkish citizens, and Canetti's father actually was born in Turkey (technically the Ottoman Empire, I feel urged to correct, but Utlu quotes Canetti's own wording here). His mother had an Italian passport and background.

But more important than these biographical data, Utlu emphasizes, is how Canetti's thought process was "permeated" ("durchdrungen") by his "wanderings" ("Wanderungen") through languages and cultures. Already in his opening statement on "The Language of the Archive" ("Die Sprache des Archivs"), Utlu references Canetti's metaphor of the "rescued" (or "liberated") tongue as evidence for his own claim that "Nobody was given their mother tongue at birth. It has to be projected/drafted; we project/draft it by throwing ourselves into the world" ("Niemand bekommt seine Muttersprache in die Wiege gelegt.

---

[22] See Mani, *Recoding* 1 and 238 on the insufficiency of unidirectional conceptualizations of movement. On multidirectional movement, see also Deniz Göktürk, *Framing Migration: Seven Takes on Movement and Borders* (Berlin: De Gruyter, 2021).

[23] Leslie Adelson, "Touching Tales of Turks, Germans and Jews: Cultural alterity, historical narrative, and literary riddles for the 1990s," *New German Critique*, vol. 80 (2000): 93–124.

Sie muss entworfen werden; wir entwerfen sie, indem wir uns selbst in die Welt werfen").[24] In the conversation with Canetti that Utlu then stages, I read Canetti's own voice as both an echo and a humorous counterpoint to the existentialist character of Utlu's opening thoughts: to his momentary emphasis on (seemingly sovereign) artistic production by way of self-creation.[25] The audio fragment that Utlu presents for Canetti is a reading of "Die Tischtuchtolle"—literally, the "table cloth maniac" or "table cloth pompadour"—one of the *Fünfzig Charaktere* (*Fifty Characters*) presented in Canetti's collection *Der Ohrenzeuge* (*The Ear Witness*), first published in 1974.[26] A satiric play on (German, or Austrian, or Swiss) obsessions with cleanliness and whiteness, the brief character portrait presents ample evidence of Canetti's poetic creativity, but in the same breath, it also warns of the hubris of feigned divine sovereignty. Ambiguously reified through the title, the "Tischtuchtolle" is compared both to a venomous snake and a forceful storm ("Orkan"). Her raging against perceived uncleanliness resembles both the Last Judgment and the days before Creation: "Things are going on like before life was created" ("Da geht es zu wie vor Erschaffung der Geschöpfe"). Per the text's dramatic closure, this raging has resulted in animals and people getting killed, and it unsettles the Creator's sovereignty as such: "God himself is no longer sure of his business there" ("Da ist Gott seiner weiteren Sache nicht mehr sicher"). In the documented reading of the piece (in Stuttgart on October 6, 1978), Canetti creates intensity by accelerating his delivery toward the end of the piece. Notwithstanding the humorous tinge I detect in his voice, my own listening experience includes disturbance about the fact that a loud collective audience laugh answers, of all sentences, the one declaring, "Animals and people have gotten washed dead" ("Da sind schon Tiere und Leute totgewaschen worden").

As we read on, however, Utlu's conceptualizations also indicate alternatives to the model of artistic creation satirized by the Tischtuchtolle's obsessive-compulsive appropriation of divine sovereignty. In the

---

[24] See Elias Canetti, *Die gerettete Zunge* (Frankfurt: Fischer Verlag, 1979). The English title is *The Tongue Set Free* (New York: Farrar, Straus and Giroux, 1983). Translations here, however, are my own.

[25] Utlu sounds more like Jean-Paul Sartre or Simone de Beauvoir here than like Martin Heidegger, to whom the terminology can be traced back, but for whom (as well as for much contemporary scholarship) the emphasis is clearly on our *being thrown into* the world/*having been* projected; see, e.g., Thomas Sheehan, *Making Sense of Heidegger: A Paradigm Shift* (London: Rowman, 2015), 207–8. See also Pheng Cheah, *What is a World?* (Durham, NC: Duke University Press, 2016).

[26] Elias Canetti, *Der Ohrenzeuge. Fünfzig Charaktere* (Frankfurt: Fischer, 1983).

opening reflection on "mother tongues," Utlu gives the example of Paul Celan, who "did not write his poetry in the language of the murderers; he overcame it" ("dichtete nicht in der Sprache der Mörder, er überwand sie"). Utlu then generalizes to assert that authors have "viele Mütter" (many mothers), from different times and places, "not tied to any one epoch or nation" ("keiner Epoche und keiner Nation verhaftet"). Celan's mothers include, among others, Rainer Maria Rilke, Alexander Puschkin, and Kabbala—and reading, Utlu adds, also means searching for these "linguistic mothers" ("Sprachmütter"). This familial metaphor allows him to develop a poetological notion of creative agency as intertextual process, embedded in the network of a tradition in which poetic creativity is "born" and "raised" by others, and in that sense non-sovereign (or non-autonomous).[27] Bodrožić develops a resonant point in her opening statement through the metaphor of alchemy: "Language cannot be imagined without amalgamations and transformations" ("Eine Sprache ohne Verschmelzungen und Verwandlungen ist nicht vorstellbar"). In the melting pot of networked creations, "any individual life, biography is always connected to the imaginary" ("Das einzelne Leben, die einzelne Biographie ist immer mit dem Imaginären verbunden"). Rather than being determined by the accidents of descent, these connections are actively configured by, as Bordrozic poetically puts it, "letter biographies of polyglot word-humans ("Buchstabenbiographien polyglotter Wörtermenschen"), which we can sketch as "a broadly-branched world map" ("eine weitverzweigte Weltlandkarte").

Making Connections and Animating Absences: The Literary Archive of Migration

Given this emphatically transnational character of tradition—and, more generally, of creative genealogy—what is "the Literary Archive of Migration" ("das Literarische Archiv der Migration")? In his statement opening the first, thus titled section of his parcours, Utlu acknowledges his ambivalence toward the notion: the archiving criterion of migration is "invalid and nonetheless legitimate" ("ungültig und trotzdem berechtigt"). It is invalid, he argues, from the perspective of the writer, insofar as migration does not determine their writing; rather, the writer actively responds to the experience of migration, among other things. Simultaneously, the archiving criterion of migration is justified insofar as authors or their texts can "become orphans" ("verwaisen") in the

---

[27] Elsewhere, I have spelled out such a notion of non-sovereign agency in dialogue with actor-network theory and phenomenology. See *Making Worlds: Affect and Collectivity in Contemporary European Cinema* (New York: Columbia University Press, 2020).

context of migration. If assembled "deliberately" ("[m]it Bedacht"), a literary archive can counteract this loss of literary parentage by widening the horizon of reception. The condition to be respected is that authors are grouped not according to the diversity of their backgrounds but, instead, in their varied literary traditions, which, again, do not equal national traditions.

In mapping these connections, the archive can "record, preserve, hold on to" ("festhalten") "stories or histories" ("Geschichten") threatened by disappearance, even as it necessarily remains "fragmented" ("fragmentiert") and "incomplete" ("unvollständig"). For example, this section of Utlu's parcours includes an empty tab for "Guest-worker poetry" ("Die Lyrik der Gastarbeiter"). The absence of an author photograph marks the archival gap: the archivist's commentary asks readers to get in touch with the Literarisches Colloquium Berlin if they have a copy of self-published poetry by authors of the guest-worker generation. Utlu's design of this archival entry reads as a balanced response to contemporary scholarly discussions on the archive. The "founding violence" inscribed in the (hegemonic) archive, as characterized by the absence or "disfiguration of any record" of subjected individuals and populations, has been debated especially in the context of American histories of slavery, for which some have suggested a fundamental questioning of "the logic and ethic of recovery."[28] What "[i]f we stopped trying to make up for what was lost?"[29] Utlu's context is a different, less brutally annihilative one, and, as indicated by his call for material, he does not question the project of recovery to the point of abandoning archival collection. Nonetheless, the visual foregrounding of absence in the design of his archival entry on guest-worker poetry resonates with the alternative ethos of "animating" archival imbalances rather than merely striving or pretending to close the gaps.[30]

As further evidence for the fragility of the archive of migration, Utlu tells the story of how he first encountered the work of Aglaja Veteranyi, who also has a tab in this section. Namely, he received a copy of her novel, *Warum das Kind in der Polenta kocht* (*Why the Child boils in the Polenta*), in a spontaneous book exchange at a reading on Audre Lorde's *Zami* that he had organized. As indicated by this story, it is the "contingent" ("zufällig[e]"), if fortuitous rather than random, event of conversation between interested readers that facilitates assembling the archive of migration. But even while emphasizing this contingency, Utlu

---

[28] Hartman, "Venus in two Acts," 10; Best, "Neither Lost nor Found," 157–8.
[29] Best, "Neither Lost nor Found," 160.
[30] Klein, "The Image of Absence," 665 (with reference to Hartman, Best, and others).

simultaneously introduces Veteranyi as one of the two authors (the other being Albert Camus) whose voices he had been familiar with before hearing them read for the first time. (I must admit that I had to Google Veteranyi, and, in the spirit of Utlu's project, I will make you Google her as needed as well.) Thus asserting an aural connection, Utlu gestures at a concept of literature that includes the level of performance and, more generally, the constitutive role of multiple senses in the processes of composition and reception: with some authors, Utlu speculates, "the sound of their voice" ("der Klang ihrer Stimme") might be transported into the text. In the audio clip chosen for Veteranyi, of a reading on September 1, 2000, in the Literarisches Colloquium Berlin, Veteranyi's first-person narrator underlines the role of smell and taste in generating a sense of home and belonging. Crossing over to Bodrožić's side of the webpage, we can conceptually spell out these indications as an insistence on "Synesthesia: knotted senses, alchemistically" ("Synästhesie: Verknüpfte Sinne, alchemistisch")—which is the title of her second section. Or, as Rita Felski puts it with reference to recent theoretical discussions in hermeneutics, the making and reading of literature is not cognitive and symbolic alone but "an embodied mode of attentiveness that involves us in acts of sensing, perceiving, feeling."[31]

According to Utlu's own, in this context decidedly skeptical, commentary, the assembly of the archive of migration from such embodied acts of reading is not just contingent but also "arbitrary" or "discretionary" ("willkürlich"): since the mere circumstance of migration does not create a sufficient connection, the assembly "reports to" ("untersteht") the archivist's subjectivity. I would caution that this claim is simultaneously too high-handed and too modest. It is too high-handed in that the archivist, like the writer herself, has "many mothers": his creativity is enabled by a network of contacts, inspirations, and conversations. It is too modest in that the range of this network, which in Utlu's case has been knit in the processes of extensive literary event management as well as individual reading, does authorize his selections. Perhaps, it is also an advantage that the scholarly establishment, with its narrow avenues of canonization and fortified gatekeeping structures, didn't have too much of a hand in Utlu's literary upbringing. The resulting archival proposal is certainly not objective, but, to borrow from Bruno Latour's alternative criteria for evaluating world assembly, it is "object-full": rich in entries, perspectives, and unexpected linkages, it expands and reconfigures my own reading archive in many places.[32]

---

[31] See Rita Felski, *The Limits of Critique* (Chicago: University of Chicago Press, 2015), 176, with reference to Marielle Macé.

[32] Bruno Latour, *Reassembling the Social: An Introduction to Actor-Network-Theory* (Oxford: Oxford University Press, 2005), 133.

An example of such unexpected linkage is the way Utlu positions the canonical GDR author Stephan Hermlin obliquely next to Tezer Özlu in this section of his parcours. The story of her oeuvre once more reinforces the theme of archival fragility. While Özlu is better known as a major voice in Turkish women's literature, she actually wrote one of her novels initially in German and won a German literary prize for it. Utlu details his lengthy quest to locate this German manuscript and, in the absence of an audio recording, documents its first two pages. Entitled "Search for the Traces of a Suicide: Variations on Cesare Pavese" ("Suche nach den Spuren eines Selbstmordes: Variationen über Cesare Pavese"), this German manuscript is part of a transnational tradition of working through the legacies of fascism. To Özlu's left on the page, we encounter Hermlin, a member of the exile generation, with a piece that describes his "return" ("Rückkehr") to Germany in 1945. In his commentary on this (hour-long) audio clip, Utlu underlines the emotional resonance of Hermlin's report on a key moment at the border: without a passport and questioned by border officials, he identified himself as a "writer" ("Schriftsteller") for the first time in his life. In conceptual terms, Utlu's entry on Hermlin emphasizes the foundational role of exile for postwar Germany (and, by extension, for German literature) on both sides of the Wall. This shared experience, he suggests, could have been deployed toward a unifying narrative after the fall of the Wall.

This is a unifying narrative that also could have included the immigrant—variously exiled—populations and writers denied a place in hegemonic conceptualizations of collective German identity after 1989. Directly above Özlu, Utlu arranges alternating tabs for four authors of the first generation of Turkish immigrants. This includes Aras Ören, whom Utlu positions in the tradition of Bertolt Brecht, Nâzım Hikmet, and Yüksel Pazarkaya: literary scholar, theater practitioner, writer, and Hikmet translator. Then there is Güney Dal, who initially came to Germany as a factory worker in 1972, following a career as a voice actor and journalist in Turkey, and, finally, Fakir Baykurt, whose long literary career in Turkey before his emigration to Germany was punctured by persecution for his political activities. Puzzlingly, the major German literary archives at Utlu's disposal did not yield audio clips for these established writers. In their absence, Utlu substitutes a video clip from his own archive, different enough to animate the absence, or dramatize it with a flamboyant gesture of literary activism. The clip documents a reading "flash mob" at the busy Kreuzberg square Kottbusser Tor. On the day marking fifty years of labor immigration from Turkey, in 2011, the performative intervention—the fleetingness of which is both undone and preserved by its video documentation—constructs a tradition by way of (as Utlu puts it) three "Ös," the "Umlaut" so prominent in Turkish while familiar to German speakers.

Reading texts by Ören (b. 1939) along with Emine Sevgi Özdamar (b. 1946) and Selim Özdoğan (b. 1971), the participants project an intergenerational connection to the present. Reading in German, Turkish, and English, they substitute their own physical voices to establish the literary presence of a tradition missing from the hegemonic archives in the public square.

Imbricating Poetics and Politics

The texts read during the documented flash mob include an essay by Ören, written for the fiftieth anniversary of labor migration, and Özdoğan's short satirical piece "Vibration background" ("Vibrationshintergrund").[33] The latter spells out, for example, what vibrators and migrants have in common: "One gets out the vibrator when one wants to satisfy a desire. One gets out the migrant when one needs a satisfying explanation" ("Den Vibrator holt man hervor, wenn man eine Lust befriedigen möchte. Den Migranten holt man hervor, wenn man eine befriedigende Erklärung braucht").[34] While these texts are programmatically political, Utlu's written commentary on the Ören–Pazarkaya–Dal–Baykurt tab urges its readers to open "unsere Sinne" (our senses) by speaking about literature, and not just about "sociology and politics" ("Soziologie und Politik"). His emphasis on aesthetics refutes the long-standing tendency among academic as well as cultural critics to discuss the literatures and cultures of immigration in primarily documentary terms.[35] Utlu develops this point in particular in the second section of his parcours, entitled "The Nonexistence of a Literature of Migration" ("Die Nichtexistenz einer Migrationsliteratur"). As indicated by the title, the section unfolds as a counterpoint to the programmatic, if qualified, proposition of "The Literary Archive of Migration" in the prior section of Utlu's parcours. "No literary movement" ("Keine literarische Strömung"), Utlu now insists more forcefully, "can be defined through the background or the apparent or assigned background of its authors alone" ("lässt sich allein über die Herkunft oder scheinbare Herkunft oder zugeschriebene Herkunft der Autoren definieren"). Doing so would rob "the aesthetic" ("das Ästhetische") of its authority.

In all likelihood deliberately, Utlu's introductory texts on individual authors in this section of his parcours withhold biographical

---

[33] Selim Özdoğan, "Vibrationshintergrund." The full text is published in *Transit*, vol. 8, no. 1 (2012), escholarship.org/uc/item/0f26f21x.
[34] Özdoğan, "Vibrationshintergrund."
[35] See, e.g., Adelson, "Touching Tales."

background information, especially for the less-known writers included (I had to do some Googling again). Instead, his assembly emphasizes poetics over sociological representation, as he both pays tribute to the (relatively) established canon of contemporary literatures of migration and significantly broadens it. To start, Utlu highlights Feridun Zaimoğlu's narration of "pain sensitivity" ("Schmerzempfindlichkeit") and "injury" ("Verwundung") in *Kanak Sprak* and Emine Sevgi Özdamar's "linguistic carpet" ("Sprachteppich"). The audio clip chosen for Özdamar, from a reading on November 19, 2004 in the Literarisches Colloquium Berlin, anchors the latter metaphor in her prose—namely, the passage from her early novel *Das Leben ist eine Karawanserei* in which the grandfather's beard weaves a carpet as he narrates twentieth-century Turkish histories.[36] In the vicinity of these (to me) familiar aesthetic contributions, Utlu positions the "atmosphere" ("Atmosphäre") of Zsuzsa Bánk's works, Katja Petrowskaja's resistance against identity "attributions" ("Zuschreibungen"), and the "intensity" ("Intensität") of Thien Tran's poetry. The audio clip for Tran, from a reading on September 7, 2010 at the Literarisches Colloquium Berlin, actually delivers the missing biographical introduction by way of the moderator's introduction, as he awkwardly wades through the swamp of hegemonic background–attribution habits and explicitly asks whether Tran sees his own oeuvre as part of the "literature of migration" ("Literatur der Migration"). "No" ("Nein"), Tran answers with some determination, even as he seems to feel obliged to add detail about his German upbringing. Tran then reads two series of reflexively poetological poems saturated with multimedia intertextuality and nature imagery, written during his stay at the Literarisches Colloquium; the first series is entitled "At the White House of Literature 1–4" ("Am White House der Literatur 1–4"). Although seemingly worlds apart in thematic focus and reference archive, Özdamar's and Tran's reading clips connect poetically, for example, in their shared emphasis on the fluid boundaries of subjectivity and the (grammatical, metaphorical, and material) agency of non-human actors.[37]

---

[36] Emine Sevgi Özdamar, *Das Leben ist eine Karawanswerei—hat zwei Türen—Aus einer kam ich rein—aus der anderen ging ich raus. Roman* (Cologne: Kiepenheuer & Witsch, 1992), 38–42.

[37] In Özdamar, the "buckets" brought along by European powers to bring home oil become agents in their own right (39), while Tran pays homage to the "intelligent states of matter" ("intelligente Agregatzustände") around and within him, and the "wind events [. . .] toward which subjectivities turn / by which subjectivities go" ("Windereignisse [. . .] nach denen sich die Subjektivitäten richten").

Importantly, Utlu's insistence on not reducing literature to politics and sociology does not categorically play linguistic experiment against experience, poetics against politics. In the first section of the parcours, he champions Ödön von Horváth for both his language and his status as a political author, asking whether the literature of migration "is ultimately nothing but the political literature of our time" ("im Grunde nichts anderes ist als die politische Literatur unserer Zeit"). In its function as counterpoint, section two of the parcours answers this question with "no, certainly not 'nothing but.'" Rather, the productive challenge is to articulate the relationship between politics and poetics in a non-reductive way. Can we make room for the multiplicity of layered—political and personal, affective and artistic, local and transnational—experiences that find their way into each writer's literary world and describe "the simultaneity of the political and the poetic" ("das Simultane des Politischen und Poetischen"), as Utlu characterizes Daniela Janjic's dramatic work in section 2?

The three remaining sections of Utlu's parcours unfold these layers and interrelations across three archival network clusters that index key fields of archival activism in the current moment: "Postcolonial Germany" ("Das postkoloniale Deutschland"), "The Opening of National History" ("Die Öffnung der Nationalgeschichte"), and "The Question of Identity" ("Die Frage der Identität"). In "Das postkoloniale Deutschland," Utlu opens with Uwe Timm. As Utlu spells out in the section's introduction, Timm's *Morenga* (1978) attended to the uprising of the Herero and Nama in what was then "German South-West Africa," today's Namibia, almost forty years before the German government would acknowledge the genocide with which the German colonial authorities answered the resistance. In the audio clip of his reading from *Morenga* on June 15, 1988, at the Literarisches Colloquium Berlin, Timm explains that his own positional implication in military perpetrator histories provided part of his motivation for the project. While acknowledging his early contribution, Utlu also articulates some hesitation about his own archival assembly here, as he marks the discontinuity of traditions: Timm works with the (by implication majority German/European) "form of the historical novel" ("Form des historischen Romans") rather than in dialogue with transnational Diasporic traditions of postcolonial critique.

The other authors honored in this section variously open up narrative form and genre by contributing to this dialogue. There is May Ayim, of course, whose pioneering poetry and scholarship hold a central place in the history of the Afro-German movement, and Sharon Otoo, who won the Ingeborg Bachmann prize in 2016 with her Afro-futurist inflection of German history and experimental narration in "Herr Gröttrup setzt sich hin" ("Mr. Gröttrup is sitting down").[38] There is also Philipp Khabo Köpsell's spoken-word poetry and Mutlu Ergün, whom Utlu highlights (right next to Timm) for how his *Kara Günlük. Die geheimen Tagebücher des Sesperado* (*Kara Günlük: The Secret Diaries of Sesperado*) connects contemporary migration histories with those of colonialism.[39] In the book, footnotes ground the hero's (docu-)fictional experiences in postcolonial theory. Like most tabs in this—central but perhaps most fragile—section of Utlu's archival *parcours*, the Ergün entry does not feature an audio clip from the Literarisches Colloquium or the Marbach archive.[40] Instead, Utlu reports on the text's performative generation in a less hegemonic venue: he recalls how Ergün wrote the text, which was published without a genre label but, per its cover text, takes the "German apprenticeship novel" ("deutschen Bildungsroman") to the next level, for and alongside a monthly

Figure 11.2 Screenshot from *Unterhaltungen deutscher Eingewanderten*. Reprinted with permission from Deniz Utlu and Literarisches Colloquium Berlin/Dichterlesen.net, www.dichterlesen.net/unterhaltungen-deutscher-eingewanderten. Photo copyright: Tobias Bohm; Renate von Mangoldt.

---

38 The text is available at bachmannpreis.orf.at/v3/stories/2773423/.
39 Mutlu Ergün, *Kara Günlük. Die geheimen Tagebücher des Sesperado*, 2nd ed. (Munster: Unrast, 2012).
40 I found a brief reading clip on YouTube: www.youtube.com/watch?v=rFYIu4WYJ7A.

reading series he had co-organized with Utlu in a Kreuzberg café. Thus, the narrative was designed in an ongoing dialogue with an audience that responded largely enthusiastically but in part also with distress to Ergün's (in Utlu's words) provocatively "open" ("offene") language about racism. With its superhero genre inspirations and its imbrication of (intimate) diary form and (public) satire, *Kara Günlük* poses insistent questions about the relations of humor and affect, aesthetics and politics, in the context of literary composition, performance, and reception. Utlu's decision to open the section on postcolonial Germany with the encounter between Timm and Ergün demonstrates how we can do the crucial work of foregrounding legacies of racism while, or in, taking questions of aesthetics seriously.

The following section, on "The Opening of National History" ("Die Öffnung der Nationalgeschichte"), only features two tabs—with, however, alternating author images for each of them (see Figure 11.2). In this way, Utlu visually stages the layering of histories that people bring along and that, as his introductory text spells out, become "part of national history" ("Teil der Nationalgeschichte"). The tab on the right side features Ilja Trojanow, Olga Grjasnowa, Nino Haratischwili, Saša Stanišić, Melinda Nadji Abonji, and Nellja Veremej. All of them are variously associated with what has sometimes been called the "Eastern European turn" in German literature: the aesthetic reassembly of the nation's—and continent's—archives, memories, and futurities through a foregrounding of histories long marginalized by hegemonic (West) European narratives.[41] On the left side, we have only two authors: Doğan Akhanlı and Edgar Hilsenrath. Their conjunction, however, opens up a whole network of intertextual links around the memory of the Armenian genocide, which was not merely "imported" into national history by Turkish-German immigrants but had long been part of it by virtue of Germany's historical involvement in the genocide and longer-standing memory work. The Ballhaus Naunynstraße and, later, the Maxim Gorki Theater in Berlin, under Shermin Langhoff's artistic direction, played crucial roles in activating this memory network with a series of productions and memorial events. In 2012, the Ballhaus Naunynstraße adapted Hilsenrath's novel *Das Märchen vom letzten Gedanken* (*The Story of the Last Thought*) (1989) for the stage. In the featured audio clip documenting a reading from March 3, 2008 in the LCB, Hilsenrath narrates how, in the wake of his previous novels on the

---

[41] See Brigid Haines, "Introduction: The Eastern European Turn in Contemporary German-Language Literature," *German Life and Letters*, vol. 68, no. 2 (2015): 145–53.

Holocaust, he was led to the Armenian topic by Franz Werfel's novel *Die vierzig Tage des Musa Dagh* (*The Forty Days of Musa Dagh*) (1933), which was adapted for the stage by the Maxim Gorki Theater in 2015. Utlu's assembly includes photographs from both productions, and his written commentary details that one of the theaters' annual memorial events was presented with Doğan Akhanlı, whose novel *Die Richter des Jüngsten Gerichts* (*The Judges of the Final Judgment*; Turkish original: *Kıyamet Günü Yargıçları*) Hilsenrath described as a "literary masterpiece" ("literarisches Meisterwerk")—this same work, it is worth mentioning, opens with two epigraph citations from Hilsenrath and Werfel.[42] As Utlu emphasizes, the connections are not merely thematic: Akhanlı is searching for a synthesis of the two forms, "fairy tale and historical novel" ("Märchen und historischer Roman"), resulting in a dreamlike poetic journey that serves as a method for finding "precise images [. . .] for the unspeakable" ("präzise Bilder [. . .] für das Unsagbare").

The concluding section of Utlu's parcours, "Die Frage nach der Identität" ("The Question of Identity"), recenters the challenge of nonreductively intertwining aesthetics and politics against the backdrop of the identity pressures exerted by hegemonic migration discourses in the contemporary German public sphere. Utlu's introductory text starts from Zafer Şenocak's observations on how German debates around immigration have focused on questions of ethnic and religious identity. Şenocak explains this national fixation with the "broken German" ("gebrochenes Deutsch") that Germans speak in relation to their own identity: in the memory ruptures enacted by shame and repression in the wake of National Socialism and the Shoah, or the "uprooting of language through the violation of its emotional capacities" ("Entwurzelung der Sprache durch eine Verletzung ihrer emotionalen Kapazitäten"). The question of identity, then, is not discarded per se but historicized and returned from a reverse perspective. Per Şenocak and Utlu, the question could become productive if directed at oneself—"Who am I?" ("Wer bin ich?")—and explored via poetic language. Utlu details Şenocak's poetic parcours that led him through Turkish and transnational modernisms, eventually toward pre-1933 German-language poetry and rare postwar exceptions, such as Paul Celan.

Utlu's own assembly of this final section of his parcours starts with Celan (positioned above Şenocak) and emphasizes poetry along with (post-)modernist writing practices across genres. For example, he foregrounds Yoko Tawada's "true" ("wirkliche") bilingualism, the defamiliarization effects of Dagmara Kraus's poetic language, and Navid

---

[42] Doğan Akhanlı, *Die Richter des Jüngsten Gerichts*, trans. Hülya Engin (Klagenfurt: Kitab, 2007).

Kermani's play with author personas. He also includes Zehra Cirak, who "sometimes translates sculptures into language" ("übersetzt manchmal aus Skulpturen in Sprache"), which, Utlu comments, is "also a form of migration" ("auch eine Form der Migration"); Jayrome C. Robinet's writing, which operates at the borders of genres, media, and genders; and the oeuvre of Max Frisch. Utlu emphasizes that for him, the question of identity has always been tied more closely to Frisch than to debates around migration. The section, as well as Utlu's parcours, concludes with Franz Kafka. The grand gesture of homage to the grand master of minor literature is, perhaps, brought somewhat down to earth by Utlu's comment that Kafka struggled to free himself from using language primarily as a means of "argumentative reasoning/presentation of evidence" ("argumentativen Beweisführung").[43] In the absence of an archival audio clip, Utlu concludes with another nod to the power of intermediality: he includes scans of three etchings by Jan Peter Tripp from a 2016 exhibition on Kafka's *Betrachtung* (*Contemplation*) at the Literarisches Colloquium Berlin. Two of these etchings play with the idea of human–bird metamorphosis (the second etching is marked as an illustration of Kafka's short "Der Ausflug ins Gebirge" ("Excursion into the Mountains"), and we may see a penguin). In this intermedial assemblage, the human voice of argumentation is displaced perhaps not with Gregor Samsa's anguished inability to communicate but with the prospect of singing. After all, "Der Ausflug ins Gebirge" begins with the narrating I's call "without sound" ("ohne Klang") but concludes with a gesture at the liberatory effect of the mountains and the words: "It is a miracle that we don't sing" ("Es ist ein Wunder, daß wir nicht singen"). Tripp's (penguin) bird may not be able to fly, but its pecker is wide open and reaching towards the sky, with its wings and chest extended to, I imagine, support its voice.[44]

Toward Non-Closure: Mobilizing the Archive

What if we took seriously the challenge of reassembling the major archives of German literature and German literary studies with the wealth of materials, the multivectoral flows of tradition, and the synesthetic affordances presented by Utlu's and Bodrožić's intermedial *parcours* of German literature? It may be high time to return to those canon debates of the late twentieth century—if in a different historical

---

[43] The Deleuze–Guattari allusion is not Utlu's but was imported by the writing representative of the "germanistischen" establishment. See Giles Deleuze and Felix Guattari, "Kafka: Toward a Minor Literature: The Components of Expression," *New Literary History*, vol. 16, no. 3 (1985): 591–608.

[44] Franz Kafka, *Betrachtung* (Leipzig: Rowohlt, 1912; Projekt Gutenberg, 2007), 38, www.gutenberg.org/files/23532/23532-h/23532-h.htm#Page_36.

moment, perhaps in a more creative than deconstructive spirit: imaginatively, specifically, materially, multisensually, and in the mode of making new connections probed by *Unterhaltungen deutscher Eingewanderten*. When I first sat down to write about this project, it occurred to me to send the web link to one of my graduate students. Particularly interested in Turkish and Kurdish German literature and film as well as in transnational approaches, more generally, the student had gently complained to me about our quite traditional MA reading list earlier in the year. In my email, I wondered in writing whether we might accept *Unterhaltungen deutscher Eingewanderten* as an alternative MA list. I quickly added a cautionary smiley and a note that I hadn't run this suggestion by my colleagues yet, and the student appreciated my comment as an indirect renewal of my earlier promise to initiate another round of revisions aimed at diversifying the list. But while realistic about the speed of institutional mobilization (not to mention the innovative energy of the overwhelmed Director of Graduate Studies writing said email), I was, in principle, more serious. Rather than just importing a few of Utlu's (and Bodrožić's) specific suggestions into an exam-resource list we call "general," the goal of reassembling the German Studies curriculum toward renewed relevance in a post-2020 world might require us to reshuffle our sense of the (heterogeneous, layered, fragmented) whole.

My point here is not a straightforward call for the institutional appropriation of Utlu's and Bodrožić's intellectual labor. Even apart from copyright concerns, I immediately grant some of my colleagues' anticipated objections. With its archival base in audio recordings, *Unterhaltungen deutscher Eingewanderten* is almost entirely lacking in pre-twentieth-century references. Rather than substituting a ready-made webpage for an old-fashioned print reading list, might we perhaps find ways of empowering our students to map their own trajectories through German literature? Could we work with them to develop new links and traditions that open up pre-twentieth-century German literature as an archive of migration and translation as well? When I did assign selected tabs from *Unterhaltungen deutscher Eingewanderten* as the basis for a departmental workshop, one of my colleagues suggested including Heinrich Heine's Jehuda Ben Halevy poem from his *Hebräische Balladen* (*Hebrew Ballads*). In other words, we got off to a good start.

The point is, obviously, about our degree of preparedness for actually mobilizing the archive—as repertoire, and vice versa—in activating intersecting vectors from "the inside" and "the outside" and dynamizing the contours of our field for the future. As indicated in the introduction, the current moment of crisis may bring radical change more quickly than many of us have foreseen. Given the field's nationalist and imperialist baggage and enduring hegemonic whiteness, should we even continue to defend the autonomy of nationally delineated departments and degrees against imminent major budget cuts?[45] I have been voting for due caution in that respect: let us not too eagerly welcome institutional dismantling while and where we still have a chance to object. Instead, I hope we can work on visions, and structures, that allow us to preserve what is valuable about these geographically and historically delineated fields—namely, the space for curating, caring for, and working with richly localized archives rather than the ostensibly global ones of World Literature alone.[46] In reassembling these localized archives (with Utlu, Bodrožić, and others), we can creatively explore how *local* does not equal *national* and how the performative activation of intermedial materiality can enhance—rather than decenter—the experience of literature.

Works Cited

Adelson, Leslie. "Touching Tales of Turks, Germans and Jews: Cultural Alterity, Historical Narrative, and Literary Riddles for the 1990s," *New German Critique*, no. 80 (2000): 93–124.

Akhanlı, Doğan. *Die Richter des Jüngsten Gerichts*, trans. Hülya Engin (Klagenfurt: Kitab, 2007).

Best, Stephen. "Neither Lost nor Found: Slavery and the Visual Archive," *Representations*, vol. 113, no. 1 (2011): 150–63.

Bluhm, Lothar. "'In jenen unglücklichen Tagen . . .': Goethes *Unterhaltungen deutscher Ausgewanderten* oder: Die Ambivalenz von Kunst und Gesellschaft," in *Erzählte Welt—Welt des Erzählens. Festschrift für Dietrich Weber*, ed. Rüdiger Zymner et al. (Cologne: edition chōra, 2000; Goethezeitportal, 2008), publikationen.ub.uni-frankfurt.de/frontdoor/index/index/docId/9442.

Bodrožić, Marica. *Tito ist tot. Erzählungen* (Frankfurt: Suhrkamp, 2002).

Bodrožić, Marica, and Deniz Utlu. *Unterhaltungen deutscher Eingewanderten*, www.dichterlesen.net/unterhaltungen-deutscher-eingewanderten/.

Breger, Claudia. *Making Worlds: Affect and Collectivity in Contemporary European Cinema* (New York: Columbia University Press, 2020).

Canetti, Elias. *Die gerettete Zunge*, 35th ed. (Frankfurt: Fischer Verlag, 1979).

Canetti, Elias. *Der Ohrenzeuge: Fünfzig Charaktere* (Frankfurt: Fischer, 1983).

Cheah, Pheng. *What Is a World?* (Durham, NC: Duke University Press, 2016).

Deleuze, Gilles, and Felix Guattari. "Kafka: Toward a Minor Literature: The Components of Expression," *New Literary History*, vol. 16, no. 3 (1985): 591–608.

Deutsches Institute für Menschenrechte. www.institut-fuer-menschenrechte.de/das-institut/team.

---

[45] See Niekerk, "Does German Cultural Studies need the Nation-State Model?"; Pfleger and Smith, *Transverse Disciplines*.

[46] See Mani, *Recoding*, 237. On curation as a (not merely conservative) contemporary humanities practice, see Stephen Muecke and Rita Felski (eds.), "Recomposing the Humanities—with Bruno Latour," *New Literary History*, special issue, vol. 47, nos. 2–3 (Spring–Summer 2016).

Ergün, Mutlu. *Kara Günlük. Die geheimen Tagebücher des Sesperado*, 2nd ed. (Munster: Unrast, 2012).
Ernst, Wolfgang. "Dis/continuities: Does the Archive Become Metaphorical in Multi-Media Space?" in *New Media–Old Media: A History and Theory Reader*, ed. Wendy Hui Kyong Chung and Thomas Keenan (New York: Routledge, 2006), 105–23.
Felski, Rita. *The Limits of Critique* (Chicago: University of Chicago Press 2015).
Felski, Rita, and Stephen Muecke, eds. "Recomposing the Humanities—with Bruno Latour," *New Literary History*, special issue, vol. 47, nos. 2–3 (Spring–Summer 2016): 215–478.
Goethe, Johann Wolfgang von. "Unterhaltungen deutscher Ausgewanderten," in *Werke. Hamburger Ausgabe*, vol. 6, ed. Erich Trunz and Benno v. Wiese (Munich: dtv, 1998), 125–241.
Göktürk, Deniz. *Framing Migration: Seven Takes on Movement and Borders* (Berlin: De Gruyter, 2021).
Gopinath, Gayatri. *Unruly Visions: The Aesthetic Practices of Queer Diaspora* (Durham, NC: Duke University Press, 2018).
Haines, Brigid. "Introduction: The Eastern European Turn in Contemporary German-Language Literature," *German Life and Letters*, vol. 68, no. 2 (2015): 145–53.
Hartman, Saidiya. "Venus in Two Acts," *Small Axe*, vol. 26 (2008): 1–14.
Kafka, Franz. *Betrachtung* (Leipzig: Rowohlt, 1912; Projekt Gutenberg, 2007), www.gutenberg.org/files/23532/23532-h/23532-h.htm#Page_36.
Klein, Lauren F. "The Image of Absence: Archival Silence, Data Visualization, and James Hemings," *American Literature*, vol. 85, no. 4 (2013): 661–88.
Latour, Bruno. *Reassembling the Social: An Introduction to Actor-Network-Theory* (Oxford: Oxford University Press, 2005).
Mani, B. Venkat. *Recoding World Literature: Libraries, Print Culture, and Germany's Pact with Books* (New York: Fordham University Press, 2017).
Niekerk, Carl, ed. "Does German Cultural Studies need the Nation-State Model?" *German Quarterly*, vol. 92, no. 4 (2019): 431–503.
Orich, Annika. "Archival Resistance: Reading the New Right," *German Politics and Society*, vol. 38, no. 2 (2020): 1–34.
Otoo, Sharon. "Herr Gröttrup setzt sich hin," *ORF*, 43. Tage der deutschsprachigen Literatur, bachmannpreis.orf.at/v3/stories/2773423/.
Özdamar, Emine Sevgi. *Das Leben ist eine Karawanserei—hat zwei Türen—aus einer kam ich rein—aus der anderen ging ich raus: Roman* (Cologne: Kiepenheuer & Witsch, 1992).
Özdoğan, Selim. "Vibrationshintergrund," *Transit*, vol. 8, no. 1 (2012), escholarship.org/uc/item/0f26f21x.
Pfleger, Simone, and Carrie Smith, eds. *Transverse Disciplines: Working Across and Beyond Academic Communities* (Toronto: University of Columbia Press, forthcoming).
Sheehan, Thomas. *Making Sense of Heidegger: A Paradigm Shift* (London: Rowman, 2015).
Taylor, Diana. *The Archive and the Repertoire: Performing Cultural Memory in the Americas* (Durham, NC: Duke University Press, 2003).
Utlu, Deniz. LinkedIn profile, de.linkedin.com/in/deniz-utlu-9794aa80.
Utlu, Deniz. Personal website, denizutlu.de/ich/.

Twelve Constructing an "Inside": Transcultural Laughter Communities in Fatma Aydemir's *Ellbogen* (2017) and Olga Grjasnowa's *Der Russe ist einer, der Birken liebt* (2012)

Lucas Riddle

Humor plays a major role in Fatma Aydemir's *Ellbogen* and Olga Grjasnowa's *Der Russe ist einer, der Birken liebt*. Protagonists and secondary characters in both novels create so-called "laughter communities," which solidify their belonging to and help draw the boundaries of their transcultural communities. Recent scholarship has investigated how multi-ethnic spaces in Europe make room for their inhabitants to construct a European identity that includes migrant and postmigrant bodies in a national or European framework previously inaccessible to them.[1] But the role of humor as a tool in this identity construction has remained largely unexamined. I argue that humor functions in these two novels as a vital tool for the construction of hybrid local identities which act to challenge and transcend national binaries in favor of belonging to hybrid local spaces.

---

[1] Among others, see: Leslie A. Adelson, *The Turkish Turn in Contemporary German Literature: Towards a New Critical Grammar of Migration* (London: Palgrave Macmillan, 2005); Fatima El-Tayeb, *European Others: Queering Ethnicity in Postnational Europe* (Minneapolis: University of Minnesota Press, 2011); Sarah Thomsen Vierra, *Turkish Germans in the Federal Republic of Germany: Immigration, Space, and Belonging, 1961–1990* (Cambridge: Cambridge University Press, 2018).

Aydemir is a Berlin-based writer and journalist. Born in 1986, she is the granddaughter of Turkish guestworkers. In addition to *Ellbogen* (*Elbows*) from 2017, she published her second novel *Dschinns* in 2022 and served as editor and contributor to the highly acclaimed essay volume *Eure Heimat ist unser Albtraum* (*Your Homeland is Our Nightmare*), published in 2019. *Ellbogen* tells of Hazal from Berlin's Wedding district; she is an eighteen-year-old second-generation Turkish-German whose transition into adulthood has been marked by disappointment, boredom, rage, and lack of options for upward mobility. With her friends, Hazal traverses early adolescence. Partying, trouble, young love, and petty arguments with her family make up her day-to-day life, until an incident with a university student on her eighteenth birthday drives her into hiding in Istanbul.

Olga Grajsnowa is also a Berlin-based writer. Like her protagonist Mascha, Grjasnowa was among the hundreds of thousands of Jewish quota refugees who arrived in Germany from the former Soviet Union (in her case, Azerbaijan) with her family in the 1990s. Aside from *Der Russe ist einer, der Birken liebt* (published in English as *All Russians love Birch Trees* in 2014), Grjasnowa published *Die juristische Unschärfe einer Ehe* (*The Legal Haziness of a Marriage*) in 2014 and *Gott ist nicht Schüchtern* in 2017 (published in English as *City of Jasmine* in 2019). *Der Russe ist einer, der Birken liebt*, her debut novel, follows Maria (Mascha) Kogan, a twenty-something from Baku, Azerbaijan, living in Frankfurt's Bahnhofsviertel. Mascha emigrated to Germany with her parents as a Jewish quota refugee when she was eight years old. Slightly older than Hazal, Mascha is studying to be an interpreter. She speaks German, Russian, French, English, Azeri, and Arabic and dreams of working for the UN. Yet, her story takes a traumatic turn when her boyfriend Elias dies following complications after a soccer injury. The plots of both *Ellbogen* and *Der Russe ist einer, der Birken liebt* are laden with tragedy, trauma, and violence, but Hazal, Mascha, and their diverse groups of friends laugh and induce laughter throughout, creating so-called "laughter communities" through shared humor.

In addition to functioning as a release and brief respite from the characters' troubling worlds, humor, joking, and laughter also build and strengthen solidarities among characters and readers—solidarities which act as the foundation for the reimagined communities present in the two novels. The humor in the novels often consists of jokes among friends rooted in defanging or repurposing the racism the characters face in their daily lives. Thus, the nature of this humor combined with the multi-ethnic make-up of the novels' friend groups create a multidirectional humor in line with Michael Rothberg's notion of multidirectional memory. Rothberg argues against the notion of a confrontational, zero-sum game when discussing encounters of unique collective histories of trauma and violence (for instance collective memory of the

Holocaust, slavery in the US, and colonialism). In opposition to what he calls "competitive memory," Rothberg, instead, views unique backgrounds of trauma and violence as dialogic and an avenue through which groups can borrow from each other and use another group's experiences to understand their own.[2] Although using this concept of multidirectional memory to read *Der Russe ist einer, der Birken liebt* and other transnational novels featuring multi-ethnic and minoritized protagonists is not a new approach, much of the existing scholarship—for instance by Elizabeth Loentz, Jonathan Skolnik, and Agnes Mueller[3]—focuses on shared trauma as the medium for, as Rothberg writes, "the creation of new communal and political identities."[4] This chapter, instead, focuses on the mechanisms of shared humor to combat racism and build community in specific excerpts centering on the characters' everyday lives in Germany.

I borrow the concept of "laughter communities" from Susanne Reichl and Mark Stein's *Cheeky Fictions: Laughter and the Post-Colonial*. They base their concept on Stanley Fish's idea of the interpretive community, which he defines as a group connected by a common, culturally informed set of references which shares a joint interpretive strategy to shape a collective reading of a given text.[5] Reichl and Stein posit that "laughter, too, presupposes shared worlds, shared codes, and shared values," or, in other words, "a shared matrix of references."[6] That is to say, a moment of shared laughter at external stimuli, between two or more parties, points to common experiences, tastes, backgrounds, or proclivities. These in turn provoke a similar interpretation of and engagement with the stimuli. In Aydemir and Grjasnowa's novels, the shared matrix is quite apparent and often is based on shared

---

[2] Michael Rothberg, *Multidirectional Memory: Remembering the Holocaust in the Age of Decolonization* (Stanford, CA: Stanford University Press, 2009).

[3] See: Elizabeth Loentz, "Beyond Negative Symbiosis: The Displacement of Holocaust Trauma and Memory in Alina Bronksy's *Scherbenpark* and Olga Grjasnowa's *Der Russe ist einer, der Birken liebt*," in *German Jewish Literature after 1990*, ed. Katja Garloff and Agnes Mueller (Woodbridge: Boydell & Brewer, 2018), 95–110; Jonathan Skolnik, "Memory without Borders? Migrant Identity and the Legacy of the Holocaust in Olga Grjasnowa's *Der Russe ist einer, der Birken liebt*," in *German Jewish Literature after 1990*, 123–45; Agnes C. Mueller, "Israel as a Place of Trauma and Desire in Contemporary German Jewish Literature," in *Spiritual Homelands: The Cultural Experience of Exile, Place, and Displacement among Jews and Others*, ed. Asher D. Biemann, Richard I. Cohen, and Sarah E. Wobick-Segev (Berlin and Boston: De Gruyter: 2019), 233–52.

[4] Rothberg, *Multidirectional Memory*, 11.

[5] See Stanley Fish, *Is There a Text in this Class?: The Authority of Interpretive Communities* (Cambridge, MA: Harvard University Press, 1980).

[6] Susanne Reichl and Mark Stein, *Cheeky Fictions: Laughter and the Postcolonial* (Amsterdam: Editions Rodopi, 2005), 13.

experiences of migration, trauma, or racism. In Aydemir's *Ellbogen*, Hazal and her friends joke about dressing as characters from the Turkish TV show *Kuzey Güney* and mock their gym teacher's exclamations that she "looooooves silk scarves" ("liiiiiiiebe Seidentücher!").⁷ And Hazal's family laughs at the inaccuracy of the Turkish-German experience in Fatih Akın film *Gegen die Wand* (*Head-On*).⁸ In Grjasnowa's novel, Mascha and her friends joke about subjects potentially damaging to their psyche: the gas station attendant who asks where they really come from; the devout Muslim, anti-Semitic, anti-Palestinian neighbor; and how, when speaking German, they are "perfectly integrated model foreigners" ("perfekt integrierte Vorzeigeausländer").⁹

Fatima El-Tayeb discusses the development of what she calls a "postethnic and translocal" European identity found primarily in neighborhoods with large populations of color or large migrant communities in European metropolises, such as Paris, Amsterdam, and Berlin.¹⁰ In these spaces, nationhood and national belonging are no longer the sole foundation for identity formation, but instead, identity is rooted in shared experiences and the alliances these shared experiences build. Often, these commonalities are similar stories of migration, economic hardship, or daily life experiences of racism.¹¹ Her preference for the terms "postethnic" and "translocal" instead of "binational" or "between two worlds" harkens back to Leslie Adelson's "touching tales" framework proposed in the late 1990s and early 2000s. Adelson sought to understand multiculturalism in Germany, specifically literary works on Turkish-German life and migration, as a convergence of cultural narratives and cultural encounters rather than two or more groups—a dominant German *Leitkultur* and "others"—living separately together. Like Adelson, El-Tayeb does not seek to deny the cultural specificities at play in European urban neighborhoods, but instead uses the above-mentioned terms in part to resist the notion that migrants of the second generation and other minoritized Europeans exist in a liminal space between two incompatible worlds.

I argue that, in the novels by Aydemir and Grjasnowa, humor is not only a significant expression of this translocal identity, but also defines

---

[7] Fatma Aydemir, *Ellbogen* (Munich: Hanser, 2017), 27, 98. All translations of *Ellbogen* are my own.
[8] Aydemir, *Ellbogen*, 78.
[9] Olga Grjasnowa, *Der Russe ist einer, der Birken liebt* (Munich: dtv Verlagsgesellschaft, 2013), 57; English edition: *All Russians Love Birch Trees*, trans. E. Bacon (New York City: Other Press, 2014), 57.
[10] Fatima El-Tayeb, *European Others: Queering Ethnicity in Postnational Europe* (Minneapolis: University of Minnesota Press, 2011), xxiii.
[11] El-Tayeb, *European Others*, 29.

terms of inclusion—however nebulous—by generating in-groups and out-groups through shared laughter. What is more, Aydemir and Grjasnowa craft laughter communities to include the reader. Humor not only functions as a means to access the community, but, for readers less familiar with the novels' milieu, functions as a social corrective in line with the humor theory of Henri Bergson. Bergson argues that the ridicule and humiliation of being laughed at helps the ridiculed overcome the social rigidity and inelasticity that evoked the laughter. Through humorous cues in the texts, readers laugh at the novels' characters who rely on stereotypes or cannot see past national or cultural binaries; this in turn offers lessons on inclusion and multicultural tolerance. In sum, shared humor gives the characters agency to construct their own "inside" and establishes a parlance to create, perform, and express identities based on a reframed notion of belonging that includes them.

Frameworks for understanding often minoritized identities in Germany that focus on a convergence and plurality of cultures are particularly productive when reading *Ellbogen* and *Der Russe ist einer, der Birken liebt*. In Aydemir and Grjasnowa's novels, the tales that "touch"—to borrow from Adelson—are not only Turkish and Russian-Jewish narratives encountering German tales within Germany. Rather, the novels present Berlin and Frankfurt as highly diverse spaces where many ethnicities, religions, cultures, and subcultures intersect. In *Ellbogen*, for instance, rather than *"Prost,"* Hazal's Bosnian friend Elma prefers the Turkish *"Şerefe."*[12] Elma, Hazal notes, "often uses Turkish words that she overheard somewhere. [. . .] She had a phase where she was really serious about belonging to us" ("benutzt häufig türkische Wörter, die sie irgendwo aufgeschnappt hat. [. . .] Sie hatte eine Phase, in der sie es richtig ernst meinte mit dem Dazugehören zu uns").[13]

Grjasnowa's protagonist, Mascha, has a circle of friends with diverse backgrounds; her boyfriend Elias is from the former German Democratic Republic, her best friend Cem is a second-generation Turkish-German, her ex-boyfriend Sami is Lebanese, and one of her lovers, Sibel, is Kurdish—to name a sampling of the novel's cast. Mascha's own identity is itself as heterogeneous as her group of friends (who are collectively in Frankfurt, and later in the novel, in Israel).[14] In Azerbaijan, she grew up as part of a Russian ethnic minority. Even among this group, she belonged to its Jewish minority—which allowed her to

---

[12] Aydemir, *Ellbogen*, 60.
[13] Aydemir, *Ellbogen*, 60.
[14] Agnes Mueller, in "Israel as a Place of Trauma and Desire," similarly analyzes Israel in Grjasnowa's novel as a "place for a collective of multiply displaced others" (246).

emigrate to Germany as a Jewish quota refugee, or *Kontingentflüchtling*. After Elias's death, Mascha also has a series of sexual relationships with men and women, in both Germany and Israel. This national and sexual fluidity, Stuart Taberner posits, "intimates her strikingly embodied desire to *know* the other, even as she herself finds it difficult to tell of her experiences in Azerbaijan."[15] Thus, Mascha's multifaceted outsider status drives her search for comradery (both in terms of friendships and sexual relationships) with those with similarly hybrid backgrounds. Beyond ethnic and national belonging, Mascha and her friends are connected through trauma and everyday experiences of exclusion in the spaces in which they reside—whether in Germany, Israel, or elsewhere.

The multi- and transculturalism extends beyond Mascha and her friends and informs the setting as well. Early in the novel, Mascha observes the goings-on in the neighborhood while on a study break:

> The boys were dressed in public housing fashion. [...] The gangsta peer group boasted with Turkish-Arabic pseudo-syntax. The underage ones bid their fellow students goodbye with "OK then ... *bunun üzerine*, bye." Fields, new buildings, and train stations now only appeared from time to time and they yelled at each other. "OK, like, bye!"

> [Die Jungs waren alle nach der Sozialbau-Mode gekleidet. [...] Die Gangsta-Peergroup gab mit türkisch-arabischen Pseudosatzkonstruktionen an, die Minderjährigen verabschiedeten sich von ihren Mitschülern mit "Also dann ... bunun üzerine tschüs." Felder, Neubauten und Bahnhäuschen tauchten nur noch in unregelmäßigen Abständen auf, und sie schrien einander "Also dann tschüs, gel!" zu.][16]

Here the neighborhood youth have developed a hybrid slang that blends Turkish, Arabic, and German—an urban creole that uses hip-hop "gangsta" aesthetic to give the youth a voice unique to their surroundings. On a sartorial level, their fashion is an expression and product of the neighborhood, social class, and the boys' ages, rather

---

[15] Stuart Taberner, "The possibilities and pitfalls of a Jewish cosmopolitanism: Reading Natan Sznaider through Russian-Jewish writer Olga Grjasnowa's German-language novel *Der Russe ist einer, der Birken liebt* (All Russians Love Birch Trees)," in *Jews on the Move: Modern Cosmopolitanist Thought and its Others*, ed. Cathy Gelbin and Sander L. Gilman (London and New York: Routledge, 2018), 144–62, here 154.

[16] Grjasnowa, *Der Russe*, 44; English: 43.

than of national belonging. Thus, the cultural contact that varying histories of migration have caused in these two novels has resulted in the creation of a hybrid culture that a "stuck-between-worlds" narrative would easily overlook.

Humor, too, reflects the meshing of cultures in these novels, and reveals solidarities as well as conflicts. In *Ellbogen*, Hazal, as the narrator, establishes her friends' laughter community through a careful exposition of their sense of humor. Shared laughter and joking among the friends construct a humor based partly on lewd, sexually charged, and often racial language and aggression coded to be funny. Similarly, characters in *Der Russe ist einer, der Birken liebt* often transform mutual experiences of micro-aggressions and moments of explicit othering into in-group humor to defang their bite. I investigate the significance of these in-group laughter communities through a close reading of how delineating such communities relates not only to the in-group, but also to the out-group and the reader. The creation of laughter communities allows the characters to draw their own borders of inclusion, shifting their group- and self-identification away from one that has foregrounded their lack of belonging. Functioning similarly to the postcolonial notion of "writing back," laughter communities assert the characters' membership of a group that offers support, gives them confidence, and whose criteria for inclusion extend beyond nationalism, shared national culture, or language.[17]

The beginning of Aydemir's *Ellbogen* in Berlin establishes the novel's social milieu—Hazal and her friends Ebru, Gül, and Elma are navigating the transition from adolescence to adulthood in the working-class, largely immigrant Berlin-Wedding. Most, if not all characters, have family issues, many with histories of abuse, chronic unemployment, and little hope for social advancement. The Berlin segment of *Ellbogen* follows Hazal from the security office of the drugstore *dm*, where she is caught stealing, through to her eighteenth birthday party, which—after Hazal is not allowed to enter a club—ends on the tracks of the U6 at Friedrichsstraße where the three girls kill a white university student who had harassed them. After the incident, Hazal flees to Istanbul to live with her internet boyfriend, Mehmet.

Early scenes with Hazal and her friends show the function of laughter communities. Much of the dialogue and many of the jokes shared are vulgar and aggressive. The chapter featuring Hazal's birthday

---

[17] In postcolonial theory and particularly in *The Empire Writes Back: Theory and Practice in Post-Colonial Literatures* by Bill Ashcroft, Gareth Griffiths, and Helen Tiffin, "writing back" is the notion of a writing that seeks: to decenter Eurocentric writing, to focus on the agency of the colonial subject, and to shift the colonial subject to the center from the margin.

party, for instance, begins with the epigraph, in English, "I'ma ruin you cunt!" repeated three times.[18] These are revealed as lyrics from the Azealia Banks song "212," which is blaring at Ebru's family's apartment where the girls are drinking before going out:

> Elma, Gül, and I are jumping around in Elma's room like we're deranged. We keep shouting the only line we know from "212," while Ebru is dancing with her eyes closed and moving her index finger to the beat, which is bumping through the apartment so loudly that the neighbors pound on the door.
>
> [Elma, Gül und ich springen wie drei Gestörte in Elmas Zimmer herum und rufen immer wieder den einzigen Satz, den wir aus "212" kennen, während Ebru mit geschlossenen Augen tanzt und ihre Zeigefinger zum Beat bewegt, der so laut durch die Wohnung knallt, dass bald die Nachbarn klopfen müssen.][19]

The laughter, drinking, and dancing are cacophonous. The friends jokingly call each other names: "Hey, I'm out of vodka! Where's my vodka, you cunts?" ("Hey, ich hab keinen Wodka mehr! Wo ist mein Wodka, ihr Fotzen?"), yells Gül.[20] Yet, the hailed insults bring the group closer together. After Ebru angrily storms to the kitchen for a towel because Gül spilled a drink, Elma falls to the floor laughing. Hazal narrates, "I start laughing because I notice how much I missed the four of us hanging out together—with a pissed-off Ebru losing her cool whenever something spins out of control" ("[i]ch fange an zu lachen, weil ich merke, wie ich es vermisst habe, zu viert abzuhängen, mit einer angepissten Ebru, die immer dann die Nerven verliert, wenn etwas außer Kontrolle gerät").[21] Here, Hazal and her friends recode vulgar insults as in-group humor and an expression of friendship.

The group's crass language is based in a stereotypically and caricaturized macho, racist vernacular, which only upon first glance appears to be simply crass.[22] Comparable to "Kanak Sprak" and the embrace in

---

[18] Aydemir, *Ellbogen*, 91.
[19] Aydemir, *Ellbogen*, 91.
[20] Aydemir, *Ellbogen*, 91.
[21] Aydemir, *Ellbogen*, 92.
[22] Though race does not come into play in this scene, the girls often refer to themselves and others as "Kanake." For instance, ethnicity and class plays a role in a conversation between Elma and Hazal. Referring to Hazal's resumé photo, Elma asks, "And what's with your *Kanake* mug? Are there any tricks you can do for the photo?" ("Und was ist mit deiner Kanakenfresse? Gibt es auch irgendwelche Tricks für das Foto?"), to which Hazal responds, "Of course, you can photoshop it" ("Klar, das kann man photoshoppen"), and laughs (54).

German minority hip-hop culture of the derogatory term "Kanake,"[23] the girls exemplify what Tom Cheesman calls "pseudo-ethnicization," referring to the "performance of a pastiche collective identity."[24] Yet, their language does not perform a specific ethnicity, but pastiches experiences of subjugation they have faced as both minorities and young women. The use of language is reminiscent of the sort of transgressive female writing Hélène Cixous called for in "The Laugh of the Medusa":

> If woman has always functioned "within" the discourse of man, a signifier that has always referred back to the opposite signifier which annihilates its specific energy and diminishes or stifles its very different sounds, it is time for her to dislocate this "within," to explode it, turn it around, and seize it; to make it hers, containing it, taking it in her own mouth, biting that tongue with her very own teeth to invent for herself a language to get inside of.[25]

As Cixous encourages women writers to use male discourse against itself to establish an empowered female discourse, Hazal and her friends' appropriate macho, racist vernacular and displace it as a parlance commonly associated with power and aggression against them. By using this slang, they express a resistance to and denial of that very subjugation. Akin to the reclamation of racial slurs in both American and German hip-hop, the girls repurpose these oppressive terms for humor and transform the terms from derogative to terms of comfort and comradery.

Eighteen-year-old girls using overly bullish language appears funny, at first because it is peculiar that young girls would speak in this way. However, when used among themselves, it has liberating properties. Drawing on Freud, Ulrike Erichsen explains that—to the "recipient of the comic stimulus"—humor and laughter function as a "release helping the person to regain his or her social and emotional equilibrium."[26]

---

[23] See Fatima El-Tayeb, "Kanak Attak! HipHop und (Anti-)Identitätsmodelle der 'Zweiten Generation,'" in *Jenseits des Paradigmas kultureller Differenz* (Bielefeld: transcript Verlag, 2015), 95–110; Elizabeth Loentz, "Yiddish, 'Kanak Sprak', Klezmer, and HipHop: Ethnolect, Minority Culture, Multiculturalism, and Stereotype in Germany," *Shofar*, vol. 25, no. 1 (2006): 33–62.

[24] Tom Cheesman, "Talking 'Kanak': Zaimoğlu Contra Leitkultur," *New German Critique*, vol. 92 (2004): 82–9, here 84.

[25] Hélène Cixous, "The Laugh of the Medusa," *Signs*, vol. 1, no. 4 (1976): 875–93, here 887.

[26] Ulrike Erichsen, "Smiling in the Face of Adversity: How to use Humour to defuse Cultural Conflict," in *Cheeky Fictions: Laughter and the Postcolonial*, ed. Susanne Reichl and Mark Stein (Amsterdam: Rodopi, 2005), 28–9.

When Hazal laughs at Ebru's anger and at her friends hailing slurs, she is reminded of the affection she feels for her friends.

In Grjasnowa's *Der Russe ist einer, der Birken liebt*, laughter communities function similarly as a means of relief for the characters. Mascha and her friends are a few years older than Hazal and the characters of *Ellbogen*. There is also a clear class difference. Grjasnowa's characters are all either pursuing or have advanced degrees at universities both in Germany and abroad. Mascha and Cem are training to be interpreters, Mascha's boyfriend Elias studied photography, and her ex-boyfriend Sami is pursuing a doctorate degree in the United States. Yet, like Aydemir's characters, they all also share often traumatic stories of migration and experiences in Germany of cultural conflict and racism. Stuart Taberner posits that in Grjasnowa's novel, "Germany exists only as a deterritorialised space in which the displaced and dispossessed reassemble and share memories of trauma."[27] Mascha and her family fled the pogroms in Baku in 1990. Sami was born in Beirut during the Lebanese civil war and relocated to France and, later, Germany with his Lebanese mother and Swiss father, who worked as a banker. Cem's brother died of cancer when Cem was young. Elias' alcoholic father abused him as a child.[28] Thus, as Agnes Mueller states, it is trauma, not "home, ethnic, cultural, or religious identity" which function as "defining markers for Masha's generation."[29] To trauma, I would also add status as outsiders (in and beyond Germany) as a point of identity formation among the characters. Yet, the trauma and shared backgrounds as outsiders also create bonds of friendship and a shared sense of humor.

A commonality nearly all Grjasnowa's characters share is that each has notably "failed" to perform correctly their culture of origin or the culture of their parents—their hybridity appears often as a shortcoming. Mascha, for instance, awkwardly stumbles through the *Schma Yisrael* while attempting to sacrifice a rabbit in her plea to God to save Elias. The German-born Cem notices, while studying abroad in Istanbul, that he speaks an unprestigious dialect of Turkish. He compensates by learning "the refined accent of the city's upper class" ("den feinen Dialekt der Istanbuler Oberschicht")[30] which then inadvertently

---

[27] Taberner, "The possibilities and pitfalls of a Jewish cosmopolitanism," 153.
[28] Skolnik writes on the anagram-like nature of character names such as Mascha, Elias, Cem, Sami, Sibel and, later, Ismael, in part as a function of Grjasnowa's "utopian postnational vision" for the novel, as they are each representative of their unique national identities, but "dissolve and join with one another" (129).
[29] Mueller, "Israel as a Place," 245.
[30] Grjasnowa, *Der Russe*, 57; English: 57.

alienates him further from his working-class parents. As a high school student in the US, Sami's Lebanese-French-German background confuses his American classmates: "In his new school none of his classmates could figure out why he had both a hard German accent and an Arabic name" ("In seiner neuen Schule konnte keiner seiner Mitschüler den harten deutschen Akzent mit dem arabischen Namen zusammenbringen").[31]

While some of these perceived cultural foibles are funnier than others and some are void of humor completely, they establish common ground among Mascha and her friends. The awkwardness or insecurities these episodes cause become more bearable once the characters can share them and laugh about them with their peers. In a call between Mascha and her ex-boyfriend Sami, he chuckles during his retelling of the story of his new Egyptian neighbor who spits on him for not being a "real Arab," because his mother is Palestinian and he has dated a Jew.[32] Mascha describes how he "imitated the Egyptian accent, pronouncing the words especially hard and talking so fast and loud that it sounded hysterical" ("imitierte [. . .] den ägyptischen Akzent, sprach die Wörter besonders hart aus und redete so schnell laut, dass es hysterisch klang").[33] At this point, Mascha cannot stop laughing, "especially since Sami normally attached such importance to his Lebanese accent, which was softer and quieter than the Egyptian one" ("insbesondere weil Sami sonst so viel Wert auf seinen libanesischen Dialekt legte, der weicher und leiser als der ägyptische war").[34] The comic element for Mascha here lies in the accuracy of Sami's imitation of the Egyptian accent; the harshness of the accent compared to the smoothness of Sami's usual Lebanese accent creates a humorous incongruity which Mascha—a fellow Arabic speaker—unpacks for the reader. Yet, the act of Sami calling Mascha, imitating his adversary, and turning it into a humorous exchange points to the social function of laughter and humor. Both Mascha and Sami have struggled to live up to others' notions of what it means to be a "real Jew" or a "real Arab." This creates a commonality between them, which allows Sami to confide in Mascha and diffuse his confrontation with the Egyptian neighbor through humor, making the Egyptian's allegations and any resulting feelings of inadequacy less harmful.

In-group humor in these two novels offers an avenue for characters to spin offensive language or personal shortcomings positively to foster

---

[31] Grjasnowa, *Der Russe*, 142; English: 128.
[32] Grjasnowa, *Der Russe*, 200–1; English: 227.
[33] Grjasnowa, *Der Russe*, 201; English: 227.
[34] Grjasnowa, *Der Russe*, 201; English: 227.

comradery. Yet, notably, incidents of humor directed at a third party also form out-groups. In *Jokes and their Relation to the Unconscious*, Freud notes that the tendentious joke (a joke which serves a purpose, as opposed to an abstract or "innocent" joke),[35] "[g]enerally speaking calls for three people: in addition to the one who makes the joke, there must be a second who is taken as the object of the hostile or sexual aggression, and a third in whom the joke's aim of producing pleasure is fulfilled."[36] So far, I have discussed laughter communities in relation to the first and third persons in Freud's schemata—the joke teller and the laughing interlocutor. Yet, focusing on the out-group, or butt of the jokes, delineates the laughter communities' borders of inclusion.

An incident between Hazal, Elma, and two German girls in *Ellbogen* shows a clash between two laughter communities. Elma is mimicking to Hazal how Gül behaves when she's drunk: "My ass is so hot, you sluts. Don't even look at me like that. You're just jealous 'cause I give so much head. You have no idea" ("Mein Arsch ist voll geil, ihr Schlampen. Ihr braucht gar nicht so zu schauen! Ihr seid doch nur neidisch, weil ich Schwänze ohne Ende lutsche. Ihr habt doch keine Ahnung").[37] Hazal laughs so hard at this that she "nearly pisses herself laughing" ("vor lauter lachen fast in die Hose mach[t]").[38] At the same moment, two white "*Ärztetöchter*" (doctor's daughters) walk by and hear Elma's imitation.[39] They do not realize Elma is mocking her friend and begin to giggle.[40] Moments later, they break into laughter. When Elma hears them laughing, she confronts them:

"What's so funny?" Elma snarls at her.
"Excuse me?"
"What's making you laugh like an idiot? I want to laugh too."

["Was gibt es zu lachen?" faucht ihr Elma ins Gesicht.
"Wie bitte?"
"Was ihr so behindert lacht? Ich will mitlachen."][41]

Elma, and later Hazal, continue to provoke the two *Ärtztetöchter*, and threaten them with violence: "I swear, I'll break your bones and hang

---

[35] Sigmund Freud, *Jokes and their Relation to the Unconscious*, trans. J. Strachey (New York: W.W. Norton & Company, Inc., 1963), 90.
[36] Freud, *Jokes*, 100.
[37] Aydemir, *Ellbogen*, 61.
[38] Aydemir, *Ellbogen*, 61.
[39] Also referred to as "Mittetussis," referring to Berlin's upper-class neighborhood Mitte.
[40] Aydemir, *Ellbogen*, 61.
[41] Aydemir, *Ellbogen*, 62.

'em around my neck" ("Ich schwöre, ich brech dir den Knochen und hänge ihn mir um den Hals").[42] The *Ärztetöchter* run away, at which point Hazal narrates, "Once they're around the corner, Elma and I die laughing" ("Als sie um die Ecke sind, lachen Elma und ich uns tot").[43]

Helga Kotthoff examines audience reception of caricaturized "macho" Turkish-German characters in Turkish-German "Ethno-Comedy."[44] Through an analysis of reviews and internet comments on comedy sketches, Kotthoff found that the exaggerated presentation of stereotypes was often understood in line with the comics' intention—as a critique of essentialism and essentialist attitudes toward minoritized groups. However, she found, specifically in comments, that the comedians' performances were also read by non-ethnic "outgroup" viewers as an affirmation of stereotypes and racist prejudices.[45] This disparity in reception, Kotthoff argues, creates a double framing of stereotyped so-called "Macho-Secondo"[46] characters, which invites both a *Lachen-Mit* (laughing with) and a *Lachen-Über* (laughing at) and unwittingly reinforces "alte Distinktionslinien zwischen 'wir' und 'ihr'" (old lines of distinction between "us" and "you"[47]).[48]

The passage above from *Ellbogen* plays out similarly to Kotthoff's case studies. The scene starts with an instance of imitation and a response of laughter between Elma and Hazal, who believe themselves to be alone. Their bawdy language could read as the language stereotypically attributed to poor, immigrant youth in Germany—acting as young female versions of Kotthoff's *Macho-Secondo*. Kotthoff explains, "[n]icht nur in vielen Ethno-Comedys, sondern auch in alltäglichen Gesprächen taucht 'Kanaksprak' als 'fun-code' auf. [. . .] Jugendliche nutzen den 'fremden' Sprechstil meist, um eine humoristische

---

[42] Aydemir, *Ellbogen*, 64.
[43] Aydemir, *Ellbogen*, 64.
[44] Helga Kotthoff, "Ethno-Comedy zwischen Inklusion und Exklusion: Komische Hypertypen und ihre kommunikativen Praktiken," in *Komik der Integration: Grenzpraktiken und Identifikationen des Sozialen*, ed. Özkan Ezli, Deniz Göktürk, and Uwe Wirth (Bielefeld: Aisthesis Verlag, 2019), 65–102, here 65.
[45] Kotthoff quotes, for example, a comment found under comedian Teddy Teclebrhan's YouTube video "Umfrage zum Integrationstest (was nicht gesendet wurde)," (Survey for the Integration Test [that was not sent]) in which the viewer states, "das traurige ist das wir wirklich so idioten wie diesen sollte das leben in deutschland verboten werden [sic]" (the sad thing is that we really have idiots like this living in germany, ignorant people like these should be banned from living in germany); "Ethno-Comedy," 88.
[46] "Secondos," Kotthoff notes, is the term used predominately in Switzerland for "die Nachfahren von migrierten Familien" (descendants of migrated families); "Ethno-Comedy," 66.
[47] Translations of Kotthoff are my own.
[48] Kotthoff, "Ethno-Comedy," 65–6.

Interaktionsmodilität einzuführen" ("'*Kanaksprak*' emerges as a 'fun code'—not only in many ethno-comedies, but also in everyday conversation. [...] Young people use the 'foreign' style of speaking in most cases to establish a humorous modality for interaction").[49] Elma's Gül impression exhibits this fun code. Yet, the two *Ärtztetöchter* take the role of Kotthoff's internet commentators; they misread the playful imitation and laugh. Elma becomes enraged. Their laugh, unlike Hazal's, is laughter *at* her for perpetuating a stereotype; Elma's imitation now becomes a reminder of her difference. To not "lose" this encounter, Elma intensifies her routine and confronts the girls to scare them. When they run away, Elma and Hazal share a laugh. Doing so, returning to Reichl and Stein, strengthens the ties between Elma and Hazal, and shows a sign of victory over the *Ärztetöchter*'s attempts to humiliate them.

Hazal and Elma's last laugh is triumphant, while functioning simultaneously as an invitation to the reader to join the laughter and, as a result, join their laughter community. Reichl and Stein suggest that because many postcolonial literatures intend to reach beyond their localities (I would argue that this extends to many minoritized literatures), there often exist "cues in the texts that enable access to their comic potential."[50] In doing so, "[l]aughter and humor are [...] 'test cases' not for cultural belonging, but for transcultural competence."[51] In terms of Kotthoff's double framing, Aydemir establishes her characters' sense of humor to teach her readers to be literate in the language of Hazal's laughter community. The ability to read Elma's Gül imitation "correctly" aligns the reader with Hazal and Elma as what Kathrin Sieg calls "in-group witnesses." On humor as a means of community building in Turkish-German stand-up, Kathrin Bower evokes Sieg's discussion of self-parody through stereotype perpetuation in *Ethnic Drag*:

> The play with and within ethnicity in ethnic drag reveals its mimetic and parodic capacity: when the "ethnic" plays an "ethnic" role it can be perceived as mimetic and thus authentic, or as parodic and thus a critique of stereotyped views of the "ethnic" other. The spectators who recognize the parody behind the ethnic drag in such cases are in on the joke, whereas those who expect or see authenticity in the performance are the dupes.[52]

---

[49] Kotthoff, "Ethno-Comedy," 80.
[50] Reichl and Stein, *Cheeky Fictions*, 13.
[51] Reichl and Stein, *Cheeky Fictions*, 13.
[52] Kathrin Bower, "Made in Germany: Integration as Inside Joke in the Ethno-Comedy of Kaya Yanar and Bülent Ceylan," *German Studies Review*, vol. 37, no. 2 (2014): 357–76, here 364.

Sieg's discussion of the passer (the person enacting the stereotype as parody), the dupe (the one who misreads the parody as authentic) and in-group witness (the spectator who understands the parody correctly) in *Ethnic Drag* is productive in demonstrating the community-building potential in Elma and Hazal's encounter with the *Ärztetöchter*. As ingroup witnesses, the reader views the *Ärztetöchter* as the butt of the joke duped into believing Elma's actions are mimetic, not parodic, based on their own preconceptions of Turkish-German stereotypes, while Elma and Hazal share a wink and a nudge with the reader. Sarah Ilott posits in her article on multicultural British film comedy that including the audience in a minority laughter community "marks an important move in seeing those often demonized in the media [...] as subjects worthy of empathy," which "reverses patterns of exclusion and temporarily recentres [...] otherwise marginalized and alienated groups."[53] Thus, the expression of identity and community-building potential created in *Ellbogen* through humor function as follows: first, humor is an avenue through which Aydemir's characters relate to each other based on commonalities using language uniquely recoded to their own in-group. Then, comic cues in the text recruit the reader to join their community, to promote comradery with often vilified, feared, or misunderstood groups and to see beyond stereotypes.

The laughter community plays a similar role in Grjasnowa's novel. After Elias's funeral, Mascha asks Sami to drive her to Elias's East German hometown to visit his grave. While there, Sami and Mascha stop at a gas station to buy ice cream. The attendant asks Sami where he is from. Sami responds "from Frankfurt," to which the attendant responds, asking where Sami is really from.[54] "The cashier was ravenous for some exoticism" ("Die Verkäuferin lechzte nach Exotik"), narrates Mascha and says to Sami, "'Come on, tell her'" ("'Komm schon, sag es ihr'").[55] Sami responds, "I'm from Madagascar [...] We all live in tree houses there and eat nothing but bananas" ("Ich komme aus Madagaskar [...] Dort leben alle in Baumhäusern und ernähren sich ausschließlich von Bananen").[56] Mascha adds that it is Sami's first time trying ice cream and the two smile.

In this passage, we once again see a laughter community based on shared experience of marginalization. Potentially damaging microaggressions are turned into fodder for in-group humor by rendering them

---

[53] Sarah Ilott, "'How is these Kids Meant to make it Out the Ghetto Now?' Community Cohesion and Communities of Laughter in British Multicultural Comedy," *Journal of Commonwealth Literature*, vol. 53, no. 2 (2018): 211–22, here 215.
[54] Grjasnowa, *Der Russe*, 142; English: 158.
[55] Grjasnowa, *Der Russe*, 142; English: 158.
[56] Grjasnowa, *Der Russe*, 142; English: 158.

laughable.[57] For Sami, the question "where are you from?" connotes a lack of belonging—and likely functions as a reminder of his otherness in Germany and, due to his dark skin, his inescapable markedness as a minority. Though Mascha's whiteness arguably allows her to pass more easily in Germany, she likely can easily relate to the question. She lives in Germany as part of a minority group and is marked as such by her surname, "Kogan." She has also likely been asked the same question and can relate to the alienation the question evokes. Yet, instead of falling victim to this alienation, Sami exaggerates the *Exotik*. Much like Elma, Sami caricaturizes himself to get Mascha to laugh. The interaction becomes positive. The passage ends with Mascha's narration: "At least things between us were good again" ("wenigstens zwischen uns war alles wieder in Ordnung").[58]

Like Aydemir, Grjasnowa also includes her readers in her laughter communities and promotes allegiances between the readers and her characters. However, Grjasnowa more clearly emphasizes humor's didactic potential in terms of cross-cultural awareness and competence, using an assumed prior knowledge of common tropes to her advantage. Mithu Sanyal notes in her essay "Zuhause" ("Home") in the 2019 essay collection *Eure Heimat ist unser Albtraum* (*Your Homeland is Our Nightmare*), the question "where are you from?" does not actually intend to ask for origin, but rather "what are you?"[59] [60] Sanyal also writes, "[e]s ist beinahe ein Klischee, noch darüber zu reden" ("[the question] is almost a cliche to still talk about"[61]).[62] Grjasnowa plays with this now well-known micro-aggression used against minorities in Germany and couples it with the in-group joke between Sami and Mascha to clue the reader in on the gas station attendant's failure to properly adapt to a multicultural Germany and properly "speak" the social language of multiculturalism. Mascha and Sami's laughter functions to alert the reader to this failure, uncovering humor's function as a corrective à la Henri Bergson.

In his essay "Laughter: An Essay on the Meaning of the Comic" (1900), French philosopher Henri Bergson sought to understand why we laugh. Specifically, Bergson's theory on humor fits into the tradition

---

[57] For a close analysis of microaggressions in *Der Russe ist einer, der Birken liebt*, see Loentz, "Beyond Negative Symbiosis," 112–14.
[58] Grjasnowa, *Der Russe*, 142; English: 158.
[59] Grjasnowa and Aydemir also contributed to this volume, with Aydemir served as editor.
[60] Mithu Sanyal, "Zuhause," in *Eure Heimat ist unser Albtraum*, ed. Fatma Aydemir and Hengameh Yaghoobifarah (Berlin: Ullstein fünf, 2019), 101–22, here 112.
[61] Translations of Sanyal are my own.
[62] Sanyal, "Zuhause," 101.

of superiority theories of humor—a family of theories of *laughing at* which generally hold that "humour springs from a gratifying sense of the frailty, obtuseness or absurdity of one's fellow beings."[63] Bergson contends that, when we laugh at someone, we laugh at their rigidity, inelasticity, inability to adapt to new situations, and their automatism: "The comic character no longer tries to be ceaselessly adapting and readapting himself to the society of which he is a member. He slackens in the attention that is due to life. He more or less resembles the absentminded."[64] As a basic example, Bergson describes a man running down the street, tripping and falling.[65] His inability to avoid the tripping hazards in the street becomes laughable as it exposes how his rigidity has caused him to fall.

To the one being laughed at, the laughter serves to humiliate and ridicule, but also to teach. Bergson asserts that laughter is a social corrective. Terry Eagleton aptly describes laughter per Bergson's theory as a way of "restraining social deviancy, tempering rigidities of character and behaviour and thus producing the psychological plasticity that modern societies demand."[66] Laughter, according to Bergson, "does not belong to the province of esthetics alone," but "pursues a utilitarian aim of general improvement."[67] Laughter as a corrective humiliates and, through humiliation, teaches one to adapt.

Bergson's focus on this utilitarian aspect of humor in a social sphere helps to understand to which ends Mascha—as the novel's first-person narrator—includes her readership in her novel's laughter community. Grjasnowa exaggerates and caricatures particular secondary characters meant to represent a line of thinking prevalent in Germany which cannot adapt—in language or action—to the multicultural space that Germany has become. Cues in the text alert the reader to the rigidity of their character by making them laughable—as if the characters have tripped and fallen over their own blind spots in cultural awareness, like asking the question "where are you *really* from?"

Mascha and Sami's interaction with the gas station attendant transforms prejudicial microaggressions into humor to be shared between characters, and between Mascha and the reader. Instances such as these in the novel, of which there are many, stand out due to the exaggerated sense of ignorance of Mascha's (or Mascha and Sami's) interlocutor. Yet,

---

[63] Terry Eagleton, *Humor* (New Haven, CT: Yale University Press, 2019), 36.
[64] Henri Bergson, *Laughter: An Essay on the Meaning of the Comic* (1900; Project Gutenberg, 2009), 55, https://www.gutenberg.org/files/4352/4352-h/4352-h.htm.
[65] Bergson, *Laughter*, 5.
[66] Eagleton, *Humour*, 41.
[67] Bergson, *Laughter*, 8.

the readership's laughter during each encounter affirms a shared sensibility between the reader and Mascha. This common sensibility provides the reader access to the laughter community of Mascha and her friends which is based on a self-evident, nuanced, and non-exoticizing view of multiculturalism. Through Bergson, we also can read these encounters as a means of testing cross-cultural competence. Can the reader laugh *with* Mascha or do they, too, need to be laughed *at*, and, thus, corrected? If the latter, Mascha's biting, sarcastic narration, and other diegetic instances of comic ridicule, light the path toward this correction, albeit through humiliation.

* * *

In this chapter, I have analyzed the function of multiethnic laughter communities in the novels *Ellbogen* by Fatma Aydemir and *Der Russe ist einer, der Birken liebt* by Olga Grjasnowa. Both novels are products of and illuminate the social milieu of many minoritized groups living in Germany today, including second- and third-generation Germans with family histories of trauma and migration. While the two novels are not without their tragic elements and while they do not ignore the continued marginalization of Germany's minoritized populations, each novel features a sense of humor that is both communal and transgressive. The multi-ethnic and multicultural groups of friends in each novel create laughter communities based on shared (trans)cultural experiences, which include shared experiences of oppression, xenophobia, sexism, classism, and racism. They reappropriate potentially hurtful language or actions and transform them into a humor that promotes comradery and brings their groups closer together. At the same time, many instances of in-group humor in these novels create out-groups. Often the butt of the joke, these out-groups function to solidify borders of belonging to the novels' laughter communities, while also signaling to readers the conditions for in-group belonging. Yet, what is important to note here is that the requisites of inclusion in the laughter communities are beyond nation and offer new pathways to an "inside" based not on a rigid national imaginary, but transcultural and transnational competence, open- and like-mindedness.

Works Cited

Adelson, Leslie A. *The Turkish Turn in Contemporary German Literature: Towards a New Critical Grammar of Migration* (London: Palgrave Macmillan, 2005).

Aydemir, Fatma. *Ellbogen* (Munich: Hanser Verlag, 2017).

Bergson, Henri. *Laughter: An Essay on the Meaning of the Comic* (1900; Project Gutenberg, 2009), https://www.gutenberg.org/files/4352/4352-h/4352-h.htm.

Bower, Kathrin. "Made in Germany: Integration as Inside Joke in the Ethno-Comedy of Kaya Yanar and Bülent Ceylan," *German Studies Review*, vol. 37, no. 2 (2014): 357–76.

Cheesman, Tom. "Talking 'Kanak': Zaimoğlu Contra Leitkultur," *New German Critique*, no. 92 (2004): 82–99.
Cixous, Hélène, "The Laugh of the Medusa," *Signs*, vol. 1, no. 4 (1976): 875–93.
Eagleton, Terry. *Humour* (New Haven, CT: Yale University Press, 2019).
El-Tayeb, Fatima. *European Others: Queering Ethnicity in Postnational Europe* (Minneapolis: University of Minnesota Press, 2011).
Erichsen, Ulrike. "Smiling in the face of adversity: How to use humor to defuse cultural conflict," in *Cheeky Fictions: Laughter and the Postcolonial*, ed. Susanne Reichl and Mark Stein (Amsterdam: Editions Rodopi, 2005), 27–42.
Freud, Sigmund. *Jokes and their Relation to the Unconscious*, trans. J. Strachey (New York: W.W. Norton & Company, Inc., 1963).
Grjasnowa, Olga. *Der Russe ist einer, der Birken liebt* (Munich: dtv Verlagsgesellschaft, 2013).
Grjasnowa, Olga. *All Russians Love Birch Trees*, trans. E. Bacon (New York City: Other Press, 2014).
Gymnich, Maron. "Writing Back," in *Handbuch Postkolonialismus und Literatur*, ed. Dirk Göttsche, Gabriele Durbeck, and Axel Dunker (Stuttgart: J.B. Metzler, 2017), 235–8.
Ilott, Sarah. "'How is these Kids Meant to make it Out the Ghetto Now?' Community Cohesion and Communities of Laughter in British Multicultural Comedy," *Journal of Commonwealth Literature*, vol. 53, no. 2 (2018): 211–22.
Kotthoff, Helga. "Ethno-Comedy zwischen Inklusion und Exklusion: Komische Hypertypen und ihre kommunikativen Praktiken," in *Komik der Integration: Grenzpraktiken und Identifikationen des Sozialen*, ed. Özkan Ezli, Deniz Göktürk, and Uwe Wirth (Bielefeld: Aisthesis Verlag, 2019), 65–102.
Mueller, Agnes C. "Israel as a Place of Trauma and Desire in Contemporary German Jewish Literature," in *Spiritual Homelands: The Cultural Experience of Exile, Place, and Displacement among Jews and Others*, ed. Asher D. Biemann, Richard I. Cohen, and Sarah E. Wobick-Segev (Berlin and Boston: De Gruyter, 2019), 233–52.
Reichl, Susanne, and Mark Stein. *Cheeky Fictions: Laughter and the Postcolonial* (Amsterdam: Rodopi, 2005).
Rothberg, Michael. *Multidirectional Memory: Remembering the Holocaust in the Age of Decolonization* (Stanford, CA: Stanford University Press, 2009).
Sanyal, Mithu. "Zuhause," in *Eure Heimat ist unser Albtraum*, ed. Fatma Aydemir and Hengameh Yaghoobifarah (Berlin: Ullstein fünf, 2019), 101–22.
Sieg, Katrin. *Ethnic Drag: Performing Race, Nation, Sexuality in West Germany* (Ann Arbor: University of Michigan Press, 2002).
Skolnik, Jonathan. "Memory without Borders? Migrant Identity and the Legacy of the Holocaust in Olga Grjasnowa's *Der Russe ist einer, der Birken liebt*," in *German Jewish Literature after 1990*, ed. Katja Garloff and Agnes Mueller (Woodbridge: Boydell & Brewer, 2018), 123–45.
Taberner, Stuart. "The possibilities and pitfalls of a Jewish cosmopolitanism: reading Natan Sznaider through Russian-Jewish writer Olga Grjasnowa's German-language novel *Der Russe ist einer, der Birken liebt* (All Russians Love Birch Trees)," in *Jews on the Move: Modern Cosmopolitanist Thought and its Others*, ed. Cathy Gelbin and Sander L. Gilman (London and New York: Routledge, 2018), 144–62.

Thirteen Screening Urban Space and Belonging in Berlin: Contemporary Berliners in Sheri Hagen's *Auf den zweiten Blick/At Second Glance* (2013), Ines Johnson-Spain's *Becoming Black* (2019), and Amelia Umuhire's *Polyglot* (2015)

Berna Gueneli

Nigerian German actor and filmmaker Sheri Hagen argues:

> [...] children and young people need stories, characters, content and images with which they can identify [... they need] role models. The German entertainment industry does not create an environment in which all creative talents can tell their stories, so only certain people [...] can see themselves reflected; others are excluded.[1]

Hagen shared similar insights in 2020 at the "Black Women Filmmakers in Germany" roundtable at the Women in German conference and at a screening of her 2013 feature film *At Second Glance*.[2] The recurrence of these remarks at these venues stresses the importance of acknowledging that mainstream German cinema—like other cultural products—does not engage enough with, let alone fully represent, the diversity of its citizens and their hi/stories. This is a concern shared by other artists

---

[1] Sheri Hagen, email message to author, October 21, 2020.
[2] Roundtable interlocutors at the WiG conference on October 16, 2020 were Karina Griffith, Ines Johnson-Spain, and Hagen. Hagen's discussion/Q&A at the University of Georgia (Athens) took place on October 20, 2020. Hereafter, the conference and the Q&A session will be referred to as WiG and Q&A, respectively.

in Germany.³ For example, Sudanese German singer Samy Delux, who thematizes growing up as a Black child without role models in the mainstream media, sings in "Superheld": "Ich wär so gern dein Superheld in brauner Haut" ("I would love to be your superhero in Brown/Black skin").⁴ And Rwandan German filmmaker/artist Amelia Umuhire remarks on the absence of audiovisual diversity in German media in general. "There is this one image of Germany, [...] you have white people speaking German if you look at the TV landscape [...]. You don't get to know people, this big part of Germany and Berlin, because they are kind of marginalized in media."⁵

Such references to marginalization in German mainstream media reflect what Fatima El-Tayeb has observed on a larger scale in Germany and Europe. The consistent marking of people of non-white ethnicities as "aliens from elsewhere," as the "eternal newcomers"—disregarding their citizenship status or their local residencies—automatically deprives ethnic minorities of being perceived as fellow citizens/residents.⁶ In this way, the idea of whiteness as the norm for a German, European identity remains continuously intact.

Yet, while mainstream German cinema still often misses many underrepresented voices, bodies, and stories, independent filmmakers and artists such as Hagen, Natasha Kelly, Johnson-Spain, Mo Asumang, recent film school graduates such as Mehmet Büyükatalay and Ilker Çatak, self-financed low-budget artists like Umuhire, and established filmmakers like Fatih Akın provide new perspectives, be it via webseries, at film festivals, in cinemas, or on television. As scholars including Deniz Göktürk, Randall Halle, Barbara Mennel, and Katrin Sieg have argued in different contexts discussing contemporary German film,⁷ these filmmakers provide stories, sounds, and visuals that create and depict hitherto less-frequently featured perspectives in German

---

³ Filmmaker Denise Ekale Kum and artist-producer Tyron Ricketts made similar comments at the roundtable "Black Spaces: Black Voices," at the University of Massachusetts Amherst on February 11, 2021.
⁴ *Dis wo ich herkomm* (*Dis Where I Come from*), Capitol Records, 2009.
⁵ "Life in Berlin: Exploring Identity, Language, and Race with Polyglot," NPR Berlin podcast, 2014, player.fm/series/npr-berlin/life-in-berlin-exploring-identity-language-and-race-with-polyglot.
⁶ With "aliens from elsewhere," El-Tayeb refers to Rey Chow's work. See Fatima El-Tayeb, *European Others: Queering Ethnicity in Postnational Europe* (Minneapolis: University of Minnesota Press, 2011), xiii–xiv. For more on "eternal newcomers," see El-Tayeb, *European Others*, xxix.
⁷ See Deniz Göktürk, "World Cinema Goes Digital: Looking at Europe from the Other Shore," in *Turkish German Cinema in the New Millennium*, ed. Sabine Hake and Barbara Mennel (New York: Berghahn, 2021); Randall Halle, *German Film After Germany: Toward a Transnational Aesthetic* (Urbana: University of Illinois

media. This is an important, ongoing conversation that extends over various disciplines. Scholars of literature and theater previously have provided critical readings of, for example, new, creative Turkish-German voices of the Cold War and post-Cold War period. Among these are seminal works by scholars Leslie Adelson, Azade Seyhan, Kader Konuk, Venkat Mani, Ela Gezen, and others.[8]

In this chapter, I wish to contribute to this conversation with a discussion of three Black women filmmakers and their work: Umuhire's webseries *Polyglot* (2015), Ines Johnson-Spain's documentary *Becoming Black* (2019), and Hagen's feature *At Second Glance* (2013). These films, set in Berlin, provide much-needed artistic engagements with still-underexplored images, hi/stories, sounds, and bodies in German film. Their unique and complex narratives convey a sense of a fundamentally diverse Germany on the screen, and particularly of urban Germany, connected to various parts of the globe. These filmic urban spaces are populated with diverse characters of varying ethnicities and races, sexual orientations, ages, differently abled bodies, varying emotional developments, and different economic, professional, and historical backgrounds.

I argue that these films—notwithstanding their individual thematic foci—become an artistic deliberation on the global city of Berlin and its contemporary inhabitants. The directors create a multi-layered, complex image of the city and its people. While doing so, they convey two things in particular: they weave the theme of "belonging" into their narratives and they portray an image of Berlin as a series of individualized local neighborhoods with multiple connections to other places. I contend that this second point in particular reflects aesthetically, in film, some of the concepts that cultural geographer Doreen Massey has developed in her work on interconnected space/place theoretically, and what sociologist Saskia Sassen has scrutinized in her deliberations on networks and global cities. I will return to these ideas below. First,

---

Press, 2008); Barbara Mennel, "Überkreuzungen in globaler Zeit und globalem Raum in Fatih Akıns Auf der anderen Seite," in *Kultur als Ereignis*, ed. Özkan Ezli (Bielefeld: transcript, 2010); Katrin Sieg, *Choreographing the Global in European Cinema and Theater* (New York: Palgrave MacMillan, 2008).

[8] See Leslie Adelson, *The Turkish Turn in Contemporary German Literature* (New York: Palgrave MacMillan, 2005); Azade Seyhan, *Writing Outside the Nation* (Princeton, NJ: Princeton University Press, 2000); Kader Konuk, *Identitäten im Prozeß: Literatur von Autorinnen aus und in der Türkei in deutscher, englischer und türkischer Sprache* (Essen: Die Blaue Eule, 2001); B. Venkat Mani, *Cosmopolitical Claims: Turkish-German Literature from Nadolny to Pamuk* (Iowa City: University of Iowa Press, 2007); Ela Gezen, *Brecht, Turkish Theater, and Turkish-German Literature: Reception, Adaptation, and Innovation after 1960* (Rochester, NY: Camden House, 2018).

however, I will provide a brief context for these Black German filmmakers and their work. Then I will use the films as case studies for the filmmakers' "aesthetics of heterogeneity,"[9] examining select scenes that provide a fresh filmic look at the city of Berlin and its residents.

Exploring the Work of Black Artists in Germany[10]

It is fair to say that the engagement with Black German themes within academia is a relatively recent field of study, notwithstanding the long history of the lives and works of Black Germans and Europeans. Early work in Germany addressing Black German subjectivities, histories, and criticism by now includes canonized anthologies such as May Ayim, Katharina Oguntoye, and Dagmar Schultz's *Farbe bekennen: Afrodeutsche Frauen auf den Spuren ihrer Geschichte* (*Showing Our Colors: Afro-German Women Speak Out*, 1986), and Ayim's important poem collection *Blues in schwarz Weiss* (*Blues in Black and White*, 1995). Initial scholarship in Black German studies began within the discipline of history, by Black German scholars such as Oguntoye and El-Tayeb. These were followed by groundbreaking works by American historians such as Tina Campt and Heide Fehrenbach.[11]

Today, scholars continue to work parallel to artists and activists, by addressing existing knowledge gaps via research rooted in an interdisciplinary context. Sara Lennox, Peggy Piesche, El-Tayeb, Natasha Kelly, Rosemarie Peña, Priscilla Layne, Kira Thurman, Tiffany N. Florvil, and Vanessa Plumly, among others, have provided significant new

---

[9] I use this term in my work on Akın; see Berna Gueneli, *Fatih Akın's Cinema and the New Sound of Europe* (Bloomington: Indiana University Press, 2019), 30, 124.

[10] For a Turkish-German cinema context, see Gueneli, *Fatih Akın's Cinema*, 20. By referring to "Black and POC artists," I would like to address the contribution of specific artists, pointing out underexplored voices and stories in mainstream film and media in Germany. Hagen argues there should be many stories told within German film, including Black, Turkish, or Vietnamese-German (Hagen, Q&A). People have vast backgrounds and bring their individual heritages, languages, and histories to their work. While categories give us tools to discuss developments within a particular field (Black German Studies), they also help us broaden others (German film and media).

[11] Fatima El-Tayeb, *Schwarze Deutsche. Der Dirkurs um Rasse und nationale Identität 1890–1933* (Frankfurt: Campus, 2001); Katharina Oguntoye, *Eine afrodeutsche Geschichte: Zur Lebenssituation von Afrikanern und Afro-Deutschen in Deutschland von 1884 bis 1950* (Berlin: Hoho, 1997); Tina Campt, *Other Germans: Black Germans and the Politics of Race, Gender, and Memory in the Third Reich* (Ann Arbor: University of Michigan Press, 2005); Heide Fehrenbach, *Race After Hitler: Black Occupation Children in Postwar Germany and America* (Princeton, NJ: Princeton University Press, 2005).

insights about Black German art, history, and activism.[12] Scholars and organizations such as the Black German Heritage and Research Association (BGHRA) contribute to the exchange of ideas, theories, and experiences, and advance scholarship.[13] These platforms also provide room for testimonials and creative works, and indicate the growing need for further study in this field. Despite the work of such scholars, and despite the history of Black Germans, which reaches back at least to colonial times,[14] the testimonials by Hagen and Umuhire at the beginning of this chapter exemplify that the portrayal of Black Germans in mainstream media often does not go beyond stereotypical tropes about figures with a "migration background" and has only a limited presence on screen.

The different films I discuss here are all made by Black artists from Berlin. Their fictive and non-fictive work challenges the expectations of mainstream audiences. They make visible a broader range of filmic characters, narratives, and aesthetics of heterogeneity, and engage with notions of identity and belonging in the global city. However, to understand Hagen's and Umuhire's criticism of mainstream media's shortcomings, let us first revisit El-Tayeb's and Kelly's work.

These scholars disentangle the racialized context of Germany and Europe that might have conditioned the exclusion of Black/POC artists

---

[12] See, e.g., Sara Lennox (ed.), *Remapping Black Germany: New Perspectives on Afro-German History, Politics, and Culture* (Amherst: University of Massachusetts Press, 2016); Peggy Piesche, "Inscriptions into the Past, Anticipations of the Future: Audre Lorde and the Black Woman's Movement in Germany," in *Audre Lorde's Transnational Legacies*, ed. Stella Bolaki and Sabine Broeck (Amherst: University of Massachusetts Press, 2016); El-Tayeb, *European Others*; Natasha Kelly, *Millis Erwachen / Milli's Awakening: Schwarze Frauen, Kunst und Widerstand / Black Women, Art and Resistance* (Berlin: Orlanda, 2019); Rosemarie Peña, "Stories Matter: Contextualizing the Black German American Adoptee Experience(s)," in *International Adoption in North American Literature and Culture*, ed. Mark Shackleton (New York: Palgrave MacMillan, 2017); Priscilla Layne, *White Rebels in Black: German Appropriation of Black Popular Culture* (Ann Arbor: University of Michigan Press, 2018); Kira Thurman, "Performing Lieder, Hearing Race: Debating Blackness, Whiteness, and German Identity in Interwar Central Europe," *Journal of the American Musicological Society*, vol. 72, no. 3 (2019): 825–45; Tiffany N. Florvil and Vanessa D. Plumly (eds.), *Rethinking Black German Studies: Approaches, Interventions and Histories* (Oxford: Peter Lang, 2018).

[13] The collective/forum "Diversity, Decolonization, & the German Curriculum" offers another platform.

[14] For discussions of the history of Black Germans, see, e.g., Robbie Aitken and Eve Rosenhaft, *Black Germany: The Making and Unmaking of a Diaspora Community, 1884–1960* (Cambridge: Cambridge University Press, 2013); Patricia Mazón and Reinhild Steingröver (eds.), *Not So Plain as Black and White: Afro-German Culture and History: 1890–2000* (Rochester, NY: University of Rochester Press, 2005).

and their work from mainstream media for so long. El-Tayeb luminously lays bare the underlying racism in Germany's and Europe's self-definition.[15] She calls attention to common misconceptions about European identities, and in particular the "[r]acialized understanding of proper Europeanness, that continues to exclude certain migrants and their descendants," thereby omitting non-white and non-Christian identities.[16] El-Tayeb informs readers about the long history of racialization in Europe.[17] Racist discourse is nothing new, but the continual refabrications of such discourse aid the perpetual construction of a white, Christian national identity.[18]

Certainly, such a conception of Europe is often reflected in the realm of culture. Kelly's artistic academic work on Black German artists aptly illustrates this point. She depicts the obstacles Black German artists have faced since the early postwar period. Her documentary *Millis Erwachen* (*Milli's Awakening*, 2018) provides a captivating filmic example. The title of the film is a reference to the Black model/muse depicted in expressionist artist Ludwig Kirchner's painting *Sleeping Milli* (1911). In her film, Kelly depicts eight Black German women artists across different generations who are active and exercise agency—quite the opposite of the passive depiction of the sleeping Milli in Kirchner's painting. These artists are self-determined, and they provide their own stories about their professional and biographical accomplishments and challenges.[19] El-Tayeb's and Kelly's criticism of the exclusion of certain people of color and their work from the European canon[20] sensitizes us to creatives whose art lies in challenging the status quo of mainstream art, despite the obstacles they often face.

---

[15] El-Tayeb, *European Others*, 12; El-Tayeb, *Undeutsch*: *Die Konstruktion des Anderen in der Postmigrantischen Gesellschaft* (Bielefeld: Transcript, 2016), e.g., 8–11, 14, 149, 157.

[16] El-Tayeb, *European Others*, xii.

[17] El-Tayeb, *European Others*, xiii.

[18] El-Tayeb, *Undeutsch*, 8–11, 14, 149, 157. Saskia Sassen also addresses xenophobic and racist longevity—see "Europe's Migrations: The Numbers and the Passions are Not New," *Third Text*, vol. 20, no. 6 (2006): 635–7.

[19] Kelly discussed her work at the Georgia Institute of Technology in Atlanta on February 25, 2019.

[20] European film/media frequently depict POC characters as others. See Yosefa Loshitzky, *Screening Strangers: Migration and Diaspora in Contemporary European Cinema* (Bloomington: Indiana University Press, 2010); Ipek Çelik, *In Permanent Crisis: Ethnicity in Contemporary European Media and Cinema* (Ann Arbor: University of Michigan Press, 2005).

Overcoming Obstacles

My selection of artists foregrounds independent filmmakers who were able to realize their projects and tell their stories. Yet, independent filmmakers often face challenges that prevent completion of their projects (e.g., access to project funding, festival screenings, and distribution mechanisms).[21] Hagen comments on the presence of "gatekeepers" at all levels who can make or break a film's very existence in different stages. She seeks "to change the system," so that diverse professionals gain access to all positions in the industry.[22] This request is not limited to film: artists from different fields also call for such change, including producer-artist-activist Tyron Ricketts.[23]

One way to overcome obstacles, Hagen states, is to apply to film schools.[24] Black filmmakers who went to DFFB, such as Skip Norman, Auma Obama, and Branwen Okpako, were able to launch their diverse careers from there.[25] Likewise, Turkish-German directors across generations such as Çatak, Büyükatalay, Akın, Tevfik Başer, and Sema Poyraz began their work in film school.[26] Not all artists will be admitted to such institutions, however. Umuhire's application to the HFF Konrad Wolf (Potsdam), for example, was rejected despite the success of her award-winning webseries *Polyglot*, which was touring festivals at that time.[27] Umuhire worked instead with alternative, open-access resources. She screened *Polyglot* through YouTube, and completed the first episode of her self-funded film with the help of family and friends.[28]

Artists like Hagen and Johnson-Spain might have profited from their previous work and connections made in the film industry. Hagen switched from a successful acting career to directing. Such paths to filmmaking do not eliminate the question of funding—Hagen uses her

---

[21] Hagen, Johnson-Spain, WiG.
[22] Hagen, WiG; Q&A.
[23] Ricketts, "Black Spaces: Black Voices."
[24] Hagen, WiG.
[25] Priscilla Layne, "All That Glitters *Isn't* Gold: Auma Obama's Nightmare of Postunification Germany," *Camera Obscura*, vol. 33, no. 3 (2018): 75–101.
[26] Çatak (Hamburg Media School) and Büyükatalay (Kunsthochschule für Medien, Cologne) began their work as students and participated in festivals. Çatak's graduation short, *Sadakat* (Fidelity, 2014), received the Student Academy Award for Best Foreign Film, among other prizes, which brought him global attention. Büyükatalay won the Berlinale's Best First Feature Award in 2019 with his graduation film, *Oray* (2019). Akın went to the Hochschule für bildende Künste (HFBK, Hamburg), where he made *Kurz und Schmerzlos* (1998) and *Im Juli* (2000). Başer, a fellow HFBK graduate, also started his career in school. Actress Sema Poyraz's beginnings were at the DFFB in Potsdam. Her graduation film, *Gölge* (Schatten, 1980), is arguably the first Turkish-German film.
[27] Umuhire, email message to author, September 9, 2018.
[28] Umuhire, email message to author, September 9, 2018.

own production company, Equality Film—but they might offer initial help. Johnson-Spain worked as a scenic painter in film and teaches at the film university in Babelsberg.[29] Johnson-Spain indicates that even the choice of genre can make a difference. A documentary, especially Black documentaries, which often are expected to be biographical, are generally associated with lower costs than feature films and might generate more interest with gatekeepers.[30]

Three Case Studies
What ultimately crystallizes in *Polyglot*, *Becoming Black*, and *At Second Glance*, in addition to their portrayals of previously untold stories, is that the filmic urban space—Berlin—with its manifold and diverse local and global connections, becomes the chosen site for identification, in particular, for Black Germans, more so than any national entity. To illustrate this, I focus on two interconnected aspects that in my view are intrinsically reflective of a contemporary global, urban experience, and that also unite these films and filmic characters. First, I emphasize the treatment of the notion of belonging, which Hagen herself mentioned specifically as a recurring thematic feature of her films, and which I also see explicitly revealed in *Polyglot* and *Becoming Black*. Second, and closely related to the first point, I examine the particular portrayal of the local and global city of Berlin and its citizens. Each filmic setting depicts an individualized, specific locality of the protagonists. Simultaneously, the works by these filmmakers show that their individual Berlin neighborhoods have multiple connections to other places, beyond Berlin, Germany, and Europe, thus creating a complex web of multifaceted networks.

On the one hand, such aestheticized connections between places bring to mind Sassen's reflections on the concrete economic and spatial implications of globalization after the 1980s, particularly as they relate to and transform subnational spaces like cities and regions.[31] Sassen further applied her concept of networks to human movements and the flow of people. Such globalized connections/networks certainly are also reflected in the city life and everyday experiences of individuals.[32] On the other hand, these connections evoke cultural geographer Doreen Massey's theoretical contemplations about space. Massey explains that these connections from one place to another are indeed how spaces and places are (re)created over time.

---

[29] Becoming Black (website), becomingblack.de/ines-johnson-spain-2.
[30] Johnson-Spain, WiG.
[31] Saskia Sassen (ed.), *Global Networks: Linked Cities* (New York: Routledge, 2016).
[32] Saskia Sassen, *Guests and Aliens* (New York: The New Press, 1999).

In her work, Massey clarifies that space refers to real places and entities, and comes into being through interrelations, interconnections of people, places, and objects. Arguing for a progressive, global idea of place, Massey states:

> Instead [...] of thinking of places as areas with boundaries around, they can be imagined as articulated moments in networks of social relations and understandings, but where a large proportion of those relations, experiences and understandings are constructed on a far larger scale than what we happen to define for that moment as the place itself, whether that be a street, or a region or even a continent.[33]

Massey says that in our frantic, global world there is a desire for "fixity," and a "security of identity." Such an idea of a homogenous locality creates boundaries.[34] Yet, with her "progressive sense of place," Massey maintains that it is ultimately the multiplicity of connections and networks that create a place.[35] She emphasizes that the "geography of social relations is changing" and that "such relations are increasingly stretched out over space."[36]

Umuhire's, Johnson-Spain's, and Hagen's filmic depictions of Berlin neighborhoods and the sense of belonging they create for their characters reiterate Massey's concept of place in film. According to Massey, it is not "some long internalized history" that constructs a place, but "a particular constellation of social relations, meeting and weaving together at a particular locus."[37] That is, if we follow Massey, "place" is not static, but fluctuates and is continuously reproduced; there are no fixed margins; and, finally, places, like our identities, are to be conceived as multiple.

After all, Berlin is not only the site of Germany's tumultuous sociopolitical history of the twentieth century (e.g. capital of the Weimar democracy, of fascism, communism, and reunified Germany; city of Magnus Hirschfeld's LGBTQ+ activism; home of Audre Lorde's Berlin

---

[33] Doreen Massey, "A Global Sense of Place," in *The Cultural Geography Reader*, ed. Timothy Oakes and Patricia Price (New York: Routledge, 2008), 262.
[34] Massey, "A Global Sense," 260, 261.
[35] Massey, "A Global Sense," 261.
[36] Massey, "A Global Sense," 262.
[37] "It is a sense of place, an understanding of 'its character,' which can only be constructed by linking that place to places beyond. A progressive sense of place would recognize that, without being threatened by it." Massey, "A Global Sense," 262.

years which originated much Black German discourse and activism; a Turkish-German cultural center, and much more), but also home to individuals who exist within and in addition to these larger phenomena with their own unique connections to other people, places, and histories that ultimately create the complex fabric of Berlin and Berliners.

Sassen's socio-economic and Massey's cultural-geographic contemplations on globalized connectivity are certainly reflected in these films; and, as we navigate the filmic narrative, we might understand better why the global city Berlin, in lieu of the nation, emerges as the preferred space of identification for several transnational urbanites in these films.

Close-up: *Polyglot*

Umuhire's webseries *Polyglot* features the Rwandan-German poet Amanda/Papaya in Berlin and London.[38] I will discuss the first two episodes, "The Bewerbungsgespräch" ("interview") and "Le Mal du Pays" ("Homesickness"), which center on contemporary Berliners and Berlin by depicting Amanda's arrival and life in the city.[39] Through Amanda's POV, the first episode portrays the theme of belonging. We follow the protagonist—who just moved to the city—traversing Berlin, scouting for a new apartment. While she navigates Berlin via the subway and on foot, the camera captures sights of the town that include iconic images such as the TV tower at Alexanderplatz and the Berlin public transportation system, but also graffiti and tagged walls, the facades of nineteenth-century apartment buildings, multiple satellite dishes on balconies associated with migrant media, independent storefronts, images of advertisements, and political messages on the streets. After the viewer becomes familiar with a particular district of Berlin—by seeing close-ups and images of a specific neighborhood—Amanda finally enters an apartment. She interviews successfully with her future roommates. The cosmopolitan roommates, each speaking English with a different accent, eventually welcome Amanda to her new home. The film ends with a calm, friendly scene with the warm light of paper lanterns in the evening. The roommates sit around the kitchen table, smoke, drink beer, and celebrate Amanda's art, as she performs one of

---

[38] The discussion on *Polyglot* is a revised version of my analysis in "Young, Diverse, and Polyglot: Ilker Çatak and Amelia Umuhire Track the New Urban Sound of Europe," in *Minority Discourses in Germany Since 1990*, ed. Ela Gezen, Priscilla Layne, and Jonathan Skolnik (New York: Berghahn, 2022), 172–95.

[39] See also Gabi Kathöfer and Beverly Weber, "Heimat, Sustainability, Community: A Conversation with Karina Griffith and Peggy Piesche," *Seminar*, vol. 54, no. 4 (November 2018): 418–27.

her poems. As a young, creative, mobile artist she belongs, as do they, to the apartment, the neighborhood, and the city.

Berlin is perpetually transforming due to political, economic, or social changes, and this is visualized in *Polyglot* through urban developments, street art, and through the residents who make this fluid, mobile, transnational experience of the place perceptible.[40] The film aesthetically reiterates the transformations of Berlin and Berliners it portrays. That is, Amanda's own move into the city and to her apartment, her multilingual new roommates, her navigating of Berlin's streets, use of the public transportation, as well as the short-lived street art on public spaces, are all indications of fluctuations that paradoxically can create a specific place of belonging for the new, transnational, urban residents.

The notion of longing for human relationships, and for belonging to places, is introduced in the first episode and more overtly attended to in the second, where the tone is less light and more emotional. "Le Mal du Pays" addresses feelings of loneliness and of a non-normative, multidirectional belonging that showcases the transnational characteristics of the city and its people. The film opens with various text messages that the protagonist writes and deletes, trying to express emotional turmoil (in English). The soundtrack features Belgian-Rwandan Cécile Kayirebwa's song "Marebe,"[41] which creates a connection between Berlin and Rwanda, and specifically to Rwandan exiles. Amanda feels low and frustrated, unable to express her emotions of homesickness and loneliness via text messages.

This episode shows segments of Amanda's life in Berlin that explain her feelings visually. We see her alone, smoking, looking out of her apartment window into the courtyard, trying to follow a YouTube video about attending to her hair, and finally taking a bus ride across Berlin to a Black German operated specialty store to purchase hair products. The second half of the film is even more emotionally laden and depicts Amanda with her hairdresser. The scene between the two Black German women allows Amanda to get a practical need resolved (her hair care), but also allows her to experience a physical and emotional closeness to a fellow Berliner who allows her to express and externalize an

---

[40] In 1910, cultural critic Karl Scheffler wrote that Berlin is always in the making, "forever becoming." Kurt Scheffler quoted in Harald Neumeyer, *Der Flaneur: Konzeptionen der Moderne* (Wurzburg: Königshausen & Neumann: 1999), 299.

[41] From Kayirebwa's album *Interuro* (Ceka, 2015; vol. 1, 1981). The artist, who lives in Belgium, says, "I want to at least work with young Rwandans who are passionate about art, so that I share and pass on the cultural heritage." Quoted in Julius Bizimungu, "Rwandan Music in Exile," Music in Africa, https://www.musicinafrica.net/magazine/rwandan-music-exile.

emotion she was not able to utter before. With only a few words, and with physical closeness, together they negotiate "belonging."

This scene is the climax of an emotional journey Amanda undertakes through Berlin. The physical closeness of the women mirrors their emotional proximity. Amanda sits on the floor, with her back leaning toward the hairdresser. They have comparable backgrounds (both left their birth countries and experienced loss or separation from loved ones). The indoor setting is calm and a contrast to the city scenes depicting busy traffic and city dwellers. In that silence the understanding between the two women emerges, starting with the hair care, that becomes caressing. The combing of the hair turns into soothing, while the camera supports this visually through close-ups of hair, hands, tears, and faces.

Ultimately, *Polyglot* subtly connects Berlin and Berliners to a much wider-reaching web of histories, places, and people, thereby transforming the diverse urban space to a place of potential solace. The women speak French, a language that evokes the Belgian (and German) colonial past, which are ultimately remembered and felt in contemporary Berlin. The Rwandan song "Marebe," which Amanda listened to earlier, concludes this scene. Through its use of language (French, German with various accents, English), the references to Rwanda in the conversation between the two women, and the diegetic/non-diegetic soundtrack of "Marebe," *Polyglot* establishes a clear connection to Rwanda, its colonial history, a history of migration, of violence, as well as to its diasporic community (we learn that Amanda's family, whom she misses, is spread out over the world). But, in Berlin, where these memories and experiences come together, Amanda is also able to find human company and share her feelings.

The first two episodes show that as a new Berlin resident, Amanda participates in and actively shapes a collective, multilingual, and multiethnic urban space. *Polyglot* introduces new audiovisual experiences to the screen, from Amanda's traversing of the city in the first episode, to her troubled text messages, and the physical and emotional closeness she feels to the Black German hairdresser in the second episode. Ultimately, this quasi-documentary-style webseries intimately displays the particular experiences of a young Black artist as she navigates her new hometown. The artist's everyday life, thoughts, and actions in Berlin subtly depict the transnational connections of one particular individual to other places and people across Europe and elsewhere. At the same time, as an individual, she expresses universal human experiences of joy, creativity, friendship, loneliness, loss, and melancholy, which posits her as a well-rounded, relatable character, complex and impervious to stereotyping. This is the result of Umuhire's resistance to using clichéd plots, figures, settings, and sounds often associated with POC and Black filmic characters, as Umuhire's above-mentioned quote addresses.[42] In this context, *Polyglot* actor and poet Amanda Mukasonga says about her character that "if I were in a TV show, normally, as me, a Black woman, I wouldn't get to be this real, as this 3D, as deep as a character."[43]

Close-up: *Becoming Black*

Berlin artist Ines Johnson-Spain arguably uses one of the most personal/direct formats to address the topic of belonging: the autobiographical documentary. Johnson-Spain's *Becoming Black* recalls Philippe Lejeune's concept of the "autobiographical pact." According to Lejeune, due to the matching name of the "author" and the "character" in the autobiographical text, the reader expects authenticity of autobiographical writing: there is an implied understanding and expectation on the part of the reader (or viewer) that the author tells their "real" story, without fabrication.[44] This is certainly a contested point. The director makes choices regarding inclusions and exclusions, and a film's editing certainly creates a specific story, a set of choices of what the director/author chooses to reveal or conceal.[45]

Johnson-Spain does not distinguish between experimental, documentary, and fiction film, however; she sees the boundaries between these genres as more "fluid," maintaining that she invents "stories by discovering them in [her] surrounding[s]." Echoing Hagen's statement, Johnson-Spain declares, "we were looking for stories we couldn't see in the film world."[46] This includes her own personal story, which includes topics not only generally underexplored in media, history, and the public sphere, but also a history previously undiscussed in her own family.

Notwithstanding our positioning as viewers—whether or not we feel bound to the "autobiographical pact," or subscribe to Johnson-Spain's claims about the fluidity of genre—*Becoming Black* is, at its core, an autobiographical documentary that visualizes the local and global connections of a particular Berliner. The film tells the story of Johnson-Spain's

---

[42] For a reference to *Polyglot* in the context of a new heterogeneous German and European film aesthetic, see, Gueneli, *Fatih Akın's Cinema*, 3; Gueneli, "Young, Diverse, and Polyglot."
[43] Quoted in Jennifer Sefa-Boakye, "'Polyglot,' A New Web Series on Young Creatives of Color in Berlin," Okayafrica, June 30, 2015, http://www.okayafrica.com/polyglot-webseries-amelia-umuhire/.
[44] Sidonie Smith and Julia Watson discuss Phillippe Lejeune's theory in *A Guide for Interpreting Life Narratives: Reading Autobiography* (Minneapolis: University of Minnesota Press, 2010), 207.
[45] Hagen, WiG.
[46] Johnson-Spain, WiG.

East German upbringing in a white family and the story of her discovery of her biological Black family, relayed through the eyes of multiple, transnational interlocutors. As the film unfolds, we see a Black German woman who talks to family members to uncover the missing and suppressed parts of her family history. Johnson-Spain grew up in East Germany without knowledge of half of her heritage. We learn that her biological father came from Togo to study in Bernau (close to Berlin) in the GDR during the Cold War. There he met Johnson-Spain's German mother, Sigrid. The couple's romantic relationship did not last, and Ines was born and grew up with her mother, stepfather, and half-brother, after a brief time in an orphanage in the GDR during the 1960s. Her skin color was not discussed, and when she inquired about it, it was quickly dismissed as something that just happens in nature.

Becoming Black provides an audiovisual document that meticulously recreates an individual and transnational family history, but it is also part of a more universal German history. Johnson-Spain's family, which the film explores in intimate conversations and imagery, has links to East German history (and especially to racial discourses and international exchange in the GDR) as well as to German history in general (e.g., to divided families and a divided Germany). The film also re-presents postwar grappling with the concepts of Germanness and race, and also with German colonial history. Through visits, interviews, and photographs, the documentary connects Johnson-Spain to different people, places, and stories. She meets and talks to family members in former East Germany, in Togo, and in now-unified Germany (her father and her ten half-siblings live or lived in the former West Germany). They speak French and German in different dialects and accents. Thereby, the film extends the protagonists' connections from Berlin to other regions of Germany and the globe.

Becoming Black highlights transnational connections between localities/regions. For Johnson-Spain, the category of the national is inherently problematic: after all, the country she was born in, the GDR, no longer exists, and the country her father came from, Togo, has changed since the Cold War, as did the FRG.[47] Johnson-Spain is similar to Hagen in this sense. Hagen states, "All my films are based on my identity, which is shaped by my heritage and my life in Lagos, Hamburg, Vienna, and Berlin. These four cities are within me and formed me in a way that is clearer than if I would name Germany and Nigeria."[48] Such notions are reflected in Johnson-Spain's and Umuhire's work, which displays a particular interest in the local neighborhoods, where people live, walk,

---

[47] Johnson-Spain, WiG.
[48] Hagen, email message to author; Hagen, WiG.

and create private and personal spaces with extensions to other places.[49] These locations are visualized in *Becoming Black* in an assembly of and cross-cutting between interior and exterior spaces specific to the individual interlocutors, whether these are at Togolese beaches, in the living rooms of East German family members, or on a western German heath with Johnson-Spain's half-siblings.

Ultimately, while *Becoming Black* is an emotional, intimate journey of self-discovery, it is also a story to which not only many East Germans of color might be able to relate, but to which nearly anyone who has an affiliation with multiple places, hi/stories, and people might identify. Ultimately, the intricate social, historical, and geo-political connections which the protagonist creates render the city of Berlin and the Berliner as simultaneously local and global.

Close-up: *At Second Glance*

An older person, approximately in his sixties, is looking down into the courtyard from his apartment window in Berlin. He sees a child and her father, who are calling a friend. From his window the elderly person yells at them to be quiet. His tone is unfriendly. He repeats his demand multiple times, as the party in the courtyard is joined by their friend.

This scene recalls the stereotypical German figure of the Berliner with his rude *Berliner Schnauze* (dialect). In more general terms, the older apartment-dweller evokes the trope of the unfriendly *Hausmeister* (janitor) in apartment buildings, typically imagined as a white, older male, surveilling his apartment's courtyard, enforcing quiet hours, and admonishing neighbors (particularly children) to be quiet. Yet, in *At Second Glance* the person exhibiting this kind of behavior is not white, but an elderly Black man by the name of "Herr Meyer."

In *At Second Glance*, Hagen manages to challenge our preconceptions as viewers. First, the character of Herr Meyer confronts us indirectly with an older generation of Black Germans who have long been part of German society, but who have been largely disregarded in German screen culture up to now. Herr Meyer is capable of being just as rude as his stereotypical white counterparts. The character's equally stereotypical name, "Herr Meyer," reveals yet another emblematic phenomenon of Hagen's film: how she plays with names and identity. Several figures, played by Black actors, have Germanic-sounding names such as Ulf, Falk, Antje, and Till. These are names that consumers of mainstream German media probably do not immediately associate with Black characters. Hagen's use of names hints at individual, untold

---

[49] For similar arguments in a Turkish-German cinema context, see Gueneli, *Fatih Akın's Cinema*, 46–7, 64–5.

stories about the characters who can be indirectly intertwined into the narrative. Specifically, we are implicitly reminded (or, we learn) that it is quite common in formerly colonized regions—including today's Cameroon and Nigeria—to find so-called German-sounding names among the Black inhabitants.[50]

Hagen also breaks with the commonly expected audiovisual composition of mainstream German screen culture, by diversifying her white and Black characters. As Hagen states, the film is often perceived as a Black film, in spite of the fact that half of the actors are white. She asserts that this perception is caused by mainstream films, which often limit POC and Black actors to no more than one or two stereotypical roles. As a consequence, audiences generally are not used to a more evenly balanced cast of characters.[51] Hagen's film not only has a cast which is 50 percent Black, but its characters have vastly different economic, generational, and educational backgrounds. While Hagen diversifies the film's cast on the formal/production level, the film's narrative—which does not primarily engage with questions of race and ethnicity, as Olivia Landry has observed[52]—continues to tell a universal narrative about human relationships and a longing to belong. The characters' skin color is thereby completely normalized.

All of the characters, individual differences notwithstanding, are united by their longing for a relationship, for love and attention, and for belonging. They all suffer from various forms of loneliness, either because they separated from or lost a partner (Falk, Kay), have an incompatible sexual and/or emotional partner (Antje, Till), or because they have a new disability (blindness) that causes them to shy away from interpersonal relationships (Kay, Elena). Ultimately, through human connections, the main characters do reach a desired place of comfort. The film shows this arrival at an interpersonal, safe place in particular through scenes that depict warm indoor spaces, which is opposed to the monochromatic outdoor scenes consisting largely of rainy, wintry city imagery.

A case in point: one scene depicts roommates and taxi driver colleagues Ulf and Frank having dinner at their home together with Frank's

---

[50] Hagen, Q&A.
[51] Hagen, Q&A.
[52] Engaging with the notions of colorblindness, visibility, invisibility, and hypervisibility, Olivia Landry stresses that the film does not "address race directly"; in fact, race appears to be of "little or no preoccupation to the narrative." Landry states that Hagen resists "identity politics": "A merging of racial difference and queerness with disability and able-bodiedness creates a context and approach of proliferation and multiplicity that works against the ascendency of whiteness, able-bodiedness and heterosexuality." Olivia Landry, "Color/blindness in Sheri Hagen's *Auf den zweiten Blick*," *Black Camera*, vol. 9, no. 1 (Fall 2017): 63, 71.

daughter and with Kay, a radio moderator. Kay recently has lost her vision in a car accident; her ex-boyfriend caused the accident and abandoned her afterwards. The warm, interior colors, soft textures, and the physical closeness of the characters indicate an initiation of human contact, friendship, and intimacy. The relationship between Falk and Kay begins to develop and the film ends with them as a romantic couple.

Set against the film's warm indoor settings, the lonely characters Benjamin and Elena also get closer to each other. Benjamin first visits Elena, a psychologist, for health reasons. Elena—in denial about her own deteriorating eyesight—and Benjamin—open about his blindness and the senses that are more pronounced for him as a result (touch, sound, etc.)—ultimately fall in love. Not only does Elena slowly come closer to accepting her progressing disability through Benjamin, but she also finds a romantic partner in him. Benjamin, in turn, is seemingly cured of his psychological condition once the romantic relationship begins. Although the film ends with an accident—Benjamin is run over by a car and the outcome of the accident for him is left uncertain—Elena and Benjamin's loving relationship is foregrounded. Elena rushes to Benjamin's side and accompanies him to the hospital, a reversal of the accident at the beginning of the movie, which separated Kay from her former partner and which left her similarly emotionally abandoned until she met Falk.

The third romantic relationship the film depicts is the one of Pan, a blind piano tuner, who meets Till, an owner of an antiques store. Till is in an unhappy relationship with Antje, and engages in adulterous relationships with men. Pan and Till's partnership develops out of their initial physical and musical connection (they play piano together). After initial misunderstandings, they work toward being a romantic couple by the end of the film.

By means of these three relationships, the film brings together differently-abled bodies, Black and white Berliners, different economic, professional, and educational backgrounds, as well as different generations of Berliners. The choices made by the director not only diversify filmic images of the main characters, but also help to paint a multiethnic, complex image of the city of Berlin. In Hagen's rendition of the city, the local and the global overlap and connect in the form of the film's diverse ensemble of Berlin residents.

The heterogeneous, urban filmic imaginary transforms, once more, to a place where solace can be found. *At Second Glance* portrays Berlin as a cold, monochromatic, rainy, impersonal city replete with heavy city traffic, busy public transportation, and industrial sites. Nonetheless, Berlin is also depicted as a place with personal, local neighborhoods, where the protagonists live, work, share their feelings, and find love. Berlin is depicted as a mix of nineteenth-century and modern buildings, and the camera dwells on the building facades behind which the protagonists' lives unfold. The characters' homes' interiors highlight their individual tastes and styles, whether cold, minimalist, and modern like Antje's home, or crowded, colorful, and warm like Falk's home. Hagen's Berliners play at individual local playgrounds, sit in apartment courtyards, and walk in streets that connote actual neighborhoods and create unique atmospheres.

Crucially, the manifold global connections of Berlin are subtly woven into the fabric of the story and the characters. This rendition of Berlin and its inhabitants might have colonial, postwar, or migratory experiences and histories that connect them to places outside of Berlin and Germany, but these are implied and not explicitly thematized. In this way, these complex connections are normalized and not used to set the characters apart. Compared to the previous examples I discussed above, where these connections take center stage, they merely serve as a backdrop in Hagen's film.

Conclusion

Films such as *Polyglot*, *Becoming Black*, and *At Second Glance* diversify and infuse German media narratives by engaging with underexplored stories of a diverse society with new vigor. One way to reflect and engage with a diverse society is to normalize multi-ethnicity and multilingualism in all aspects of life. In the films discussed here, diverse filmic characters, their interactions and travels, and their links to places in and beyond Berlin depict life in a globalized world. Individual, global citizens live in and connect to their local neighborhoods in Germany, as much as to Togo, or elsewhere, and make this experience available to the audience.

Through their individual experiences, Black and other (non-)marginalized characters navigate through their city as locals and actively shape this multilingual and multi-ethnic urban space. Through them (Amanda in *Polyglot*, Ines in *Becoming Black*, and Kay, Falk, and Ulf in *At Second Glance*), transnational connections to other places and people across the globe are negotiated, while their own, local belonging to Berlin is emphasized. Hence, the films transcend traditional, national parameters and foreground the city as a place where belonging is negotiated individually. Berlin on screen—where transnational identities are core components—is exposed and experienced as a space in the sense of Doreen Massey's thinking on the subject, as a way that connects the web of individual histories, memories, and experiences of the characters, navigating between the local and the global.

Through the work of artists like Umuhire, Johnson-Spain, and Hagen, we not only begin to see "this big part of Germany and Berlin" a little bit less "marginalized in media," but we also can locate Black Berliners as core citizens in the transnational global city. Black and POC artists are creating multi-ethnic, multilingual films that are reflective of a multifaceted, transnational concept of German/European life and media. These artists' efforts allow for unexoticized, diverse casts (including Black Germans/Black Europeans, Turkish Germans, differently abled Germans, etc.), a specific diverse urban setting (a Berlin with transnational connections), and a diverse soundtrack (multiple languages, different accents and dialects from European and non-European places, e.g., Rwanda and Togo). The protagonists find belonging in the global city, and the viewer is invited to experience an inclusive and connected Berlin.

Such efforts recently have become more broadly visible. At the beginning of this chapter, I referred to artists such as Sammy Delux and Hagen who remarked on the missing "role models" for Black and POC children in mainstream media. Perhaps influenced by the work of the Black artists discussed above, we might in fact begin to notice small, but relevant recent changes in mainstream media, including children's shows. Shows such as the Westdeutscher Rundfunk's popular *Die Sendung mit der Maus* (1971–present), for example, now feature journalist Clarissa Corrêa da Silva, who grew up in Brazil and Germany, and musician Shary Reeves, who grew up in Cologne and New York, among their teams of moderators.[53] Such shows seem to have recognized and attempted to reflect the reality of their audiences by beginning to provide diverse "role models" for children.[54]

Ultimately, the films discussed here, the work by other Black artists that focus on Black and POC art and histories,[55] and even the changing casts in mainstream children's shows engage, in multiple ways, with

---

[53] "Die Sendung mit der Maus," WDR, https://kinder.wdr.de/tv/wissen-macht-ah/ahteam/wma-shary-100.html.

[54] See also *Pia und die wilden Tiere* (2020–present), hosted by Pia Amofa-Antwi, on BR (Bayrischer Rundfunk), "Natur und Tierreportagen für Kinder," BR Kinder, November 29, 2020, https://www.br.de/kinder/schauen/anna-paula-pia-wilde-tiere-und-natur/paula-anna-und-die-wilden-tiere-104.html.

[55] From television talk shows to cultural and academic venues, we observe a revived debate around Black art and activism, and about racism and discrimination against Black and POC residents in Germany/Europe. Such intensified debates certainly were influenced by the Black Lives Matter protest movement across the USA, motivated in part by the killing of George Floyd, on May 25, 2020, and by other deaths at the hands of police before and after. This had resonance in Germany and led to an increased public reconsideration of racism, racial profiling, and police violence in Europe—this debate also has contributed to a new public discourse on representation, inclusivity, and diversity in media and elsewhere in public life. See Billy Perrigo and Mélissa Godin, "Racism Is Surging in Germany. Tens of Thousands Are Taking to the Streets to Call for Justice," *Time*, June 10, 2020, time.com/5851165/germany-anti-racism-protests/.

contemporary questions and debates. These hopefully will lead in the future to more widely pursued critical engagement with questions related to equity, inclusivity, and representation in German media and public life.

Works Cited

Adelson, Leslie. *The Turkish Turn in Contemporary German Literature* (New York: Palgrave MacMillan, 2005).

Aitken, Robbie, and Eve Rosenhaft. *Black Germany: The Making and Unmaking of a Diaspora Community, 1884–1960* (Cambridge: Cambridge University Press, 2013).

Ayim, May. *Blues in schwarz Weiss* (Berlin: Orlanda, 2005).

Bizimungu, Julius. "Rwandan Music in Exile," *Music Africa*, March 8, 2016, www.musicinafrica.net/magazine/rwandan-music-exile.

Campt, Tina. *Other Germans: Black Germans and the Politics of Race, Gender, and Memory in the Third Reich* (Ann Arbor: University of Michigan Press, 2005).

Çelik, Ipek A. *In Permanent Crisis: Ethnicity in Contemporary European Media and Cinema* (Ann Arbor: University of Michigan Press, 2015).

El-Tayeb, Fatima. *Schwarze Deutsche. Der Diskurs um Rasse und nationale Identität 1890–1933* (Frankfurt: Campus, 2001).

El-Tayeb, Fatima. *European Others: Queering Ethnicity in Postnational Europe* (Minneapolis: University of Minnesota Press, 2011).

El-Tayeb, Fatima. *Undeutsch: Die Konstruktion des Anderen in der Postmigrantischen Gesellschaft* (Bielefeld: Transcript, 2016).

Fehrenbach, Heide. *Race After Hitler: Black Occupation Children in Postwar Germany and America* (Princeton, NJ: Princeton University Press, 2005).

Florvil, Tiffany N. *Mobilizing Black Germany: Afro-German Women and the Making of a Transnational Movement* (Urbana: University of Illinois Press, 2020).

Florvil, Tiffany N., and Vanessa D. Plumly, eds. *Rethinking Black German Studies: Approaches, Interventions and Histories* (Oxford: Peter Lang, 2018).

Gezen, Ela. *Brecht, Turkish Theater, and Turkish-German Literature: Reception, Adaptation, and Innovation After 1960* (Rochester, NY: Camden House, 2018).

Göktürk, Deniz. "World Cinema Goes Digital: Looking at Europe from the Other Shore," in *Turkish German Cinema in the New Millennium*, ed. Sabine Hake and Barbara Mennel (New York: Berghahn, 2021), 198–211.

Gueneli, Berna. *Fatih Akın's Cinema and the New Sound of Europe* (Bloomington: Indiana University Press, 2019).

Gueneli, Berna. "Young, Diverse, and Polyglot: Ilker Çatak and Amelia Umuhire Track the New Urban Sound of Europe," in *Minority Discourses in Germany Since 1990*, ed. Ela Gezen, Priscilla Layne, and Jonathan Skolnik (New York: Berghahn, 2022), 172–95.

Halle, Randall. *German Film After Germany: Toward a Transnational Aesthetic* (Urbana: University of Illinois Press, 2008).

Kathöfer, Gabi, and Beverly Weber, "Heimat, Sustainability, Community: A Conversation with Karina Griffith and Peggy Piesche," *Seminar*, vol. 54, no. 4 (November 2018): 418–27.

Kelly, Natasha. *Afrokultur: "der raum zwischen gestern und morgen"* (Munster: Unrast, 2018).

Kelly, Natasha. *Millis Erwachen / Milli's Awakening: Schwarze Frauen, Kunst und Widerstand / Black Woman, Art and Resistance* (Berlin: Orlanda, 2019).

Konuk, Kader. *Identitäten im Prozeß: Literatur von Autorinnen aus und in der Türkei in deutscher, englischer und türkischer Sprache* (Essen: Die Blaue Eule, 2001).
Landry, Olivia. "Color/blindness in Sheri Hagen's *Auf den zweiten Blick*," *Black Camera*, vol 9, no. 1 (Fall 2017): 62–79.
Layne, Priscilla. "All That Glitters *Isn't* Gold: Auma Obama's Nightmare of Postunification Germany," *Camera Obscura*, vol. 33, no. 3 (2018): 75–101.
Layne, Priscilla. *White Rebels in Black: German Appropriation of Black Popular Culture* (Ann Arbor: University of Michigan Press, 2018).
Lennox, Sara, ed. *Remapping Black Germany: New Perspectives on Afro-German History, Politics, and Culture* (Amherst: University of Massachusetts Press, 2016).
Loshitzky, Yosefa. *Screening Strangers: Migration and Diaspora in Contemporary European Cinema* (Bloomington: Indiana University Press, 2010).
Mani, B. Venkat. *Cosmopolitical Claims: Turkish-German Literature from Nadolny to Pamuk* (Iowa City: University of Iowa Press, 2007).
Massey, Doreen. "A Global Sense of Place," in *The Cultural Geography Reader*, ed. Timothy Oakes and Patricia Price (New York: Routledge, 2008), 257–63.
Mazón, Patricia, and Reinhild Steingröver, eds. *Not So Plain as Black and White: Afro-German Culture and History: 1890–2000* (Rochester, NY: University of Rochester Press, 2005).
Mennel, Barbara. "Überkreuzungen in globaler Zeit und globalem Raum in Fatih Akıns Auf der anderen Seite," in *Kultur als Ereignis*, ed. Özkan Ezli (Bielefeld: Transcript, 2010), 95–118.
Neumeyer, Harald. *Der Flaneur: Konzeptionen der Moderne* (Wurzburg: Königshausen & Neumann, 1999).
Oguntoye, Katharina. *Eine afro-deutsche Geschichte: Zur Lebenssituation von Afrikanern und Afro-Deutschen in Deutschland von 1884 bis 1950* (Berlin: Hoho, 1997).
Opitz, May, Katharina Oguntoye, and Dagmar Schultz, eds. *Farbe bekennen: Afro-deutsche Frauen auf den Spuren ihrer Geschicht* (Berlin: Orlanda, 1986; Frankfurt am Main: Fischer, 1992).
Peña, Rosemarie. "Stories Matter: Contextualizing the Black German American Adoptee Experience(s)," in *International Adoption in North American Literature and Culture*, ed. Mark Shackleton (New York: Palgrave McMillan, 2017), 197–220.
Perrigo, Billy, and Mélissa Godin. "Racism is Surging in Germany. Tens of Thousands Are Taking to the Streets to Call for Justice," *Time*, June 10, 2020, time.com/5851165/germany-anti-racism-protests/.
Piesche, Peggy. "Inscriptions into the Past, Anticipations of the Future: Audre Lorde and the Black Woman's Movement in Germany," in *Audre Lorde's Transnational Legacies*, ed. Stella Bolaki and Sabine Broeck (Amherst: University of Massachusetts Press, 2016).
Sassen, Saskia. *Guests and Aliens* (New York: New Press, 1999).
Sassen, Saskia. "Europe's Migrations: The Numbers and the Passions are Not New," *Third Text*, vol. 20, no. 6 (November 2006): 635–45.
Sassen, Saskia, ed., *Global Networks: Linked Cities*, 2nd ed. (New York: Routledge, 2016).
Sefa-Boakye, Jennifer. "'Polyglot,' A New Web Series on Young Creatives of Color in Berlin," *Okayafrica*, June 30, 2015, www.okayafrica.com/polyglot-webseries-amelia-umuhire/.
Seyhan, Azade. *Writing Outside the Nation* (Princeton, NJ: Princeton University Press, 2000).

Sieg, Katrin. *Choreographing the Global in European Cinema and Theater* (New York: Palgrave MacMillan, 2008).

Smith, Sidonie, and Julia Watson. *A Guide for Interpreting Life Narratives: Reading Autobiography*, 2nd ed. (Minneapolis: University of Minnesota Press, 2010).

Thurman, Kira. "Performing Lieder, Hearing Race: Debating Blackness, Whiteness, and German Identity in Interwar Central Europe," *Journal of the American Musicological Society*, vol. 72, no. 3 (Fall 2019): 825–45.

Fourteen Bertolt Brecht's *Me-ti* or the Aesthetics of Translation: Universal Love, Mutual Benefits, and Transience

Chunjie Zhang

Mi-en-leh taught: Introducing democracy can lead to dictatorship; introducing dictatorship can lead to democracy.

[Mi-en-leh lehrte: Das Einführen der Demokratie kann zur Einführung der Diktatur führen. Das Einführen der Diktatur kann zur Demokratie führen.][1]

Bertolt Brecht's aphorism in *Me-ti. Buch der Wendungen* (*Me-ti. Book of Transformation and Usage*) expresses the dialectic of two seemingly antithetical political systems.[2] Mi-en-leh is meant to be Lenin, whose name Brecht reinvents in a Chinese-like style. Likewise, the book itself is allegedly Brecht's own German "translation" of *Mozi*, a book of ancient Chinese philosophy of Mohism, from an English translation. Yet Brecht's

---

[1] Antony Tatlow (ed.), *Bertolt Brecht's Me-ti: Book of Interventions in the Flow of Things* (London: Bloomsbury, 2016), 85; Bertolt Brecht, "Prosa 3. Sammlungen und Dialoge," in *Bertolt Brecht Werke. Berliner und Frankfurter Ausgabe*, ed. Jan Knopf (Berlin, Weimar, and Frankfurt am Main: Aufbau/Suhrkamp, 1995), 88.

[2] I translate the word *Wendung* as both transformation, in terms of "wenden," and usage, in terms of "Redewendung," because both elements are prominent in *Me-ti*. I believe that Brecht intentionally uses this word to connect the double meaning in the word *Wendung*. The English translator of *Me-ti*, Antony Tatlow, translates the title as *Book of Interventions in the Flow of Things*, which doesn't reflect the aspect of usage or practicality, which is important for Brecht's dialectic. There are also various translations by other scholars.

self-stylization as the German translator and the alleged English translation of *Mozi* are both fictive. His creative negotiation with Mohism contains an aesthetics of translation through which he connects ancient Chinese philosophy, Marxism, and socio-political situations in the twentieth century in *Meti*.

Although *Me-ti* first was published posthumously in 1965, Brecht began working on it in the 1930s.[3] This project accompanied Brecht throughout his exile and his late years in East Germany. Despite its fragmentary status, *Me-ti* maintains an essential position in Brecht's oeuvre. Fredric Jameson reads it as Brecht's "principal work in the dialectic" and also as "a set of political commentaries on the leftist politics of the period."[4] Hans-Peter Krüger interprets *Me-ti* as a major intervention in the dialectic of art, comparable to Hegel's dialectic of thinking and Marx's dialectic of capitalism, because Brecht sees in art its own limits and thus seeks its liberation from its ritualist and cult-like functions.[5] Foregrounding Marxist dialectic, Jameson and Krüger do not mention the role of Chinese Mohism in *Me-ti*, despite the obvious relation between the two. Roland Jost argues that Mohism serves as an exotic garment covering twentieth-century issues; this helps achieve the V-effect of the materialistic dialectic.[6] Thus the Chinese element merely provides a narrative form and has little to do with the philosophical content of *Me-ti*. More recently, Markus Wessendorf has argued that Mohism, along with Confucianism, contains "respected counterparts and foils that allowed [Brecht] to develop and articulate his own

---

[3] See Brecht, "Prosa 3," 486–7.
[4] See Fredric Jameson, *Brecht and Method* (London and New York: Verso, 1998), 140. Theo Stammen views *Me-ti* as Brecht's most comprehensive reflection and discussion about Marxist dialectic among his writing. Theo Stammen, "'Me-ti'—Große Methode—Große Ordnung," in *Bertolt Brecht—Aspekte seines Werkes, Spuren seiner Wirkung*, ed. Helmut Koopmann and Theo Stammen (Munich: Ernst Vögel, 1994), 147.
[5] See Hans-Peter Krüger, "Brechts Dialektik-Konzept in >Me-ti<," in *Brecht und Marxismus. Dokumentation* (Berlin: Henschelverlag Kunst und Gesellschaft, 1983), 210.
[6] See Jan Knopf (ed.), *Brecht Handbuch. Prosa, Filme, Drehbücher*, vol. 3 (Stuttgart and Weimar: Metzler, 2002), 242. Also see Klaus-Detlef Müller, "Brechts *Me-ti* und die Auseinandersetzung mit dem Lehrer Karl Korsch," *Brecht-Jahrbuch*, vol. 7 (1977): 9–29. Müller disputes any real connection to China or Chinese philosophy and contends that *Me-ti* is a discussion with Brecht's friend and philosophical interlocutor Karl Korsch. See also Mei-Ling Luzia Wang, *Chinesische Elemente in Bertolt Brechts "Me-ti. Buch der Wendungen"* (Frankfurt am Main: Peter Lang, 1990), who confirms that, even though Brecht is inspired by Mohism, his dialectics still should be understood in the context of Marxism and the socialist movement in Germany and the Soviet Union because there are major differences between Mohist and Brecht's dialectics.

materialist-ethical positions. Because of their cultural difference and historical remove from Brecht's own context they provided an echo chamber and testing ground that allowed him to estrange and historicize his own ideas as well as the Marxist discourse of his time, thereby rendering both developable."[7] I propose to take Wessendorf's argument about the general "echo chamber" one step further and inquire what Brecht precisely does on the "testing ground," without falling back into the same argument that he is merely concerned with Marxism and socialism. Interestingly, Günther Heeg suggests that *Me-ti* is not an amalgamation of Chinese philosophy and Marxism, but a creation without context, because Brecht takes both out of their contexts and rearranges them in a third constellation.[8] Yet Heeg's analysis remains work-immanent only. To understand the role of Mohism in *Me-ti*, we need to engage with the question of translation.

Translation, an issue that hasn't been properly addressed in *Me-ti* scholarship, promises to take us to different contexts and to yield a deeper understanding of Brecht's textual and contextual practice. Even though Brecht's work is not a translation from one language to another, it is a "translation" of philosophical ideas between ancient Mohism and twentieth-century Marxism. *Me-ti* is the result of the interpolation and extrapolation of thought experiments between Mohism and Marxism. Moreover, the narrative style of *Me-ti* also resembles that of the Chinese book *Mozi* in that it collects an eclectic number of anecdotes, aphorisms, statements, and comments. *Me-ti* is thus also a trans-literation. If we take seriously Brecht's aesthetic practice of translation, then we need to close-read the related texts and detect the intertextual traces to render Brecht's meticulous art of translation visible and intelligible. *Me-ti* provides a unique opportunity to read Brecht in intercultural and global contexts that hasn't yet been deeply explored. Instead of reading from the perspective of Marxist dialectic, I venture to read *Me-ti* from the major vantage points of Mohism and its philosophy of universal love, mutual benefit, and the transience of life. I argue that Brecht's vision of socialism, called the Great Order in *Me-ti*, reflects the Mohist ideals of

---

[7] Markus Wessendorf, "Brecht's Materialist Ethics between Confucianism and Mohism," *Philosophy East & West*, vol. 66, no. 1 (January 2016): 122–45, here 138.

[8] Günther Heeg, "Brechts chinesische Wendungen: *Me-ti* und die Praxis kultureller Flexionen," *Brecht Yearbook*, vol. 36 (2011): 135–50, here 141. Even though Heeg highlights *Me-ti* as a transcultural experiment that resides in a realm between one's own and foreign cultures, he still concludes that Master Mo is not the primary philosopher ("Hauptphilosoph") in Brecht's *Me-ti*. And, Chinese philosophies including Confucianism and Taoism are not well integrated with Marxism: "Aber die chinesische Philosophie geht nicht als Lehre, als philosophische Doktrin in das Buch der Wendungen ein" (141).

universal love based on the logic of mutual benefit; Brecht's understanding of dialectic, called the Great Method in *Me-ti*, stresses metamorphosis and the transience of things in different forms and times. Before the analysis of the Great Order and the Great Method, I will first discuss the historical context of the translations of *Mozi* from Chinese into European languages. I also will show that Brecht's interest in Mohism is not singular, because there was a renaissance of Mohism among Chinese intellectuals, which prompted the translation of *Mozi* into European languages. We thus should take Mohism more seriously than it has been regarded in *Me-ti* scholarship. It is too limiting to merely read *Me-ti* within the Western context. Mohism is not merely an external function of the V-effect, but also an internally integrated philosophical content that Brecht brings into dialogue with Marxism to articulate his own dialectic.

Brecht's "Translation" and the Renaissance of Mohism as a Global Moment

In the foreword to *Me-ti* in the edition published after his death in 1965, Brecht claims that he used Charles Stephen's English translation of *Mozi* (墨子) for his German translation. *Mozi* contains the teachings of the philosopher Mo Zi, meaning Master Mo, and his followers in later times.[9] Master Mo, actually named Mo Di (墨翟), supposedly lived in the fifth or fourth century BCE, during the Warring States Era in Chinese history. Mo was most probably a contemporary of Confucius. While Brecht's claim about the English translation sounds plausible, as many books in Chinese were first translated into English and from there into other European languages, in reality, the English translator Stephen did not exist. Brecht, of course, is not the German translator of *Mozi* in the literal sense.

The first comprehensive translation of *Mozi* into a European language is Alfred Forke's, from Chinese into German in 1922: *Mê Ti, des Sozialethikers und seiner Schüler philosophische Werke* (*Me Ti, Philosophical Works by the Social Thinker and his Students*).[10] Forke's translation is based on the 1895 edition of *Mozi Jiangu* (墨子間詁, *A Concise Commentary of Mozi*) by the Chinese scholar Sun Yirang (孫詒讓, 1848–1908). Sun was an eminent Confucian philologist around 1900, toward the end of the Qing Dynasty (1636–1912). His critical edition of *Mozi* has been considered

---

[9] See Bertolt Brecht, *Me-ti, Buch der Wendungen* (Frankfurt am Main: Suhrkamp, 1965). In the 1995 edition, this foreword is identified as the last text Brecht wrote for this project. See "Prosa 3. Sammlungen und Dialoge," 194.

[10] Alfred Forke (ed.), *Mê Ti, des Sozialethikers und seiner Schüler philosophische Werke* (Berlin: Vereinigung wissenschaftlicher Verleger, 1922).

the most authoritative modern Chinese edition of the classic to date. *Mozi*'s English translator, Ian Johnston, mentions that there are four partial translations of *Mozi* before Forke's, with the earliest dating back to 1861: two into English, one into German, and one into French.[11] Several other partial translations into English and German occurred after Forke's, until the most complete English translation by Johnston appeared as late as 2010.[12] No translator, however, was named Charles Stephen, in contrast to Brecht's claim. Brecht owned, however, a copy of Forke's translation and used it intensively to study Mohism. He even had it bound in black leather. "Me-ti in leather" ("ME-TI in Leder") was one of the few things Brecht took with him in his Swedish exile.[13] Obviously, Mohism remained important to Brecht for decades.

Then why did Brecht invent such an English translator—a question few scholars have asked so far? Why did he portray himself as a fictive German translator? He could just simply claim that the stories and aphorisms in his book were inspired by his reading of *Mozi* in Forke's translation. Perhaps the desire to be a translator goes beyond the obvious joy of literary creation and reveals a deeper insight in merging philosophical thinking with literary creation, the present with the past, and the East with the West. It is a non-binary and non-normative attempt by Brecht that welds ancient Chinese Mohism with Marxism and twentieth-century politics to create a new form of thinking characterized by intertextuality. Brecht's *Me-ti* bridges the gap between what he claimed was ancient Chinese socialist thinking and the twentieth-century international socialist movement. Brecht's self-portrayal as the German translator of a fictive English translation manifests his creative method of "translating" the ancient Mohist philosophy into a twentieth-century model of thinking as well as his awareness that this type of "translation" has gone through layers of interpretations and is farther from its original. It is also a transliteration because Brecht transforms phrases in Forke's translation into his own and, at times, makes Master Mo comment on the socio-political situations in Germany and the Soviet Union,

---

11   Johnston doesn't mention that the earliest study of Mohism in a European language was probably J. Edkins's five-page *Notice of Character and Writings of Meh-tsi*, published in the *Journal of the North-China Branch of the Royal Asiatic Society* in Shanghai in 1859. Joseph Edkin, "Notice of Character and Writings of Meh Tsï," *Journal of the North-China Branch of the Royal Asiatic Society*, vol. 2 (May 1859): 165–9.
12   MoZi, *The Mozi: A Complete Translation* (New York: Columbia University Press, 2010), lxxix.
13   Werner Mittenzwei, "Nachwort. Der Dialektiker Brecht oder die Kunst 'Me-ti' zu lesen," in Brecht, *Prosa*, vol. 4, ed. Werner Mittenzwei (Berlin and Weimar: Aufbau, 1975), 182.

creating a V-effect and jumping a huge time gap of more than 2,000 years. Mohism is visible in both form and content of *Me-ti*.

Brecht also invents a series of Sinicized names for countries, well-known personalities, and his friends. For example, Germany is Ga or Ge-el; the Soviet Union is Su; Lenin is Mi-en-leh; Karl Marx is Ka-meh; Hegel is Meister Hü-jeh or He-leh; Stalin is Ni-en; Hitler is Hi-jeh, Hu-ih, Hui-jeh, or Ti-hi; Brecht's friend and teacher Karl Korsch is Ko or Ka-osch; his lover and collaborator Ruth Berlau is Lai-tu, and Brecht himself is Kin, Kin-jeh, or Kien-leh. These names are "translations" from the twentieth century to antiquity and from German or Russian to their Chinese-like versions. Toward the end of the foreword, Brecht endeavors to strengthen the readers' impression of the authenticity of his claims by claiming that some chapters in the book, such as those on music and conduct, are really written by Master Mo while some other chapters are not, even though these too are ancient teachings; the remaining chapters, however, are written more recently but use the old style of the text.[14] Brecht reflects that from a strictly scientific ("streng wissenschaftlich") point of view, books like *Me-ti* might not qualify as a serious book. But if the readers do not merely care about the stamp of authenticity ("Echtheitsstempel") but rather focus on the content, then they may very well gain something valuable through reading this eclectic collection.[15] In conclusion, Brecht hopes, his insertions of modern thoughts and the comparisons between modern history and the ancient Chinese philosophy could also amuse his readers. Indeed, the word "eclectic" reveals Brecht's aesthetic method and practice of "translating" Mohist ideas into something that can be used for contemporaneous issues. Brecht's argument about authenticity as not necessary also indirectly points to his idea of borrowing and applying philosophical ideas from one context to another.

Brecht also claims that the Chinese classic *Mozi* had suffered from an almost complete repression ("fast völlige Verdrängung") by Confucianism and thus is not part of the classics of Chinese antiquity. Brecht reports that the teachings of Master Mo, however, experienced a renaissance in the nineteenth century because some elements resembled certain Western philosophical trends and appeared almost modern. Even

---

[14] In fact, there are no chapters on music in Brecht's fragments, but there are chapters on music in *Mozi*. It is also true that *Mozi* is a collection of both Master Mo's works and his later followers. Forke also comments on this in the introduction to his translation: "Mê-tsi ist nicht ein einheitliches Werk, sondern eine Sammlung mehistischer Schriften," in *Mê Ti, des Sozialethikers und seiner Schüler philosophische Werke*, 2.

[15] Brecht, *Me-ti, Buch der Wendungen*, 8.

though one could doubt the veracity of Brecht's claim after discovering the fictionality of the English translator, the marginalization of Mohism in Chinese intellectual history, as Brecht ascertains, is confirmed by scholarly consensus. Johnston considers Mohism "the most serious challenge" to the dominance of Confucianism and its neglect a consequence of the firm establishment of Confucianism as the orthodox state philosophy and social value system until the mid-nineteenth century.[16] The lack of interest in Mohism in the West reflects the Chinese paucity. Hence Johnston's complete translation of *Mozi* (2010) serves the purpose of reviving the study of Mohism as late as the twenty-first century. Forke also claims that:

> The answer to the question of what are the most important philosophical or religious systems in ancient China has until now been commonly: Confucianism and Taoism. Yet there was a third system that is usually completely ignored or merely mentioned in passing: Mohism, the teaching of Mê Ti. He challenged the status of his rivals, Confucius and Laozi, for centuries; then his teaching disappeared, and he was almost forgotten for two millennia.[17]

Forke further comments that Chinese scholars began to pay more attention to Mohism after their intensive and violent encounters with Western powers and China's own social reform; both challenged the absolute authority of Confucianism. After Chinese students had studied in the West, they began to observe China's intellectual history from a different perspective. Thus came *Mozi*'s renaissance in the early twentieth century. Forke's view is confirmed by his Chinese contemporary, scholar Fang Shouchu (方授楚, 1898–1956). In his well-known study on Mohism, *Moxue Yuanliu* (墨学源流, *The Origin and Trends of Mohism*, 1936), Fang contends that Mozi was the only classical Chinese thinker who was seriously read and discussed among Chinese intellectuals around 1900. Due to disappointment with a Confucian tradition that had not succeeded in debunking Western imperialist encroachment, the younger generation in the early twentieth century started to actively study European thinkers and reassess the Chinese tradition. Indeed, with the downfall of the ancient dynastic system in 1912, Confucianism lost its unquestionable authority as a political philosophy and a bedrock of cultural value in a country that had been challenged by Western imperialism and industrial modernity. Confucianism was

---

[16] MoZi, *The Mozi: A Complete Translation*, xvii.
[17] Forke, *Mê Ti, des Sozialethikers und seiner Schüler philosophische Werke*, vii. All translations from this work are mine.

not considered effective in defending China against imperialist invasions. Hence, Mo Zi as an anti-Confucianist came into favor. His twin ideas of universal love (兼爱, jian ai) and distaste of warfare (非攻, fei gong), as well as his attention to the ordinary and the poor people beyond familial and national boundaries, impressed Chinese scholars who were looking for new points of orientation for China in the world. Well-known scholars and politicians including Liang Qichao (梁启超), Hu Shi (胡适), Zhang Binglin (章炳林), Qian Mu (钱穆), and Feng Youlan (冯友兰) all published monographs discussing Mohism's usefulness for modern China.[18] Unlike Confucius who was an impoverished aristocrat, Master Mo was a low-status craftsman. Mo's personal name *Di* (翟) means "dark" or "black" in classical Chinese, referring to his low-status dirty work as an artisan. Fang stresses Mo Zi's low social status as a decisive factor in his thinking, contending that Confucius's perspective aligned with that of the ruling class while Mozi established his philosophy from the position of the less privileged.[19] Fang argues that Mohism was revolutionary in the turbulent and conflicted period of the Warring States in Chinese history. Fang considers equality the most important element in Mozi's teaching.

Against this backdrop, Brecht's claims about the marginalization and the renaissance of Mohism are not only true, but also reflect his own social and intellectual interests, concurring with those of Chinese intellectuals. Brecht's argument about Mohism's affinity with Western philosophy and modernity is closely connected to the renaissance of Mohism in both China and the West. Forke recounts that many European sinologists such as Ernst Faber, Cognetti de Martiis, and Alexandra David considered Master Mo the oldest socialist in East Asia. Chinese and Japanese scholars concurred with this view. Forke argues, however, that Mo Zi is not a socialist as understood in terms of social democracy, but rather a socially minded aristocrat, because he does not renounce social classes and monarchism. As the title of Forke's translation already demonstrates, he sees Mo Zi as a social moral philosopher ("Sozialethiker"). According to Forke, Master Mo and his followers promote an ethical socialism that fosters universal and equal love for everyone, transcending the social boundaries that Confucianism strictly observes.[20] Forke comments that Mohism's universal love contains "an essential communist quality because, if one should love those who are

---

[18] See Shouchu (方授楚) Fang, *Mo Xue Yuan Liu* 墨學源流 (Beijing: Beijing Library Press (Beijing Tushu Guan Chuban She), 2003), 231–3.
[19] Shouchu, *Mo Xue Yuan Liu*, 74–6.
[20] Forke, *Mê Ti, des Sozialethikers und seiner Schüler philosophische Werke*, 73.

at some distance ('Fernstehende') as much as those who are closely related to oneself, then all sanguine relations, friendships, and patriotism would be dissolved and sublated. A complete equality exists for all."[21] Mohism's universal love is reminiscent of Christianity—Forke mentions that Chinese scholars even call Mo Zi the Chinese Jesus and are proud that socialism, a set of internationally influential ideas, also is intellectually echoed in East Asian antiquity. In addition to the twin ideas of universal love and opposition to warfare, Forke also considers two other principles crucial for Mohism: respect for and promotion of capable people in state affairs regardless of their social backgrounds and status, and reduction and elimination of superfluous luxury and the arts. This, Forke comments, is in line with the communist theories of François-Noël Babeuf and Robert Owen.[22]

Given the interest in socialist thinking and Mohism in both Europe and China, it is a global intellectual historical moment to which Brecht refers. Forke's translation not only provided a more or less complete textual foundation for Mohism in a European language, but also opened up a channel for Europeans to understand the recent intellectual movement in China. Without the renaissance of Mohism in China and the recession of Confucianism in the early twentieth century, if it had not been edited and discussed by Chinese intellectuals, Forke might not have made the effort to translate the complete *Mozi*, as Fang informs us. Hence Brecht's creative engagement with Mohism further contributes to the global circulation of knowledge and creates a new aesthetics for philosophical "translation" between the East and the West and between antiquity and modernity.

The global intellectual historical context, in which Brecht's *Me-ti* is deeply embedded, calls our attention to Brecht's aesthetics of translation. It also raises questions about Brecht's practice of translation in creating a meaningful inter-text connecting both Mohism and dialectic materialism. Since *Me-ti* basically remains a fragment, it is a very difficult task to interpret or even to make sense of it. Brecht researcher Werner Mittenzwei confirms that no other manuscript among Brecht's papers is as difficult for the editors of Brecht's works as the *Me-ti* material. Brecht left behind neither a general plan for publication nor a clear order for all the stand-alone chapters in the manuscript folders. The four different editions of *Me-ti* are organized in different ways. The editors of the first two editions of *Me-ti* (published in 1965 and 1967), Uwe Johnson and Klaus Völker, more or less followed the order in which *Me-ti* was found in the Brecht archive. Mittenzwei, the editor of the third

---

[21] Forke, *Mê Ti, des Sozialethikers und seiner Schüler philosophische Werke*, 73.
[22] See Forke, *Mê Ti, des Sozialethikers und seiner Schüler philosophische Werke*, 74.

edition (1975), however, divides the materials over five sections based on the themes in Forke's translation, because this organization reflects "the inner order and the compositional principle of all the *Me-ti* materials."[23] Jan Knopf, the editor of the *Berliner und Frankfurter Ausgabe* (1995), followed the chronological order in which the episodes were written. But Mittenzwei's edition gives *Me-ti* a philosophically meaningful structure and situates Brecht's writing within the context of Mohism.

Even though Mittenzwei's edition reflects the essentiality of Mohism in Brecht's fragment, he does not discuss the intertextual connections between Forke's translation and Brecht's *Me-ti*, let alone their relation to the Chinese original of *Mozi*. Instead, he warns against treating Forke's translation of *Mozi* as the foil or foundation for *Me-ti* and argues that Brecht's dialectic and ethics are better than Mohism. Then he follows a track similar to other critics by interpreting *Me-ti* within the context of Western socialist art movements and Marxism. He argues that *Me-ti* experiments with a new philosophy through art and literature and demonstrates a materialist dialectic through the V-effect.[24] Mittenzwei contradicts himself by first emphasizing and then downplaying the importance of Mohism for Brecht. Given the philosophical significance of *Me-ti* and the historical background of Mohism, it is indispensable to trace Brecht's practice of philosophical translation in the intertextuality between the Chinese original, Forke's German translation, and Brecht's *Me-ti*. Among the five sections, the "Book of the Great Method" and the "Book of the Great Order" are the two sections on which I will focus next because they both reflect Brecht's vision about how to reach the ideal of a socialist order through dialectics.[25]

The Great Order: Socialism

In the anecdote "Gespräche über Su" ("Conversations about Su"), Kin-jeh (Brecht) tells Ko (Karl Korsch) about a legal case in Su (the Soviet Union). A farmer goes to a city to work in a blacksmith's shop. The farmer lives with a family that has a vacant room in their house. Both

---

[23] Forke, *Mê Ti, des Sozialethikers und seiner Schüler philosophische Werke*, 236.
[24] Mittenzwei, "Nachwort. Der Dialektiker Brecht oder die Kunst 'Me-ti' zu lesen," 192–4.
[25] The five sections are comprised of the following: the first section, the "Book of the Great Method" ("Buch der Großen Methode"), is about dialectics; the second section, the "Book of Experience" ("Buch der Erfahrung"), is about ethics; the third, the "Book about Disorder" ("Buch über die Unordnung"), is about fascism; the fourth, the "Book of Upheaval" ("Buch der Umwälzung"), is on socialist revolution; and the fifth, the "Book of the Great Order" ("Buch der Großen Ordnung"), is about socialism.

parties agree that the farmer will move out when the family's son comes home. Yet, when the son returns, the farmer refuses to move out because it is very difficult to find other lodgings. The house management takes the case to the local court. The judge, however, does not pass any verdict on the case. Instead, the judge commissions the house management to find an apartment for the farmer and promises that he himself will also look out for an apartment for him. Kin-jeh praises the judge because he understands that moving out of one place means moving into another. Ko, however, does not believe that such a story could happen because it is too good to be true. Ko argues that, in Su, too many things are not done according to the principles required by the masters, who are supposedly Marx, Engels, and Lenin.[26] When Kin-jeh insists that this story indeed happened because he has witnessed it, Ko contends that the judge only faked it because Kin-jeh was present. Kin-jeh answers that, even though the judge does so merely because of his presence, it is still a great achievement of the judge, even to make such a sound ("vernünftig") decision only once. Kin-jeh draws an analogy: if Ko hears that a man can run faster than everyone else but only does so when Ko is present, isn't it still a great achievement of the runner?[27]

Yun-Yeop Song points out that Brecht has generally integrated the Mohist idea of universal love and usefulness ("Nützlichkeit") into his thinking about socialist social order.[28] Indeed, the story of the farmer and the apartment is a concrete application of the Mohist principle of universal love and the equal care for the rich and the poor in a socialist society. The equal treatment of both family members and non-family members corresponds to the second chapter on Universal Love in *Mozi*. Master Mo asks a question about the causes that harm the state and then responds:

> It arises through lack of mutual love. Nowadays, feudal lords know only to love their own states and not to love the states of others, so they have no qualms about mobilizing their own state to attack another's state. Nowadays, heads of houses know only to love their own house and not to love the houses of others, so they have no qualms about promoting their own house and usurping another's house. Nowadays, individual people know only to love their own person and not to love the persons of others, so they have no qualms about promoting their own person

---

[26] See the comment on the masters in Brecht, "Prosa 3," 511.
[27] Brecht, "Prosa 3," 57–8.
[28] See Yun-Yeop Song, *Bertolt Brecht und die chinesische Philosophie* (Bonn: Bouvier, 1978), 290–3.

and injuring the persons of others. [...] When the people of the world do not all love each other, then the strong inevitably dominate the weak, the many inevitably plunder the few, the rich inevitably despise the poor, the noble inevitably scorn the lowly, and the cunning inevitably deceive the foolish.[29]

The only cure, Master Mo argues, lies in the "methods of universal mutual love and exchange of mutual benefit." Mo Zi explains that if people view others as their own, either in terms of political state, household, or individual, then they would attack less, discriminate less, and deceive less. "Within the world, in all cases, there would be nothing to cause calamity, usurpation, resentment and hatred to arise because of the existence of mutual love."[30] Mohist universal love transcends the borders of states, the barriers between families, the hierarchies between nobility and commoners, and the difference between the rich and the poor. Mohist love imagines an absolute equality among all peoples and communities. It radically breaks with social hierarchy and conventional boundaries between groups and individuals. More importantly, this love is immediately bound to the pragmatic realm of benefit. It is thus not merely a theoretical construction or an abstract idea, but rather a concrete suggestion about how to practice universal love and for what purpose. In other words, without mutual benefits mutual love can't be expressed and demonstrated. Only through the deeds that lead to mutual benefits is the principle of universal love confirmed, visible, and tangible. At the same time, the foundation for mutual benefits should be firmly rooted in universal love, not in any other sentiment or motivation.

Kin-jeh's interpretation of the farmer's story follows the Mohist philosophy of mutual love and benefit. The story challenges the common understanding of family and justice in a twentieth-century bourgeois society. Usually, the family's son is considered closer to the family than the farmer, a stranger. The farmer's room is situated in the family's apartment, which causes a breach in this family-based unity. The agreement to move out acquiescently accepts the convention of familial love and its boundaries. When the farmer refuses to follow this logic, the boundary of love is being challenged and the bourgeois convention needs to defend its validity. The judge, however, does not support this bourgeois convention in the Soviet Union. Instead, he practices universal love in demonstrating understanding for both the farmer's and the

---

[29] MoZi, *The Mozi: A Complete Translation*, 137–9.
[30] MoZi, *The Mozi: A Complete Translation*, 139. Universal love (兼相爱) and mutual benefit (交相利) in Forke's translation are "das Mittel der allumfassenden gegenseitigen Liebe und [...] [der] Austausch gegenseitiger Vorteile" (245).

family's situations. His instruction to the house management and his own promise to find housing for the farmer reveal his intention to address the needs of both sides. According to the passage in *Mozi* cited above, since the family only loves their own son and does not care about the farmer, the conflict emerges due to the lack of universal love. Justice thus should be achieved on the basis of equality and love, not on the boundaries of love. The judge, however, also does not demand that the family continue to provide housing for the farmer. This solution would not be as useful for the family's son who also needs housing. The establishment of justice thus needs a pragmatic and forward-looking spirit that seeks to solve problems collectively as a society. The farmer who then becomes a worker in a blacksmith's shop clearly is a member of the industrial proletariat. The family with a spare room probably belongs to a more privileged class. With the Mohist sense of universal love, the judge moves beyond the boundaries of class and family and avoids conflicts caused by bourgeois conventions.

Furthermore, Kin-jeh and Ko's conversation about practicing good deeds only in the presence of others resembles a conversation between Master Mo and his student Wu Ma Zi (巫马子):

> Wu Ma Zi spoke to Master Mo Zi saying: "You, Sir, practice righteousness but I don't see people submitting to you and I don't see ghosts blessing you. Still you practice it. You must be mad!" Master Mo Zi said: "Suppose now there were two officials—one who carried out his duties when he saw you, but not when he did not see you, and one who carried out his duties whether he saw you or not. Which of these two men would you value?" Wu Ma Zi replied: "I would value the one who carried out his duties whether he saw me or not." Master Mo Zi said: "In that case, then, you would also be valuing one who is mad!"[31]

Master Mo praises the honesty of working diligently whether or not it is visible to others. It is a kind of honesty that one chooses for oneself and, in Mohist understanding, for heaven and the spirits. Yet Brecht's story takes a different turn to argue that even if the event is singular, it is still remarkable. The recognition of both parties' needs and the willingness to help both, even if it only happens once in Kin-jeh's presence, is still a great insight and practice, and it has the potential to develop into more established legal routines in Su. This corresponds to the pragmatic tendency of Mohism in that it does not merely insist on the moral

---

[31] MoZi, *The Mozi: A Complete Translation*, 645–7; Forke, *Mê Ti, des Sozialethikers und seiner Schüler philosophische Werke*, 540–1.

principles of love and honesty as something abstract but also recognizes the meaning and importance of the ideas in the practice itself. Indeed, Kin-jeh's argument about the fastest runner contains the encouragement to do so more often because this man already has the potential to run fast, while many others don't even have the ability to do so.

In Forke's translation, we read, "A smaller good deed is the same as the generosity of a great deed. By extension [. . .] People love their fellow humans not because of praise. Analogy in: caring for the elderly."[32] Obviously, Kin-jeh's argument about the importance of even a one-time good deed echoes the statement about extending the good deed from a smaller to a larger dimension. The analogy between the judge and the runner in Brecht's story also imitates the style in this passage, presenting an argument first and then an analogy. Both the content and form of *Mozi* are reflected in Brecht's writing. The Mohist ideas and practice of universal love and mutual benefits correspond to Brecht's vision of socialism, as described in this story.

Brecht's emphases on the individual practice, extension, and encouragement of universal love and mutual benefits can be found in many other episodes in *Me-ti*. In the chapter "The Great Order and Love" ("Die Grosse Ordnung und die Liebe"), Me-ti defends love as something that inherently belongs to the Great Order because the enemies of the Great Order eliminate love.[33] Similar to Master Mo, Brecht understands universal love as the foundation for a socialist society. In "A female cook should be able to lead the State" ("Die Köchin soll den Staat lenken können"), Mi-en-leh, referring to Lenin, promotes the idea that the state should be organized and reformed like a kitchen and vice versa. Every female cook has the ability to organize a kitchen as well as a state.[34] This anecdote reveals Brecht's belief in the power of an individual in the realization of a collective plan. The comparison of a female cook with the head of a state also breaks class boundaries and social hierarchies, and empowers women. The female cook reminds us of the noble character of Grusche in Brecht's drama *The Caucasian Chalk Circle*, (*Der kaukasische Kreidekreis*, 1944). Individual effort induces colossal changes. A commoner with a "low" social status can perform a "high" status job just as well. Here Brecht already expresses his dialectics, the Great Method that guarantees or leads to the Great Order: socialism with universal love and mutual benefit.

---

[32] Forke, *Mê Ti, des Sozialethikers und seiner Schüler philosophische Werke*, 524–6.
[33] Brecht, "Prosa 3," 105.
[34] Brecht, "Prosa 3," 162. Editor Jan Knopf mentions a poem by Majakowski as the source for the metaphorical figure of a female cook in his comment. See "Prosa 3," 553.

The Great Method: Dialectics

In "The principle of inequality in the Great Method" ("Der Ungleichheitssatz in der großen Methode"), Brecht discusses the dialectic between identity and change or between a linguistic concept and its changing object in reality. The speaker, Me-ti himself, reflects on the philosophy of He-leh, referring to Hegel, and states:

> The sentence "one is not equal to one" points to certain difficulties but is in itself tricky. It ought really to be "one is not only equal to one but is also not equal to one." It expresses the thought that you can't find one thing that you can induce to be true to itself over a long period of time; nor can you find a concept that proves ready to stick to the point at least for as long as you're speaking if you're saying more than one sentence.

> [Der Satz "Eins ist nicht gleich eins" weist auf viele Tücken hin, enthält aber selber Tücken. Er müßte eigentlich heißen "Eins ist nicht nur gleich eins, sondern auch nicht gleich eins." Er drückt aus, man kann nicht ein Ding finden, das man veranlassen kann, längere Zeit sich selber treu zu bleiben; noch kann man einen Begriff finden, der sich bereits zeigt, wenigstens solang, als man spricht, wenn man mehr als einen Satz spricht, bei der Sache zu bleiben.][35]

According to Knopf's commentary, the sentence "one is not equal to one" could allude to Hegel's *Wissenschaft der Logik* (*The Science of Logic*), in which Hegel points out that the absolute laws of thinking ("absolute Denkgesetze") are caught in a constant contradiction between a thesis and an antithesis and their sublation.[36] Brecht's text, however, refers to the temporality of a concept, the fluidity, the ephemerality, and the flexibility between an idea and what it refers to in a constantly changing reality. Even though an indirect reference to Hegel's dialectic of thinking could be contained in Brecht's statement, it also reveals Brecht's negotiation with a Mohist idea.

The Mohist dialectic expresses itself laconically:

> Completely applicable: There is only either being at rest or being in motion. [. . .] A beginning: Time in some cases has duration and in some cases does not. A beginning is a specific instant of time

---

[35] Brecht, "Prosa 3," 98; Tatlow, *Bertolt Brecht's Me-ti: Book of Interventions in the Flow of Things*, 84.
[36] Brecht, "Prosa 3," 528–9.

without duration. [. . .] A transformation: Like a water frog becoming a quail. [. . .] Stopping: Not stopping when there is no duration corresponds to "ox is not horse" and is like "an arrow passing a pillar." Not stopping when there is duration corresponds to "horse is not a horse" and is like "a man passing a bridge."[37]

The frog and quail are biologically completely different creatures. But, from the perspective of the transformation of life energy, Mohism does not preclude the possibility of metamorphosis through which one form of life could change into another. A horse is not equal to a horse because time changes despite the duration of a life. Even though the horse still remains the horse, it is no longer the same horse, because the horse could have become older or thinner or slower during the years. Conceptually speaking, a horse is thus not equal to a horse. This point could have inspired Brecht's statement about the change of a thing over time and the instability of a concept ("Begriff"). Temporality plays an important role in Mohist dialectics. The movement of time, however, is not conceived of as conflict and synthesis, as it is in the Hegelian manner; rather, it is conceived of as a transformation and transition from one form of existence to another. Of course, the Hegelian conflict and its synthesis are themselves movements within time. Yet Mohist dialectics stresses the changes that one entity or one form of existence undergoes during time.

Brecht once contemplated using the title *Buch über den Fluß der Dinge* (*Book on the Flow of Things*) for *Me-ti*, which reflects the Mohist dialectic about motion, duration, and transformation. Yet again, Brecht doesn't remain at the abstract level but seeks to put this idea into practice. In "Über den Fluss der Dinge" ("On the Flow of Things"), To-tsi, referring to Trotsky, observes that workers in a blacksmith's shop have first organized strikes against the exploitation by the shop owners and demanded better payment. Yet, when the shops are closed due to a lack of iron, the workers insist on the continuation of exploitation ("Fortführung der Ausbeutung").[38] To-tsi comments that life means for the workers to be exploited, and now they are afraid of losing their lives. They are now angry with the shop owners and drive them away because the owners refuse to continue exploiting the workers. While it is satiric to conclude that the workers desire to be continuously exploited because their existence is otherwise in danger, this anecdote reveals the changing historical realities in different scenarios during the proletariat's revolution.

---

[37] MoZi, *The Mozi: A Complete Translation*, 411–17; Forke, *Mê Ti, des Sozialethikers und seiner Schüler philosophische Werke*, 449–50.
[38] Brecht, "Prosa 3," 73.

While exploitation in and of itself should be condemned and in principle prevented, if its elimination induces unemployment and jeopardizes livelihood, then being able to work is considered more practical and more important than the bare theory about exploitation and resistance. Social reality is more complex than ideological thinking based on fixed principles. Ideology needs to be constantly adjusted to changing social reality. One needs to recognize the most pressing need at the moment and act accordingly. Nothing is cast in stone. Just as a frog could become a quail and a horse does not remain a horse, the fact of exploitation is in principle to be condemned, but could also become desirable and even occasionally save lives.

Brecht writes in another episode with the same title, "Über den Fluss der Dinge," that nothing is completely dead, not even those who have died. Even dead stones, which can't really die, still breathe and induce changes.[39] Brecht argues that we need to call the things, for example the moon, "dead" for the sake of a concept. If we don't do so, we lose a description, the word "dead," and the possibility to name something that we experience.[40] At the same time, since we notice that the moon is not completely dead, we need to keep both sides in mind and treat it as "something that is both dead and not dead, though actually more dead, in a certain sense deceased, in this sense absolutely and irretrievably deceased, but not in every sense."[41] While Brecht discusses the delicate balance between death and life and argues here about life in death, in a later episode he warns not to focus too much on the transience and disregard the duration of things and its possible harm. In "Dangers of the idea about the Flow of Things" ("Gefahren der Idee vom Fluss der Dinge"), Brecht reflects that one might see something as less severe based on the assumption that it would eventually disappear ("vorübergehen"), but these things can do damage.[42] Changes don't happen by themselves. Changes need to be made so that harmful things can be forced to disappear ("zum Vergehen gezwungen").[43] A conscious choice in life is still necessary even though the flow of things is inevitable. This idea echoes a statement in *Mozi*: "Promote benefit and do away with harm; the analogy lies in stopping a leak."[44] The flow of water is

---

[39] Brecht, "Prosa 3," 73.
[40] Brecht, "Prosa 3," 73.
[41] Tatlow, *Bertolt Brecht's Me-ti: Book of Interventions in the Flow of Things*, 55; Brecht, "Prosa 3," 74.
[42] Brecht, "Prosa 3," 113.
[43] Brecht, "Prosa 3," 113.
[44] MoZi, *The Mozi: A Complete Translation*, 615; Forke, *Mê Ti, des Sozialethikers und seiner Schüler philosophische Werke*, 525.

often compared to the flow of time. The dripping of water is change, but it is a change that disadvantages the container, which could symbolize the resources in a society. It is dangerous if one merely thinks that all things change and neglects to plug the hole that causes the leak. Stopping the leak is necessary for the restoration of good social order.

The practical application of this idea is echoed in the statement "Frieden und Krieg" ("Peace and War") in *Me-ti*. Brecht writes that imperialism must be eradicated by the proletariat's revolution, because imperialism will not vanish by itself, but must be forced to disappear:

> We saw that the nation, which lived in peace with other nations, fostered a war between its own classes. But the war against other nations, which was caused by the war between its own classes, brought about a truce among the classes. And yet at the same time it worsened the war of the classes; so the truce collapsed and the war of the classes ended the war between nations.
>
> [Wir sahen: Das Volk, das mit andern Völkern in Frieden lebte, nährte einen Krieg seiner eigenen Klassen. Aber der Krieg mit andern Völkern, welcher durch den Krieg der eigenen Klassen hervorgebracht wurde, erzeugte den Burgfrieden der Klassen. Und dennoch verschärfte er den Krieg der Klassen zugleich; so zerfiel der Burgfrieden und der Krieg der Klassen beendete den Krieg der Völker.][45]

According to Knopf's commentary, the war of the classes in the first sentence alludes to the class struggles against exploitation in Germany before World War I, while the same phrase in the last sentence refers to the Russian Revolution in 1917 and the German Revolution in 1918. The German political party SPD (*Sozialdemokratische Partei Deutschlands*), in this reading, projected internal conflict outward and passed a bill to allow Germany to follow imperialist foreign policies, to which the war with other nations in the quote refers.[46] Brecht argues here instead that German imperialism abroad does not pacify the class struggles in the country itself but rather intensifies them. To stop the leak of the logic of war pursued by the German Social Democratic Party, the international proletariat's revolution is necessary, since it will end these wars in a timely manner. It is dangerous to passively wait for the right time to make changes. The dialectic between peace and war works in favor of

---

[45] Tatlow, *Bertolt Brecht's Me-ti: Book of Interventions in the Flow of Things*, 91; Brecht, "Prosa 3," 113.
[46] Forke, *Mê Ti, des Sozialethikers und seiner Schüler philosophische Werke*, 535.

the future Great Order of socialism that promises universal love and equality, not only in one country but in an international order. International class solidarity is the cure for leaking imperialism worldwide.

Conclusion

Reading about the Great Order and the Great Method in *Me-ti* alongside *Mozi* enables the reconstruction of Brecht's aesthetics of "translation" between ancient Mohism and contemporaneous Marxism, between theory and practice, and between art and reality. *Me-ti* evinces an intertextuality inflecting both *Mozi*'s teaching and Brecht's own understanding of universal love, mutual benefit, and the dialectic of transience. Of course, Brecht did not translate *Mozi* from English into German. Instead, he translated the content and the spirit of *Mozi* from its ancient context into the twentieth-century setting of the international communist movement. Hence translation should not be seen as merely a transaction from one language to another, but also as a trans-situational movement between historical periods, ideological orientations, and civilizations. Translation is always also a political and ideological act, an engagement that stresses the practical and ethical function of literature in intellectual debates and political movements. Brecht's self-stylization as the German "translator" and his imitation of the aphoristic style of *Mozi* reveal his translation as transliteration, moving beyond linguistic, historical, ideological, national, cultural, and class boundaries. *Me-ti* represents a form of world literature that is translation and transliteration both in form and content. This translational perspective allows us to place *Me-ti* within the realm of dialectic without reducing Mohism to an exotic garment merely used as a V-effect or overemphasizing materialist dialectics as the text's only real content. Translation thus functions as a perfect medium and time machine for Brecht to negotiate with ancient Mohist philosophy and find his own vocabulary. He in turn gives Mohism a new life in Europe after more than 2,000 years. Without the renaissance of Mohism in China around 1900, however, Forke wouldn't have translated *Mozi* into German and Brecht wouldn't have had the opportunity to write *Me-ti*. Hence *Me-ti* is also a product of a global intellectual history that conceals and reveals more connections and cross-currents than we could have realized. In his copy of Forke's translation, Brecht underlined in red pencil the sentence "One can find pleasure in the benefit of the world" ("Man kann an dem Wohl der Menschheit seine Freude haben").[47]

---

[47] Forke, *Mê Ti, des Sozialethikers und seiner Schüler philosophische Werke* 511. MoZi, *The Mozi: A Complete Translation*, 593. Johnston's translation is "The world's benefit is pleasing." But I find it in this case preferable to translate the German version back to English to better reflect what Brecht has read.

Indeed, Brecht articulates a generous love of the world through his *Me-ti* that creatively connects, wittily translates, and dialectically infuses aesthetics and politics beyond the divide between inside and outside.

Works Cited

Brecht, Bertolt. *Me-ti, Buch der Wendungen* (Frankfurt am Main: Suhrkamp, 1965).
Brecht, Bertolt. *Prosa*, vol. 4, ed. Werner Mittenzwei (Berlin and Weimar: Aufbau, 1975).
Brecht, Bertolt. "Prosa 3. Sammlungen und Dialoge," in *Bertolt Brecht Werke. Berliner und Frankfurter Ausgabe*, ed. Jan Knopf (Berlin, Weimar, and Frankfurt am Main: Aufbau/Suhrkamp, 1995).
Edkin, Joseph. "Notice of Character and Writings of Meh Tsï," *Journal of the North-China Branch of the Royal Asiatic Society*, vol. 2 (May 1859): 165–9.
Fang, Shouchu (方授楚). *Mo Xue Yuan Liu* 墨學源流 (Beijing: Beijing Library Press (Beijing Tushu Guan Chuban She), 2003).
Forke, Alfred, ed. *Mê Ti, des Sozialethikers und seiner Schüler philosophische Werke* (Berlin: Vereinigung wissenschaftlicher Verleger, 1922).
Heeg, Günther. "Brechts chinesische Wendungen: *Me-ti* und die Praxis kultureller Flexionen," *Brecht Yearbook*, vol. 36 (2011): 135–50.
Jameson, Fredric. *Brecht and Method* (London and New York: Verso, 1998).
Knopf, Jan, ed. *Brecht Handbuch. Prosa, Filme, Drehbücher*, vol. 3 (Stuttgart and Weimar: Metzler, 2002).
Krüger, Hans-Peter. "Brechts Dialektik-Konzept in >Me-ti<," in *Brecht und Marxismus. Dokumentation* (Berlin: Henschelverlag Kunst und Gesellschaft, 1983), 203–11.
Luo (罗炳良), Bingliang, and Hu Xiyun (胡喜云), eds. *Mozi Jieshuo* (墨子解说) (Beijing: Huaxia Chuban She, 2007).
Mittenzwei, Werner. "Nachwort. Der Dialektiker Brecht oder die Kunst 'Me-ti' zu lesen," in Bertolt Brecht, *Prosa*, vol. 4, ed. Werner Mittenzwei (Berlin and Weimar: Aufbau, 1975), 182–234.
MoZi. *The Mozi: A Complete Translation* (New York: Columbia University Press, 2010).
Müller, Klaus-Detlef. "Brechts *Me-ti* und die Auseinandersetzung mit dem Lehrer Karl Korsch," *Brecht-Jahrbuch*, vol. 7 (1977): 9–29.
Song, Yun-Yeop. *Bertolt Brecht und die chinesische Philosophie* (Bonn: Bouvier, 1978).
Stammen, Theo. "'Me-ti'—Große Methode—Große Ordnung," in *Bertolt Brecht— Aspekte seines Werkes, Spuren seiner Wirkung*, ed. Helmut Koopmann and Theo Stammen (Munich: Ernst Vögel, 1994), 147–66.
Sun (孙以楷), Yikai, and Zhen Changsong (甄长松), eds. *Mozi Quan Yi* (墨子全译), vol. 19, Mozi Da Quan (墨子大全) (Beijing: Beijing Tushuguan Chubanshe (北京图书馆出版社), 2000).
Sun, Yirang (孫詒讓), ed. *Mozi Jiangu* (墨子閒詁, *A Concise Commentary of Mozi*), vol. 1 (Beijing: Zhonghua Shu Ju (中华书局), 2009).
Tatlow, Antony, ed. *Bertolt Brecht's Me-ti: Book of Interventions in the Flow of Things* (London: Bloomsbury, 2016).
Wang, Mei-Ling Luzia. *Chinesische Elemente in Bertolt Brechts "Me-ti. Buch der Wendungen"* (Frankfurt am Main: Peter Lang, 1990).
Wessendorf, Markus. "Brecht's Materialist Ethics between Confucianism and Mohism," *Philosophy East & West*, vol. 66, no. 1 (January 2016): 122–45.

Fifteen Clowns in Exile: *Hamletmaschine* and the (In)human

Olivia Landry

What does it mean to encounter a clown? How does this figure challenge perceptions of the human? The 2017 production of Heiner Müller's *Hamletmaschine* (*Hamletmachine*) by the Exil Ensemble foregrounds and intensifies the playwright's original treatment of the figure of the clown. All performers don Grimaldi-style clown costumes and partake in whimsical antics and object-oriented tricks. The Exil Ensemble's *Hamletmaschine* stretches far beyond the clowning aesthetics of its famous precursors in the productions of Robert Wilson (premiere 1986) and, in the German context, Dimiter Gottscheff (premiere 2007). This more recent staging invites an extensive engagement with the ontology of the clown and its inhuman qualities.

With a focus on the figure of the clown, this chapter examines the Exil Ensemble's *Hamletmaschine* as an exploration of the fragile division between humanity and inhumanity. Loosely set during the Syrian civil war, this production upholds a timeliness and specificity of politics of contemporary war and exile. Yet the ethical questions it sets forth call on a critical discourse long in place and far-flung in its entanglements. This is the discourse of the (in)human. Drawing on a range of conceptual insights from Eunjung Kim's "becoming an object" to Giorgio Agamben's *homo sacer*, Hannah Arendt's "rights to have rights," and finally Emmanuel Levinas's "being-for-the-other," this chapter seeks to deepen our understanding of the stakes of this complex production and of the boundaries of the human in the state of exile.

When it was founded in November 2017, the Exil Ensemble was a group composed of seven professional actors and theater makers from Syria, Palestine, and Afghanistan living in exile in Berlin. Ayham Majid

Agha, Mazen Aljubbeh, Karim Daoud, Tahera Hashemi, Kenda Hmeidan, Maryam Abu Khaled, and Hussein Al Shatheli were the founding members. The name of the Ensemble was inspired by Bertolt Brecht and his own exile work during World War II as well as the legacy of his political theater. The Ensemble provided a platform to not only continue making theater but also to probe contemporary political topics of war, migration, exile, and racism through art. Several other similar ensembles were initiated at different theaters across Germany, such as the Open Border Ensemble at the Munich Kammerspiele, the Boat People Project in Göttingen, and other smaller-scale projects. While the membership of the Exil Ensemble has fluctuated, and only a few of the original members are still active in the Ensemble, since its founding the group has been based at the Maxim Gorki Theater in Berlin. Not the first or the only theater to establish such a course, since 2013 the Gorki has nevertheless become a central place for transnational theater and performance, and a new and more permanent home for what many have labeled "postmigrant theater" under the direction of Shermin Langhoff (and the erstwhile co-direction of Jens Hillje). At its inception, the impulse of postmigrant theater was a practical intervention in a history of theater exclusion. Minoritized Germans and immigrants had been systematically excluded from established German theater scenes for not being "German enough" to participate in "national" high culture, so they decided to make their own theater.[1] Despite the institutional collaboration of the Exil Ensemble and the Maxim Gorki Theater, one of the main founding members of the Ensemble, Ayham Majid Agha, has distanced himself from postmigrant theater as an inadequate label, not least because immigration and exile are two distinct realities.[2] He maintains that the work of the Ensemble in many regards differs

---

[1] A growing body of scholarship exists on the topic of "postmigrant theater," and one could certainly write at length on the topic and the debate regarding its label. However, what I seek to highlight here is simply the basic motivating element of this theater movement. Rüdiger Schaper, "Nach dem Theatercoup: Wie Langhoff und Hillje das Gorki leiten wollen," *Tagesspiegel*, May 23, 2012, www.tagesspiegel.de/kultur/nach-dem-theatercoup-wie-langhoff-und-hillje-das-gorki-leiten-wollen/6661782.html. This is something I discuss at length in my study *Theatre of Anger: Radical Transnational Performance in Contemporary Berlin* (Toronto: University of Toronto Press, 2020).

[2] Agha also cites the distinct history of Turkish immigration and the vicissitudes of citizenship, which underpin the inception of "postmigrant theater." Yana Meerzon, "On Dramaturgy of Care and Encounter in the Theatres of Multilingualism: Interview with Ayham Majid Agha," *Critical Stages/Scènes critiques*, no. 20 (2019), www.critical-stages.org/20/on-dramaturgy-of-care-and-encounter-in-the-theatres-of-multilingualism-interview-with-ayham-majid-agha/.

from that of postmigrant theater, and defines the endeavor of the former more broadly as a striving to negotiate the past and the present.[3] To this end, no German playwright provides a better model than Heiner Müller.

In 2018, the Exil Ensemble set itself the challenging task of adapting and producing Müller's 1977 play *Hamletmaschine*, a short five-act play, loosely based on themes from Shakespeare's *Hamlet*. This was the third theater project of the Ensemble but the first to directly adapt a canonical German play. Engaging with the work of Müller, a well-known East German dramatist, to explore the events of the present—in particular, the ongoing civil war in Syria—should not be construed as an Orientalist exercise of trying to make sense of war (elsewhere) in a place of peace (Germany) through Western grammar. The product of a translation project, Müller's unstable, absurd, and violent text provided the appropriate impetus for an exploration of the horror of civil war. In this new adaptation, *Hamletmaschine* is extended and transmogrified through different perspectives, experiences, and histories. As Agha contends:

> In Heiner Müller's short sentences, there is the knowledge of many generations and literatures; his play presents the soul of the German people in 1977, one of its darker periods. Müller asks an important question of how to be an intellectual in his time [. . .] As an artist, whether a refugee or a migrant, I feel a responsibility to be in dialogue with the great minds of world literature, not to fall into the traps of identity theatre. For Exil Ensemble, it has always been my goal to produce the repertoire. So, if I want to tell my own story, I will use the work of Brecht, Müller or Turgenev.[4]

Müller's *Hamletmaschine* may be a reckoning with the Hungarian uprising of 1956, but as Agha also suggests, it is a direct product of the period of the German Autumn and thus temporally and spatially a much closer contemplation of the state of (West) Germany than it might at first seem.[5] For Agha, to work with *Hamletmaschine* is to engage with remarkable literature as well as with what Agha refers to (not without a dash of irony) as "the soul of the German people."

Müller's *Hamletmaschine* is without doubt one of his most celebrated and perplexing plays. What is most compelling for the present study is

---

3 Meerzon, "On Dramaturgy of Care."
4 Meerzon, "On Dramaturgy of Care."
5 David Barnett, "*Die Hamletmaschine*," in *Hamlet-Handbuch*, ed. Peter W. Marx (Stuttgart: Metzler, 2014), 422.

its marking and performance of crises: crises of the intellectual, of the political, of European culture, of gender, and so forth. Many regard the play as manifesting a moment of crisis for Müller himself, one that produced a shift in his work.⁶ According to Jeanette Malkin, *Hamletmaschine* ushered in a later and more serious phase of Müller's oeuvre, a phase not only postmodern but also post-ideological, expressing total collapse and precarity: the collapse of enlightenment, revolution, socialism, intellection, and the unified self.⁷ Among these crisis points, the concept of the human certainly can be included. In Müller's text, Hamlet's notable identification with the machine (in Act 4, Müller quotes Andy Warhol's claim "I want to be a machine" from 1963) offers an expression of human fragility and vulnerability in the embrace of becoming an object.⁸ From this site of the crisis of the human and its state of unbecoming, I follow the Exil Ensemble's turn to the clown.

The concept of the clown is drawn out in the dramaturgy of the performance. For this production, Exil Ensemble teamed up with Gorki director Sebastian Nübling, known for his dynamic, even athletic dramatizations. Nübling brings the focus to the body and corporeal movement onstage. His overarching approach fits and underpins the atelic whimsy, slapstick, and circus skills that typically comprise the performance of the clown, and which are recalibrated in this production. The choreography of *Hamletmaschine* is full of bursts of energy and movement. With minimal text, the clowns express themselves through objected-oriented tricks and pantomimes of death scenes. Bodies are brought forth with exuberance onstage, rather than as people with individualized identities. Doris Kolesch and Matthias Warstat point out that the clown costumes in *Hamletmaschine* serve to cloak the bodies of the performers in masquerade, so that attributions of nationality and ascribable emotions are no longer legible.⁹ Indeed, all seven of the performers are dressed in garishly colorful costumes, including form-fitting onesies, colorful neck ruffs, and grotesque joker-like masks or

---

[6] Jonathan Kalb, *The Theater of Heiner Müller* (Cambridge: Cambridge University Press, 1998), 107.

[7] Jeannette Malkin, *Memory-Theater and Postmodern Drama* (Ann Arbor: University of Michigan Press, 1999), 72. See also Nicholas Zurbrugg, "Post-Modernism and the Multi-Media Sensibility: Heiner Müller's *Hamletmachine* and the Art of Robert Wilson," *Modern Drama*, vol. 31, no. 3 (1988): 439–53, here 441.

[8] References to Müller's text are indicated by their act and taken from Heiner Müller, "Die Hamletmaschine," in *Der Auftrag und andere Revolutionsstücke*, ed. Uwe Wittstock (Stuttgart: Reclam, 1988), 38–46.

[9] Doris Kolesch and Matthias Warstat, "Affective Dynamics in the Theatre: Towards a Relational and Poly-Perspectival Performance Analysis," in *Analyzing Affective Societies: Methods and Methodologies*, ed. Antje Kahl (London: Routledge, 2019), 221.

white face-paint topped with bulbous red foam noses. But beyond the potential aim of covering up or anonymizing the bodies onstage, the costumes form a significant part of the performance of the clown. If the clown had only been represented (if at all) by a single figure in previous productions of *Hamletmaschine*, here its role has proliferated to include the entire ensemble.

Clowns and the Inhuman

From the buffoons, fools, and court jesters of ancient Greek, medieval, and Elizabethan theater alike, to the harlequins of commedia dell'arte, and finally to the pantomimes of modern theater still most familiar to audiences today, clowns and clown-like figures have been staples of the Western stage. Despite this long tradition, defining the identity of a clown is not a simple matter. Throughout these different periods, clowns have assumed nuanced roles and tasks. Earlier figures of the clown often served as messengers of the abstract and objective truth, according to Mikhail Bakhtin.[10] This is especially evident in the Shakespearean fools, who are even permitted to use blasphemy in the name of truth. Consider, for instance, *Hamlet*'s two grave diggers in Act 5, as they irreverently contemplate the fate of Ophelia's corpse. More modern examples frequently demonstrate a transition to physical comedy and the clown acts common to circuses. The famous Swiss clown "Grock" embodies many of the qualities of this later period. In addition to physical comedy, he performed a whole repertoire of spectacles, including juggling, acrobatics, and the playing of instruments.[11] Embedded in theater, however, modern clown figures, such as those found in Samuel Beckett's plays, are more nuanced and marginal. Mary Bryden describes them as wholly dispossessed, alien beings.[12] Appropriately, the qualities of the modern clown seem to circle around deprivation, including a lack of purpose, of subjective experience, and of history.[13]

Throughout their various renditions, clowns remain liminal figures, both in the theater and in other contexts. This liminality allows them to transgress all kinds of boundaries and embody a myriad of paradoxes. In more recent definitions, clowns are often perceived as part-human

---

[10] Mikhail Bakhtin, *Rabelais and His World*, trans. Hélène Iswolsky (Bloomington: Indiana University Press, 1984), 93.
[11] Jon Davison, *Clown: Readings in Theatre Practice* (London: Palgrave Macmillan, 2013), 9–10.
[12] Mary Bryden, "Clowning with Beckett," in *A Companion to Samuel Beckett*, ed. S. E. Gontarski (Malden, MA: Wiley Blackwell, 2010), 358–71, here 366.
[13] Joshua Delpech-Ramey, "Sublime Comedy: On the Inhuman Rights of Clowns," *SubStance*, vol. 39, no. 2 (2010): 133–4.

and part-thing, or, as some would suggest, even part-monster. It is not surprising that the contemporary clown figure is frequently taken up in the realm of horror.[14] In scholarly discourse, Noël Caroll's account of the clown has advanced this turn toward horror, which insightfully addresses the ontological ambiguity of this elusive figure:

> The clown is a monster [. . .] It is a fantastic being, one possessed of an alternate biology that can withstand blows to the head by hammers and bricks that would be deadly for any mere human, and the clown can sustain falls that would result in serious injury for the rest of us. Not only are clowns exaggeratedly misshapen and, at times, outright travesties of the human form—contortions played on our paradigms of the human shape—they also possess a physical resiliency conjoined with muscular and cognitive dysfunctionalities that mark them off as an imaginary species.[15]

For Caroll, the clown represents a kind of superhuman monster, which fascinates through its defiance of categories. Able to withstand deadly violence, clowns represent the undead, condemned to a kind of immortality. Yet the clown is still uncannily human-like in bodily appearance and expression. At once human and inhuman, then, clowns reveal much about our own judgments of what constitutes a human and what determines its degradation. Not only does Caroll's definition raise these critical issues, it also directs us back to the Exil Ensemble's *Hamletmaschine*, whose foregrounding of the clown borrows the frame of this protracted tradition in theater history to address the complex ontology and ethics of the (in)human.

In a brief but rich text on clowns, theater, and philosophy, Joshua Delpech-Ramey similarly characterizes the clown primarily as inhuman.[16] He notes that in the ancient rule of theater, the clown cannot be killed. What is more, it cannot kill itself. Drawing on examples from Shakespeare to Beckett and Charlie Chaplin to Rainspan '43, Delpech-Ramey elucidates this claim. Modern clowns descend from Shakespeare's "holy fool," and, in this tradition, he writes, "The fool at court is allowed to blaspheme, to ridicule the king, and to indulge in behavior

---

[14] One could name numerous examples here. Stephen King's paradigmatic *It*, also adapted for the screen, is particularly noteworthy. See the recent "Special Issue on Violent Clowns," ed. Anna-Sophie Jürgens, Jarno Hietalahti, Lena Straßburger, and Susanne Ylönen, in *Comedy Studies*, vol. 11, no. 1 (2020).
[15] Noël Caroll, "Humor and Horror," *Journal of Aesthetics and Art Criticism*, vol. 57, no. 2 (1999): 155.
[16] Delpech-Ramey, "Sublime Comedy," 132.

that would otherwise get him killed. The modern clown is something like a superfool, who appears to have not a protected sacrosanct life, but one that is strangely, uncannily *immortal*."[17] But the immortality of the clown should not be mistaken for a sort of deified invincibility. Rather, immortality is the inescapable domain of the undead.[18] The inhumanity of the modern clown results in part from its purgatory existence between life and death.

A better understanding of the ontology of the clown can be achieved with reference to political philosophy and Giorgio Agamben's concept of bare life. Deriving from the Greek term *zoē*, at its most basic, bare life presents "the simple fact of living common to all living beings (animals, men, or gods)."[19] But beyond the potential non-anthropocentrism of *zoē* (indeed, elsewhere Agamben rejects what he calls "the anthropological machine of humanism"),[20] the concept also indicates a living being without political or legal rights and privileges. *Zoē* stands in contrast to *bios*, the political life of a person or group. The two are, however, not opposites; rather, they are irrevocably intertwined. As Agamben puts it, "Bare life remains included in politics in the form of exemption, that is, something that is included solely through an exclusion."[21] This logic serves to account for the marginalization, neglect, and mistreatment of certain groups and individuals beyond the pale of the jurisdiction of the state. It constitutes precarious and dispossessed populations that subsist outside the representational capacities of the state but who are still confined within the state's political life, or *bios*.

Agamben identifies refugees as well as Jews and Roma under the Nazis as examples of populations throughout history thrust into a state of exception. They live a brute existence within the state but essentially possess no political or legal rights. In *Remnants of Auschwitz*, Agamben presents the example of the *Muselmann*, the barely living death camp detainee, as indicative of radical bare existence—the absolute living dead.[22] On the face of it, comparing victims of the Nazis and refugees to clowns seems not only inconceivable but also in bad taste. Yet the Exil Ensemble's production of *Hamletmaschine* urges us to account for the clown and all that it could represent in this context. Certainly, the

---

[17] Delpech-Ramey, "Sublime Comedy," 132–3.
[18] Delpech-Ramey, "Sublime Comedy," 134.
[19] Giorgio Agamben, *Homo Sacer: Sovereign Power and Bare Life*, trans. Daniel Heller-Roazen (Stanford, CA: Stanford University Press, (1995) 1998), 1.
[20] Giorgio Agamben, *The Open: Man and Animal*, trans. Kevin Attell (Stanford, CA: Stanford University Press, (2002) 2004), 29.
[21] Agamben, *Homo Sacer*, 11.
[22] Giorgio Agamben, *Remnants of Auschwitz: The Witness and the Archive*, trans. Daniel Heller-Roazen (New York: Zone Books, (1998) 1999), 54.

catastrophe and barbarism of the Syrian civil war have not only made the country uninhabitable, but also subjected its inhabitants to terrible pain and suffering. The war has stretched the limits of humanity and arguably nearly destroyed its self-worth. What is left, then, but bare existence, exemption, inclusion only via exclusion? As clowns, the performers represent aspects of this "bare life" status while displaying, in Delpech-Ramey's words, an "inhuman drive to exist beyond every [human] limitation."[23]

Inhuman Objects (of Comedy and Violence)

In theater performance, the inhumanity of the clown manifests itself through a proximity to the object world of things, of inert matter.[24] Eunjung Kim has argued convincingly for the imbrication of the inhuman and objecthood. Writing within the context of disability and queer studies, Kim maintains that when bodies are brought into relation with objects, this frequently becomes a condemning act of dehumanization. The denial of one's humanity based on the attachment to an object can transpire in the form of epithets of comparison and mistreatments. However, Kim also suggests that the deliberate embrace of objecthood, that is, an assertive act of "unbecoming human," can also bring with it a critical "ethics of proximity that reveals the workings of the boundary of the human."[25] This ethics of proximity between humans and objects assumes yet another dimension in the context of clowns, whose objects are almost without fail objects of comedy. This is manifested in *Hamletmaschine*, as the clowns brandish balloons, dolls, pencils, and Coke bottles. With these objects, they also perform tricks. When comedy is introduced to the fragile divide between humans and objects, the scale tips toward inhumanity. Comedy and horror alike belong to the realm of the inhuman.[26] This nexus of objects, comedy, and inhumanity reverberates most vehemently in the play's third act, "Scherzo."

The "Scherzo," already an established genre of musical levity, playfulness, and comical interlude, sets up the potential for comedy onstage. Act 3 in Müller's original text is composed almost entirely of descriptive stage directions and has long presented both a challenge and an opportunity for directors. In the Exil Ensemble's performance of this act, all the clowns position themselves downstage from a barely visible scrim, which serves to divide upstage and downstage and upon which the text

---

[23] Delpech-Ramey, "Sublime Comedy," 136.
[24] Delpech-Ramey, "Sublime Comedy," 134.
[25] Eunjung Kim, "Unbecoming Human: An Ethics of Objects," *GLQ: A Journal of Lesbian and Gay Studies*, vol. 21, no. 2–3 (2015): 296.
[26] Delpech-Ramey, "Sublime Comedy," 137.

is projected in translation. If spoken in German, it is translated and projected in Arabic. If it is in Arabic, then it is translated and projected in German. (English translation of all text appears in the surtitles positioned to the left and right of the proscenium arch.) The scrim is the only permanent physical object of the otherwise dark and minimalist set.

Yet in this act the strange repertoire of mobile objects of the clowns proliferate. Now there is also a wheelchair, a clown doll, an ironing board and iron, a toothbrush, a spray bottle, a cup, and a sledgehammer. Vigorous Dabke-style music ushers in the scene. One clown, Agha, remains upstage behind the scrim, mounted on a pedestal and holding a microphone. Unlike the other clowns, Agha only appears on three occasions during the performance, and each time recites from his own texts. In "Scherzo" he appears for the second time and emulates a kind of outlandishly morbid television entertainment program host. From behind the scrim, he enthusiastically introduces Ophelia and Hamlet as if they were contestants on his show. Repeating their names several times, he gives them various tragic biographies for the present, containing death, flight, and migration. Consider one example:

> That is Ophelia. Her father is Agamemnon. At the end of the thirties he had close ties to the fascist party. Her mother is a contemporary Palestinian artist. Ophelia was born in 1976 in Tehran and was murdered there in 1991.
>
> [Das ist Ophelia: Ihr Vater ist Agamemnon. Ende der Dreißigerjahre stand er der faschistischen Partei nahe. Ihre Mutter ist eine zeitgenössische, palästinensische Künstlerin. Ophelia wurde im Jahre 1976 in Tehreran geboren, und wurde dort 1991 ermordet.][27]

Agha's introductions continue in this way. He only pauses for brief interludes to join his fellow clowns in dance. Mixing religious texts with Greek mythology, and Levantine and African history, Agha reimagines Ophelia and Hamlet in a strange mix of history and fiction, past and present.

Finally, Agha introduces himself with a high-pitched ululation. With his own variation, he draws on Müller's text in Act 1: "And I?" "I am the third clown in the Arab Spring" ("Und ich?" "Ich bin der dritte Clown im Arabischen Frühling"). Agha then launches into an account

---

[27] Agha's texts have not been published. These are cited directly from the play. I am grateful to Anna Bause for providing a digital copy of the play's premiere at the Maxim Gorki Theater. Unless otherwise indicated, all translations from the German are mine.

of what it means to be the "clown of the Arab Spring," an uprising for justice whose rejoinder has been years of absolute tyranny and massacre.

> To survive does not mean to live. My friends and I, we died eight times, but we survived. At the same time, the old dictator lived the last eight years of his life, although he was actually dead. The edge of death is death.
>
> [Überleben bedeutet nicht leben. Meine Freunde und ich, wir starben acht Mal aber wir überlebten. Gleichzeitig lebte der alte Diktator die letzten acht Jahre seines Lebens, obwohl er eigentlich tot war. Der Rand des Todes ist der Tod.]

The curse of survival is the condemnation of immortality for the clown, which has nothing to do with eternal life but instead with a bare life existence. At the precipice of death is only more death. Under a dictatorship and the annihilation of human rights, the dignity of life ceases to exist for anyone but the dictator. Agha continues:

> We dig for the dead, we bury them and bid farewell. But we survivors died without having received the calm of a grave. The future belongs to the dead under the earth, because only those who rest in a grave will be reborn. But we live as unburied dead without a future and without a past [. . .] Give us our weapons, give us our daily war and a chest riddled with bullets. Amen.
>
> [Wir graben für die Toten, wir begraben sie und nehmen Abschied von ihnen. Wir Überlebenden aber sind gestorben, ohne die Ruhe eines Grabes geschenkt bekommen zu haben. Den Toten unter der Erde gehört die Zukunft, denn nur jene, die in einem Grab ruhen, werden wiedergeboren. Wir aber leben als unbegrabene Tote ohne Zukunft und ohne Vergangenheit [. . .] Gib uns unsere Waffen, unseren täglichen Krieg und einen Brustkorb, gefüllt mit Munition. Amen.]

Grave diggers, survivors, the living dead—the clowns of the Arab Spring are all of these things. Their existence is one without past or future because they have even been deprived of a grave, a final resting place. Again evoking Müller, Agha concludes his own macabre prayer for daily war and death. His texts are the basis for a grotesque performance of musical comedy.

Downstage, against the thematic backdrop of unbounded violence, the other clowns perform an obscene variety show. They each engage in the repetition of a singular activity with their individual objects. Karim Daoud irons his hand, Mazen Aljubbeh sprays his hair, Kenda Hmeidan appears to brush her teeth, and so forth. Eventually, all the clowns begin to dance. The "crazy clown hour," in the phrase of one performer, concludes with a series of pantomimed mass killings. The aforementioned objects transform into imaginary weapons, which the clowns direct at each other in an orgy of mass murder. After each execution, there is a brief pause of silence and stillness. Müller's text is projected onto the scrim. Then the music suddenly starts again, the clowns are revived, and they begin interacting with their objects and dancing as before. They dramatically repeat this act of mass murder and subsequent revival several times. Although Agha is no longer visibly present behind the scrim, the soundtrack is punctuated by his voice in Arabic and his excited ululations. The undead dimension of the clown is brought forth in this uncanny and violent repetition of murder. Performing Agha's text, the clowns are marked for death, but are nonetheless unable to die. This scenario echoes in the production's recurring mimed scenes of murder and mass suicide just behind the scrim. These acts forge a shadowy landscape of grisly violence and death. Driven by objects, excess, and repetition, the clowns demonstrate their inhuman dimension as both a result of brutal dehumanization through violence and dispossession and as a consequence of their uncanny proximity to banal objects.

Clowns, Refugees, and the Theater of Confrontation

Kim's ethics of the inhuman leads us to what could be called a critical inhumanist position, but while she promptly moves beyond the human and toward diverse ontologies, the Exil Ensemble's work revisits the questions of universal humanism and human rights.[28] This unfolds especially with regard to the status of the refugee in today's world. At this juncture, a return to Agamben and his concept of the *homo sacer* offers both further insight and finally leads us to Hannah Arendt, whose famous argument for "a right to have rights" still reveals much about what it means to be human and the standards by which humanity is measured and boundaries are drawn.

Agamben declares the refugee to be the contemporary incarnation of the *homo sacer*, the human being that cannot be ritually offered, but can be killed with impunity. The *homo sacer* is a subject not only stripped of the juridico-political rights of a citizen but also excluded from the category of human. It is relegated to bare life existence. Yet the *homo sacer* is intrinsic to the state's very exercise of power; it occupies a state of

---

[28] Kim, "Unbecoming Human," 305.

exception from within the state. In Agamben's words, "*homo sacer* names something like the originary 'political' relation, which is to say, bare life insofar as it operates in an inclusive exclusion as the referent of the sovereign decision."[29] If the concentration camp detainee, the so-called *Muselmann*, under the Nazis is the prototype of the modern *homo sacer*, then the refugee is its progeny. In his brief sketch "We Refugees," a homage to Hannah Arendt's earlier essay of the same name, Agamben draws this connection:

> [I]nasmuch as the refugee unhinges the old trinity of state/nation/territory—this apparently marginal figure deserves rather to be considered the central figure of our political history. It would be well not to forget that the first camps in Europe were built as places to control refugees, and that the progression—internment camps, concentration camps, extermination camps—represents a perfectly real filiation. One of the few rules of the Nazis faithfully observed in the course of the "final solution" was that only after the Jews and [Roma] were completely denationalized (even of that second-class citizenship that belonged to them after the Nuremberg laws) could they be sent to extermination camps.[30]

The biopolitics—or better necropolitics—of the Nazis and their extermination camps was, as Agamben elucidates, not an aberration or anomaly of history but rather a practice central to the fiction of nation-state sovereignty.[31] According to Agamben, this is also a practice to which denationalized refugees are subject, for they are similarly denied the rights of citizens. Depriving persons of rights is the first step in targeting them for death.

The Exil Ensemble's production of *Hamletmaschine* does not explore the status of the refugee directly. This later project is distinct from the Ensemble's first production with director Yael Ronen, titled *Winterreise* (*Winter Journey*, 2017), which is a kind of autoethnographic exploration of life as a refugee in contemporary Germany. *Hamletmaschine* instead offers a much more perplexing and searing perspective, through its

---

[29] Agamben, *Homo Sacer*, 85.
[30] Giorgio Agamben, "We Refugees," *Symposium* vol. 49, no. 2 (1995): 117.
[31] Regarding "biopolitics," see Michel Foucault, *Discipline and Punish: The Birth of the Prison*, trans. Alan Sheridan (New York: Vintage, (1975) 1991). It bears noting that Agamben's text precedes Achille Mbembe's famous theorization of "necropolitics," and he employs the term "thanatopolitics" to refer to politics of death. Regarding "necropolitics," see Achille Mbembe, "Necropolitics," trans. Libby Meintjes, *Public Culture* vol. 15, no. 1 (2003): 11–40.

staging of bare life existence. The vicissitudes of the refugee, deprived of rights, humanity, and ultimately marked for death, are represented through the performance of the clown. Positioned between the human and the inhuman, the clown offers more than a simple metaphor. Through the chronicle of war, flight, and exile, this production confronts the audience with a tale of dehumanization. It is the tale of "becoming clown."

In his final scene, Agha borrows the form of Hamlet's letter to Ophelia, read by her father Polonius in Shakespeare's *Hamlet*, which begins "O dear Ophelia," to narrate a story not of sexual desire but of paramilitary violence and control that turned into interminable flight: "Dear Ophelia, my drama took place on February 3 at 12 noon in front of the parliament building in Damascus" ("Liebe Ophelia, am 3. Februar, 12 Uhr mittags fand mein Drama in Damaskus vor dem Parlamentsgebäude statt"). He relates events connected with being picked up by security officers for protesting. Implicit details of torture and coercive confessions follow. But his final monologue ends with a return to Müller. Not only is there a mood of circularity in these last lines, but there is also a proclamation of global entanglements and of the continuity of violence:

> Berlin is a port on a sea of blood that reaches to Damascus. I have begun digging a hole under Alexanderplatz. Maybe it will be a grave, maybe a tunnel under the sea.
>
> [Berlin ist eine Hafenstadt an einem Meer aus Blut, das bis Damaskus reicht. Ich habe begonnen, ein Loch in den Alexanderplatz zu graben. Vielleicht wird es Grab, vielleicht ein Tunnel unter dem Meer.]

Remnants of Müller's opening text pierce these last lines by Agha. By comparison, Müller writes, "I stood at the shore and talked to the surf BLABLA, the ruins of Europe behind me" (Ich stand an der Küste und redete mit der Brandung BLABLA, im Rücken die Ruinen von Europa) (Act 1).[32] Agha mobilizes Müller's evocation of the past and history, with what Malkin notes is a reference to Walter Benjamin's "Theses on the Philosophy of History" and the ruins of history violently accruing on the heels of progress, and brings it into the multidirectional politics

---

[32] The English translation is borrowed from Heiner Müller, "Hamletmachine," trans. Carl Weber, *Performing Arts Journal*, vol. 4, no. 3 (1980): 141.

of the present.³³ From start to finish, Agha's epistolary monologue narrates a scenario of near death that results in flight. However, flight provides no permanent solution. As a refugee, the struggle for the legitimacy of existence continues well beyond the scene of original terror. Notwithstanding the weight of his own words, Agha as a clown continues to perform, apparently inured to their horror. The clown is no tragic hero; he has no access to history or transcendence. Here again the clown's uncanny and even comical performance undermines narrative tragedy. As he reads, Agha dramatically, indeed clownishly, wipes away tears. Unsettling as the action seems, it altogether matches the clown's antics. The scene intentionally alienates in more ways than one.

Theater, especially since Brecht, is often about confrontation. The spectator is "made to face something."³⁴ Even in her much later phenomenological treatise for theater, Erika Fischer-Lichte maintains that confrontation is critical, albeit in a different way. For her, the bodily co-presence of performers and spectators in a given space impels both confrontation and interaction: "The performance emerges from their [performers' and spectators'] encounter—as a result of its confrontation, its interaction" ("Die Aufführung entsteht aus ihrer Begegnung— aus ihrer Konfrontation, aus ihrer Interaktion").³⁵ In theater, whether a site of ideology or a site of phenomenology, spectators are drawn into an encounter and must reckon with what is on the other side and in what relationship they stand to that object of encounter. While some might argue for the distinction between theater and real life, Bert O. States reminds us that "[p]erformances may well go on in the theatre but they are *transitive* in nature"; in other words, performance in the theater can bear a purpose beyond its immediate context and follow us well past its hallowed walls.³⁶

This chapter opened with questions about encounter and the challenge such an encounter might pose to our perceptions. Theater provides the occasion for this encounter, this confrontation. Following Arendt, the encounter with the clown and the refugee presents the breakdown of the conception of human rights. Arendt recognized that

---

[33] Walter Benjamin, "Theses on the Philosophy of History," in *Illuminations: Essays and Reflections*, ed. Peter Demetz, trans. Harry Zohn (New York: Schocken, (1955) 1968). See also Malkin, *Memory-Theater and Postmodern Drama*, 27.

[34] Bertolt Brecht, *Brecht on Theatre: The Development of an Aesthetic*, ed. and trans. John Willett (New York: Hill and Wang, (1957) 1964), 37.

[35] Erika Fischer-Lichte, *Die Ästhetik des Performativen* (Frankfurt: Suhrkamp, 2004), 58. My translation. The published English translation of this passage is quite different. For this reason, I have cited the original German version.

[36] Bert O. States, "Performance as Metaphor," *Theatre Journal*, vol. 48, no.1 (1996): 9.

not only were human rights profoundly ambiguous and divisive, but that they were also extremely precarious—even conditional. In *The Origins of Totalitarianism*, she writes that "The conception of human rights based upon the assumed existence of humans as such, broke down at the very moment when those who professed to believe in it were for the first time confronted with people who had indeed lost all other qualities and specific relationships—except that they were still human."[37] *Hamletmaschine* creates this confrontation, and in the tradition of Brecht, it asks what it means to be human; indeed, this has never been a stable category.[38] While Brecht never relinquished the idea of the human and the human's capacity for action, he also never took it for granted.

For Arendt, the Declaration of the Rights of Man in the late eighteenth century was a historical turning point. It indicated for the first time that man and not God's command would be the source of law. However, as Arendt articulates it, there was a paradox at the heart of this declaration of inalienable human rights because, in her words, "it reckoned with an 'abstract' human being who seemed to exist nowhere."[39] Enacted within the terms of the French Revolution, universal human rights thus quickly became blended with national emancipation and were ultimately inapplicable to those living in tribal communities or other social orders distinct from emancipated sovereignty. Indeed, as Gayatri Chakravorty Spivak importantly reminds us, human rights are not only Eurocentric, they long have been an alibi for intervention and violations of all sorts.[40] They are in effect rights reduced to a passport. Universal human rights therefore became inextricably linked to the nation-state and citizenship. Ratified by the United Nations in 1948, the Universal Declaration of Human Rights (UDHR) made another attempt at the promise to uphold the accordance of inalienable rights to all humans in the aftermath of the horrendous catastrophe that was World War II. But Arendt remained skeptical about its renewed capacity to defend and uphold these rights de facto. In her oft-invoked formulation "a right to have rights," she maintained that when national rights were dispossessed, as in the case of the Jews under the Nazis, human rights followed.[41] Deprived of legal personhood, the stateless were also rightless. This presented not only a conceptual gray area but also a juridical loophole. In a more recent

---

[37] Hannah Arendt, *The Origins of Totalitarianism* (Orlando, FL: Harcourt, (1951) 1968), 299.
[38] Brecht, *Brecht on Theatre*, 37.
[39] Arendt, *The Origins of Totalitarianism*, 291.
[40] Gayatri Chakravorty Spivak, "Righting Wrongs," *South Atlantic Quarterly*, vol. 103, no. 2–3 (2004): 524.
[41] Arendt, *The Origins of Totalitarianism*, 296.

critical revisiting of Arendt's theories for the present condition of migrants, refugees, and otherwise undocumented individuals, Ayten Gündoğdu unambiguously states that "[e]xpulsion from their political communities entailed an expulsion from humanity, as they lost not only their citizenship rights but also their human rights."[42] Humanity suddenly had grades of identification and value. Arendt patently anticipates Agamben (and certainly her work was a significant influence) with the words, "The world found nothing sacred in the abstract nakedness of being human."[43] Beyond the more abstract concept of national belonging, statelessness or bare life implies an inactive life without the possibility of participating in the political life of a community and of working, what Arendt has described elsewhere as the crux of *vita activa* (the tripartite of work, labor, and action), the foundation for the general conditions of human existence.[44] Refugees are denied all, if not most, of these rights.[45] Following Arendt, confronted with the clown and the refugee—the human stripped of human rights and therefore humanity—the theater audience encounters the absolute impossibility of the human as such.

Broadly speaking, critics have emphasized the work of the Exil Ensemble as a promotion of the humanity of refugees and an appeal to an ethics of universalism.[46] In the wake of the so-called "Welcoming Culture" ("Willkommenskultur") moment in Germany in 2015, we witnessed a strong discursive return to universal humanism. Recall for instance Amnesty International's short film campaign "Look Beyond Borders" of 2016, in which European citizens sit face to face with refugees and make

---

[42] Ayten Gündoğdu, *Rightlessness in an Age of Rights: Hannah Arendt and the Contemporary Struggle of Migrants* (Oxford: Oxford University Press, 2015), 2.
[43] Arendt, *The Origins of Totalitarianism*, 299.
[44] Hannah Arendt, *The Human Condition* (Chicago: University of Chicago Press, 1958), 7–8.
[45] In the German context and elsewhere, there are restrictions on when and how much refugees may work. Work permits are of course only obtainable by refugees with official refugee status. It may be noted that according to the Dublin Regulation, not all refugees are permitted to apply for asylum status in a given country and the application process for asylum can take months, even years. For further information, see Jan-Paul Brekke and Grete Brochmann, "Stuck in Transit: Secondary Migration of Asylum Seekers in Europe, National Differences, and the Dublin Regulation," *Journal of Refugee Studies*, vol. 28, no. 2 (2015): 145–62. For an account of refugee rights and politics in Germany, see Olivia Landry, "'Wir sind alle Oranienplatz!' Space for Refugees and Social Justice in Berlin," *Seminar*, vol. 51, no. 4 (2015): 398–414.
[46] Marike Janzen, "The Gorki Theater's *Exil Ensemble* as State-Sponsored Repudiation of Citizenship," in *Writing Beyond the State: Post-Sovereign Approaches to Human Rights in Literary Studies*, ed. Alexandra S. Moore and Samantha Pinto (Cham, Switzerland: Palgrave Macmillan, 2020), 258–9, 265–90.

uninterrupted eye contact for a total of four minutes. The video experiment sought to reinforce the human connection between the pairs with the implicit message of similarity and universality beyond borders, language, and culture and was praised for its promotion of empathy and humanitarianism.[47] The Exil Ensemble's aforementioned production, *Winterreise*, also presented a compelling example of such a commitment. Based on a bus trip the Ensemble members take through Germany, *Winterreise* is a performance of discovery and a journey of hope for life in Germany. It applies goodwill, humorous anecdotes about encounters with cultural stereotypes, and even concludes with a reconciliatory hug and the implication that "everything is going to be alright." But this optimism was cursory, as were the humanitarian politics that underpinned it.[48] Moreover, the very fact that civil war still rages in Syria and elsewhere cannot simply be forgotten. After this first production, the Ensemble subsequently took things in a dramatically different direction. Preceding *Hamletmaschine*, in 2017 the Ensemble performed Agha's play *Skelett eines Elefanten in der Wüste* (*Skeleton of an Elephant in the Desert*). Against a war-ravaged setting, the startling account of a sharpshooter unfolds. This brutal and absurd tale provides a thematic precursor to *Hamletmaschine*. Müller's piece is already wrought with despair, violence, and a biting critique that is far less reconciliatory than it is provocative. As I argued in the introductory pages, *Hamletmaschine* is an edict for the crisis of the human. Thus, the conceit of the encounter as an opportunity for universal understanding and human connection notably advanced by Emmanuel Levinas (and evoked in the "Look Beyond Borders" project) is turned on its head through this performance of *Hamletmaschine*. As Levinas unambiguously puts it, "To be in relation with the other face to face—is to be unable to kill."[49] In other words, the encounter—the meeting of the face—is thought to be the site and enactment of "moral consciousness."[50] Yet Levinas's ethical-ontological approach of being-with-the-other still holds as a method, notwithstanding its conceptual limitations from within an explicitly Judeo-Christian framework. Read against the grain, the encounter does not serve merely to subtend the

---

[47] The video project is still available to watch on the Amnesty International website: www.amnesty.org/en/latest/news/2016/05/look-refugees-in-the-eye/.

[48] Already in 2016, Beverly Weber wrote convincingly about the abrupt end to humanitarian discourse, in the wake of the sexual violence at the Cologne New Year's Eve gathering, and the resulting more restrictive immigration policies. See Beverly Weber, "The German Refugee Crisis After Cologne: The Race of Refugee Rights," *English Language Notes*, vol. 54, no. 2 (2016): 77–92.

[49] Emmanuel Levinas, *Entre-Nous: Thinking-of-the-Other*, trans. Michael B. Smith and Barbara Harshav (New York: Columbia University Press, (1991) 1998), 10.

[50] Levinas, *Entre-Nous*, 11.

universality of the human, but rather to propose that there is actually no such thing. What is revealed in this performance is not that "refugees are humans just like 'us'" but that the human is a mere abstract concept of the juridico-political structure.

Conclusion

The clowning in *Hamletmaschine* opens up a nuanced exploration of the category of the human and where it begins to fall apart. Human-like, but also dispossessed of human qualities, the clown drifts between the human and the inhuman. It is a liminal and transgressive figure, associated with violence, the immortality of the undead, and the world of inanimate objects. The clown is reminiscent of Agamben's *homo sacer*, a being included within the political life of a community only by way of systematic exclusion and exemption. The *homo sacer* has no rights within or protection by the state. This figure simply exists. The status of bare existence evoked by the performance of the clown in turn appeals to the juridico-political situation of the refugee, or what Agamben refers to as the contemporary epitome of the *homo sacer*. For the statelessness of the refugee significantly reduces a person's scope of possibility and action. Although the Exil Ensemble itself includes artists in exile and war refugees, this chapter has focused on the context and qualities of the clown in order to gain insight into a particular performance of exile and refugee status, rather than to offer a predetermined reflection on the status of the troupe members.

But theater is not simply about spectacle; the encounter and even confrontation of performance is critical to *Hamletmaschine*. The clown reminds us of the arbitrary and precarious nature of the human. If, according to Arendt, human rights are soldered to the rights endowed by a nation-state, then the clown, like the refugee, has no rights. If the universality of human rights is a fiction, for not all humans globally have de facto access to the same rights, then the very concept of what it means to be human is also troubled. *Hamletmaschine* provokes by enigmatic means. The clown is transformed into a political category that flies in the face of humanitarian complacency and the failure to recognize profound inequalities. What is more, it compels us to question our very existence as humans.

Works Cited

Agamben, Giorgio. "We Refugees," *Symposium*, vol. 49, no. 2 (1995): 114–19.
Agamben, Giorgio. *Homo Sacer: Sovereign Power and Bare Life*, trans. Daniel Heller-Roazen (Stanford, CA: Stanford University Press, (1995) 1998).
Agamben, Giorgio. *Remnants of Auschwitz: The Witness and the Archive*, trans. Daniel Heller-Roazen (New York: Zone Books (1998) 1999).
Agamben, Giorgio. *The Open: Man and Animal*, trans. Kevin Attell (Stanford, CA: Stanford University Press, (2002) 2004).

Arendt, Hannah. *The Human Condition* (Chicago: University of Chicago Press, 1958).
Arendt, Hannah. *The Origins of Totalitarianism* (Orlando, FL: Harcourt, (1951) 1968).
Bakhtin, Mikhail. *Rabelais and His World*, trans. Hélène Iswolsky (Bloomington: Indiana University Press, 1984).
Barnett, David. "Die Hamletmaschine," in *Hamlet-Handbuch*, ed. Peter W. Marx (Stuttgart: Metzler, 2014), 422–8.
Benjamin, Walter. "Theses on the Philosophy of History," in *Illuminations: Essays and Reflections*, ed. Peter Demetz, trans. Harry Zohn (New York: Schocken, (1955) 1968), 253–64.
Brecht, Bertolt. *Brecht on Theatre: The Development of an Aesthetic*, ed. and trans. John Willett (New York: Hill and Wang, (1957) 1964).
Brekke, Jan-Paul, and Grete Brochmann. "Stuck in Transit: Secondary Migration of Asylum Seekers in Europe, National Differences, and the Dublin Regulation," *Journal of Refugee Studies*, vol. 28, no. 2 (2015): 145–62.
Bryden, Mary. "Clowning with Beckett," in *A Companion to Samuel Beckett*, ed. S. E. Gontarski (Malden, MA: Wiley Blackwell, 2010), 358–71.
Caroll, Noël. "Humor and Horror," *Journal of Aesthetics and Art Criticism*, vol. 57, no. 2 (1999): 145–60.
Davison, Jon. *Clown: Readings in Theatre Practice* (London: Palgrave Macmillan, 2013).
Delpech-Ramey, Joshua. "Sublime Comedy: On the Inhuman Rights of Clowns," *SubStance*, vol. 39, no. 2 (2010): 131–41.
Fischer-Lichte, Erika. *Die Ästhetik des Performativen* (Frankfurt: Suhrkamp, 2004).
Foucault, Michel. *Discipline and Punish: The Birth of the Prison*, trans. Alan Sheridan (New York: Vintage, (1975) 1991).
Gündoğdu, Ayten. *Rightlessness in an Age of Rights: Hannah Arendt and the Contemporary Struggle of Migrants* (Oxford: Oxford University Press, 2015).
Janzen, Marike. "The Gorki Theater's *Exil Ensemble* as State-Sponsored Repudiation of Citizenship," in *Writing Beyond the State: Post-Sovereign Approaches to Human Rights in Literary Studies*, ed. Alexandra S. Moore and Samantha Pinto (Cham, Switzerland: Palgrave Macmillan, 2020), 265–90.
Kalb, Jonathan. *The Theater of Heiner Müller* (Cambridge: Cambridge University Press, 1998).
Kim, Eunjung. "Unbecoming Human: An Ethics of Objects," *GLQ: A Journal of Lesbian and Gay Studies*, vol. 21, no. 2–3 (2015): 296–320.
Kolesch, Doris, and Matthias Warstat. "Affective Dynamics in the Theatre: Towards a Relational and Poly-Perspectival Performance Analysis," in *Analyzing Affective Societies: Methods and Methodologies*, ed. Antje Kahl (London: Routledge, 2019), 214–29.
Landry, Olivia. "'Wir sind alle Oranienplatz!' Space for Refugees and Social Justice in Berlin," *Seminar*, vol. 51, no. 4 (2015): 398–414.
Landry, Olivia. *Theatre of Anger: Radical Transnational Performance in Contemporary Berlin* (Toronto: University of Toronto Press, 2020).
Levinas, Emmanuel. *Entre-Nous: Thinking-of-the-Other*, trans. Michael B. Smith and Barbara Harshav (New York: Columbia University Press, (1991) 1998).
Malkin, Jeannette. *Memory-Theater and Postmodern Drama* (Ann Arbor: University of Michigan Press, 1999).
Mbembe, Achille. "Necropolitics," trans. Libby Meintjes, *Public Culture*, vol. 15, no. 1 (2003): 11–40.

Meerzon, Yana. "On Dramaturgy of Care and Encounter in the Theatres of Multilingualism: Interview with Ayham Majid Agha," *Critical Stages/Scènes critiques*, no. 20 (2019), www.critical-stages.org/20/on-dramaturgy-of-care-and-encounter-in-the-theatres-of-multilingualism-interview-with-ayham-majid-agha/.

Müller, Heiner. "Hamletmachine," trans. Carl Weber, *Performing Arts Journal*, vol. 4, no. 3 (1980): 141–6.

Müller, Heiner. "Die Hamletmaschine," in *Der Auftrag und andere Revolutionsstücke*, ed. Uwe Wittstock (Stuttgart: Reclam, 1988), 38–46.

Schaper, Rüdiger. "Nach dem Theatercoup: Wie Langhoff und Hillje das Gorki leiten wollen," *Tagesspiegel*, May 23, 2012, www.tagesspiegel.de/kultur/nach-dem-theatercoup-wie-langhoff-und-hillje-das-gorki-leiten-wollen/6661782.html.

Spivak, Gayatri Chakravorty. "Righting Wrongs," *South Atlantic Quarterly*, vol. 103, no. 2–3 (2004): 523–81.

States, Bert O. "Performance as Metaphor," *Theatre Journal*, vol. 48, no.1 (1996): 1–26.

Weber, Beverly. "The German Refugee Crisis After Cologne: The Race of Refugee Rights," *English Language Notes*, vol. 54, no. 2 (2016): 77–92.

Index

acting, actor, 112, 121, 123, 249, 281, 293, 295, 296, 287, 323–24; as strategy, 144–45, 274–75
Adelson, Leslie, 110n1, 228–29, 244, 250n35, 261n1, 264, 265, 283
Adorno, Theodor, 112, 113–14, 125
affect, 26, 41, 124, 157, 192, 194, 197, 200–208, 252, 254,
Afghanistan, 14, 17, 28–30, 323–24
Africa, Africans, 24, 26, 92, 158–59, 162, 331; North Africa, 102
Afro-Brazilians, 158–161
Afro-Germans, *see* Black Germans
afterlife, *see* immortality
Agamben, Giorgio, 323, 329–30, 333–34, 338, 340
Agha, Ayham Majid, 323–25, 331–33, 335–36, 339
Akın, Fatih, 115, 264, 282,
alienation, 86, 87, 92, 93, 94, 124, 138, 157, 188, 191–94, 201–02, 207–09, 271, 275, 276, 336
allegory, 86, 102, 114
alterity, 48, 164n41, 191, 200, 242,
America, *see* United States
American Friends Service Committee, *see* Quakers
Amnesty International, 338
anthropology, 26, 91, 131, 230–31, 232–33, 239, 329
anti-Semitism, 79n52, 138, 170, 172, 174, 180, 192, 199, 264

appropriation, 45, 55, 165, 238, 245, 257, 269, 278,
Arab, Arabic, 123, 216, 218, 223, 225, 262, 266, 271, 331–32, 333
archive, 17, 22–28, 32, 43, 44, 46, 47, 110, 116, 123, 126, 141, 146, 150, 237–39, 240–42, 243–44, 246–54, 256–58; v. Internet, 240–41; arkhe, arkheion, 25, 33, 241–42
Arendt, Hannah, 155n12, 323, 333, 334, 336–38, 340
Arndt, Ernst Moritz, 156
aristocracy, aristocratic, 41–42, 44, 49, 243, 310
assimilation, 134; of Jews in Europe, 155; of European Jews in the U.S., 173–80
asylum, 13–14, 338n45
Auerbach, Erich, 17, 19, 30–32, 99, 134
Auschwitz, 201n24, 329
Australia, 85, 87, 100, 102
Austria, 69, 86, 102–3, 118, 130, 174, 244, 245; annexation of (*Anschluß*) and consequences for Jews, 170–78, 188
Austria-Hungary, 55
autobiography, autobiographical, 38, 43, 44, 53, 120–21, 130, 131, 133, 151, 192, 193, 196n11, 201, 206, 207, 293–94

Aydemir, Fatma, 261–62, 263–65; works by: *Ellbogen* (*Elbows*), 265, 267–70, 271, 272–75, 276, 278

Baggesen, Jens, 40n4, 49, 61n1, 82
Basque, Basque country, 125
belonging, 1, 5, 16, 41, 42, 110, 126, 133–35, 151, 156, 158, 191, 248, 261, 264–67, 274, 276, 278, 281, 283, 285, 288, 289, 290–92, 293, 296, 298–99, 338
Benjamin, Walter, 113, 115, 133, 143, 215, 218, 228, 335
Bergen-Belsen, 200n20, 201
Bergson, Henri, 265, 276–78
Berlin, 68, 72, 74, 115, 117, 188, 192, 216, 217–19, 225, 226, 231, 262, 264, 265, 267, 281–85, 288–99, 335; East, 118
Berliner Ensemble, 121, 123
Berlin Wall, 1, 13
biblical, 100, 137, 162
bibliomigrancy, bibliomigrant, 28, 244
Bildung, *see* education
Black German Heritage and Research Association, 285
Black Germans, 252–53, 281–99
Black Lives Matter, 299n55
blackness, 81, 131, 159, 160, 162–65, 285n12, 310
Bodrožić, Marica, 237–39; works by: *Unterhaltungen deutscher Eingewanderten* (*Conversations of German Immigrants*), 238–58
border, 1–3, 5n9, 13–17, 19–20, 23–25, 27, 30, 32–33, 62, 80–81, 100, 103, 111, 113, 116, 124–26, 130, 143, 146, 147, 196n10, 238, 242, 243, 256, 267, 272, 278, 314, 338; Dutch-German, 129; French-Spanish, 136; Spanish-Portuguese, 140–45, 147, 148

bourgeois, bourgeoisie, 47, 89n13, 163, 165, 314–15
Brazil, 131, 151–66, 220, 299
Brecht, Bertolt, 21, 109, 112, 115, 120, 123, 126, 249, 303–22, 324, 325, 336, 337; works by: *Der kaukasische Kreidekreis* (*The Caucasian Chalk Circle*), 316; *Me-ti. Buch der Wendungen* (*Me-ti. Book of Transformation and Usage*), 303–22; "Der Ungleichheitssatz in der großen Methode" ("The principle of inequality in the Great Method"), 317
Bruckner, Beatrice, 129–30, 131–32, 135, 136–40, 141–48
Brun, Friederike, 37–56; works by: "Ich denke Dein" ("Thinking of You"), 45–46; *Lieder für Hellas* (*Songs for Hellas; also Scherflein für Hellas*), 51–56; *Prosaische Schriften* (*Prosaic Writings*), 42–43, 45; *Wahrheit aus Morgenträumen* (*Truth in Morning Dreams*), 44–45, 52

camp, concentration, 94, 101, 172, 177, 179, 187, 188, 199–204, 220, 329, 334; transit, 199
Canetti, Elias, 244–45
canon, canonical, 2, 5, 7, 39n3, 41, 44n16, 45, 46, 48–49, 89, 90, 99, 102, 111–13, 115, 134n11, 151, 156, 218, 242–43, 248, 249, 251, 256–57, 284, 286, 325
capital, capitalism, 6–7, 94, 97, 124, 229, 234, 304
Catholic, Catholicism, 100, 141, 160–61, 162, 171, 174–75; Catholic Committee for Refugees from Germany, 176, 178–79, 180, 181; National Catholic Welfare Council, 186
Celan, Paul, 17, 218, 246, 255

censorship, 47, 53, 115, 116, 118, 120, 123, 184
China, Chinese, 23, 123, 218, 224, 303–16, 321; philosophy, *see* Mohism
Christianity, 54–55, 80, 91, 103, 125, 137, 138, 225n27, 286, 339
cinema, German, 281–84, 284n10
citizen, citizenry, citizenship, 13–14, 20, 76, 117, 152, 156, 176, 192, 193, 208, 282, 324n2, 333, 334, 337–38
city, *see* urban
Classicism, 50–51
climate, 17, 63, 244
clown, 323, 326–40
Coetzee, J.M., 98; works by: *Doubling the Point: Essays and Interviews*, 92; *Elizabeth Costello*, 85–89, 92–98, 100–102, 103; *The Lives of Animals*, 88
Cold War, 29, 283, 294
collage, 157, 173, 240
colonial, colonialism, colonies, 25–27, 29, 41, 74, 94, 98–99, 102, 114, 154, 227–28, 238, 252, 253, 263, 267n17, 285, 292, 294, 298
Communism, Communist, 115, 116, 289, 310–11, 321
comparative literature, 90, 99, 100, 231
Conrad, Sebastian, 22–23, 30
contingency, 18, 67, 195, 224, 229, 247–48
cosmopolitan, cosmopolitanism, 5, 37–38, 39n3, 41, 55, 56, 69, 74, 76, 87, 88, 91, 92n22, 99, 147, 266n15, 290
community, 1, 5, 6, 7, 16, 63, 70, 134, 146, 147, 180, 194, 200, 201, 202n29, 230, 263, 265, 292, 338, 340; laughter and, 267, 274–78
Confucianism, 304–05, 306, 308–11
Congress of Vienna, 118
Copenhagen, 37–38, 40–42

coronavirus, *see* pandemic
Czech, 215, 220

Dachau, 172, 187
Damascus, 335
Damrosch, David, 19
democracy, democratic, 27, 64, 75, 118, 120, 289, 303, 310
Denmark, Danish (*see also* Copenhagen), 38, 40, 41, 43, 44, 49, 56
deracination, 195, 196, 197, 208
Derrida, Jacques, 25, 220
Detering, Heinrich, 196–97
Deutsches Literaturarchiv Marbach, 238, 253
dialect, 126, 157, 270, 294, 295, 299
dialectic, dialectical, dialectics, 192, 194, 207, 303–06, 311, 312, 316, 317–22
diary, 254
diaspora, diasporic, 147, 191, 194, 195, 244, 252, 292
difference, 76, 113, 131, 147, 164n41, 220, 229, 230–31, 232, 274, 296n52; cultural, 160, 166, 305
disability, 283, 296–97, 299, 330
distant reading, 90, 126
displacement, 1, 5, 7, 8, 17, 24, 30, 39, 56, 111, 113, 116–19, 124, 147, 169, 203, 240, 270
diversity, 6, 91, 173, 196n10, 230, 238, 242, 247, 281, 282, 299n55
documentary, 293–94
drama, *see* play, playwriting
dramaturgy, 326
Dutch, *see* Netherlands, the

East Germany, *see* German Democratic Republic
ecological, 94
economics, 5, 23, 44, 62, 70, 94, 101, 102, 180, 230, 231, 264, 283, 288, 290, 291, 296, 297

editing, editor, 39n3, 41, 43, 44–50, 53, 56, 239, 262, 293, 311–12
education, 20, 21, 50, 53–54, 70–73, 74, 75, 79, 82, 166, 193, 204–06; language, 2n2, 8n14, 157
El-Tayeb, Fatima, 264, 282, 284–86
emigration, 192–95, 243; from Nazi Vienna, 170–88
empathy, 145–46, 165, 207, 275, 339
empire, 4, 16, 28, 32, 51, 123, 156, 244
Enlightenment, 67, 75, 225, 230, 326
enslaved people, *see* slavery
ethnic, ethnicity, 123, 126, 255, 261–66, 268n22, 269–70, 273–75, 278, 282–83, 292, 296–99; ethnic nationalism, 68, 71, 80
ethnography, 157, 161, 334
epistolary writing, 42–56, 336
Eurocentric, Eurocentrism, 16, 97, 100, 103, 216–19, 221–27, 267n17, 337
European, identity, 2–3, 16–32, 49n32, 80–81, 137–38, 152–66, 217, 229–31, 261–64, 282, 286, 298–99
exclusion, 5, 16, 50, 133, 147, 242–43, 266, 275, 285–86, 293, 324, 329–30, 334, 340
Exil Ensemble, 323–40
exile literature, 32, 112
exile studies, 4, 7

fascism, 166, 192, 194, 208, 249, 312n25
Federal Republic of Germany, 20, 294, 325
Fichte, Johann Gottlieb, 61–82
film industry, in Germany, 287–88
Flusser, Vilém, 215–16, 220–22; works by: *Die Schrift. Hat Schreiben Zukunft? (Does Writing Have a Future?)*, 222–26, 234

foreign, foreigner, foreignness, 38, 70, 79, 118, 153, 157, 160n31, 164–65, 194, 197, 264, 274
France, French, 5, 40–41, 65, 67, 69–70, 78–79, 89n13, 116, 146, 157, 162, 177, 180, 220, 243, 271, 292, 294, 307
Franco (Francisco Franco Bahamonde), 132, 136–37, 139–41, 143, 144
Frankfurt (am Main), 262, 265, 275
Frankfurt School, 113, 133
French language, *see* France
French Revolution, 61, 63, 65, 68, 78, 89n13, 125, 243, 337
Freud, Anna, 204n33
Freud, Sigmund, 3, 133, 147n34, 192, 198–99, 205, 269, 272

gender, 101, 159, 256, 326; and language, 268–70; studies, 91
German Culture Nation (*Kulturnation*), 38
German Democratic Republic, 29–30, 73, 74n39, 87, 249, 265, 275, 293–95, 304, 325
Germanistik, *see* German Studies
German language, 1, 18, 37, 42, 48–52, 89, 91, 102, 110, 151, 157, 194–97; literatures, 42, 49, 87–92, 102–03, 151, 156, 255
German Literature Archive Marbach, *see* Deutsches Literaturarchiv Marbach
German Studies, 1–8, 44n16, 87, 88–91, 237, 257, 284
Germany, united, 29, 38
Germany, East, *see* German Democratic Republic
Germany, West, *see* Federal Republic of Germany
global; city, 283, 285, 288, 290, 298–99; history, 17, 22–28; literature, 15, 17, 23–24, 28–30, 102
globalization, 3, 24, 230, 238, 288

Goethe, Johann Wolfgang von, 21, 40, 43n11, 45, 47n25, 111, 122, 155, 218, 242–43
Grjasnowa, Olga, 254, 262; works by: *Der Russe ist einer, der Birken liebt* (*All Russians love Birch Trees*), 264–67, 270–72, 275–78
guest worker, 121–26, 247
guilt, 41–42, 197
Gumbrecht, Hans Ulrich, 19, 22, 89n13, 90–91, 99
grief, 206

Hagen, Sheri, 281–88; works by: *Auf den zweiten Blick* (*At Second Glance*), 283, 288–90, 295–300
Hegel, Georg Wilhelm Friedrich, 109, 304, 308, 317–18
hegemonic, hegemony, 88, 99–100, 229, 242, 247, 249–51, 253, 254, 255, 257–58
Heine, Heinrich, 2, 21, 49, 50n36, 52, 109–26, 257; works by: *Almansor*, 114; *Atta Troll. Ein Sommernachtstraum* (*Atta Troll, a Midsummer Night's Dream*), 116–26; *Deutschland, ein Wintermärchen* (*Germany, a Winter Tale*), 116–20; *Französische Zustände* (*Conditions in France*), 119–20; *Hebräische Balladen* (*Hebrew Ballads*), 257; *Romanzero*, 118; *Vitzliputzli*, 114
Hermand, Jost, 20–21
Hikmet, Nâzım, 111–112, 115, 116–18, 126; works by: "En guzel deniz" ("The Most Beautiful Sea"), 115; *Memleketimden İnsan Manzaraları* (*Human Landscapes from my Country*), 116, 118, 119, 120
Hitler, Adolf, 130, 132, 136–37, 138, 143, 170, 192, 308
Hofmannsthal, Hugo von, 88, 89, 102, 103; works by: *Ein Brief* (*A Letter*), 101

Hölderlin, Friedrich, 81
Holocaust (Shoah), 7, 173, 199, 201, 244, 255, 263,
Holocaust studies, 173
home, 14, 15, 32–33, 40, 42, 109, 110, 114, 117–18, 132, 134, 155–56, 165, 180, 194, 195, 197, 207, 248, 270, 276, 298
homeless, homelessness, 14, 112, 114, 117–18, 125, 133, 134, 160, 199
Homer, 31; works by: *The Odyssey*, 99
homesickness, 41, 119, 193, 290, 291
human, v. the inhuman, 323, 326–40
human rights, 61, 65, 239, 332, 333, 336–40
Humboldt, Alexander von, 73–74, 74n37
Humboldt, Wilhelm von, 71, 73n33, 74
Humboldt University (University of Berlin), 70, 71, 72–73, 74
humor, 217, 227, 228, 245, 254, 261–78
hybrid, hybridity, 24, 261, 266–67, 270
hyperlink, 15, 17, 19, 22, 28, 30–31

Idealism, 61–72, 62n4, 62n5, 69n21, 76, 78n48, 80, 81
identity, 3–4, 8, 24, 67, 80, 81, 86, 130–33, 135, 136, 139–41, 232, 241–42, 251, 252, 255, 256, 264–65, 269, 270, 275, 285, 289, 294, 317, 325, 327; cultural, 125; European, 3n5, 261, 264, 282; German, 119, 163, 249, 255, 282; hyphenated, 112; Jewish, 192, 203; and language, 112, 140, 295; national, 1, 48, 89n13, 114, 129–33, 135, 136, 139, 140–41, 202n29, 286; and perception

(of and by others), 130; politics, 3, 296n52
immigration, 240, 242–49, 250, 255, 324, 339n48; policy during 1930s-1940s, 171, 175–86
immortality, 77–79, 80, 121, 122, 328, 329, 332, 340
imperialism, 5, 114, 309, 320–21
improvisation, 44, 45–46, 123
inclusion, 6, 16, 18, 110, 147, 264–67, 272, 278
India, 13, 14, 23–24, 28, 225, 226–28
indigeneity, indigenous, 100, 160–62, 193
Indonesia, 131
insider, 3, 7, 146
intermediality, 115, 216–18, 225–27, 232, 234, 256–58,
intertextuality, 102, 196, 242, 246, 254, 305, 312
Iran, 30, 115
Islam, 55
isolationism, 19, 70
Italy (*see also* Rome), 42n8, 42n9, 55, 153

Japan, Japanese, 215–17, 310
Jewish German, 191, 208
Jewishness, 164n41
Johnson-Spain, Ines, 218–83, 287–88; works by: *Becoming Black*, 283, 288–89, 293–95, 298–99

Kaddish, 199, 202, 206–07
Kafka, Franz, works by: *Ein Bericht für eine Akademie* (*A Report for an Academy*), 85–96; *Betrachtung* (*Contemplation*), 256; "Vor dem Gesetz" ("Before the Law"), 101
Kant, Immanuel, 71, 74
Keilson, Hans, 191–209
Kermani, Navid, 30, 110, 255–56
Kim, Eunjung, 323, 330
kinship, 87, 158
Kittler, Friedrich, 220

Lacan, Jacques, 199, 201, 205n36
Latin, 26, 50–51, 101, 141, 216, 224, 234
laughter, *see* humor
law, 69n24, 133, 142–44, 159n25, 170, 177, 337
Lebanese, Lebanon, 265, 270, 271
Lehnert, Nelly, 173–74
Lenin, Vladimir, 303, 308, 313, 316
Levinas, Emmanuel, 323, 339
LGBTQ, 238, 289, 296n52, 330
Literaturhaus Basel, 238
Literaturhaus Stuttgart, 238
Literarisches Colloquium Berlin, 238, 247, 248, 251, 252, 253, 256
literary history, 15–33, 38–41, 44–45, 49, 85n1, 87–99, 102–03, 120
local, 5n9, 6–7, 8n14, 19, 20, 23–24, 28, 38, 41, 44–45, 56, 87, 91, 102, 117, 238, 252, 258, 261, 264, 283, 288–89, 293–95, 297–98
logographic, 219–24
Lorde, Audre, 247, 285n12, 289–90
loss, 116, 119, 153, 154, 156, 162, 165, 196, 197, 200, 206, 208, 238, 247, 292
love, 109, 113–14, 146n32, 156, 296, 305–06, 310–16, 320–22

magnetism, 81
Mallorca, 129–30, 132, 141, 142
Mann, Heinrich, 152n1, 154n8, 155n11, 156n15; works by: *Zwischen den Rassen* (*Between the Races*), 155, 164–65
Mann, Julia, 151–66
Mann, Thomas, 31, 129, 135, 151–52, 155–56, 163, 164, 165
Marx, Karl, 6–7, 109, 120, 122, 313; Marxism, 74n39, 124–25, 304–22
Massey, Doreen, 283, 288–90, 298
machine, 326, 329
materialism, 64–65, 241, 304–05, 311–12, 321

Maxim Gorki Theater, 239, 254–55, 324, 326
media studies, media theory, 215–16, 220–23, 234
memoir, 7, 52, 132–48, 151–66, 196–97
memory, 7–8, 14, 73, 76, 96, 110, 111, 121, 145–48, 156, 161, 163, 197–98, 241–42, 254–55; studies, 262–63
metaphysics, 64, 71, 76, 77
Mexico, 114, 138
Middle East, 102, 123, 223
Midwest, 173–74, 178, 179–81, 183
migration (*see also* emigration, immigration), 1, 4, 5, 13–15, 20, 27, 30, 33, 91, 116, 119, 126, 151, 208, 217, 242, 246–53, 255–57, 264, 267, 270, 278, 285, 292, 324, 331; literature of, 21–22, 216, 239, 250, 252; voluntary v. forced, 238–39
minoritized, minority, 14, 238, 263, 264, 265, 269, 273–76, 278, 282, 324
miscegenation, 155–56
mobility, 4, 5, 24, 31, 111, 130, 132, 135–36, 142, 146, 217, 234, 262
modernism, 117, 151
modernity, 87, 111, 113, 133, 155, 156, 159–60, 309, 310, 311
Mohism, 303–15, 318, 321
monolingual, 15, 80, 87, 102
monster, 327–28
morality, 65, 68, 71, 76–77, 80, 91, 94, 97, 119, 161, 208n45, 315–16, 339
Moritz, Karl Philipp, works by: *Magazin zur Erfahrungsseelenkunde (Journal of Empirical Psychology)*, 64–68, 81
mourning, 199, 202, 206–07
Mozambique, 153
Mudimbe, Valentin Y., 26–27
mulatto, 158

Müller, Heiner, works by: *Hamletmaschine (Hamletmachine)*, 323, 325–27, 328–40
multiethnic, *see* ethnic
multilingual, 20, 28, 89–90, 91, 99, 102, 103, 115, 117, 157, 162, 215, 220, 238, 291, 292, 298, 299
music, 45, 152, 153, 155, 161, 162–63, 218, 231, 291n41, 297, 299, 308, 330, 331–33
Muslim, 13–14, 30, 264
Muslim Ban, *see* Travel Ban

Namibia, 252
national, character, 70, 73, 79; literature, 15, 17, 19, 21, 24, 91, 243
nationalism, 2–7, 6, 13–14, 62, 68–69, 71, 74, 76, 80n53, 82, 91, 119, 133, 180, 238, 267
nation-state, 2–8, 14, 16, 24, 32, 135, 337, 340
National Refugee Service, 177, 178
National Socialism, 94, 97, 101, 113, 130, 132, 136–37, 138, 139, 142–45, 169–88, 191, 202–09, 255, 329, 334, 337
native, 15, 32; language, 41, 111–12
Native American, 138
Netherlands, the, 129–31, 192–208
New York City, emigrants arriving in, 174–83
Nigeria, Nigerian, 281, 294, 296
North, 165
North Africa, 102
nostalgia, 116, 240, 241
Nuremberg Laws, 170–71, 174, 334

orphans, 198–99, 202–08, 246–47, 294
Özdamar, E.S., 110, 112, 115–16, 120–21; works by: *Karagöz in Alamania/Schwarzauge in Deutschland (Blackeye in Germany)*, 122–26; *Das Leben ist*

eine Karawanserei (*Life is a Caravansery*), 120
outsider, 3, 7, 24, 38, 119, 125, 133–35, 137–38, 142–44, 146, 166, 188, 196, 266, 270

painting, 61, 63, 65, 116, 221, 243, 286, 288
Palestine, 323
pandemic (coronavirus), 8, 15, 16, 114, 238
parcours (media term), 239
passport, 139, 170, 172, 177, 244, 249, 337
patriotism, 69, 156, 311
Pazarkaya, Yüksel, 109, 110, 112, 115, 249, 250
pedagogy, *see* education
PEN Center of German-Speaking Writers Abroad, 194
Philhellenism, 39, 46, 51–52, 54–55
philology, 16, 39, 41, 46, 47, 48–54, 56, 89, 100, 113, 242
plantation, 4, 41, 152, 158, 163
POC, 284n10, 285–86, 292–93, 296, 298–99
police, 120, 123–24, 132, 136, 139, 140, 143, 185, 299n55
populism, 14, 33
Portugal, Portuguese, 152, 157, 161–62, 220
postcolonial, postcolonialism, 4, 25–26, 27, 32, 88, 90, 91, 92, 97, 98, 100, 102, 103, 130, 229, 252, 253, 254, 267, 274
postmigrant, 239, 261, 324–25
postmodern, 102, 326
poverty, 16, 244
power, and violence, 133, 141–45
primitivity, 155, 160, 163
Protestant, Protestantism, 161, 171
Prussia, 102, 119, 174
psychoanalysis, 4, 81, 192–209, 239

psychology, empirical, 62–67, 81–82
psychopolitics, 67–68

Quakers, and American Friends Service Committee (AFSC), 169–88
queer, see LGBTQ

race, racial, 101, 138, 152, 155–56, 158–60, 162–66, 267, 268n22, 269, 283, 285–86, 294, 296, 299n55
racism, 15, 68, 138, 157, 254, 262–64, 268, 270, 273, 278, 324
rationality, lack of, in human behavior, 145
realism, 32, 92, 94–97, 99, 102, 135
refugee, refugees, 13–17, 22–30, 32–33, 114, 117, 130–39, 146–47, 169–88, 262, 266, 325, 329, 333–40; United Nations High Commission for, 13
religion, religious, 7, 13, 16, 42–44, 55, 76–78, 123, 125, 153, 160–62, 174–75, 255, 265, 270, 309, 331
Romanticism, 50, 61–62, 69n21, 75, 121
Rome, 38, 42, 46, 48, 49n32, 117
Rothberg, Michael, 7n12, 262–63
Rousseau, Jean-Jacques, 64–65, 67, 68
Russia, 28–29, 42n8, 116, 117, 169, 262, 265, 308, 320
Rwanda, Rwandan, 282, 290, 291, 292, 299

Said, Edward, 3–5, 16–17, 19, 32, 81, 89n13, 98–101, 102, 133–35, 147
salon, 37–38, 41–44, 47, 53–54, 56
Sassen, Saskia, 283, 288, 290
Scattergood (refugee hostel in Iowa), 179–80, 182, 185
Schiller, Friedrich, 21, 40, 109, 110, 115

Schreck, Dora, 173–75, 183–88
Schreck, Rudolf J., 169–88
self, *see* subject
sex, sexuality, 162, 165, 266, 267, 272, 283, 296, 335, 339n48
sexism, 278
Shakespeare, William, 122, 327, 328; works by: *Hamlet*, 325, 327, 335
Shoah, *see* Holocaust
simultaneity, 216, 229, 252
slang, 266; as resistance, 269
slavery, 4, 41–42, 43, 74, 77, 80, 153, 154, 157–65, 247, 262–63
Smith, Helmut Walser, 2, 6, 62n4, 69, 81n56
socialism, 304n6, 305, 307, 310–16, 320–21, 326
sound, 162, 218, 222–24, 238, 240, 241, 248, 256, 269, 271, 282, 283, 291, 292, 295–96, 297, 299, 333
South, Southern, 42n9, 152, 160n31, 161n35, 162, 165
South Africa, 87, 100
South America, 74, 130, 138
Soviet Union, 29, 101, 262, 304n6, 307–08, 312, 314
Spain, Spanish, 74, 101, 114, 117, 121, 130–32, 136–41, 143–45, 161
Spivak, Gayatri Chakravorty, 26–27, 337
state, *see* nation-state
State Department, U.S., 172, 183–86
statelessness, 13, 14, 337, 338, 340
Stoler, Ann Laura, 26–27
subaltern, 27, 86
subject, subjectivity (search for self, ich), 22, 32, 63–69, 76, 81–82, 95, 111, 132–33, 135, 157, 192, 194, 197, 206, 207, 229, 230, 231, 233, 248, 251, 267n17, 275, 284, 298, 327, 333–34
sugar, 41, 42, 152
Suriname, 131

Switzerland, 102, 129, 130, 140, 244, 273n45
synesthesia, 248, 256
Syria (*see also* Damascus), 29, 30, 225, 323, 325, 330, 339

Tawada, Yoko, 215–18, 232, 234, 255; works by: *Sprachpolizei und Spielpolyglotte* (*Language Police and Play Polyglot*), 216–34; *Überseezungen* (*Overseatongues*), 217
teleology, 24, 87n8, 90, 195, 216, 223, 231
temporality, 18, 92, 198, 199n18, 201–07, 220, 225, 229, 231–34, 317–18; linear, 31, 216, 220–26, 229, 231, 232; belatedness, 199, 205, 207, 228–29, 233
terrorism, 16
Thelen, Albert Vigoleis, 129–48; works by: "Grenzstein der Freiheit" ("Border Stone of Freedom"), 136–37 ; "Der Hirtenbrief" ("Pastoral Letter"), 136–48; *Die Insel des zweiten Gesichts* (*The Island of Second Sight*), 130; *Der schwarze Herr Bahßetup* (*Black Mr. Bahssetup*), 131
Third Reich, *see* National Socialism
transatlantic trade, 43; slave trade, 163
transcultural, transculturation, 102, 111, 130, 261, 266, 274, 278, 305n8
translation, 19, 28, 49, 50n33, 85n1, 87–89, 143–44, 193, 215, 217, 257, 325, 330–31; aesthetics of, 303–22; fictive, 303–22
transliteration, 305, 307, 321
transnational, transnationalism, 3, 4, 7, 8, 15, 18, 38, 42, 45, 46, 55, 56, 74, 88–90, 91, 238, 249, 252, 255, 257, 278, 290–94, 298–99; literature, 87, 88–90, 92, 98, 103,

110–12, 115, 126, 242–46, 263; theater, 324
trauma, traumatic, 7, 99, 109, 113, 147, 151, 155, 156, 165–66, 191, 197–209; traumatization, sequential, 202, 208
travel, 41, 43, 47n25, 49, 56, 117, 119, 122, 217, 219, 230
Travel Ban (Muslim Ban), 13
Treblinka, 188
Trotsky, Leon, 318
Turkish-German, 109–10, 112, 115, 254, 262, 264, 265, 273–75, 283, 284n10, 287, 290
Turkey, 116, 120, 134, 244, 249

Umuhire, Amelia, 282, 287, 289, 298; works by: *Polyglot*, 283, 290–95
uncanny, 101, 119, 153, 164, 192, 333, 336
United States, 1, 13, 14, 15, 21, 114, 171–87, 270
universalism, 86, 89n13, 205n36, 207, 232, 338–40
university, 8, 15, 66, 67, 69, 71–72, 74, 75, 78, 82
urban, urbanity, 44, 56, 123, 218, 264, 283, 285, 288, 290–92, 298–99
Utlu, Deniz, 239; works by: *Unterhaltungen deutscher Eingewanderten* (*Conversations of German Immigrants*), 238–58

Veteranyi, Aglaja, 247–48
Vienna, 169–77, 181–88, 294
visa, 14–15, 174, 176–77, 183–87
Vormärz, 118

webseries, 282; *Polyglot*, 283, 287, 290, 292
Weimar, 40n4, 56, 192, 196, 198, 206, 289
Wellbery, David, 17–19
West Germany, *see* Federal Republic of Germany
West Indies, 4, 40, 41
working class, 120, 125, 182, 249, 267, 271, 315, 318
world literature, 5, 6, 15, 17–19, 23, 28, 32, 86, 87, 90–91, 93, 99–100, 110–14, 115, 117, 126, 242–43, 258, 321, 325
World War I, 29, 114, 156n15, 171n6, 320
World War II, 94, 114, 131, 132, 134, 135, 187, 198, 199, 202, 206, 220, 324, 337
writing, 215–29, 231–34; as resistance, 92, 135, 220, 225, 232

xenophobia, 54, 82, 94, 133, 174, 278, 286n18

Yiddish, 49

zero, 226–29
Žižek, Slavoj, 6–7

Volumes in the Series:

1. *Improvisation as Art: Conceptual Challenges, Historical Perspectives*
by Edgar Landgraf

2. *The German Pícaro and Modernity: Between Underdog and Shape-Shifter*
by Bernhard Malkmus

3. *Citation and Precedent: Conjunctions and Disjunctions of German Law and Literature*
by Thomas O. Beebee

4. *Beyond Discontent: 'Sublimation' from Goethe to Lacan*
by Eckart Goebel

5. *From Kafka to Sebald: Modernism and Narrative Form*
edited by Sabine Wilke

6. *Image in Outline: Reading Lou Andreas-Salomé*
by Gisela Brinker-Gabler

7. *Out of Place: German Realism, Displacement, and Modernity*
by John B. Lyon

8. *Thomas Mann in English: A Study in Literary Translation*
by David Horton

9. *The Tragedy of Fatherhood: King Laius and the Politics of Paternity in the West*
by Silke-Maria Weineck

10. *The Poet as Phenomenologist: Rilke and the* New Poems
by Luke Fischer

11. *The Laughter of the Thracian Woman: A Protohistory of Theory*
by Hans Blumenberg, translated by Spencer Hawkins

12. *Roma Voices in the German-Speaking World*
by Lorely French

13. *Vienna's Dreams of Europe: Culture and Identity beyond the Nation-State*
by Katherine Arens

14. *Thomas Mann and Shakespeare: Something Rich and Strange*
edited by Tobias Döring and Ewan Fernie

15. *Goethe's Families of the Heart*
by Susan E. Gustafson

16. *German Aesthetics: Fundamental Concepts from Baumgarten to Adorno*
edited by J. D. Mininger and Jason Michael Peck

17. *Figures of Natality: Reading the Political in the Age of Goethe*
by Joseph D. O'Neil

18. *Readings in the Anthropocene: The Environmental Humanities, German Studies, and Beyond*
edited by Sabine Wilke and Japhet Johnstone

19. *Building Socialism: Architecture and Urbanism in East German Literature, 1955–1973*
by Curtis Swope

20. *Ghostwriting: W. G. Sebald's Poetics of History*
by Richard T. Gray

21. *Stereotype and Destiny in Arthur Schnitzler's Prose: Five Psycho-Sociological Readings*
by Marie Kolkenbrock

22. *Sissi's World: The Empress Elisabeth in Memory and Myth*
edited by Maura E. Hametz and Heidi Schlipphacke

23. *Posthumanism in the Age of Humanism: Mind, Matter, and the Life Sciences after Kant*
edited by Edgar Landgraf, Gabriel Trop, and Leif Weatherby

24. *Staging West German Democracy: Governmental PR Films and the Democratic Imaginary, 1953–1963*
by Jan Uelzmann

25. *The Lever as Instrument of Reason: Technological Constructions of Knowledge around 1800*
by Jocelyn Holland

26. *The Fontane Workshop: Manufacturing Realism in the Industrial Age of Print*
by Petra McGillen

27. *Gender, Collaboration, and Authorship in German Culture: Literary Joint Ventures, 1750–1850*
edited by Laura Deiulio and John B. Lyon

28. *Kafka's Stereoscopes: The Political Function of a Literary Style*
by Isak Winkel Holm

29. *Ambiguous Aggression in German Realism and Beyond: Flirtation, Passive Aggression, Domestic Violence*
by Barbara N. Nagel

30. *Thomas Bernhard's Afterlives*
edited by Stephen Dowden, Gregor Thuswaldner, and Olaf Berwald

31. *Modernism in Trieste: The Habsburg Mediterranean and the Literary Invention of Europe, 1870–1945*
by Salvatore Pappalardo

32. *Grotesque Visions: The Science of Berlin Dada*
by Thomas O. Haakenson

33. *Theodor Fontane: Irony and Avowal in a Post-Truth Age*
by Brian Tucker

34. *Jane Eyre in German Lands: The Import of Romance, 1848–1918*
by Lynne Tatlock

35. *Weimar in Princeton: Thomas Mann and the Kahler Circle*
by Stanley Corngold

36. *Authors and the World: Literary Authorship in Modern Germany*
by Rebecca Braun

37. *Germany from the Outside: Rethinking German Cultural History in an Age of Displacement*
edited by Laurie Ruth Johnson

www.ingramcontent.com/pod-product-compliance
Lightning Source LLC
Chambersburg PA
CBHW052141300426
44115CB00011B/1468